Claude Monet's water lily paintings are a beloved works of art of the past century. Y were created at a time of terrible private turmoil and sadness for the artist. The dramatic history behind these paintings is little known; Ross King's *Mad Enchantment* tells the full story for the first time and, in the process, presents a compelling and original portrait of one of our most popular and cherished artists.

By the outbreak of war in 1914, Monet, then in his mid-seventies, was one of the world's most famous and successful painters, with a large house in the country, a fleet of automobiles and a colossal reputation. However, he had virtually given up painting following the death of his wife Alice in 1911 and the onset of blindness a year later. Nonetheless, it was during this period of sorrow, ill health and creative uncertainty that – as the guns roared on the Western Front – he began the most demanding and innovative paintings he had ever attempted.

Encouraged by close friends such as Georges Clemenceau, France's dauntless prime minister, Monet would work on these magnificent paintings throughout the war years and then for the rest of his life. So obsessed with his monumental task that the village barber was summoned to clip his hair as he worked beside his pond, he covered hundreds of yards of canvas with shimmering layers of pigment. As his ambitions expanded with his paintings, he began planning what he intended to be his legacy to the world: the 'Musée Claude Monet' in the Orangerie in Paris.

Drawing on letters and memoirs and focusing on this remarkable period in the artist's life, *Mad Enchantment* gives an intimate portrayal of Claude Monet in all his tumultuous complexity, and firmly places his water lily paintings among the greatest achievements in the history of art.

COMHAIRLE CHONTAE ÁTHA CLIATH THEAS
SOUTH DUBLIN COUNTY LIBRARIES

CLONDALKIN BRANCH LIBRARY
TO RENEW ANY ITEM TEL: 459 3315
OR ONLINE AT www.southdublinlibraries.ie

Items should be returned on or before the last date below. Fines, as displayed in the Library, will be charged on overdue items.

MAD ENCHANTMENT

CLAUDE MONET *and the* PAINTING *of the* WATER LILIES

ROSS KING

BLOOMSBURY CIRCUS

LONDON · OXFORD · NEW YORK · NEW DELHI · SYDNEY

Bloomsbury Circus
An imprint of Bloomsbury Publishing Plc

50 Bedford Square
London
WC1B 3DP
UK

1385 Broadway
New York
NY 10018
USA

www.bloomsbury.com

BLOOMSBURY and the Diana logo are trademarks of Bloomsbury Publishing Plc

First published in Great Britain 2016

British Library Cataloguing-in-Publication Data
A catalogue record for this book is available from the British Library.

ISBN: HB: 978-1-4088-6195-0
ePub: 978-1-4088-6196-7

2 4 6 8 10 9 7 5 3 1

Designed by Sara Stemen
Printed and bound in Great Britain by CPI Group (UK) Ltd, Croydon CR0 4YY

To find out more about our authors and books visit www.bloomsbury.com.
Here you will find extracts, author interviews, details of forthcoming events
and the option to sign up for our newsletters.

In loving memory of Claire King

CONTENTS

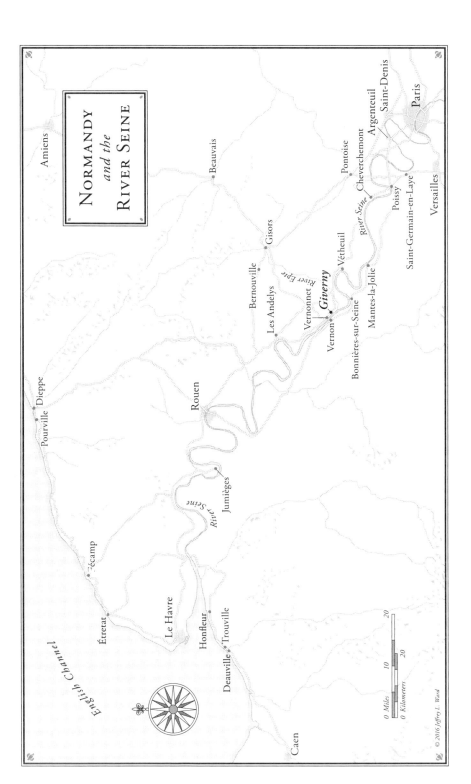

NORMANDY
and the
RIVER SEINE

English Channel

Amiens

Dieppe
Pourville

Beauvais

Fécamp

Étretat

Le Havre

Honfleur
Trouville
Deauville

Rouen

Jumièges

River Seine

Caen

Bernouville

Les Andelys

Gisors

Vernonnet
Vernon

River Epte

Giverny

Vétheuil

Bonnières-sur-Seine

Mantes-la-Jolie

Pontoise

Cheverchemont

River Seine

Poissy

Saint-Germain-en-Laye

Versailles

Argenteuil
Saint-Denis

Paris

0 Miles   10   20
0 Kilometers   20

© 2016 Jeffrey L. Ward

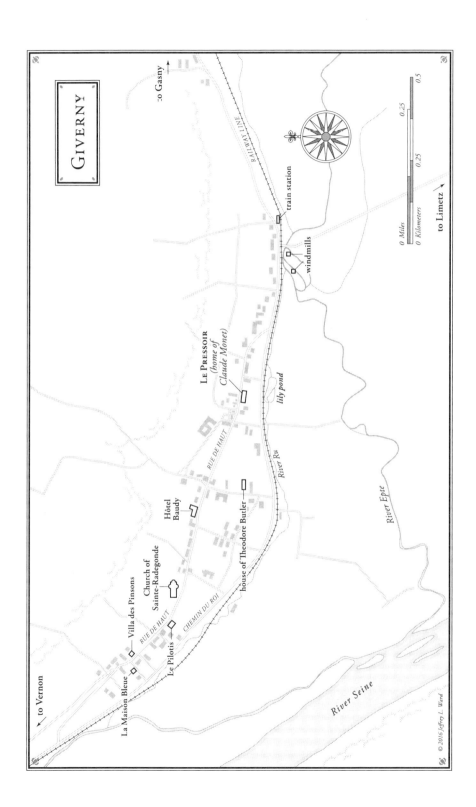

GIVERNY

to Gasny →

RAILWAY LINE

train station

windmills

LE PRESSOIR
(home of Claude Monet)

lily pond

RUE DE HAUT

River Ru

Hôtel
Baudy

Church of
Sainte-Radegonde

house of Theodore Butler

RUE DE HAUT

Villa des Pinsons

La Maison Bleue

Le Pilotis

CHEMIN DU ROI

← to Vernon

River Seine

River Epte

to Limetz →

0 Miles   0.25   0.5

0 Kilometers   0.25

© 2016 Jeffrey L. Ward

RUE DE HAUT

RUELLE DE L'AMSICOURT

PLAN OF THE GARDENS

A The "Clos Normand"
  1 The house
  2 The second studio and garage (built ca. 1897)
  3 The *Nymphéas* studio (built 1915)
  4 The greenhouses
  5 The rose alley
  6 Head gardener's cottage
B The water garden
  a Water duct for the pond
  b Water lily pond
  c Dock
  d Japanese footbridge
C Underground passage connecting the gardens
D Railroad
E Road to Vernon
F Road to Gasny
G River Ru

COMMUNAL LANDS

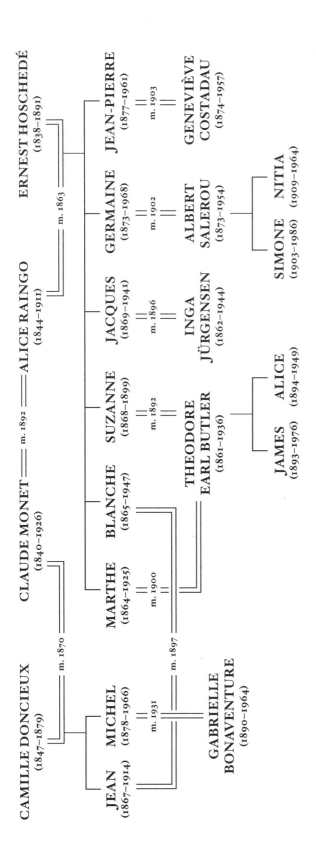

MONET-HOSCHEDÉ FAMILY TREE

CAMILLE DONCIEUX (1847–1879)

CLAUDE MONET (1840–1926) — m. 1892 — ALICE RAINGO (1844–1911)

ERNEST HOSCHEDÉ (1838–1891)

m. 1870

m. 1863

JEAN (1867–1914)

MICHEL (1878–1966)

m. 1931

m. 1897

GABRIELLE BONAVENTURE (1890–1964)

MARTHE (1864–1925)

BLANCHE (1865–1947)

m. 1900

THEODORE EARL BUTLER (1861–1936)

SUZANNE (1868–1899)

m. 1892

JACQUES (1869–1941)

m. 1896

INGA JÜRGENSEN (1862–1944)

GERMAINE (1873–1968)

m. 1902

ALBERT SALEROU (1873–1954)

JEAN-PIERRE (1877–1961)

m. 1903

GENEVIÈVE COSTADAU (1874–1957)

JAMES (1893–1976)

ALICE (1894–1949)

SIMONE (1903–1986)

NITIA (1909–1964)

══ MARRIAGES

CHAPTER ONE

THE TIGER AND THE HEDGEHOG

WHERE WAS GEORGES CLEMENCEAU? The day of the French election had arrived—Sunday, April 26, 1914—and the newspaper *Gil Blas* announced in astonishment that the seventy-two-year-old former prime minister had disappeared from Paris. "His departure does not fail to cause surprise," reported the paper. "Is this vigorous polemicist no longer interested in the political battle?"[1]

Gil Blas was always remarkably well informed about the comings and goings of Clemenceau, whose fearsome personality had earned him the nickname the Tiger. Two years earlier the paper had reported how firefighters came to Clemenceau's rescue when his bathroom caught fire as he took a hot soak; another time it informed readers how, despite the fact that he was France's most notorious anti-Catholic, he had recuperated from an operation at a convalescent home run by nuns.[2] And indeed, on this occasion, the paper quickly managed to track him down, reporting that he had gone to enjoy springtime in the countryside. "It is whispered that he wants rest at all costs, and that, little concerned with electoral results, he will sleep late, in rustic silence."

Clemenceau's rustic retreat was fifty miles northwest of Paris, in the Normandy village of Bernouville. Six years earlier, while still prime minister, he had bought a half-timbered hunting lodge whose garden he planted with white poplars and Spanish broom, and whose ponds he stocked with trout and sturgeon. A few weeks after he left office in the summer of 1909, *Gil Blas* ran an admiring poem describing how, "spry as a stripling," he was hard at work in his garden.[3] It was no doubt this love of gardening that, as the election loomed, drew him to Bernouville and that, so he could talk flowers instead of politics, then took him to Giverny to see his friend, the painter Claude Monet.

1

*

GIVERNY WAS TWENTY miles from Bernouville, but the chauffeur would have covered the distance quickly: Clemenceau, who loved speed, always urged his drivers to go faster, racing along bone-shaking country roads at speeds in excess of 100 kilometers (62 miles) per hour.[4] He often unhooked the speedometer to allay the alarm of his passengers.[5] The car would have entered the tiny village of Vernonnet and then, as it reached the right bank of the Seine, turned left for Giverny along a road bordered on the right by meadows and, on the left, by the steep flank of a hill. The hill was gouged with whitish streaks from sandstone quarries and sown here and there with vines that produced the local vintage. To the right was the river Ru, a thin rivulet in which, not long ago, a visiting journalist had marveled at the sight of washerwomen.[6] Beyond, a line of tall poplars snaked across meadows that in May were stippled by poppies and that in autumn were populated by towering stacks of wheat.

A couple of miles from Vernonnet, a cluster of houses suddenly appeared. Clemenceau's driver would have swung left at the fork, heading toward a small church with a squat, octagonal tower and a black witch's hat of a steeple. Giverny was a village of some 250 inhabitants, with one hundred or so rustic cottages interspersed with more imposing homes set in orchards behind moss-covered walls.[7] The effect, especially for someone coming from Paris, was magical. Visitors unfailingly described Giverny as charming, quaint, picturesque, and an "earthly paradise."[8] One of Monet's visitors later enthused in her journal: "This is the land of dreams, the realization of a fairyland."[9]

Monet had first arrived in Giverny three decades earlier, at the age of forty-two. The village was forty miles as the crow flies northwest of Paris, in the valley of the Seine. In 1869 a set of railway tracks had appeared beside the Ru, and a railway station sprouted in the shadow of the two windmills on Giverny's eastern outskirts, where the willows lazily arranged themselves over the riverbank. Soon four trains were puffing through the village every day except Sunday. Early in the spring of 1883, one of them carried a house-hunting Monet. He was then a widower with two boys to think about, along with a middle-aged mistress

GIVERNY, près Vernon
Vue prise sur la Côte

Phot. A. L., Vernon

Postcard of Giverny in Monet's time

and her own brood of six children. From his seat he watched, entranced, as the steam train hissed to an unscheduled halt beside a wedding party waiting by the side of the road. Led by a violinist, the newlyweds and their guests happily embarked, oblivious that their festivities decided the painter on his domestic surroundings.[10]

A short time later, Monet and his blended family took possession of one of the largest homes in the village, an old farmhouse known as Le Pressoir (the Cider Press). For the next seven years he rented the property from Louis-Joseph Singeot, a trader with dealings in Guadeloupe. Pink with grey shutters, it overlooked on its north side the rue de Haut (High Street), and on its south side a walled garden planted with vegetables and an apple orchard. Monet soon painted the shutters green, a color that quickly became known in the village as "Monet green."[11] For a studio he took over a dirt-floored barn connected to the house. In 1890, a few days after his fiftieth birthday, he purchased Le Pressoir from Singeot, adding an adjoining plot of land a few years later. He began

Postcard of Monet's second studio with the greenhouses in the foreground

uprooting the vegetables and apple trees, replacing them with irises, tulips, and Japanese peonies. On the northwest corner of the property he constructed a two-story building—described by one visitor as a "rustic pavilion"[12]—on whose top floor he arranged a high-ceilinged, skylit studio. On the ground floor was an aviary stocked with parrots, turtles, and peacocks, as well as a photographer's darkroom and a garage for his collection of motorcars.

The large house, the light-filled studio, the fleet of automobiles—such luxuries had come late. Monet's early years as a painter occasionally featured irate landlords and shopkeepers, out-of-pocket friends and enforced economies. "For the past eight days," he lamented in 1869, aged twenty-nine, "I've had no bread, no wine, no fire for the kitchen, no light."[13] That same year he claimed to have no money to buy paints, and bailiffs seized four of his paintings from the walls of an exhibition to settle his numerous debts. Over the next decade his canvases sometimes went for as little as 20 francs each—at a time when a blank canvas cost 4 francs. He was once forced to give paintings to a baker in return for bread. A draper proved "impossible to appease." His laundress sequestered his bedsheets when he failed to pay her bill. "If I don't come up with 600 francs by tomorrow night," he wrote to a friend in 1877, "my furniture and all I own will be sold and we'll be thrown into the street."[14] When a butcher sent round the bailiffs to impound his possessions, Monet vengefully slashed two hundred of his canvases. He once, so the legend went, spent a winter living on potatoes.[15]

Monet often exaggerated his plight. Even in the early days, his paintings had sometimes attracted astute collectors and fetched respectable prices. In 1868 the esteemed critic Arsène Houssaye paid 800 francs for one of his paintings—enough to pay the rent on a house for an entire year. Moreover, his privations were offset by generous friends: the painter Frédéric Bazille; the novelist Émile Zola; a pastry chef and novelist named Eugène Murer; and Dr. Paul Gachet, who would later have on his hands another frustrated and even more impecunious artist, Vincent van Gogh. All of them, over the years, received begging letters detailing Monet's allegedly precarious financial state and his miserable prospects. In 1878, aged thirty-eight, he lamented to another benefactor, Georges de Bellio, a homeopath: "It's sad to be in such a situation at my age, always obliged to ask for favours." Then, a few months later: "I'm absolutely disgusted and demoralized by this existence that I've led for such a long time…Each day brings new sorrows and new difficulties from which I'll never extricate myself."[16]

Monet's career had actually begun with great promise. In 1865 his two views of the Normandy coast caused a sensation at the Paris Salon: one critic called them "the finest seascapes seen in recent years," while another declared them the best in the entire exhibition.[17] However, the following years proved difficult as subsequent works—whose blurry images and seemingly casual brushwork violated prevailing conventions—were regularly spurned by Salon juries. His critical notoriety seemed to be sealed when, in 1874, he showed work in Paris with a group of artistic rebels who included Pierre-Auguste Renoir, Edgar Degas, and Paul Cézanne. They were pejoratively dubbed "Impressionists," with one of Monet's seascapes mockingly denounced as "less skilful than crude wallpaper."[18] Conservative critics condemned his paintings as "incoherent," as "false, unhealthy and comical" and as "studies in decadence." "When children amuse themselves with paper and crayons," sniffed one of his critics in 1877, "they do a better job."[19] Monet kept a scrapbook of these reviews—a veritable catalogue, a friend observed, of "shortsightedness, ignorance and indifference."[20] An 1880 interview called him "one of those wild beasts of art."[21] A collector who bought one of his canvases was so ridiculed by his friends that, according to Monet, he removed the work from his wall.[22]

MONET'S ARRIVAL IN Giverny had not been particularly auspicious. In April 1883, the very month that he moved into the village, a reviewer claimed that his work was simply beyond the comprehension of the general public. Monet enjoyed the esteem of a small band of admirers, the critic admitted, but the public at large still held out stubbornly against him. "Monet paints in a strange language," he claimed, "whose secrets, together with a few initiates, he alone possesses."[23]

Besides this unintelligible style, Monet had brought a whiff of scandal to Giverny. Following the death of his wife Camille in 1879— and possibly before—he had taken up with a married woman named Alice Hoschedé. She was the estranged wife of a bankrupt businessman, Ernest Hoschedé. Among Hoschedé's ruinous investments had been sixteen Monet paintings, including *Impression, Sunrise*, the work whose title, according to a myth as persistent as it is erroneous, gave the Impressionists their name.[24] Hoschedé purchased the work for 800 francs in 1874, only to sell it at a loss, four years later, for 210 francs.[25] Monet had moved into Le Pressoir with Alice, his own two boys, and Alice's children: four girls and two boys. The large clan was notable in Giverny because all of them dressed, as one of them later recalled, "rather haphazardly in loud colors, wearing hats... We were, in the eyes of the villagers, newcomers who were observed with distrust."[26]

Yet by 1914, three decades later, matters had changed. Monet was no longer a notorious "wild beast." He was seventy-three years old. Forty years had passed since the controversial 1874 group exhibition

The Monet-Hoschedé families at Giverny ca. 1892. Clockwise from lower left: Michel Monet, Alice Hoschedé, Claude Monet (*standing*), Jean-Pierre Hoschedé, Marthe Hoschedé, Jean Monet, Jacques Hoschedé, Blanche Hoschedé (*foreground*), Germaine Hoschedé, Suzanne Hoschedé.

at which his work had been mocked by the critics. Success and acclaim had come slowly enough, but after Monet arrived in Giverny his quintessentially French scenes—rows of poplars beside the river, the vaporous morning light breaking over the Seine—eventually began attracting the enthusiastic attention of critics and collectors alike. Complaints about his sketchiness and incompetence with a paintbrush disappeared as critics suddenly became sensitive not only to the prototypical Frenchness of his scenes but also to the mysteriously beautiful qualities of his canvases. He was praised as a "powerful poet of nature" whose works "resonate with the mysterious sounds of the universe."[27] In 1889 a reviewer noted that critics who once had nothing but sarcasm and jokes for Monet now "glorify him as one of the most illustrious of men." In 1909 a critic called him "the greatest painter we possess today," while the novelist Remy de Gourmont declared: "We stand here in the presence of perhaps the greatest painter who has ever lived."[28] Monet's old comrade Paul Cézanne had put it more succinctly: "Fuck, he's simply the best."[29]

Monet had exchanged notoriety for celebrity. His fame brought journalists flocking to Giverny, which a newspaper dubbed "the Mecca of Impressionism."[30] Even more plentiful were painters, many of them young American students hoping (as a journalist reported) "to catch a glimpse of this god" and to perfect what became known as the "Giverny trick": painting in bright colors with a prevalence of purple and green.[31] Monet condescended to interviews with select journalists but held himself disdainfully aloof from the invasion of young painters. He curtly rebuffed the attentions of inquisitive Americans and earned himself what a newspaper called "a reputation for savagery."[32] Relations with the American painters were not improved when, in the early 1890s, several of them proposed to Alice's daughters. "*Sacrebleu!*" he exclaimed after learning that one young American, Theodore Earl Butler, had asked for the hand of Suzanne Hoschedé. "To marry a painter," he wailed to Alice, "how annoying."[33] He even threatened to move from Giverny to scupper the nuptials, which took place when, bowing to the inevitable, he finally relented. His reputation for unsociability did little to deter the curious. An American woman, daring to approach him, once asked for a paintbrush as a souvenir. "Really," Monet complained to a friend, "people have the most idiotic ideas."[34]

Along with the acclaim came great wealth. Few wealthy and status-conscious Americans could resist finishing their buying trips to Europe without adding a new Monet to their collections. In New York, Louisine Havemeyer, widow of a sugar baron and one of the first Americans to buy a Monet, adorned the Tiffany-designed rooms of her mansion on East Sixty-Sixth Street with twenty-five Monet canvases. A Chicago collector, Bertha Palmer, wife of a department store and real estate tycoon, once bought twenty-five Monets in a single year. But even their collections were dwarfed by that of the art dealer James F. Sutton, founder of the American Art Association, who owned fifty Monet paintings.

In 1912 alone Monet earned 369,000 francs from sales of his works—a vast sum, considering that the average laborer in Paris earned 1,000 francs a year, and that, a few years earlier, the Hope Diamond changed hands for 400,000 francs.[35] As a result he was, as a visitor enviously noted, "surrounded by every comfort."[36] By 1905 his fleet of vehicles had been worth 32,000 francs. A year later he added to his collection both a Peugeot and a brand-new four-cylinder Mendelssohn costing 6,600 francs.[37] Such was Monet's passion for speed that the mayor of Giverny was obliged to publish a notice stating that automobiles passing through the village should go no faster than "the speed of a horse at a regular trot."[38] Monet received his first speeding ticket in 1904.[39]

Claude Monet in his Panhard et Levassor.

Besides a chauffeur, the domestic staff at Giverny included a butler and a cook, as well as a six-strong team of gardeners to look after his flowers, trees and pond. Along with the automobiles, he owned four riverboats. Visitors were struck by his "lordly bearing."[40] Alice, whom he had finally married in 1892, and whom he dressed in Worth gowns, called him, because of his grand airs, *le marquis*.[41]

YET ALL WAS not well on that April day in 1914 when Clemenceau arrived in Giverny. According to one of his closest friends, Monet had suffered "the terrible grief that breaks the heart and ravages the mind."[42]

Tragedies had indeed befallen Monet: what he called "an endless succession of troubles and anxieties."[43] Worst of all had been Alice's death from leukemia in 1911. "I am annihilated," he wrote to a friend in what became a constant refrain.[44] A quarter century earlier, in 1886, when it looked as if Alice might return to her husband, he had been distraught: "The painter in me is dead...Work would be impossible now."[45] But now she truly was gone, and work did indeed become impossible. Two months after her death he wrote to his friend, the sculptor Auguste Rodin: "I ought to be able to work to conquer my grief, but I cannot."[46] A year after her death he wrote to his stepdaughter Germaine: "The painter is dead and what remains is an inconsolable husband." To another stepdaughter, Blanche, he wrote that his paintings were a "horrible joke." He declared that he was going to stop painting altogether.[47]

Work became even more impossible a year after Alice's death when, in the summer of 1912, he suddenly began losing his eyesight. "Three days ago," he wrote to a friend, "when I was getting down to work, I made the dreadful discovery that I was no longer able to see anything out of my right eye."[48] It was a terrible blow for someone whose almost preternaturally acute eyesight—what an admiring poet called his "fabulously sensitive retina"[49]—was held to be one of the great secrets of his genius. In 1883 a reviewer had claimed that Monet "sees differently from the rest of humanity," speculating that he was acutely sensitive to colors at the ultraviolet end of the spectrum.[50] Cézanne had famously declared: "Monet is only an eye, but, good Lord, what an eye!" To another friend he said that Monet possessed "the most prodigious eye in the history of painting."[51]

But now—such was the malice of fate—this phenomenal vision was muddy, bland, indistinct. A cataract was diagnosed soon afterward. His doctors and friends tried in vain to reassure him that he was in no danger of going blind, but Monet's deep pessimism and sullen depression remained. Shortly after his diagnosis, a violent thunderstorm pummeled the village. "In Giverny," a newspaper solemnly reported, "the property of the famous painter Claude Monet was destroyed."[52] Repairs were duly made, but a year later, in the summer of 1913, *Gil Blas* reported that "the great Monet" had decided, once and for all, to retire his paintbrushes.[53]

Then yet more sorrow. In February 1914 his son Jean died at the age of forty-six. Jean Monet had been the child of his impecunious, struggling youth, born to his model (later his first wife) Camille Doncieux. The infant Jean appeared in many of Monet's early paintings: asleep with a doll in his cradle, sitting at the table during a family luncheon, riding a "horse tricycle," or sprawled on the grass with his mother in the garden.

In the summer of 1912 he suffered a stroke, possibly the result of syphilis. A year later, increasingly incapacitated, Jean was forced to move from Beaumont-le-Roger, where he had been operating a trout farm, and into the Villa des Pinsons, a house in Giverny that Monet purchased for him. "What torture for me to witness his decline," Monet wrote to a friend a few days before, when after much suffering, Jean finally died.[54]

In 1905 a visitor wrote of Monet, then at the height of his powers: "He constantly seeks new worlds to conquer and nothing seems too difficult."[55] But a decade later it appeared that his conquests had reached an end. This was the Claude Monet—wealthy and celebrated yet listless, despondent and idle—that Georges Clemenceau, in late April 1914, came to Giverny to visit.

CLEMENCEAU AND MONET had known each other since they were young men in Paris in the 1860s.[56] Theirs was, in some respects, an unlikely friendship. Monet claimed his only two interests in life were painting and gardening. He certainly had little interest in politics, never even bothering to cast his vote.[57] Clemenceau, on the other hand, had many interests and many talents, chief among them politics. In 1914 he was both a member of the Senate and the editor of a daily newspaper, *L'Homme Libre*, for which he wrote lengthy and forthright editorials. He was absolutely irrepressible, a bustling and seemingly unconquerable force of nature. Monet, by contrast, was volatile, insecure, and prone to petulance, frustration, and despair. There were, nonetheless, strong similarities: pride, stubbornness, passion, a vigorous youthfulness that belied their years, and what a mutual friend, referring to Monet, called "an invincible force that was not merely physical."[58]

Clemenceau called Monet by an assortment of nicknames: "old lunatic," "poor old crustacean" and "frightful old hedgehog."[59] He had come by his own nickname, the Tiger, quite honestly. As a newspaper reported the previous January, he was "a man before whom the whole world trembles."[60] His political enemies liked to refer to him by the full title that he never actually used: Georges Clemenceau de la Clemencière. He had been born in the Vendée, along France's Atlantic coast, and raised in the massive Château de l'Aubraie, a moated manor house with a ring of walls and four towers. This grim castle and the ornate title could be traced back to a certain Jehan Clemenceau who, sometime after 1500, was ennobled by King Louis XII for having served as the "beloved and trusty bookseller"of the bishop of Luçon.[61] Later generations of the family loved books but were, as far as both church and state were concerned, much less beloved and trusty. Georges's father, Benjamin, was a rabid republican and anti-Catholic. "The natural state of my father was indignation," Georges once observed.[62] Master of all he surveyed, squire of many acres of farmland tilled by peasants, Benjamin seethed with revolutionary fervor in his gloomy castle, which he decorated with portraits of Robespierre and other heroes of 1789. He was an outspoken opponent of the Emperor Napoleon III, who once had him arrested on suspicion of participating in an assassination plot. "I will avenge you," vowed the seventeen-year-old Georges as his father was marched away to prison.[63]

Much of the rest of Clemenceau's life had been spent exacting revenge on his and his father's enemies. "I feel very sorry for those people who want to make friends with everyone," he once said. "Life is a combat."[64] He had indeed made many enemies and experienced much combat, sometimes literally: he had fought a total of twenty-two duels with swords and pistols. A journalist once claimed there were only three things to fear about Clemenceau: his tongue, his pen, and his sword.[65] He was a master of the witty put-down. About the young journalist Georges Mandel he quipped: "Mandel has no ideas, but he will defend them until death."[66]

Clemenceau studied medicine in Paris in the early 1860s, writing a dissertation on the soon-to-be-disproved theory of spontaneous generation. His true vocation, however, was radical politics. For many years he was leader of the Radical Party, whose members saw themselves as latter-day Jacobins fighting to preserve the French Republic established in 1789. Like his father, he was a fierce enemy of the Church and an ardent republican, and for several months in 1862 he had likewise been a political prisoner thanks to having distributed pamphlets critical of the emperor. In 1865 the emperor's crackdown on dissidents drove him into voluntary exile in the United States, where for several years

Georges Clemenceau

he supported himself by teaching French, fencing, and horseback riding at the Catharine Aiken School for girls in Stamford, Connecticut. Here he found a wife, Mary, the daughter of a New Hampshire dentist. The marriage would not be a happy one, not least because of Clemenceau's numerous dalliances with beautiful actresses. "What a tragedy that she ever married me," he later reflected in a rare moment of regret.[67]

Clemenceau had returned to France in the summer of 1869 to work as a country doctor in the Vendée. His political career began in earnest with the fall of Napoleon III during the Franco-Prussian War. In September 1870 an old friend of his father, Étienne Arago, who had just become mayor of Paris, appointed him mayor of the working-class hilltop suburb of Montmartre. WE ARE CHILDREN OF THE REVOLUTION, Clemenceau's posters on the steep streets proudly declared.[68] He doubled as a doctor, opening a clinic through which filed, he sorrowfully observed, a "procession of human miseries" from the slums.[69] After six years, he got himself elected as Montmartre's representative in the Chamber of Deputies, where his reputation for bringing down governments (thirteen collapsed in the 1880s alone) brought him the nickname *tombeur de ministères* (toppler of ministries). He had little respect for his fellow politicians, later telling Rudyard Kipling that he obtained his eminence in politics not through any excellent qualities of his own "but through the inferiority of my colleagues."[70] Active in journalism since his student days, in 1880 he launched a radical newspaper, *La Justice*, whose first issue declared his intention to "destroy the old dogmas."[71] However, the newspaper folded and his political career imploded in the wake of the liquidation in 1892 of the Panama Canal Company amid charges of swindling and bribery in which he was implicated. That same year his marriage likewise collapsed. "I have nothing, nothing, nothing," he wrote in a fleeting moment of despair.[72]

But scandal, disgrace, poverty, and divorce were no match for Clemenceau. He returned to prominence through his support in a series of articles in his new newspaper, *L'Aurore*, for Alfred Dreyfus, the Jewish artillery officer unjustly convicted of spying for the Germans. After a decade in the political wilderness he was elected to the Senate in 1902, then appointed minister of the interior in 1906. Later that year, at the age of sixty-five, he became prime minister, serving until the summer of 1909. He pushed through social reforms, including holidays for workers and the creation of a ministry of labor. But the campaigning journalist who had been a champion of the poor and the suffering took a brutal approach with dissenters who threatened revolution. His ruthless suppression of striking miners and winegrowers earned him yet another nickname, *briseur de grèves* (strikebreaker) and even Clemenceau le Tueur (Clemenceau the Murderer). And it was in these years that he was given the sobriquet by which all France came to know him—the Tiger—a comment on the terror that he inspired in virtually everyone. As a friend wrote, "People were unfailingly petrified of him."[73]

Yet Clemenceau also had immense charm and culture. The wife of a British statesman found him "swifter in thought, wittier in talk, more unexpected in what he said, than anyone I ever knew... No one was ever such fun as he was. We hung upon his every word."[74] If he was anathema to most politicians, who hated and feared him, he was a great friend to artists and writers. Clemenceau patiently sat for two portraits by Édouard Manet, reporting that he had "great times" talking with the infamous painter.[75] He had artistic pretensions of his own, writing novels and short stories (one collection was illustrated by Henri de Toulouse-Lautrec). In 1901 his play *Le Voile de Bonheur* was performed at the Théâtre de la Renaissance in Paris. He was also a connoisseur, amassing a huge collection of Japanese art and artifacts: swords, statuettes, incense boxes, tea bowls, woodblock prints by Utamaro and Hiroshige, all of which he lovingly crammed into his small apartment across the Seine from the Eiffel Tower. Japanese art was yet another passion that he shared with Monet, whose house displayed his collection of 231 woodblock prints.

Most of all, Clemenceau was a connoisseur and admirer of Monet's works. The series of paintings of Rouen Cathedral, painted in 1892 and 1893 and exhibited in Paris in 1895, compelled him to write a long and ecstatic review in *La Justice*. The subject of these canvases was an ironic one to appeal to a notorious priest-gobbler and republican like Clemenceau: the façade of the ancient cathedral in which during the Middle Ages the dukes of Normandy were crowned. But Clemenceau was intoxicated. "It haunts me," he wrote on the front page of the newspaper. "I must talk about it." He regarded Monet—who possessed, he said, "the perfect eye"—as the herald of nothing less than a revolution in human vision, "a new way of looking, feeling and expressing." Who could doubt, looking at Monet's canvases, "that today the eye sees in another way than before?" He ended his article by imploring France's president, Félix Faure, to buy all twenty of the paintings in the show for the nation in order to mark a "moment in the history of mankind, a revolution without gunshots."[76] Faure declined to purchase any works, but the idea of having a cycle of Monet's paintings serve as a national monument became a mounting obsession among Clemenceau and his artistic friends.*

---

* Clemenceau would exact revenge on Faure, an anti-Dreyfusard, with a famous pun. After Faure died in 1899 while being fellated by his mistress, Marguerite Steinheil, Clemenceau quipped: *"Il voulait être César, il ne fut que Pompée."* The literal meaning is: "He wanted to be Caesar, but only ended up as Pompey." However, the phrase is a *double entendre*, since the French verb *pomper* (to pump) was slang for oral sex.

As Clemenceau and Monet transformed from enfants terribles to grand old men, becoming two of the most famous men in France, the affection between them grew. There was a steady stream of letters, lunches together in Paris, and regular visits by Clemenceau to Giverny. Clemenceau's dedication to Monet became even greater after the death of Alice. He provided endless encouragement, issuing invitations to Bernouville, escorting Monet around gardens, and persuading him to take holidays. Most of all, he urged him to keep painting. "Remember the old Rembrandt in the Louvre," he wrote two months after Alice's death. "He clings to his palette, determined to hold out until the end through terrible adversities."[77]

CHAPTER TWO

DU CÔTÉ DE CHEZ MONET

"AS SOON AS you push on the small door on the main street of Giverny," wrote one of Monet's best friends and most frequent visitors, the writer Gustave Geffroy, "you can believe…that you have stepped into paradise."[1]

On that April day in 1914 the door to this paradise—a "slightly worm-eaten door," as one guest noted[2]—would have been opened by Blanche Hoschedé-Monet, whom Monet affectionately called "my daughter."[3] Blanche was, in fact, his stepdaughter but also, by virtue of her marriage to his son Jean, his daughter-in-law. Plump, blue-eyed, blond, and cheerful, the forty-eight-year-old Blanche was the vision of her mother. She was also the only one of Monet's children or stepchildren with artistic interests or aspirations. As a young woman she had been his faithful assistant, helping to carry his easel and canvases into the fields for him. She had also painted side by side with him, setting up her easel next to his and hewing closely to his Impressionist style. Occasionally she managed to exhibit or sell her work, although she suffered in comparison to her stepfather, "a master," as a critic pointed out in a review of her paintings at the 1906 Salon des Indépendants, "whom it is dangerous to imitate."[4] Jean's illness had brought her back to Giverny, where she attended to her husband's needs and then, following Jean's death, to those of her stepfather. Clemenceau called her the "Blue Angel": a reference to her blue eyes and sweet, generous nature. Her younger brother Jean-Pierre Hoschedé—another faithful and beloved stepchild—noted that after Jean's death she was "at Monet's side, always and everywhere."[5]

Among Monet's numerous blessings was a close and sympathetic extended family. Another stepdaughter, Marthe, lived nearby with her American husband, the painter Theodore Earl Butler, whose first wife,

Michel Monet on his
quadricycle in front of the
Hôtel Baudy in Giverny.

Suzanne, Marthe's younger sister, had died in 1899. Butler and Suzanne
had two children together, the eldest of whom, Jacques, had exhibited
landscapes at the 1911 Salon d'Automne, aged only eighteen. Jean-Pierre,
thirty-six years old, lived nearby with his wife, as did Monet's surviving
son, Michel, likewise thirty-six, a quiet and reclusive bachelor. Michel
added an intoxicating whiff of petrol and engine oil to the scent of the
flowers in Giverny. Sharing Monet's love of motorcars, he bought and sold
a succession of automobiles, motorcycles, auto parts, and once a six-seater
omnibus. A clever engineer, he built his own motor-powered "quadricycle" on which he navigated the streets of Giverny.[6] He possessed an enthusiasm for speed that surpassed his father's and alarmed even Clemenceau.
"Unfortunately there he is, in his car, running about the country—he'll
break his neck one of these days," the Tiger once complained.[7]

Jean-Pierre was yet another speed freak. He operated a garage, auto
dealership, and cycle shop in Vernon, even assisting with the 1910 Tour
de France when it passed through the area.[8] He also shared Monet's love
of plants, parlaying youthful expeditions with his stepfather through
Giverny's marshes and meadows into a career as an amateur botanist.
A corresponding member of the Linnean Society of Normandy since
the age of nineteen, he published articles in distinguished journals on
the weeds and flowers of Vernon and surrounding area. He also raised

prizewinning Irish water spaniels—although Monet banned dogs and cats from his garden "because," as Jean-Pierre explained, "he feared the damage they would cause."⁹

Guests to Giverny would be conducted into the presence of this extended household's paterfamilias, who was usually found in his garden, "in shirt sleeves, suntanned, his hands black with earth," as one friend described him.¹⁰ Clemenceau's 1895 article in *La Justice* had celebrated Monet as *le paysan de Vernon* (the peasant of Vernon). A visitor once described him as looking like "a rough farmer, a hunter of wolves and bears, the sturdy branch of an ancient lineage."¹¹ It must have seemed appropriate that this greatest of French landscapists, the man who so intuitively interpreted the country's rural delights, should have looked like a robust, weather-beaten, hardworking man of the soil. Others compared him to, or mistook him for, a sailor or sea captain.¹² This comparison, too, seemed apt. He was such a renowned painter of seascapes that Rodin, seeing the ocean along the Brittany coast for the first time, exclaimed: "Oh, how beautiful—it's a Monet!"¹³

Although born in Paris, Monet had, in fact, grown up beside the sea in the bustling port of Le Havre on the Normandy coast, 125 miles downstream from Paris, at the mouth of the Seine. Here his father had worked for a wholesale grocer supplying the local clipper ships, and the family lived in the working-class suburb of Ingouville, known for its brothels, cabarets, and "shady places of all kinds."¹⁴ Monet later told a friend that the sea, with its waves and clouds, had been the backdrop to his entire existence.¹⁵ Some of his earliest known sketches were coastal scenes with sailboats, and his attachment to the sea—which he continued to paint throughout his life—was such that he said that when he died he wanted to be buried in a buoy.¹⁶

Monet had moved from Le Havre to Paris at the age of eighteen, in the spring of 1859, to study painting. Here he quickly immersed himself in the cosmopolitan world of art, politics, and literature. He soon left this bohemian world of his youth behind, moving to the Paris suburbs following his marriage to Camille, and then afterward to Giverny. However, something of the eccentric dress sense of his companions

of the boulevards and brasseries—the capes and caftans of the critic
Théophile Gautier, the suede gloves and "intentionally gaudy trousers"
of Édouard Manet[17]—stayed with him. His hardy, rugged looks were offset by his herringbone tweed suits, which came from a fine English tailor
in Paris, and by his made-to-measure boots of ruddy leather from a firm
that supplied the French cavalry. His ruffled shirts were of pastel hues
with cuffs of frilly tulle that gave him what one visitor called a "touch of
dandyism."[18] Jean-Pierre aptly summed up this unusual look as *campagnard chic* (rustic chic).[19]

Clemenceau later offered a picture of his friend: "Medium sized,
with a beautifully poised, well-built frame, an aggressive but twinkling
eye, and a firm and sonorous voice."[20] Monet was, in fact, short, and wide
of girth, with a thick crumb catcher of a beard in the yellow-stained middle of which burned an "eternal cigarette."[21] His aquiline nose reminded
one visitor of an Arabian sheik's.[22] His advancing years and roly-poly
physique belied his bustling energy. Everyone noted his keen, intelligent
eyes, although no one could agree on their color. Clemenceau called
them "black steel" and Edmond de Goncourt found them a "frightening
black"; others described them as blue, steel-gray, or chestnut brown.[23]
The ambiguity was perhaps fitting for someone who believed that our
perception of color was always affected by light, and that the visual
effect varied from one minute to another.

"LUNCH FIRST," MONET used to tell his guests.[24] The words must
always have been welcome. One of the great attractions of Giverny was
the food. "You get the best cuisine in France at his house," enthused an
art dealer who was forever trying to wangle invitations for himself.[25] The
meals were prepared by Monet's cook of many years, Marguerite, whose
husband, Paul, the butler and general factotum, ferried steaming dishes
from the kitchen while the chauffeur, Sylvain, fetched bottles of wine
from the cellar.

Clemenceau would have been conducted into a room he knew
well, the *salle à manger*, the entirety of which—walls, sideboards, chairs,
ceiling beams, wainscoting—was painted what a guest called "a Monet

yellow." The copper hood of the fireplace was so bright it made people squint.[26] More than fifty of Monet's Japanese prints hung on the walls, spilling into the other rooms and progressing up the stairs of the studio. Monet owned several Manet lithographs, but visitors encountered these little masterpieces only when visiting the *cabinet de toilette*.[27] Lunch chez Monet was a delightful but demanding gastronomical odyssey. Renoir used to seize upon the fish, fruits, and vegetables brought back from the market by his cook—not to eat but to paint, his dinner having to wait until the painting was finished.[28] Monet's voracious appetite kept him from detaining his cook or from producing many still lifes. Jean-Pierre claimed that Monet was not a gourmand: someone who ate and drank in huge quantities. He was, Jean-Pierre insisted, a gourmet: someone with refined and discriminating tastes.[29] But Monet was actually a combination: he ate and drank in huge quantities the kinds of food and wine that satisfied his refined and discriminating tastes. "He eats like four," one amazed guest reported. "I promise you, that's not just a manner of speaking. He'll take four pieces of meat, four servings of vegetables, four glasses of liqueur."[30] He loved foie gras from Alsace, truffles from Périgord, mushrooms that he picked himself at dawn in a chestnut grove outside Giverny. Dishes that featured at his groaning table included beef tongue, oxtail stew with frankfurters, calf's liver in aspic, chicken in a crayfish sauce, and a bouillabaisse whose recipe came courtesy of Cézanne. He ate feathered game that had been hung for at least a week—the gamier the better. On one occasion Clemenceau gave him a woodcock, which he stuffed into the pocket of his overcoat and promptly forgot about. Several days later, when he discovered the festering bird, "he did not disdain taking it to the kitchen, where it was cooked and he ate it with pleasure."[31]

In the middle of a hearty meal, Monet observed *le trou Normand* (the "Norman break"), a shot of apple brandy that served to cleanse the palate and stimulate the appetite for further bouts of gluttonous indulgence. Wine was served, of course—not the local plonk but better vintages brought up from his cellar. For a digestif there was his homemade plum brandy. Coffee was taken in the erstwhile barn-studio, which had long since been converted into an unpretentious drawing room and

Monet in the alley of roses in his flower garden.

furnished with rustic chairs, a marble statue by Rodin, and an old mirror into whose frame he inserted creased and yellowed photographs of
friends. The walls were crammed with the master's unframed paintings.
A bay window overlooked the garden into which, once the coffee was
finished, Monet would conduct his well-fed guests.

Monet's garden was what, in truth, most visitors hoped to see.
Numerous newspaper articles had been written about it, scores of photographs taken, profuse requests for viewings granted (and many others
declined). The chief attraction was not even the section of garden seen
from the windows of the house, spectacular though it was: the former
orchard and vegetable patch that Monet had transformed with islands
of multicolored flower beds and, at the center, a grand alley flanked by a
pair of yew trees and festooned with roses spiraling over metal frames.
The main attraction, beyond, was reached by means of an underground
passage in the southwest corner. The passageway led under a road, the

chemin du Roy, on which automobiles often stopped so their occupants could stare in wonder through a gap in the stone wall that Monet, in a concession to his celebrity, had opened to offer weary travelers a glimpse of his garden.[32] The tunnel also passed beneath the railway tracks from which, on that fateful expedition in 1883, Monet had first spotted the pink grandeur of Le Pressoir. Emerging from the tunnel, one reached what a journalist called "the domain of the water lilies."[33]

MONET HAD BEGUN creating this magical domain in 1893, when he bought a parcel of marshland on the other side of the road and railway tracks, beside the river Ru, and immediately sought planning permission to divert part of the river to create a lily pond. But because the river was used to water cattle, wash laundry, and power two mills on Giverny's eastern outskirts, the townspeople complained, fearful that Monet's exotic flowers—which had, as far as they could see, no commercial value—might overrun the banks and poison the water. Monet was unsympathetic to their concerns: "To hell with the natives of Giverny," he retorted.[34]

Monet's relations with the locals had never been especially good. He was what they called a *horzin*—an outsider or incomer. As an artist, he was an object of suspicion. Little impressed by his celebrity, the locals were largely unsympathetic to his artistic pursuits. Farmers charged him a fee to cross their pastures or paint in their fields. A few years earlier, when one of his paintings of a wheat stack was half-finished, the farmer informed him that the twenty foot-high rick would be demolished for threshing unless he paid for a stay of execution.* The villagers,

---

* These enormous conical ricks with their thatched crowns were, technically speaking, *meules de blé* (stacks of wheat) rather than haystacks (*meules de foin*). They functioned as silos for the storage of the wheat harvest during the winter. For protection from the elements, the stalks were arranged with the ears facing inward toward the center, while the top, like the roofs of many houses in Giverny at the time, was thatched. What to call *meules de blé* in English (grain stacks, wheat stacks, stacks of wheat?) has been subject to much art historical variation, with haystacks now definitively ruled out. I shall follow recent custom and call them wheat stacks.

who called themselves *cultivants*, could not understand the point of his flower garden, which yielded nothing to eat or sell. He for his part did not condescend to participate in what Jean-Pierre called "the exchange of banal pleasantries," which he found pointless and uninteresting.[35]

Permission for the pond was quickly granted, thanks to Monet having some strings to pull with local journalists and politicians. He was good friends with the mayor of Giverny, Albert Collignon, another *horzin*. Collignon was a distinguished writer and intellectual who had founded a journal, *La Vie littéraire*, and published important works on Stendhal and Diderot.[36] He was sympathetic to Monet's aspirations, and by the end of the year the painter had been allowed to divert the river and, by means of a system of sluices and grilles, create a small pond over a narrow stretch of which—probably inspired by his Hokusai wood-cuts—he had an elegant Japanese bridge constructed.

The first water lilies arrived in 1894, courtesy of Joseph Bory Latour-Marliac, a skilled and enterprising botanist with a nursery near Bordeaux. By cross-breeding white water lilies from northern climes with more vivid tropical varieties from the Gulf of Mexico, Latour-Marliac had created the first viable colored water lilies in Europe. He showed these exotic cultivars, with their palette of yellows, blues, and pinks, at the Exposition Universelle in Paris in 1889, in a garden at the Trocadéro, across the Seine from the Eiffel Tower, likewise unveiled to the world in 1889. The sight of these gorgeous new hybrids had inspired Monet. He wished to create a garden, he wrote, to "please the eyes"; but he also wanted, from that first glimpse at the Trocadéro, to provide himself with what he called "motifs to paint."[37]

Monet's original order from Latour-Marliac included six water lil-ies—two pink and four yellow—along with various other aquatic plants, such as water chestnut and bog cotton.[38] He also ordered four Egyptian lotuses, which, despite Latour-Marliac's assurances that they were capable of surviving in Normandy, quickly perished. However, the water lilies thrived, and Monet subsequently placed orders for red varieties. In the winter of 1895 he set up his easel beside the water and began to paint his pond for the first time. A year later he was visited by a journalist,

Monet beside his
newly expanded
water lily pond in
1905, around the time
he began painting his
"landscapes of water."

Maurice Guillemot, who enthused over the "strangely unsettling" blossoms floating among glassy reflections. Monet confided to Guillemot that he hoped to decorate a circular room with these green and mauve blossoms and reflections.[39]

Nothing came of this plan, and Monet's paintings of his pond went into storage. He set about expanding the water garden a few years later, buying an adjacent parcel of land that, once more earth was moved, further sluices added, and the Ru once again diverted in its bed, effectively tripled the size of the pond. Meanwhile he constructed four new bridges, while to the existing Japanese bridge he added a trellis for wisteria. Bamboo, rhododendrons, and Japanese apple and cherry trees joined the willows artfully disposing themselves along the margins of the pond.

The running costs were, of course, fabulously expensive. Greenhouses were constructed, including one dedicated to the water lilies, complete with its own heating system. The team of gardeners toiled through the seasons. In 1907, when passing automobiles showered his water lilies with dust, Monet paid for the chemin du Roy to be tarmacked rather than—as he had been doing—instructing his gardeners to give the lily pads a daily dunking. Altogether he spent some 40,000 francs per year on his gardens. Monet's lavish means meant, however, that he could easily meet these extravagant costs, since his bank accounts, chock-full from the sales of his works, meant he was earning some 40,000 francs in annual interest payments alone.[40]

EARLIER IN HIS career, Monet had roved widely around France, palette and paintbrush in hand. In 1886 he worked along the windswept cliffs of Belle-Île-en-Mer, ten miles off the coast of Brittany. In 1888 he went with Renoir to Antibes, in the South of France, returning with gorgeous portraits of the Côte d'Azur. The following year he spent three months at Fresselines, painting beside the steep gorge of the river Creuse, 220 miles south of Paris.

After buying Le Pressoir in 1890, Monet still made the occasional painting expedition: to Norway to visit a stepson, to the Normandy coast, to London three times between 1899 and 1901 and a trip to Venice with Alice in 1908, where the two of them, looking every inch the tourists, posed for photographs among the pigeons in the Piazza San Marco. However, the vast majority of Monet's paintings after 1890 were done within a mile or two of his house. In the 1890s he began devoting himself to local subjects such as the wheat stacks in the nearby meadow, the poplar trees beside the river Epte, and scenes of the Seine downstream at Vernon and upstream at Port-Villez. He painted the ancient church of Notre-Dame perched above the river at Vernon, and in the summer of 1896 he began rising at three thirty in the morning and paddling onto the Seine in a flat-bottomed boat so he could capture the dawn mists.

Local these scenes might have been, but the Monet scholar Paul Hayes Tucker has shown that they possessed powerful national resonances as evocations of an essential Frenchness. Monet's paintings of wheat stacks, for instance, were images of the bountiful and enduring landscape, what Tucker calls a "rural France that is wholesome and fecund, reassuring and continuous."[41] Likewise the poplars, which were a crop planted for both firewood and the building industry. Indeed, the poplars Monet painted beside the Epte were due to be chopped down before he finished his canvases, forcing him to purchase the entire crop (which, unsentimentally, he sold to a timber merchant once his works were done). The poplar was, moreover, the "tree of liberty" in France, adopted as such, Tucker notes, because its name came from *populus*, which meant both "people" and "popular."[42] The Gothic cathedral of Rouen was even more obviously a symbol of France, the representative of an architectural style, born on the Île-de-France, that spread across Western Europe during the Middle Ages. As a critic wrote in December 1899, with these paintings Monet "expressed everything that forms the soul of our race."[43]

There was a certain irony in the fact that this catering to a yearning for visions of rural France was done by a man whose own rustic neighbors scorned him as an intruder unsympathetic to their age-old country ways. Indeed, Monet was not unlike the exotic water lilies whose existence depended on the diversion of the natural course of a river essential to rural life: he, too, was an exotic import whose presence in Giverny was not in keeping with, or conducive to, the traditional ways of life that he made his fortune from depicting on canvas.

Despite these canvases making him wealthy and famous, by the end of the century Monet abruptly abandoned these patriotic and quintessentially French scenes of the countryside near Giverny. Instead, his subjects became even more circumscribed as he turned almost obsessively, and at the expense of all else, to his garden. As his friend Gustave Geffroy wrote: "The powerful landscapist who so strongly expressed the greatness of the sea, cliffs, rocks, ancient trees, rivers and cities, took pleasure in a sweet and charming simplicity, in this delightful corner of a garden, this tiny pond where blossoms some mysterious petal."[44] The turning point, as Tucker points out, had been 1898, a date that coincided with the climax of the Dreyfus Affair, the political scandal and miscarriage of justice in which the wrongful conviction for espionage of Alfred Dreyfus revealed an ugly anti-Semitism at the highest levels of French society.⁴⁵ Monet's friends Clemenceau and Émile Zola took leading and, indeed, heroic roles in the affair, with the former publishing the latter's famous article "J'Accuse"—a master class in speaking truth to power—in his newspaper *L'Aurore*. "Bravo and bravo again," Monet wrote to Zola, who was promptly convicted of libel and forced to flee across the channel to England.⁴⁶ No more patriotic scenes of the French countryside, no more expressions of the soul of the French race, issued forth from Monet's brush. How could a Dreyfusard such as Monet celebrate or even represent France after the nation's glory had been, as Zola wrote, "threatened by the most shameful and most indelible of stains"?⁴⁷ Indeed, following Zola's trial, he stopped painting altogether for eighteen months.

"Il faut cultiver notre jardin," wrote Voltaire at the end of *Candide*. Monet proceeded to do precisely that: he cultivated his garden, whose Japanese bridge, rose alley, weeping willows, and water lilies—none of which was evocative of the French countryside or the soul of the French race—would provide, over the next quarter of a century, material for some three hundred paintings. This narrowing of geographical range to the boundaries of his own property did not mean a curtailing of his artistic vision. Far from it, as astute critics quickly realized. "In this simplicity," wrote Geffroy, "is found everything the eye can see and surmise, an infinity of shapes and shades, the complex life of things."⁴⁸ If William Blake saw the world in a grain of sand, Monet could glimpse, in the mirrored surface of his lily pond, the dazzling variety and abundance of nature.

MONET'S PAINTINGS OF his garden eventually became even more critically and commercially successful than his canvases of wheat stacks, poplars, and cathedrals. In 1909 he unveiled forty-eight of them at an exhibition in Paris entitled *Les Nymphéas: Séries de paysages d'eau par Claude Monet* (*The Water Lilies: Series of Waterscapes by Claude Monet*). With rapid and lucrative sales, it was the most resoundingly triumphant exhibition of his career. A critic in the *Gazette des Beaux-Arts* declared: "For as long as mankind has been around, and for as long as artists have painted, no one has ever painted better than this." Another critic crowned Monet as "the greatest painter we possess today."[49] His work was compared to Michelangelo's frescoes in the Sistine Chapel and to Beethoven's last quartets.[50]

Monet's renown as France's greatest painter—not to mention France's most famous gardener—was complete. But after such success, of course, came the deluge of sorrow: the deaths of Alice and Jean, the trouble with his eyes, the forced retirement of his brushes. Monet must have wondered, too, about his artistic fate. In 1905 the influential critic Louis Vauxcelles wrote that Monet reminded him of Ernest Meissonier.[51] He was referring to Monet's physical appearance: his long white beard and robust frame. But Monet's tremendous wealth and success, together with his imposing country house and his obstreperous temperament, bore uncomfortable comparison with the arrogance and extravagance of France's mightiest artistic titan in the years of Monet's youth—the Meissonier whose paintings drew huge crowds and changed hands for vast sums, who spent a fortune on his splendid mansion in Poissy, who used his vast property as a stage set for his paintings, and who was celebrated as the most renowned artist of his age. But following his death in 1891, Meissonier had vanished into almost unrelieved obscurity. "Many people who had great reputations," Meissonier had once observed with an anxious eye on the prospects for his own posterity, "are nothing but burst balloons now."[52] Monet could have been forgiven for worrying that his balloon would likewise burst and that, like Meissonier, he would pay for the Olympian success of his lifetime with disdain and anonymity after his death.

The warning signs were already flashing. The legacies of Monet and his fellow Impressionists were still in doubt. In 1912, Vauxcelles declared: "It is generally agreed that Impressionism has passed into history. Younger artists, while paying their respects, must seek other things."[53] The movement had indeed passed into history. The Impressionists had exhibited together for the last time in 1886, more than a quarter of a century earlier. The participants had passed, or were passing, from the scene. Édouard Manet had died in 1883, the very week that Monet moved to Giverny. Berthe Morisot followed in 1895, Alfred Sisley in 1899, Camille Pissarro in 1903, and Paul Cézanne in 1906. The surviving members were largely inactive due to the infirmities of age. The seventy-three-year-old Renoir, arthritic and wheelchair-bound, had retired to the South of France, where he presented a "frightful spectacle" to visitors.[54] Edgar Degas, approaching eighty, was in a worse condition: a bitter and misanthropic recluse. "Death is all I think of," he announced to the few souls who could stand his company.[55] Mary Cassatt described him as a "mere wreck."[56] She, like him, was virtually blind and, also like him, had stopped painting altogether—a fate that it appeared Monet was about to share.

Monet was in danger of becoming an anachronism. As early as 1898 an anonymous critic had written that the art of "Monsieur Monet" would have no future. "The fact is," he wrote, "that the master of true Impressionism…no longer conquers the youth."[57] That was not entirely true, since young artists such as Henri Matisse and André Derain were greatly inspired by his example. But the most vocal opposition to Impressionism was led not, as in the old days, by conservative art critics but by a new and rising Parisian avant-garde, in particular by the Cubists and their supporters. These and other younger painters, including Pointillists such as Georges Seurat, were labeled "Post-Impressionists" by the English critic Roger Fry in 1910—a name suggesting that they had superseded the Impressionists. Many of them, especially the Cubists, claimed to look to Cézanne rather than Monet as their master. Cézanne, they believed, showed a "calculated and intentional effort" in his rigorously constructed compositions, as opposed to the formless and "hasty fantasy" produced by Monet.[58] In 1908, when the Cubist painter Georges Braque staged his first one-man exhibition in Paris, Guillaume Apollinaire, a friend of Pablo Picasso, wrote in the catalogue's preface that Impressionism was nothing but "ignorance and frenzy." There was now, he declared, "a place for a nobler art—more measured, more orderly, more cultivated."[59] By which, of course, he meant the Cubism of Braque and Picasso. Another critic, André Salmon, a friend of Apollinaire and Picasso, claimed that the "modern landscapist, as soon as he looks at nature and before he even picks up his brush, pronounces the condemnation of Impressionism."[60]

*

THE PURPOSE OF Clemenceau's visit to Giverny in 1914 was not merely to escape from Paris and its incessant talk of the election in order to enjoy the delights of Monet's table and the sight of his garden. He had come, as usual, to offer comfort and encouragement.

Monet was as fortunate with his friends as he was with his family. Old comrades had been rallying around him for the previous three years. "You still have great and beautiful things to do," urged Gustave Geffroy, who, along with Clemenceau and the novelist Octave Mirbeau, was Monet's closest friend and greatest supporter.[61] Another sympathetic friend was the young man-about-town Sacha Guitry, whom *Gil Blas* called an "author, actor, lecturer, caricaturist, man of the world, model husband and delightful friend."[62] The twenty-eight-year-old Guitry and his wife, Charlotte Lysès, had begun enticing Monet to their country home, Les Zoaques, which stood in the shadow of a picturesquely ruined abbey in the charming village of Jumièges, near Rouen. Fearing that Monet was unlikely to do much more painting, they had coaxed him from his torpor in the summer of 1913 by having him redesign their garden. Monet enjoyed the company of "les Guitry," as he called them. They were generous hosts, sending luxurious automobiles to collect guests as they disembarked from the train, then plying them with lobster and champagne. "Life here is always delicious," Monet wrote to Blanche during a stay that August.[63] One other guest at Les Zoaques that summer witnessed a hearty-looking Monet, with typical gusto, downing a bottle of Burgundy and devouring a whole partridge.[64]

Monet had taken with relish to the task of creating a garden at Les Zoaques. Readers of the gossip columns—in which Sacha, a tireless self publicist, always featured conspicuously—could follow his progress closely. "Louis XIV had Le Nôtre," reported *Gil Blas*. "Sacha Guitry has Claude Monet. Sacha Guitry has nothing for which to envy to Louis XIV."[65] Sacha was bedridden in the spring of 1914, seriously ill with pneumonia. (The society pages kept readers apprised of every change in his parlous condition.) But in April, Monet was still making occasional trips to Les Zoaques, armed with drawings and plants from

Monet's "delightful friend," Sacha Guitry

his garden. Charlotte wrote him affectionate letters, telling him to "stay happy" and calling him her "dear and great gardener."[66]

Gardening was one thing, painting quite another. None of Monet's friends had surrendered hope of him taking up his brushes again. In the summer of 1913, during one of his stays at Les Zoaques, the "affectionate exhortations" of Guitry and Mirbeau sent him back to his easel.[67] A few months later a Paris weekly duly printed a reassuring photograph of the master, resplendently turned out in his Old England tweeds, sitting before the easel in his studio and dabbing away at a canvas depicting the pergola of roses behind his house. "I went three years without painting because of a terribly cruel loss," he told the interviewer. "I only went back to my easel two or three short months ago."[68] But any work he did was desultory, sporadic and without any of the old enthusiasm. One problem was that he thought he had accomplished everything he could possibly do with a paintbrush. "I always wanted to believe," he wrote to one of his picture dealers in 1913, "that I would make headway and finally do something worthwhile. But, alas, I must now bury that hope."[69]

It was with the determined plan of disinterring that hope that, on the day of his visit to Giverny, Clemenceau at some point—no doubt after lunch and a tour of the gardens—descended with Monet, according to legend, to the cellar. Here in the dank gloom he saw Monet's first paintings of the water lily pond, the canvases done almost twenty years earlier, shown to Maurice Guillemot in 1897 but never put on public display. Working up an enthusiasm, Clemenceau told Monet that he was amazed by the paintings, although he later confessed that he found these first efforts, although quite pretty, "not very interesting and quite sober."[70] But he hoped to revive in Monet the old dream, confessed to Guillemot, of decorating a room with a series of large-scale canvases. "Monet," Clemenceau told him, "you ought to hunt out a very rich Jew who would order your water lilies as a decoration for his dining-room."[71]

Clemenceau must have been surprised but delighted by Monet's positive reaction. Indeed, he responded in a way Clemenceau did not anticipate, because rather than doing something with these decades-old canvases he decided to create an entirely new and even more ambitious set of paintings of his pond. Several days later Monet wrote to Geffroy, telling him of Clemenceau's visit and declaring that he was "in good shape and possessed by the desire to paint." The poor weather, he said, had prevented him from making a start, but he intended "to undertake great things."[72]

These words must have come as a huge relief to Geffroy, who, as one of Monet's greatest cheerleaders, had been trying to convince him that, despite everything, his artistic powers remained undiminished. But neither Geffroy nor Clemenceau could in their wildest dreams have imagined the artistic odyssey that their exhortations had unleashed. "You have launched a projectile toward infinity," Clemenceau would later write. He also described Monet, with his new project, as a man who was "madly striving for the realization of the impossible."[73]

CHAPTER THREE

LANDSCAPES OF WATER

MUCH OF CLAUDE MONET'S life and work had been a mad striving for the impossible. His goal, which he frankly admitted was unattainable, was to paint his carefully chosen object—the cathedral, cliff, or wheat stack before which he raised his easel—under singular and fleeting conditions of weather and light. As he told an English visitor, he wanted "to render my impressions before the most fugitive effects."[1]

In 1889 a critic had scoffed that Monet's paintings were nothing more than a matter of "geography and the calendar."[2] This was, however, to miss the point of Monet's work. Since objects changed their color and appearance according to the seasons, the meteorological conditions, and the time of day, Monet hoped to capture their visual impact in these brief, distinctive, ever-changing moments in time. He concentrated not only on the objects themselves but also, critically, on the atmosphere that surrounded them, the erratically shifting phantoms of light and color that he called the *enveloppe*. "Everything changes, even stone," he wrote to Alice while working on his paintings of the façade of Rouen Cathedral.[3] But freezing the appearance of objects amid fleeting phantoms of light and air was no easy task. "I am chasing a dream," he admitted in 1895. "I want the impossible."[4]

Recording the fugitive effects of color and light was integral to Monet's art. Setting up his easel in front of Rouen Cathedral, or the wheat stacks in the frozen meadow outside Giverny, or the windswept cliffs at Étretat on the coast of Normandy, he would paint throughout the day as the light and weather, and finally the seasons, changed. To reproduce the desired effects accurately according to his personal sensations, he was forced to work outdoors, often in disagreeable conditions. In 1889 a journalist described him on the stormy beach beneath the cliffs at Étretat, "dripping wet under his cloak, painting a hurricane in the salty spray" as he tried to capture the different lighting conditions on two or three canvases that he shuttled back and forth onto his easel.[5]

Because lighting effects changed quickly—every seven minutes, he once claimed[6]—he was forced, in his series paintings of wheat stacks and poplars, to work on multiple canvases almost simultaneously, placing a different one on his easel every seven minutes or so, rotating them according to the particular visual effect he was trying to capture. Clemenceau once watched him working in a poppy field with four different canvases. "He was going from one to the other, according to the position of the sun."[7] In the 1880s the writer Guy de Maupassant had likewise witnessed Monet "in pursuit of impressions" on the Normandy coast. He described how the painter was followed through the fields by his children and stepchildren "carrying his canvases, five or six paintings depicting the same subject at different times and with different effects. He worked on them one by one, following all the changes in the sky."[8]

This obsession with capturing successive changes in the fall of light or the density of a fogbank could lead to episodes that were both comical (for observers) and infuriating (for Monet). In 1901, in London, he began painting what he called the "unique atmosphere" of the river Thames—the famous pea-souper fogs—from his room in the Savoy Hotel.[9] Here he was visited by the painter John Singer Sargent, who found him surrounded by no fewer than ninety canvases, "each one the record of a momentary effect of light over the Thames. When the effect was repeated and an opportunity occurred for finishing the picture," Sargent reported, "the effect had generally passed away before the particular canvas could be found."[10]

One irony of Monet's approach was that these paintings of fleeting visual effects at single moments in time actually took many months of work. "I paint entirely out of doors," he once airily informed a journalist. "I never touch my work in my studio."[11] However, virtually all of Monet's canvases, although begun on the beaches or in the fields, were actually completed back in the studio, often far from the motif and with much teeth-gnashing labor.[12] Octave Mirbeau reported that a single Monet canvas might take "sixty sessions" of work.[13] Some of the canvases, moreover, were given fifteen layers of paint.[14] His London paintings were finished not beside the banks of the Thames but as much as two years later in his studio in Giverny, beside the Seine, with the assistance of photographs. The revelation that Monet used photographs caused something of a scandal when this expedient was revealed in 1905 thanks to the indiscreet and possibly malicious comments of several of Monet's London acquaintances, including Sargent. Monet had risked a similar kind of scandal when he took one of his Rouen Cathedral paintings to Norway.

There was another irony to Monet's paintings. Many of them evoked gorgeous visions of rural tranquility: sun-dappled summer afternoons along a riverbank or fashionable women promenading in flowery meadows. As Mirbeau wrote, nature appeared in Monet's paintings in "warm breaths of love" and "spasms of joy."[15] His pleasingly bucolic scenes were combined with a flickering brushwork that produced delicious vibrations of color. The overall result was that many observers regarded his paintings as possessing a soothing effect on both the eye and the brain—and Monet himself as *le peintre du bonheur* (the painter of happiness). Geffroy believed Monet's works could offer comforting distraction and alleviate fatigue, while Monet himself speculated that they might calm "nerves strained through overwork" and offer the stressed-out viewer "an asylum of peaceful meditation."[16] The writer Marcel Proust, an ardent admirer, even believed Monet's paintings could play a spiritually curative role "analogous to that of psychotherapists with certain neurasthenics"—by which he meant those whose weakened nerves had left them at the mercy of fast-paced modern life.[17] Proust was not alone. More than a century later, an Impressionist expert at Sotheby's in London called Monet "the great anti-depressant."[18]

This "great anti-depressant" was, however, a neurasthenic who enjoyed anything but peaceful meditation as he worked on his paintings. Geffroy described Monet as "a perpetual worrier, forever anguished," while to Clemenceau he was *le monstre* and *le roi des grincheux*—"king of the grumps."[19] Monet could be volatile and bad-tempered at the best of

times, but when work at his easel did not proceed to his satisfaction—
lamentably often—he flew into long and terrible rages. Clemenceau
neatly summed up the quintessential Monet scenario of the artist throwing a tantrum in the midst of blissful scenery: "I imagine you in a Niagara
of rainbows," he wrote to Monet, "picking a fight with the sun."[20]

Monet's letters are filled with references to his gloom and anger.
Part of his problem was the weather. Monet could pick a fight with the
sun, the wind, or the rain. Painting in the open air left him at the mercy
of the elements, at which he raged like King Lear. His constant gripes
about the wind and rain had once earned him a scolding from Mirbeau:
"As for the nauseatingly horrible weather we have and that we will have
until the end of August, you have the right to curse. But to believe that
you're finished as a painter because it's raining and windy—this is pure
madness."[21]

It was a strange contradiction of Monet's practice that he wished
to work in warm, calm, sunny conditions, and yet for much of his
career he chose to paint in Normandy: a part of France that was, as a
nineteenth-century guidebook glumly affirmed, "generally cold and
wet…subject to rapid and frequent changes, and fairly long spells of
bad weather that result in unseasonable temperatures."[22] Working on
the windswept coast of Normandy in the spring of 1896, he found conditions exasperating. "Yesterday I thought I would go mad," he wrote.
"The wind blew away my canvases and, when I set down my palette to
recover them, the wind blew it away too. I was so furious I almost threw
everything away."[23] Sometimes Monet did in fact throw everything away.
On one occasion he hurled his color box into the river Epte in a blind
rage, then was obliged to telegraph Paris, once he calmed down, to have
a new one delivered.[24] On another occasion, he flung himself into the
Seine. "Luckily no harm was done," he reassured a friend.[25]

Monet's canvases likewise felt his wrath. Jean-Pierre Hoschedé
witnessed him committing "acts of violence" against them, slashing
them with a penknife, stamping them into the ground or thrusting his
foot through them.[26] An American visitor saw a painting of one of his
stepdaughters with "a tremendous crisscross rent right through the

centre"—the result of an enraged Monet giving it a vicious kick. Since he had been wearing wooden clogs at the time, the damage was considerable.[27] Sometimes he even set fire to his canvases before he could be stopped. On occasion his rages became so intense that he would roam the fields and then, to spare his family, check into a hotel nearby in Vernon. At other times he retreated to his bedroom for days at a time, refusing both meals and attempts at consolation. Friends tried to coax him from his gloom with diverting trips to Paris. "Come to Paris for two days," Mirbeau pleaded with him during one of these spells. "We shall walk. We shall go here and there...to the Jardin des Plantes, which is an admirable thing, and to the Théâtre-Français. We shall eat well, we shall say stupid things, and we shall not see any paintings."[28]

There was another contradiction in Monet's practice. He loved to paint and, indeed, he lived to paint—and yet he claimed to find painting an unremitting torment. "This satanic painting tortures me," he once wrote to a friend, the painter Berthe Morisot.[29] To a journalist he said: "Many people think I paint easily, but it is not an easy thing to be an artist. I often suffer tortures when I paint. It is a great joy and a great suffering."[30] Monet's rage and suffering before his easel reveal the disingenuousness of his famous comment about Vincent van Gogh. Mirbeau, who owned Van Gogh's *Irises*, once proudly showed the work to Monet. "How did a man who loved flowers and light so much," Monet responded, "and who painted them so well, make himself so unhappy?"[31]

Some of Monet's friends regarded his torture and suffering as a necessary condition of his genius—as a symptom of his search for perfection, or what Geffroy called the "dream of form and color" that he pursued "almost to the point of self-annihilation."[32] After witnessing yet another fit of dyspepsia, Clemenceau wrote to Monet that "if you were not pushed by an eternal search for the unattainable, you would not be the author of so many masterpieces."[33] As Clemenceau once explained to his secretary apropos of Monet's dreadful fits of temper: "One must suffer. One must not be satisfied...With a painter who slashes his canvases, who weeps, who explodes with rage in front of his painting, there is hope."[34]

Clemenceau must have realized that in persuading Monet to paint large-scale canvases of his water lily pond he had not only rekindled the painter's hopes but also, as a sore temptation to fate, his exasperation and rage.

OVER THE DECADES, Monet experienced various difficulties and privations. Early on, he endured bouts of poverty and critical derision. Later, he suffered from rheumatic pains—"the price of my time in the rain and snow"[35]—and cataracts, which may have been partly the price of his time in the bright sunshine staring at reflective, sparkling waters. However, no paintings had ever given him so many difficulties—and been the cause of so much anguished self-doubt and so many shredded canvases—as those of his water lilies. The 1909 exhibition *Les Nymphéas: Séries de paysages d'eau par Claude Monet* may have been his greatest critical and commercial triumph, but creating these magical waterscapes had plunged him into terrible anxiety and depression.

Monet had begun painting his newly expanded water garden in 1903. A year later a visiting journalist found him at the side of the pond working on twelve separate canvases, which he rotated according to the light.[36] An exhibition was scheduled for the spring of 1907, but things did not go well, and one month before the opening he asked for a postponement of a year, informing the gallery's proprietor, Paul Durand-Ruel, that he had just destroyed thirty canvases.[37] Matters were made even worse when, that spring, a violent storm damaged his garden. A year later, with the paintings still not ready, Monet dramatically renounced the projected exhibition "once and for all."[38] Forsaking his lily pond, he began painting baskets of eggs.

Monet's wife, Alice, began to despair of him as the black moods endured. "He punctures canvases every day," she lamented.[39] An American newspaper reported with incredulity that in a single day in May 1908 Monet destroyed $100,000 worth of paintings, raising the questions about whether (as the paper put it) he was an artist or a fool.[40] He began refusing to eat his lunch—a bad sign in such a gourmand—and stayed in his bedroom all day long. He began suffering headaches, fits of dizziness and blurred vision. His friends, as always, rallied and cajoled. Mirbeau gently chastised him for canceling the exhibition, noting that such behavior was "insane and painful" in someone who was "without doubt the greatest and most magnificent painter of our time."[41] Buoyed by such praise, Monet finally returned to his canvases. "These land-scapes of water and reflections have become an obsession," he wrote to Geffroy in the summer of 1908.[42]

In 1909, two years later than planned, Monet exhibited a total of forty-eight paintings of his lily pond. By this time Monet's anguished struggles were well publicized. A critic for *Le Gaulois* noted that the paintings were being shown to the public only after "much hesitation, anxiety and modesty" on the part of the artist, while another critic, Arsène Alexandre, informed his readers that Monet had become the victim of fatigue and neurasthenia.[43] Neurasthenia was a malady more usually associated with women, Jews, male weaklings, homosexuals, and the morally debauched.[44] It must have come as a shock to many that Monet, the hale and hearty "peasant of Vernon," with his wooden clogs and robust physique, was suffering from this nervous affliction.

Monet's nervous fatigue was not merely the result of the winds that billowed his canvases or the rains that pelted and pummeled his pre-cious garden. Nor was it simply caused by sitting in the same spot and staring at the same scene, day after day—the kind of sedentary activity that, the experts were agreed, could result in neurasthenia and that, in Rouen in 1892, had left him with disagreeable nightmares of the cathe-dral falling on his head. Monet's anguish was caused more than anything by his attempt to do something entirely new and different, indeed rev-olutionary. His own description of the project was typically laconic: "The crucial thing is the mirror of water whose appearance changes constantly with the reflections from the sky."[45] The water did indeed change in appearance in his paintings, turning from pale green or dusky mauve to salmon pink and fiery orange. But how he composed his motif of water and sky revealed a gradual change in his artistic vision—the bold experiment that, as Geffroy claimed, had driven him to the brink of self-annihilation.

Monet was unique in attempting to paint a still, reflective surface of water in a steep, close-up perspective. Painters of water usually concentrated on more distant effects, such as moonlight shimmering on ruffled rivers or waves crashing heavily on the beach. Monet himself was an acknowledged master of these sorts of waterscapes: Édouard Manet once called him the "Raphael of water."[46] But Monet beside his lily pond was in search of more intimate impressions as he registered not only the surface vegetation and reflections but also the water's half-hidden depths. He had already tried his hand at capturing these subtle underwater effects. "I am troubled by impossible things," he complained to Geffroy as he painted beside the river Epte in 1890, "such as water with vegetation undulating in its depths."[47] The upshot of these subaqueous preoccupations had been a canvas showing his stepdaughters Blanche and Suzanne in a rowboat, drifting through (as Mirbeau poetically described the scene) "the liquid transparencies of an extraordinary world of underwater flora, of long filaments of algae, muddy and untamed, which, under the pressure of the current, tremble and twist."[48]

The difficulty of painting these "impossible things"—of capturing not only the fleeting shadows and surface reflections but also the murky, half-hidden depths of trembling vegetation—was one of the things that drove Monet to despair. His success when the paintings were finally exhibited in 1909 was the result of a sophisticated technique of applying his paints.[49] Monet was not, as Cézanne had claimed, "only an eye," for his incredible acuity of vision was combined with an equally adroit hand capable of subtle but masterful techniques. The painter André Masson—himself a master of spontaneous applications of paint—later rhapsodized over Monet's "touch of many accents: crisscrossed, ruffled, speckled. You have to see it in close-up. What a frenzy!" His brushwork was, Masson declared, "the wildest whirlwind."[50]

Close examination of these waterscapes reveals a magnificently varied technique. Monet chose canvases with a pronounced weave, one whose weft threads were thicker than the warp. He then applied a series of undercoats, allowing each one to dry before adding the next. He brushed his paint at right angles to the weft so that its threads trapped more of the pigment, creating a series of corrugations and giving the canvas what has been called a "textural vibration."[51] In other words, he used his pigments and the texture of the canvas to suggest both the ripples of water on the surface and, in the declivities marked by the warp threads, the underlying depths. Paradoxically for a man who wished to give the impression of the spontaneous capture of a fleeting moment in time, he sometimes used a dozen or more layers of paint on a canvas. He often scraped off one or two layers, leaving behind an uneven texture to further enhance the shimmering appearance of the subsequent applications.[52]

This sort of brushwork was a virtuoso performance, especially in combination with how Monet composed his scenes. Many of his earliest paintings of his water garden, such as those of his Japanese bridge done in the late 1890s, showed a traditional perspective. The landscape receded from the foreground, which was composed of water and floating water lilies, and into a middle ground, across which the Japanese bridge gracefully arched. In the background was the distant bank with its lush vegetation, and in some of the paintings, a snatch of sky. But gradually water, land, and sky began to blend and exchange places, or even disappear entirely as, standing beside the pond, Monet lowered his gaze to focus with increasing intensity on the water. By 1904 the sky was cropped from his views of the pond. It appeared only in reflection, with the expanse of water bordered at the top of the canvas by the opposite bank. A year later, the opposite bank disappeared as Monet concentrated on the surface of the water, whose reflections were interrupted by the shimmering archipelagoes of lily pads. The view became even more dizzyingly confusing in 1907—Monet's frustrating annus horribilis—as he rotated his canvases 90 degrees and began painting views that were taller than they were wide. Water lilies were strewn across murky reflections of willow trees, while a gap of mirrored sky in various hues occupied the center of the painting.

One of the critics in 1909, Louis Gillet, noted what was remarkable about these waterscapes: they were "upside-down paintings" because the sky was at the bottom and the landscape—present only in the topsy-turvy reflections of willows and other foliage—at the top. Landscape painting had been turned on its head. There was no firm mooring for the viewer, only a vertiginous gaze into what Gillet called "a mirror without a frame"⁵³—a mirror that offered an inverted view of the world and the half-hidden depths beneath. The viewer was left with no perspective and little means of gauging space or distance. Land, trees, and sky had all disappeared, glimpsed only in streaky reflections agitated by the breeze, set ablaze by the sun or dimmed by the falling day. The only solid forms left were the blurry clusters of water lilies with their bright pinpricks of color. As the reviewer for the *Gazette des Beaux-Arts* exclaimed, no one had ever painted like this before. Little wonder that, in the midst of these discombobulating visions, Monet should briefly have turned to painting baskets of eggs.⁵⁴

Louis Gillet made another point about Monet's 1909 waterscapes. What made these scenes so innovative, he suggested, was their abstraction. Indeed, he declared that "the pure abstraction of art can go no further."⁵⁵ Monet may have protested that his art was not an abstraction from nature but, rather, an attempt to reproduce it as faithfully as possible—indeed, with an almost fanatical attention to visual evidence, however transient. Jean-Pierre Hoschedé later claimed that Monet never worked "abstractly."⁵⁶ However, critics such as Gillet, as well as certain avant-garde painters, saw things differently. For them, Monet's delicious formal qualities—the shimmering brushstrokes and fields of harmonized color—had liberated themselves from any mundane descriptive function. That is, a realistic depiction of the pond was far less important than both the formal means through which it was conveyed and the emotions that these mesmerizing swipes of color evoked in the viewer. If Monet had been written off by some critics as an irrelevance, Gillet's claim about "pure abstraction" placed him, in 1909, at the forefront of modern art.

THE GREAT SUCCESS of Monet's 1909 exhibition led to calls for the forty-eight paintings to be kept together as part of a decorative ensemble. The appeal was similar to the one that Clemenceau had made in

1895 regarding the Rouen Cathedral paintings, when he urged the government—to no avail—to purchase the collection and keep it intact. Monet himself wrote a letter to Geffroy expressing his desire to have his water lily paintings decorate a room, creating a "flowery aquarium" in which the owner could relax and restore himself. He envisaged the canvases "covering the walls, unifying them, giving the illusion of an endless whole, of a wave with no horizon and no bank."[57] The press adopted this ambition, with journalists from at least five newspapers appealing for someone to come forward and purchase the works, thereby re-creating and preserving the immersive experience enjoyed by visitors to the Galerie Durand-Ruel. "Will the millionaire who is needed read these lines?" asked one newspaper.[58]

It should not have been difficult to find a millionaire in need of some tranquil yet bewitching interior decoration. Large-scale paintings for private homes had been all the rage in Paris for the previous few decades, with artists such as Édouard Vuillard and Maurice Denis adorning the salons, studies, and dining rooms of wealthy plutocrats with canvases specially commissioned to create decorative ensembles. Denis claimed in 1903 that the word *décoratif* was the "*tarte à la crème*," or watchword, among young French painters.[59] Three years later, a French critic argued that the greatness of a work of art must not be denied simply on the grounds that "it could be of some use or ornament in our homes" and he noted that the annual Paris Salon, with numerous decorative murals on display, was beginning to look more and more like "a veritable furnished apartment."[60]

Monet already had some experience of his own creating pictorial ensembles in domestic spaces. In the late 1870s he executed at least four landscapes on canvases almost six feet high and six feet wide to embellish the wood-paneled grand salon of Ernest Hoschedé's country home, the Château de Rottembourg. These works featured the grounds of Hoschedé's magnificent estate: a rose garden, a shimmering pond, a flock of turkeys glowing whitely on the lawn. They were never installed due to bankruptcy proceedings against Hoschedé (whose wife soon decamped with Monet). But a few years later the artist painted thirty-six panels of varying sizes to adorn the doors in Paul Durand-Ruel's Paris apartment using his garden at Giverny for inspiration.

In 1909, however, no millionaire stepped forward to rescue the collection of water lily paintings. "Never again," lamented *Le Gaulois*, Paris's biggest-selling morning newspaper, "nowhere else, will anyone see them grouped as we see them now. They will scatter to the four corners of the earth, all of them exquisite, but each one yielding only a part of the secret of them all."[61] The comment may have exasperated Monet and his supporters, given that the proprietor of *Le Gaulois*, Gabriel Thomas, had just paid Maurice Denis to decorate the dining room of his pink-bricked mansion in Meudon, Les Capucins, with pastoral scenes inspired by his garden.

The prophecy that the paintings would be dispersed was fulfilled soon enough. The critic for the *Gazette des Beaux-Arts* pointed out that several of the paintings were going to "eager America, which is forever stealing our masterpieces."[62] As early as 1889 a reviewer feared that the "rapacity of the Yankees" might mean that Monet's best works would go to the United States[63]—a fear that seemed very real when, two years later, Bertha Palmer's European shopping spree saw her return to Chicago with twenty-five Monets. The transatlantic flight of Monet's works continued in 1909. Two of the water lily paintings were bought from the exhibition by Alexander Cochrane, a chemical manufacturer, to grace the Boston mansion built for him by Stanford White. Other buyers of the canvases included Hunt Henderson, a New Orleans sugar baron, and Cornelius Newton Bliss, a former secretary of the interior, a wall in whose mansion on East Thirty-Seventh Street in New York already displayed one of Monet's Étretat paintings. The Worcester Art Museum bought one on the advice of Desmond FitzGerald, a Brookline-based hydraulic engineer and inveterate Monet collector. Another went to Katherine Toll, the widow of a prominent Colorado lawyer. Still another would join the bountiful collection of Monets in the home in Naugatuck, Connecticut—also built by Stanford White—of the iron manufacturer Harris Whittemore. In 1890, Whittemore had begun collecting Monet so assiduously that his father complained: "We will have more of the

Monets than I think we will care for."[64] Undeterred, Whittemore eventually acquired thirty of his canvases. A discerning collector, he also owned Whistler's *Symphony in White, No. 1: The White Girl*, which hung on a staircase landing.

Whatever disappointment Monet experienced with the loss of the opportunity to install a "flowery aquarium" in a domestic setting may have been assuaged by the fact that in 1909 the sales of his paintings amounted to 272,000 francs. But it was this old dream of a complete decorative ensemble—one of the few things that Monet had not yet truly realized—that Clemenceau, with his vision of "a rich Jew," revived almost five years later.

CHAPTER FOUR

A GREAT PROJECT

MONET'S GUESTS AT Giverny were often conducted up the stairs and into the master bedroom. Gustave Geffroy called this spacious, light-filled room, with its views of the garden, "the museum of Monet's most admired companions."[1] The walls featured, among other works, a Degas bather, three Pissarro landscapes, four works by Édouard Manet, and two watercolors by Eugène Delacroix. There were a pair of bronzes by Auguste Rodin and, above the simple bed, a "voluptuously beautiful" Renoir[2] and Cézanne's *Château Noir*. Cézanne had been Monet's most admired companion of all, and no fewer than fourteen of his paintings hung on the walls of his bedroom and studio. "Yes, Cézanne, he is the greatest of us all," Monet once declared.[3] Whenever his work was not going well, he was forced to drape his Cézannes, unable to work in the presence of such genius. "I felt a pygmy at the foot of a giant," he once explained.[4]

The sight of these admired companions meant that Monet enjoyed waking up each morning. He was by long habit an early riser. Whenever he was painting he kept hours with the sun, retiring at dusk and rising at dawn, not even bothering to shutter the bedroom windows. After a bath—always cold, no matter the weather—he descended for breakfast and the first of many cigarettes. He ate a grilled eel or else bacon and eggs, the latter courtesy of the chickens cooped in the garden. Sometimes he enjoyed an English-style breakfast of marmalade on toast and Kardomah tea, delights he had discovered during his stays in London. Sacha Guitry claimed that he also started the day with a glass of white wine, keeping a venerable French working-class tradition.[5] Then it was off to work in the open air or, on inclement days, in his studio. A bell at eleven thirty A.M. precisely summoned him to lunch, which began with a glass of homemade plum brandy. He was back before his easel two hours later, working through the afternoon until he was physically exhausted. When in the throes of painting, he had no time for such time-consuming trivialities as getting a haircut, and so the village barber would be summoned to the side of the pond to crop the master's locks as he painted—though the scissors were forbidden to touch his great tobacco-stained beard.[6]

Monet appears to have resumed work with his old intensity within days of Clemenceau's April visit, working almost daily throughout May and June. "I'm getting up at four in the morning," he wrote to one of his picture dealers in June 1914.[7] Around the same time he wrote to the art critic and gallery director Félix Fénéon: "I'm hard at work and, whatever the weather, I paint... I have undertaken a great project that I love."[8]

One of the first things Monet did was to make a number of drawings. He once declared that he never drew "except with a brush and paint."[9] He liked to promote the idea that drawing had no real place in his art—unlike, for example, the nineteenth-century painter J.-A.-D. Ingres, who claimed that drawing was "seven-eighths of what makes up painting" and who made more than five thousand drawings in the course of his long life.[10] Monet downplayed the role of drawing in his art because it smacked of forethought and went against the Impressionist ideal of spontaneously capturing an impression. However, he was actually a talented draftsman with charcoal, pen, and pencil, often making sketches in pencil or crayon as preparatory studies for his paintings. He first made his reputation as an artist with a pencil rather than a brush, since as an adolescent in Le Havre he had attracted notice with the caricatures of local worthies that he sketched and then displayed, much to the delight of passersby, in the window of a stationery shop. Later, in Paris in the 1860s, he made pencil sketches of his bohemian comrades in the brasseries.[11]

Following Clemenceau's visit, Monet evidently dug out several of his old sketchbooks.[12] One of them was, incredibly, fifty years old, and some of its ten-by-thirteen-and-a-half-inch pages were covered in rough drawings he had made as long ago as the 1860s. It was a well-traveled book, too, since others of the drawings were of the windmills he had captured in Holland in 1871. There was also, poignantly, a sketch of his

Caricatures by a youthful Claude Monet

son Jean as a schoolboy—a sight that, a few months after Jean's death, must have brought him up short.

Onto the blank pages of these well-worn sketchbooks, Monet began drawing views of his irises, willows, and water lilies, rehearsing in pencil and wax crayon—sometimes violet in color—the motifs he was planning to paint. The last page of one of the books featured a smudgy sketch, made in pencil many years earlier, of the church steeple and distant rooftops of the neighboring village of Limetz. In need of space, he turned the sketchbook upside down and in the sky over Limetz began adding—as if they were large, buoyant clouds—great clusters of water lilies. His line was swift, loose, almost dreamy. It was also assured and, it is possible to imagine, joyous—the modest and squiggly beginnings of his great project.

Monet sketch in violet crayon for one of his water lily paintings

*

MONET WAS ABLE to resume work in the spring of 1914 because his vision had stabilized since the "dreadful discovery" almost two years earlier that he was losing the sight in his right eye. He was undergoing treatment from an ophthalmologist to delay an operation, and Clemenceau had for the moment allayed his fears of imminent blindness. "A cataract is less unpleasant than prostate trouble, I can assure you," he informed Monet.[13] Clemenceau knew whereof he spoke, having had his prostate gland removed in 1912.

Monet still suffered from poor vision in his left eye and, as a result, limited depth perception. His color vision, too, was distorted, but he compensated, as he later told an interviewer, by "trusting both the labels on my tubes and the method I adopted of laying out my pigments on my palette." But he also confessed that his "infirmity" gave him various remissions, periods of visual clarity that allowed him to tinker with the color balance of his canvases.[14] In any case, in the spring of 1914, his worries and complaints about his eyesight ceased for the moment, and he took the wise precautions of avoiding direct sunlight and wearing a wide-brimmed straw hat when out of doors.

Word of Monet's sudden revival made the news in Paris, where in the middle of June a journal published an article headlined THE HEALTH OF CLAUDE MONET. The author immediately sought to reassure his readers: "Claude Monet is in perfect health. However, this has not always been the case over the years, and admirers of the great artist deeply regretted that he had stopped all work. The master of Giverny no longer painted, an extremely unfortunate situation for French art, as well as for Claude Monet himself, who spent long hours in meditation, unable to take up his brushes." But those in any doubt that the master was now back at his easel were invited to take the train through Giverny: from the window of their carriages they would be able to spot the master beside his pond, capturing "with his amazing sensitivities the marvellous colours that enchant his eyes anew."[15]

Those peering out of the window of passing locomotives may have been surprised not only by the sight of a busy Monet but also by the size of his canvases. A measure of his excitement about his "great project" was the fact that many of the canvases on which he began working in 1914 loomed over him. Early in his career, when trying to attract public attention and to get paintings accepted into the Paris Salon, he attempted several monumental paintings—the kind of showstoppers known as *grandes machines* because of the pulleys, wires, and other equipment needed to move them around the studio. In 1865 he had begun *Luncheon on the Grass*, a picnic scene filled with life-sized modern-dress figures (the women wear fashionable crinolines) that would have come in at thirteen feet high by twenty feet wide. Slathering 260 square feet of canvas with pigment ultimately proved too complex and he was forced to abandon the project unfinished.

Seemingly undaunted by this failure, in 1866 he began another large-scale canvas, *Women in the Garden*, which stood eight feet high and almost seven feet wide. His commitment to plein air painting meant—so the legend goes—that he was obliged to dig a trench in the garden of his house in Ville-d'Avray, outside Paris, and raise and lower the oversized canvas by means of a system of pulleys. His herculean efforts proved in vain, since the work was rejected by the jury for the 1867 Salon. In 1914 it featured prominently in his studio, as did the remnants of *Luncheon on the Grass*. In 1878 he had offered *Luncheon on the Grass* as security to his landlord in Argenteuil, a certain Monsieur Flament, who promptly rolled it up and put it in the cellar. Monet redeemed the canvas six years later, by which time it had been so badly damaged by damp and mold that he cut it into three pieces.

Since then, Monet's canvases had shrunk dramatically in size. Virtually all his paintings since the mid-1860s had been no more than three feet wide—in part, no doubt, because of his commitment to painting outdoors. The few exceptions were several paintings of his stepdaughters Blanche and Suzanne floating in skiffs on the river, done at Giverny in the late 1880s after he told his picture dealer that he hoped "to get back to big paintings."[16] But even these canvases were less than five feet wide. The works that made his reputation and his fortune—his paintings of wheat stacks, poplars, Rouen Cathedral, London—barely ever exceeded three feet in either height or width. The water lily paintings in his spectacular 1909 Paris exhibition had been similarly modest in dimension. Most of these works were roughly three feet by three feet, with the largest still less than three and a half feet wide.

In 1914, however, Monet began working on canvases that were five feet high by more than six and a half feet wide, and his ambitions would presently stretch well beyond even these dimensions. How precisely he worked on these large canvases, especially in the early days of his great project, is difficult to know. He may have begun with small canvases on an easel beside the water, then moved into his studio and scaled up the design on the large canvases. If he began painting on large canvases in the open air beside the water, he would have needed assistance to carry them, as well as the wooden easels and his box of paints, down the steps of his studio and then more than a hundred yards through the garden and tunnel to the lily pond.

Monet may have been aided in these tasks by his gardeners, but Blanche also gave him practical assistance as in the old days when she used to follow him through the fields, pushing his canvases in a wheelbarrow and then painting her own compositions at his side. One visitor to Giverny later recalled that Blanche would "tackle the weighty easels" for Monet.[17] He could not have hoped for a more sympathetic or knowledgeable assistant. She had enjoyed some artistic success of her own: Bertha Palmer bought one of her landscapes in 1892, and she showed her work at the Salon des Indépendants—and, like her stepfather, was rejected by the Salon.* If she had given up on her own painting, she now turned her attentions to helping Monet. "She's not going to leave me at present," Monet had written to Geffroy back in February, a week after Jean's death, "which will be a consolation for the both of us."[18]

Indeed, the presence of Blanche, who offered both companionship and support, were as vital to Monet's artistic resurrection in the spring of 1914 as the encouragement of Clemenceau. As Geffroy later observed, Monet "found the courage to live and the strength to work thanks to the presence of the woman who became his devoted daughter." After Jean's death, she began taking the place of her mother by maintaining the house for Monet and hosting friends such as Clemenceau when they came to visit. Crucially, she also "encouraged him to take up his brushes,"[19] thereby helping to end his years of sorrow and inactivity.

"MONET PAINTS IN a strange language," the reviewer had claimed in 1883, "whose secrets, together with a few initiates, he alone possesses." This language was understood much better by the first decades of the twentieth century. Impressionism in general, and Monet in particular, had been the subject of numerous books and articles explaining their secrets: the seemingly impulsive brushwork and random compositions of everyday subjects of middle-class leisure and beautiful but otherwise undistinguished snatches of countryside. As early as 1867, readers of Edmond and Jules de Goncourt's novel *Manette Salomon* were given, through the depiction of a painter named Crescent, a clear-sighted account of the aspirations of Monet and his friends. Crescent differs from the members of the "serious school," who are "enemies of color." These painters, trained at the École des Beaux-Arts, distrust spontaneous impressions and instead approach paintings "by reflection, through an operation of the brain, through the application and judgment of ideas."

---

*Blanche Hoschedé-Monet's works can be found in a number of public collections in France: the Musée Clemenceau and the Musée Marmottan Monet, both in Paris; the Musée Toulouse-Lautrec in Albi; the Musée des Beaux-Arts in Rouen; the Musée des Augustins in Toulouse; the Musée de la Cohue in Vannes; and the Musée A.G. Poulain in Vernon.

Crescent, by contrast, instinctively records his sensations of grass and trees, the freshness of a river, the shade along a path. "What he sought above all," the narrator says, "was the vivid and profound impression of the place, of the moment, the season, the hour."[20]

This passage gives a remarkable account of what was soon to become Monet's practice. But how were these scenes—with their subtle and often short-lived visual effects such as quavering leaves, fleeting shadows and glints of light—to be reproduced by pigment on canvas? How could the immaterial and impermanent be given materiality and permanency? How could the artist capture what the human eye perceived in the brief sparkle of a second?

The technical procedures of the Impressionists varied from painter to painter, and in most cases they evolved over the decades. But their "strange language" involved, among other things, conspicuously calling attention to their brushes and their paints. They fragmented their brushstrokes into flickering touches of color that seemed to dissolve their painted worlds into shimmering mirages. Most critics and gallery-goers were taken aback by these apparently slipshod and incoherent dashes and commas, which were so different in application from the smooth and precise touches of established and successful painters, such as Meissonier, whose meticulous attention to minute detail was savored by one collector through the lens of a magnifying glass. Impressionist canvases were not meant to be seen at such close range. In 1873 a young critic named Marie-Amélie Chartroule de Montifaud, who wrote under the pseudonym Marc de Montifaud, noted that the apparently "crude simplicity" of a Manet painting actually disguised a sophisticated visual experience. "Stand back a little," she urged in her review. "Relations between masses of color begin to be established. Each part falls into place, and each detail becomes exact."[21] The ideal viewing distance for Impressionist paintings soon became a topic of scientific discussion. Camille Pissarro—who by the 1880s had hoped to use "methods based on science" in his art—eventually came up with a formula whereby the viewer should stand at a distance measured at three times the diagonal of the canvas.[22]

Paradoxically for a painter who wished to give the impression of spontaneity, Monet's painting technique actually required a good deal of forethought and groundwork. His supposedly impulsive canvases were actually the result of much advance preparation and fastidious organization. A visitor to his studio once counted seventy-five paintbrushes and forty boxes of pigments.[23] Each of his canvases—which arrived regularly on the train from Paris—was first of all primed with a layer of lead white, giving a luminous ground for the layers of bright color that he would then apply. One of the innovations of Édouard Manet and the Impressionists in the 1860s had been this pale, luminous base layer on which they worked. Their technique broke all of the artistic rules established by the "serious school," since artists had always painted over top of a darker ground in order to enhance the appearance of depth. Titian and Tintoretto, for example, had used brown or dark red undercoats, and even Gustave Courbet—a good friend of Monet's and an early influence on him—sometimes painted over a black primer coat. But the Impressionists in their quest for an airy brightness abandoned not only these dark bases but also the bitumen-based glazes with which so many of their predecessors had slathered the tops of their painted canvases in order to achieve a darkish Old Master patina. As a connoisseur once informed John Constable: "A good picture, like a good fiddle, should be brown."[24] Many color merchants even stocked for use by painters the same amber glaze with which instrument makers varnished their lutes.

Those who prized the well-varnished Old Master look were highly suspicious of colorful pyrotechnics. The nineteenth-century art theorist Charles Blanc once declared that painting "will fall through color just as mankind fell through Eve."[25] But the Impressionists had been only too happy to be seduced by the bright new colors that nineteenth-century chemistry was creating. Early in his career, Monet had captured the sparkling effects of sunlit water on the Thames thanks to a palette that included cobalt violet, invented in 1859, and chromium oxide green, created in 1862.

Monet was also anxious to use pigments that would survive the test of time—ones that would not fade or yellow, as he knew so many pigments were prone to doing. According to an art dealer, Monet was always thinking about "the chemical evolution of colors" as he painted.[26] By the time he resumed work in the spring of 1914, his palette of colors had therefore been narrowed to those pigments he believed to be the most stable. In order to enhance their preservation, he also mixed them much less than he had done in the 1860s and 1870s. Moreover, he took to squeezing his pigments onto absorbent paper to extract some of the poppy oil binder, since he knew that oils, as they rose to the surface, were responsible for the yellowing of many Old Masters—a murky posterity from which he hoped his paintings would be spared.

BY JUNE, MONET was working so intently on his work that only with the greatest difficulty could he be persuaded to leave Giverny. He even turned down an invitation to Jumièges to supervise the garden he had designed at Les Zoaques. Only the most momentous occasion—the entrance of fourteen of his paintings into the Louvre—convinced him to take the train to Paris. The honor was truly magnificent. Artists ordinarily needed to have been dead for at least ten years before their works could be displayed in the Louvre. Monet would therefore be one of a very few living artists ever to see his work hung in what one of France's most eminent curators called "that great Pantheon of Art."[27]

Monet disliked crowds, traveling, public events and even Paris itself. He described himself, with good reason, as a *casanier*—a homebody.[28] "City life doesn't really suit me," he once claimed.[29] Unlike Manet and Degas, he preferred the country lanes of Normandy to the boulevards of Paris. A decade earlier a journalist noted that Monet's celebrity was one of the things that made Paris odious to him: he was unable to walk a hundred yards "without being accosted by importuners, boors, pretentious ignoramuses and snobs."[30]

Monet did, however, make regular trips to Paris. One thing that could always entice him was the prospect of eating oysters with friends at the restaurant Prunier in the rue Duphot—the most fashionable seafood restaurant in Paris—as well as going to wrestling matches. "The effort is always a beautiful thing," he said of wrestling.[31] His visits to Paris did not fail to cause a stir. A friend once visited the theater with him and Geffroy. "I remember walking beside Claude Monet, squat, solid and quiet, as he struck his cane vigorously on the pavement. He had the appearance of a proud and free *campagnard* on a boulevard." Inside the theater, packed with "brilliantly shallow" Parisians, such was his compelling presence and forceful charisma that all eyes turned to him. "When he took his seat, the ushers, without being able to name this powerful figure, had the confused sensation that a true man had just entered the box."[32]

At first Monet used his work as a convenient excuse to avoid the throng of the grand opening: *Gil Blas* reported that he could not attend because he was "in the middle of working and could not leave the motif."[33] The sight of his paintings adorning the walls of the Louvre was, however, far too seductive to pass up. Moreover, spurned for many years by the artistic establishment, Monet had long been determined that he and his friends and allies should be conspicuously represented in the national collections. In 1890 he had waged a long and vigorous campaign to get Manet's *Olympia* — the scandal of the 1865 Paris Salon — into the Luxembourg Museum, Paris's museum of contemporary art. In 1907 he convinced Clemenceau, then the prime minister, to move the painting into the Louvre for its ultimate consecration. Seven years later, he was about to join Manet in the Louvre.

Monet did therefore make one of his rare forays into Paris, where a curator at the Louvre arranged a private viewing of the Camondo rooms.[34] In early June, he boarded the train at Bonnières-sur-Seine, five miles from his house. The journey on the Paris–Le Havre line took a little more than an hour, but the route of the chugging train would have plunged Monet back into his vanishing past. His life had run parallel, so to speak, to this railway line, which stretched from the Gare Saint-Lazare to the Normandy coast. The first rails had been laid in 1841, one year after his birth, and the line reached Le Havre, his childhood home, in 1847, a year or two after his family relocated there from Paris. This had been the railway line that had transported him, in May 1859, aged eighteen, along its 140 miles of track to study in Paris, and then carried him back to Normandy many times to paint at Rouen, Sainte-Adresse, Honfleur, and Trouville-sur-Mer.

On that June day in 1914 Monet caught the train from the Paris bound platform at Bonnières. The locomotive traveled east, taking him on what must have been a fond, familiar, and at times, poignant journey. It went through the valley of the Seine and into Paris's western suburbs—into the heartland of Impressionism, whose twin arteries, for Monet, were the river and the railway, with their splendid, colorful paraphernalia of rowboats and cafés, bridges and bathers, and locomotives releasing their black plumage into the sky. "Impressionism was born," a critic would write more than a dozen years later, "in the suburbs of the capital."[35] No one had loved this landscape of suburbs and villages, of pleasure spots and happy exertions, of dappled sunlight and reflections on wrinkled surfaces of water, more than Monet, or depicted it so distinctly and enticingly.

From Bonnières the railway swung south across the meadows, avoiding a meander in the Seine, and after passing through a two-thousand-yard-long tunnel emerged at Rosny-sur-Seine, where flashes of river could be seen through dense riverbank foliage. A few minutes later came Mantes-la-Jolie and a glimpse of its old stone bridge, once painted by Camille Corot, whom Monet called "the greatest landscape painter" of all.[36] Twenty minutes later, on the opposite side of the river, the white limekilns of Triel-sur-Seine appeared. High above them, screened by a green cloister of poplars, stood the villa of Monet's friend Octave Mirbeau. A few minutes later, rattling through Médan, Monet could have seen the house of another writer and friend of the Impressionists, the late Émile Zola, its shutters and towers visible above the trees on the right. Next came Poissy—"that horrible place," as Monet called it[37]—where he had lived briefly before moving to Giverny and where, uniquely, he found nothing to paint.

The locomotive then puffed through the Forest of Saint-Germain-en-Laye and crossed the looping Seine. Downstream to the right, as the train clattered through Carrières, were the islands, cafés, and other landmarks that almost a century later the local municipalities would shrewdly christen the "Pays des Impressionnistes"—the Land of the Impressionists. The Restaurant Fournaise, immortalized in 1881 by Renoir in *The Luncheon of the Boating Party*, had closed its doors almost a decade earlier, but farther downstream the boatyard, café, and ballroom of La Grenouillère, "the Frog Pond," were still operating. Here Monet and Renoir had painted side by side on the riverbank in the summer of 1869, capturing bathers bobbing in the river and reflections quivering around the tiny island known as Le Camembert.

To the left, three miles upstream from the bridge, where the breadth of the Seine expanded to two hundred yards, the masts and smokestacks of Argenteuil appeared. Here, newly married, Monet had lived from 1871 to 1874 in the rue Pierre Guienne, and then for the next four years in the boulevard Saint-Denis (later renamed, in honor of a subsequent Argenteuil resident, boulevard Karl Marx). Here he used to paint Camille in their garden, against spectacular profusions of flowers. Other times he carried his canvases and easel down to the riverbank or onto the highway bridge and painted sailboats, the railway bridge, the port of Argenteuil. Or he plied the broad stretch of river in his floating studio, a rowboat onto which, with the help of his friend, the painter Gustave Caillebotte, he constructed a makeshift cabin. As water sloshed against the hull and Camille sat inside the cabin, he would sit cross-legged on the foredeck, happily painting—which was precisely how, one golden day in the summer of 1874, Édouard Manet depicted him at work. Manet also painted him tending his garden in the rue Pierre Guienne, bent over his flowers with Camille and seven-year-old Jean reposing nearby on the lawn. "Those wonderful moments," Monet later remembered of that time, "with their illusions, their enthusiasm, their fervor, ought never to end."[38]

The train crossed the Seine for the last time at Asnières, upstream from the Île de la Grande Jatte, on the bridge that thirty years earlier Georges Seurat depicted in the background of *Bathers at Asnières*. To the left, once this bridge was crossed, lay the scrubby patch of ground that a century later another local municipality, equally shrewd, would christen "Le Parc des Impressionnistes." Then Paris finally hove into view, the Arc de Triomphe visible in the distance and, beyond it, the

Henri Fantin-Latour's *A Studio at Les Batignolles* (1870). Monet is on the far right.

Eiffel Tower. The train passed the smokestacks and gasholders of Clichy and immediately entered the Batignolles, where Monet and his friends had once gathered each night at their table in the Café Guerbois to discuss "art with a capital A"[39] and plan their conquest of Paris. The café stood close to Manet's studio, the interior of which had been depicted in 1870 by Henri Fantin-Latour in *A Studio at Les Batignolles*, featuring Monet and his friends grouped about the elegant, blue-cravatted Manet as he sat at his easel. Fantin-Latour had now been dead for a decade, and of the eight determined young men he portrayed, only Monet and Renoir survived.

The train was swallowed by the Batignolles tunnel and then emerged into daylight to offer a last sight—the Pont de l'Europe, directly overhead—before shunting across the fanwork of tracks and into the Gare Saint-Lazare. Early in 1877 Monet had received permission to set up his easel on the station's platforms, from where he painted a series of canvases capturing the clamor of smoke and steam. For one critic, hostile but astute, these works revealed the "disturbing ensemble" of qualities that distinguished Impressionism: "the crude application of paint, the down-to-earth subjects, the appearance of spontaneity, the conscious incoherence, the bold colors, the contempt for form."[40] It was only fitting that Impressionism should have been so well-defined at this alpha and omega of Monet's existence, the soaring, sooty building in which so many of his journeys began and ended.

THE FOURTEEN MONET paintings entering the Louvre had been the property of Count Isaac de Camondo, a Paris-based Jewish financier and collector who originally came from Constantinople, held Italian citizenship and possessed "an extraordinary capacity for making money."[41] According to one cynical observer, Camondo's bid for acceptance and respectability had seen him abandon the "slippers and fezzes" of his ancestors for a bowler hat, a subscription to the Opéra, a stable of race horses and a "nobiliary particle."[42] He also became a connoisseur of paintings, amassing in his lavish apartment in the avenue des Champs-Elysées one of the finest collections of Impressionist works in France. When he died suddenly in 1911 at the age of fifty-nine, he left the entire collection—which included work by Manet and Cézanne as well as Monet—to the Louvre. He also left 100,000 francs for the installation and display of the paintings in a special set of rooms, which in the early summer of 1914 was ready to receive them.

It must have been a triumphant moment for Monet to witness himself and his friends colonizing a corner of the Louvre with paintings that had once been so vigorously despised by the artistic establishment and so controversial with the public. Even Camondo had not been overly keen on some of them: it took a letter from Monet to convince the collector to purchase Cézanne's *The Hanged Man's House*. After buying the painting, Camondo, as if to justify this purchase, preserved the letter from Monet in a leather pouch stitched onto the back of the frame.[43]

The moment was also one for Monet to remember with fondness—as, perhaps, on the train journey—his own, smaller struggles and victories. For here were more poignant waymarkers, paintings representing every period of his career and, indeed, of his adult life: from a snow-covered road near Honfleur that he painted as a young man, through scenes of Argenteuil and Vétheuil, to his triumphant Rouen Cathedral paintings (of which Camondo owned four) and a canvas of the water lily pond. A newspaper reported that before his canvases "he had flashes of joy, and he was pleased to recall the year, the date, the smallest circumstances of his works."[44]

SOON AFTER MONET'S visit to the Louvre that June, a catastrophic thunderstorm struck Paris. A newspaper headline declared: LE SOL S'EFFRONDRE (THE GROUND SHATTERS). Torrential rains, together with "negligence and defects,"[45] caused the Gare Saint-Lazare to flood. Sewers burst and overflowed, the Métro broke down, cracks and holes opened in the streets. One crevasse swallowed a taxi with its driver and passenger; both died. Lightning strikes killed a team of railway workers and sent debris from rooftops cascading into the streets. Gas lines exploded in flames, with a particularly violent detonation in the rue Saint-Philippe-du-Roule blasting a hole twenty-five yards deep that engulfed an upholstery shop. An ox fell into another fissure in the boulevard Ney, while nine horses working underground at the Porte de la Chapelle drowned when water ten feet deep flowed into the railway tunnel. Yet one journalist, venturing out that night to watch the rescue efforts of the frantic firefighters in their acetylene headlamps, was astounded to see lights blazing and music blaring in a building in the rue La Boétie where couples, cheerfully oblivious to the destruction everywhere around them, danced "languorous waltzes and voluptuous tangos."[46]

It is hard not to see in this carefree waltzing on the edge of the yawning abyss what the journalist could not: a parable of France in the summer of 1914—an insouciant, fun-loving world about to be engulfed by tragic events. Later, people would look back nostalgically at the prewar years as a golden age of gaiety and joyous innocence, as the period of blissful nonchalance and elegant artistry that gave rise to the German expression "as content as God in France" and much later, after it had all disappeared, to the French expression *la belle époque*. The belle époque was a retrospective construction, to be sure, but an image of this land of soon-to-be-lost content—a contemporary portrait of the delightful enchantments of what Parisians themselves called *la vie douce* (the sweet life)—had been offered to readers of *Le Figaro* exactly one year earlier. In June 1913 one of the newspaper's journalists asked a troop of forty-seven Boy Scouts visiting from San Francisco their opinions of Paris. The Scouts had been impressed by the Eiffel Tower and the gargoyles on Notre-Dame but also by the fountains and public gardens, the tree-lined boulevards, and the outdoor cafés where, while having a drink, one could watch people passing in the streets. They admired the red trousers of the French soldiers, the beards on the young men (who, hats in hand, sometimes embraced one another), the long loaves of bread, the extraordinary number of automobiles (there were six hundred car manufactories in Paris alone), and naturally "the fine young ladies of fashion," who, the young Scouts observed with awed incredulity, smoked cigarettes in the street.[47]

This image of Paris, with its boulevards, gardens, cafés, and women of fashion, was that of Monet and the Impressionists: the happy world of beauty and elegance, of casual everyday leisure, that they had brought to life and commemorated under their brushes. Monet's garden, for some, as well as his paintings of his garden, were as much a part of the visual vocabulary of Paris as the Art Nouveau entrances to the Métro stations and the dancers at the Folies-Bergère. "When I think of the beautiful times of peace," a novelist turned soldier would write to Monet from the trenches barely eight months later, "I see often the gorgeous garden and the large dining room at Giverny."[48]

Monet's gorgeous garden appears to have come through the great storm of June 1914 more or less unscathed. He noted the "terrible weather" in a letter to Charlotte Lysès, but two days after the deluge he informed another friend that he was in "a fever of activity" and had no time to leave home. "My work before everything," he wrote in a declaration that might have served as his manifesto, and one on whose resolution he would need to call many times in the years to come.[49]

Several weeks later he wrote two more letters: one to a certain Madame Cathelineau, to whom he offered to show his water lilies in their full June bloom; and the other to one of his picture dealers in Paris, Paul Durand-Ruel. He informed Durand-Ruel that he was back at work, that his eyesight was better, and that "everything goes well."[50]

The date of these remarkably upbeat letters was June 29. On that same day the front pages of all the French newspapers were reporting the assassination in Sarajevo of the Austrian archduke Franz Ferdinand.

GEORGES CLEMENCEAU HAD not been one to dance on the edge of the abyss. He saw and feared the gathering storm. In March, while unveiling a statue to an Alsatian politician in Metz, he had declared of Germany: "Her fury for the leadership of Europe decrees for her a policy of extermination against France. Therefore, prepare, prepare, prepare."[51] It was an audacious speech considering that Metz had been part of the German Empire since 1871. Throughout the first half of 1914, his daily editorials for his latest newspaper, *L'Homme Libre*, deployed his considerable rhetorical power to warn against what he called "German Caesarism." All the forces of the German Empire were, he wrote, "advancing in a formible array of coordinated activities toward the goal of world domination—which will be peaceful if the world resigns itself to submission, but violent if resistance is given."[52] He deplored the poor state of French munitions and the fact that the Germans had 3,500 heavy guns compared to France's paltry 300. He advocated an extension of compulsory military service from two years to three, the better to maintain a large, well-drilled army. When soldiers in the eastern garrisons mutinied at this proposal, he published a pamphlet asking them: "While you throw away your arms, do you not hear the clatter of the field-guns on the other side of the Vosges?"[53]

Clemenceau's editorial for June 23 had declared: "There is no point in denying that Europe lives in a state of permanent crisis." That crisis became ever more acute with the assassination of Franz Ferdinand. Yet even Clemenceau could not foresee how events would unfold. Two days later his editorial on the "appalling tragedy in Sarajevo" bore the title

"Into the Unknown." The leader of the French socialists, Jean Jaurès, was less hesitant to predict where events might lead. Jaurès was the only politician in France with the charisma, intellect, and rhetoric to match Clemenceau, to whom he was a considerable and inveterate opponent. If Clemenceau was the most brilliantly forceful writer in French politics, Jaurès was by far the most spellbinding orator—according to some, the greatest of all time.[54] In July 1914, Jaurès turned his formidable oratorical skills against French involvement in the "wild Balkan adventure," believing that war could still be averted. He exhorted his audience in a speech in Vaise, near Lyon, on July 25: "Think of what that disaster would mean for Europe…What a massacre, what destruction, what barbarism!"[55]

Much of France was, however, distracted from issues of Serbian politics and impending massacres by l'Affaire Caillaux—the murder trial of Henriette Caillaux, the second wife of Joseph Caillaux, formerly Clemenceau's minister of finance and, from June 1911 to January 1912, prime minister. In March 1914 the editor of Le Figaro, Gaston Calmette, in a campaign against Caillaux, published some of his private correspondence—including letters written to Henriette while he was still married to his first wife—as proof of his having used dishonourable means to achieve personal goals. "He is unmasked," Calmette triumphantly announced. "My task has been accomplished."[56] Madame Caillaux accomplished her own task three days later, entering Calmette's office in the rue Drouot and discharging six shots from the Browning automatic pistol concealed in her fur muff. She came to trial for his murder in July.

As Europe teetered on the brink, far more ink was devoted to the trial of Madame Caillaux than to the worsening political situation. One newspaper, L'Écho de Paris, cleared its pages of virtually all other news. Even the front page of L'Homme Libre offered its readers the smallest details of the case, including the fact that Madame Caillaux, wearing a black dress and a hat of black straw, sustained herself on the first day of her trial by eating a luncheon of jellied eggs and salt-marsh lamb washed down with a bottle of Évian water.[57] After a trial that drew in two former prime ministers, along with various cabinet ministers past and present, she was acquitted on July 28. The announcement came only hours before

Austria-Hungary declared war on Serbia and began bombing Belgrade. It came three days before another shocking event: the assassination of Jaurès by a French nationalist in a café in the rue Montmartre.

On the following day, August 1, the general mobilization order arrived by telegram at the Assemblée Nationale, where it was immediately put on display. Outside, in the newspaper kiosks along the quai d'Orsay, Clemenceau's headline in *L'Homme Libre* declared: THE RACE INTO THE ABYSS. Two days later, at six fifteen P.M., as thunderstorms shook Paris and pelted the streets with rain, Germany declared war on France.[58]

CHAPTER FIVE

INTO THE UNKNOWN

—————

"**AS FOR ME,** I shall stay here regardless, and if those barbarians wish to kill me, I shall die among my canvases, in front of my life's work."[1]

So wrote Claude Monet almost a month into the war. Two weeks later he echoed this solemn defiance in a letter to Geneviève Hoschedé, the wife of his stepson Jean-Pierre, who, like 3 million other Frenchmen, was already in uniform. "If there is disorder or danger," he informed her, "I would understand if Blanche leaves, but I shall stay regardless. Too many memories keep me here. More than half of my life has been spent here and, in short, I should prefer to die here in the midst of my work rather than to save myself and leave everything that has been my life to thieves or enemies."[2]

Monet's determination to stand fast in the face of the enemy contrasted starkly with his behavior in 1870, the last time German soldiers set foot on French soil. On that occasion he had been honeymooning with Camille and three-year-old Jean in the seaside resort of Trouville. When two hundred thousand heavily armed Prussian troops descended on Paris and began besieging the city, he hastily slipped across the channel to England. There he sat out the entirety of the Franco-Prussian War strolling through London's parks—of which he made several fine canvases—and developing tastes for Constable, Turner, and marmalade.

In August 1914 the situation looked equally bleak for the French. Hundreds of trains had rushed to the German frontier the French soldiers in the kepis and red pantaloons that had so impressed the visiting Boy Scouts. The cavalry wore shining breastplates and the officers brandished canes. "All the men sang," reported *Le Matin*, "because they knew themselves to be serving a sacred cause—the cause of human civilization."[3] They were also, of course, serving the cause of their country.

A French bayonet charge,
Battle of the Marne, 1914

"Mourir pour la Patrie," they sang. *"C'est le sort le plus beau ... "* Tens of thousands met this supposedly enviable fate as German guns — the massive
field guns that Clemenceau had heard clattering on the other side of
the Vosges — remorselessly scythed them down. On August 22, twenty
thousand French soldiers died in the Battle of Charleroi, the largest
single-day loss in the history of the French Army. Two days later a million
German troops poured across the French frontier.

A French newspaper reported that Parisians were reacting to events
with *"le superbe sang-froid."*[4] But in fact panic was the order of the day. By
the end of August, German gunfire was audible in Paris and a Taube airplane was dropping bombs on the city. Parisians anxiously scanned the
sky for Zeppelins. As the minister of war predicted the arrival of the
Germans in Paris within the week, the evacuations hastily commenced.
As in 1870, the government decamped to Bordeaux, while Parisians
flocked to the Gare d'Austerlitz and the Gare d'Orléans, turning them
into hubbubs of luggage-stacked motorcars and embattled gendarmes.
Others tried to catch boats to Rouen or Le Havre, where base hospitals
were hastily prepared to deal with the wounded. Thousands of others
took to the roads in farm carts, on bicycles, or pushing perambulators.[5]
Works of art joined the exodus. More than 2,500 paintings were taken
from the Louvre, packed in boxes sealed with passwords and guarded by
soldiers, and dispatched for safekeeping to Toulouse and Blois. Included
among the evacuees were the fourteen Monet paintings in the Camondo
collection, which had lasted little more than two months on the walls of
the Louvre.[6]

In Giverny, trains carrying troops in cattle-cars trundled along the bottom of Monet's garden, heading east. Meanwhile, many farmers and villagers headed west, fleeing Giverny and environs for safety in what Monet later called "a moment of terrible and ridiculous panic."[7] One witness described the roads of Giverny that August as "filthy with dust and invaded by hordes of poor people driving their flocks before them, with children weeping noisily on carts and old people, broken by pain and emotion, sobbing silently, heads buried in their hands."[8] Soon a family of Belgian refugees arrived in the village, accommodated in the house owned by Delphin Singeot, from whose family Monet had bought Le Pressoir.[9]

More than thirty men in Giverny had enlisted or been mobilized. The American colony vanished virtually overnight. Among them were Monet's stepdaughter Marthe, with her husband Theodore Earl Butler and his two children: they fled Giverny for New York City. One American who remained, at least for a few more months, was Frederick William MacMonnies, a sculptor from Brooklyn who since 1901 had occupied a seventeenth-century monastery near the church. He improvised a fourteen-bed hospital in an ivy-covered house named Le Pilotis. It quickly filled with wounded soldiers.

Giverny's makeshift hospital soon found itself with a celebrity for its head nurse: Eugénie Buffet, a "street singer" whose performances in Parisian cabarets and cafés-concerts had made her a national sensation in the 1890s. Having qualified as a nurse a few weeks earlier, Mademoiselle Buffet, now forty-eight, was sent to change bandages and comfort wounded soldiers in Giverny. "God, what a sight!" she later wrote. "What nights I spent listening to the moaning of the poor soldiers... Those who went mad in the first offensive used to get up in the middle of the night, despite our surveillance, screaming as if they were still in the trenches." She noted that many of the young soldiers gave the same pitiful cry: "*Maman.*" One night she began singing to them and, "lulled, relieved and calmed, they fell asleep."[10]

This hospital with its grim scenes of misery and death stood less than half a mile from Monet's house. The people of Giverny donated linen and mattresses, and Monet, too, made his own contribution: the wounded and shell-shocked soldiers were nourished on vegetables from his garden. These peas and beans came not from the famous garden of Le Pressoir but rather, because Monet believed vegetable foliage to be unsightly, from the vegetable patch his gardeners cultivated in the garden of a house he rented nearby, La Maison Bleue. Monet's gardens were threatened with some distress due to the war, since several of his gardeners had gone off to the front. "We are well and continue to receive good news about our loved ones," he wrote to Joseph Durand-Ruel, the son of his longtime picture dealer, "but we live in constant anguish and worry."[11]

IN EARLY JULY, in buoyant spirits, Monet had announced to Gustave Geffroy that he was at "the beginning of a great work."[12] Now, however, in the first terrible weeks of conflict, with Jean-Pierre in uniform along with his stepdaughter Germaine's husband, Albert Salerou, he had more to worry about than the fate of his grand new project. "Be brave and careful," he wrote to Jean-Pierre, "and know that our hearts are with you."[13] His son Michel had been exempted on medical grounds, possibly due to either a surgical operation a few months earlier or an old injury, a broken femur suffered when he crashed his car in Vernon in 1902.[14] He was, however, once again attempting to enlist. Monet also worried about his friends. He sent telegrams to inquire after Sacha and Charlotte, tried to track down Octave Mirbeau, and wrote friends in Paris to discover news of Renoir, two of whose sons were in uniform.[15]

Monet also worried about his paintings. With the enemy only thirty miles from Paris, and with airplanes bombing the capital and dropping sacks of sand with notes attached announcing the forthcoming arrival of the Germans, he fretted that his canvases might fall prey to the Huns, whose destruction in 1870 of many of Camille Pissarro's paintings he no doubt remembered: the Prussians had used his house at Louveciennes as a butcher shop and his canvases as carpets. On the last day of August he wrote to Joseph Durand-Ruel, asking if a "secure place" might be found for "a certain number of my canvases…Perhaps you could rent an automobile," he suggested, "that would come with a reliable person who could take whatever might be possible."[16] Monet's canvases, if he got his way, were, like the treasures of the Louvre, about to join the mass exodus.

No automobile came from Paris to evacuate the paintings, but on the following day one did arrive carrying Octave Mirbeau from his home at Cheverchemont, twenty-five miles upstream from Giverny. Few visitors could have been as welcome, especially in such a time of such anxiety. Mirbeau had undoubtedly been sincere when he wrote to Monet that "of all human beings, you're the one I like the best."[17] For Sacha Guitry, their mutual affection was touching: "Nothing has ever seemed more beautiful than the look in their eyes when they exchanged a glance."[18]

Their friendship stretched back more than thirty years, when Mirbeau wrote his first rapturous lines of prose about Monet's paintings in the early 1880s. One of France's most astute and articulate art critics, he made himself the most hated man in Paris, according to Guitry, thanks to his early support for Monet, Cézanne, and Van Gogh.[19] Monet called him "a discoverer in painting."[20] He was also a novelist of striking and sometimes bizarre originality. In 1913 a newspaper called him "the great Octave Mirbeau, the most powerful writer of our time."[21] Above all, he was a tireless campaigner for the causes of truth, justice, and the downtrodden—a man with (as the same newspaper reported) "very advanced ideas."[22] A fellow novelist once said of him that every morning he got up angry and then spent the rest of the day looking for excuses to stay that way.[23] As a child he used to bombard unsuspecting passersby with apples from his family's orchard,[24] and for the rest of his life he continued to lob missiles at moving targets. Chief among them was the Church, whose cover-up of sexual abuse by its priests (a fate he suffered as a schoolboy in Brittany) he exposed with horrifying frankness in his 1890 novel *Sébastien Roch*, subtitled *The Murder of the Soul of a Child*.

Mirbeau shared Monet's love of food. In the 1880s he had founded a literary dining club, the Bons Cosaques (Good Cossacks), to which Monet was promptly invited. Gardening was another shared passion,

Monet's great
friend, the writer
Octave Mirbeau

with Mirbeau by the 1890s becoming almost as fanatical a gardener as Monet. "I love flowers with an almost single-minded passion," he declared in a newspaper in 1894. "Flowers are my friends...All joy comes from them."[25] He also loved the earthier aspects of gardening, once confiding to Monet: "I find a clod of earth admirable and can contemplate it for hours on end. And compost! I love compost as one loves a woman. I spread it and see in the steaming pile the beautiful forms and gorgeous colors that will emerge from it!"[26] Mirbeau spread his compost on a number of gardens as he moved from one home to another, with Monet offering him endless advice and in return receiving comical accounts of his failures and frustrations ("I do not have a flower, not one!...As for the poppies, the slugs eat the tops, the grubs their roots").[27] When Mirbeau's father died in 1900, he had recommended the family gardener, Félix Breuil, to tend Monet's plants—and, more than a decade later, Breuil was still in Giverny, ensconced in a small house on the property.

In his younger days, Mirbeau's passionate intensity was combined with an intimidating appearance: fiery red hair, fierce, sky-blue eyes, and an imposing physique. A journalist described him as having "the wide shoulders and the muzzle of a mastiff who barked loudly and bit hard."[28] One of his eccentricities was a savage-looking dog that he used to parade about Paris on a lead—a beast of mysterious origins (purportedly a dingo) whose tenacious fidelity to its master reflected Mirbeau's own devotion to friends such as Monet.[29] As a reflection of his gentler side, he also owned a more placid pet, a hedgehog whose death left him bereft.

In the old days, Mirbeau used to bicycle along the Seine to Giverny. By 1914, at the age of sixty-six, he was, sadly, a shadow of his former self, partially paralyzed by a stroke two years earlier. He had become known as the "hermit of Cheverchemont,"[30] able to travel only with difficulty and—more seriously—unable to write. To raise funds for the upkeep of his house, he was reduced to selling his beloved collection of paintings. Three of his Van Goghs went to auction in 1912, including *Irises* and *Three Sunflowers*, both bought by Mirbeau a year after the artist's death from Père Tanguy, whose portrait by Van Gogh he also owned. "Ah! How he has understood the exquisite soul of flowers!" Mirbeau wrote in one of the earliest appreciations of Van Gogh.[31] He sold the paintings with much reluctance, although the fact that *Three Sunflowers* was hammered down for 50,000 francs, 166 times what the price he paid for it, provided some consolation.

The visit from Mirbeau, however welcome, may not have been especially cheerful. Convinced that his death was nigh, the stricken writer had taken to telling his friends and visitors: "You won't see me again. Oh, no! I'm done for!" On one occasion he told Monet: "We won't see each other again, Monet. I'm finished, this is the end!"[32] His mood was bleak for other reasons as well. He was one of France's most prominent and articulate antimilitarists, his novels frequently expressing a horror of war, nationalism, and patriotism. The title character in *Sébastien Roch*, for example, denounces patriotism as vulgar and irrational, while military heroism he finds nothing but "a bleak and dangerous banditry and murder." Sébastien ultimately dies ingloriously on the battlefield, illustrating Mirbeau's belief that, in wiping out the youngest and strongest, war does nothing but destroy "the hope of humanity."[33] Unsurprisingly, the outbreak of war left him despondent. "The war weighs on me," he was to tell a journalist a few months later. "It haunts my nights and days."[34]

Mirbeau must have been cheered, however, by the sight of Monet's new paintings, comforted in the knowledge that Monet, at least, could still work even if he himself could not. An essay on Mirbeau, written by a friend and published in 1914, said of him: "Noble of heart and demanding of spirit, he eagerly sought in the minds of men, and in their works, an impossible beauty for which, as a paladin of justice and beauty, he was prepared to break his lances."[35] Monet was, above all, the artist in whom Mirbeau found this impossible beauty, and for whom he was willing to break his lances. From his pen, over the years, there had issued a constant stream of reassurance and encouragement, espe-cially during Monet's various periods of crisis. "You are, without doubt, the greatest, most magnificent painter of our time," he wrote as the despairing Monet canceled his 1907 exhibition and shredded his water lily paintings.[36] And in the summer of 1913 he had gone with Monet to Les Zoaques, joining Guitry's "affectionate exhortations" for him to take up his brushes again.[37]

Fittingly, Mirbeau was among the first to see the beginnings of the grand new project. Monet was eager to show the work to friends. He had invited Gustave Geffroy back in July to see "the start of the vast work,"[38] but on two occasions that month the visit failed to materialize. Nor was he any luckier with Clemenceau, who, as a senator, the chairman of the Senate's army and foreign affairs committees, and editor of *L'Homme Libre*, was likewise detained in Paris and, in fact, preparing to follow the government to Bordeaux. Meanwhile, Sacha Guitry had remained seri-ously ill with pneumonia throughout the spring and early summer, and at the start of July he went to convalesce at Évian-les-Bains. By September he and Charlotte were preparing to join the evacuees, arranging a villa for themselves in the safety of Antibes.

What exactly there was for Mirbeau to see—that is, how far Monet's work had progressed by early September—is difficult to know. Monet claimed in early July that he had been at work for two months "with no interruptions, in spite of the unhelpful weather."[39] Scorching temperatures and thunderstorms in early to mid-July gave way to cooler days and frequent downpours toward the end of the month.[40] If he did accomplish more work in July, he appears to have stopped painting altogether in August and September, amid the panic and uncertainty. What Mirbeau saw in those frantic early days of the war was the beginnings of a work that, however impressive, had temporarily been suspended.

BY THE MIDDLE of September, the threat had eased and the military situation, from a French point of view, looked almost optimistic. The "Victory of the Marne," in which more than six hundred taxicabs carried reinforcements to the front, meant that the threat to Paris disappeared. "They return home by the road of defeat and shame," a newspaper exulted of the German retreat from the Marne.[41] The Germans did not, of course, return home; rather, in the middle of September they began digging their first trenches on the northern banks of the Aisne, while the British, on the opposite side of the river, began entrenching themselves along the chemin des Dames: the first muddy burrows of the network that would ultimately stretch from the North Sea to Switzerland. Already the conflict had been christened with names—"La Grande Guerre," "La Guerre Mondiale"—that suggested its terrible magnitude.[42]

After the heart-stopping events of the previous six weeks, an unreal and uneasy life returned to Giverny. The village was still eerily empty of people. "All the world fled," Monet wrote in October.[43] To a friend in Paris he wrote that he saw no one, "unless it's the unfortunate wounded, who are found everywhere here, even in the smaller towns."[44] However, Mirbeau paid him another visit early that month, and Monet reported to Geffroy that their ailing friend was "in good health and very excited by events"[45]—that is, by Monet's grand new project, on which, however, he had still not resumed work.

In November, Monet made a trip to Paris, his first visit since the outbreak of hostilities. The city presented a sober aspect in the first months of the Grand Guerre. Many evacuees had returned by this

point, and the city was filling with Belgian refugees and wounded soldiers. The wounded were so numerous that part of the Ritz had been
requisitioned and turned into a makeshift hospital. Only a handful of
other hotels remained open.[46] The streets were largely deserted, the
theaters closed, the Louvre empty, the streets dark after sunset. There
was virtually no art to be seen anywhere. As a newspaper put it on the
day Monet arrived: "Throughout the terrible tests imposed on us by
the abominable war, art can hardly raise its voice except to make a com-
plaint. Art is in mourning for the marvels of Louvain, Malines, Arras
and Reims,"[47] cities whose art and architectural treasures had been
damaged or destroyed. The sole exhibition on offer, sponsored by a
Franco-Belgian association, was Henri-Julien Dumont's "Impressions
of War: Senlis in Ruins"—paintings that, as a reviewer declared, "spoke,
screamed and wept for justice violated and punishment too long in
coming."[48] The time for blissful and beautiful scenes of ponds and gardens, it must have seemed, had passed.

In Paris, Monet enjoyed a lunch with Geffroy. The pair had been
friends since first meeting in September 1880, when they found themselves staying in the same small hotel at the foot of a lighthouse on Belle-
Île-en-Mer and Geffroy mistook Monet—with his beard, beret, chunky
sweater, and weather-beaten appearance—for a sea captain.[49] That same
year Geffroy had started working as a journalist on Clemenceau's *La
Justice*. Like Clemenceau and Mirbeau, he had become an articulate,
forceful, and lifelong crusader. According to one friend, he was "the man
who puts the just in justice."[50] To other friends, he was known affectionately as "Le bon Gef." His "sweet, care-worn face," as a fellow critic
described it,[51] had been painted by Cézanne and sculpted by Rodin. A
prolific author of books on artists and museums, since 1908 he had served
as the director of the Manufacture Nationale des Gobelins, the tapestry
factory in Paris. There he lived in an elegant apartment with his beloved
mother, his invalid sister Delphine, and his library of thirty thousand
books. One of the many things he had in common with Clemenceau and
Mirbeau was the conviction that Monet was one of the greatest artists
in history—"among the race of masters," as he confidently declared.[52]

A pleasure denied to Monet and Geffroy during their visit was the company of Clemenceau, who was in Bordeaux running *L'Homme Libre* from a tiny flat with a skeleton crew: three-quarters of the newspaper's staff had gone to war.[53] Monet had not heard from the Tiger since the first week of the war, when he wrote from Paris: "I am very tense, but I am convinced that if everyone stays in good spirits—and this is what I see around me—we shall do very well. Only it will take time."[54] That August he had written stirringly in *L'Homme Libre* of the need to set aside political enmity and division: "Today there must be no hatred among the French. Now is the time for us to discover the joy of loving one other."[55] A few days later he wrote optimistically to a friend in England: "We are experiencing difficult times, but I think we shall come out of it well. The country is admirable. Not a cry, not a song. Nothing but the tranquillity of resolutions."[56]

Portrait of Gustave Geffroy (1895–6) by Paul Cézanne

This joy of loving and tranquillity of resolutions did not last. By the end of August, when Paris looked ready to fall to the Germans, Clemenceau met with Raymond Poincaré, the French president, who found himself subjected to a spectacularly forceful attack. "He spoke with the hatred and violent incoherence of a man who had completely lost control of himself," claimed Poincaré, "and with the fury of a disillusioned patriot who thought that he alone could bring victory."[57]

Poincaré was not the only one to suffer the Tiger's wrath. In 1887, Clemenceau had declared: "*La guerre! C'est une chose trop grave pour la confier à des militaires.*"[58] In 1914 he quickly became confirmed in his belief that war was too important to be left to the generals. By September he had launched fierce attacks on France's military elite. He criticized the army's medical services in *L'Homme Libre* after witnessing wounded soldiers shipped from the front in cattle cars and horse boxes, with the result that many contracted tetanus. However, the government had enacted State of War regulations, suspending civil liberties and granting the military authorities wide-ranging powers to censor any newspapers deemed liable to endanger public order or deplete morale. Clemenceau was accused by one general of waging a "vicious and misleading campaign."[59] All copies of the newspaper were seized and *L'Homme Libre* was suspended for a week. The paper eventually reappeared, albeit with a sarcastic new name on the masthead: *L'Homme Enchaîné*. The "Free Man" thus became "The Man Enchained."

MONET, ON THE other hand, had slipped his fetters: by the end of November he was painting again. "I have returned to work," he announced in a letter to Geffroy on the first of December. "It is still the best way to avoid dwelling on the present calamities, though I feel a little embarrassed about making investigations into shape and colour while so many people are suffering and dying for us."[60]

Monet's embarrassment was understandable. A year later, in November 1915, the English art critic Clive Bell would complain in an article entitled "Art and War": "From every quarter comes the same cry—'This is no time for art!'"[61] Indeed, many French painters had downed brushes and donned uniforms, leaders of the avant-garde among them. "Today almost all of our artists are at the front," announced *Le Figaro*.[62] That was true, at least, of the younger generation. Monet's friend Charles Camoin, a thirty-five-year-old Fauve who lived nearby in Vernon, had been mobilized in August and immediately dispatched to the front, as had another sometime visitor to Monet's house, the Cubist Fernand Léger. Likewise in uniform were the Fauves Maurice de Vlaminck and André Derain, and Georges Braque, the Cubist.

Many other French artists, especially the older generation, had already begun serving their country—or would soon be doing so—in a different capacity: with their brushes and paints. At the Battle of the Marne in September 1914, a forty-three-year-old artist named Lucien-Victor Guirand de Scévola, a former student at the École des Beaux-Arts, was serving in the artillery when his unit—all dressed in their bull's-eye-red pantaloons—came under heavy enemy fire. "It was at this moment," he later wrote, "that, vaguely at first, then more and more precisely, the idea of camouflage came to me. There had to be, I thought, a convenient way to disguise not only our unit but also the men who served in it." Guirand de Scévola therefore began working on ways to make his fellow soldiers and their environment "less clearly visible" by means of experiments in "shape and color."[63]

Guirand de Scévola's ideas were quickly ratified by the Ministry of War. The first camouflage team would be established early in 1915, initially with thirty artists but ultimately drawing on the services of three thousand *camoufleurs*, all wearing handsome uniforms adorned with their insignia designed by Guirand de Scévola himself: a golden chameleon on a red background. Included in their ranks was Braque, rescued from the trenches along with other Cubists such as Jacques Villon, Roger de La Fresnaye, and André Mare. The Cubists had been reviled in the prewar years as unpatriotic and anti-French, but Guirand de Scévola claimed their style was absolutely vital to his enterprise: "To completely deform the object, I employed the methods of the Cubists, which allowed me to hire a number of talented painters who, because of their very special vision, could disguise any object whatsoever."[64]

As Guirand de Scévola's team was about to start its work of concealing French soldiers by replacing their proud kepis with paint-spattered *cagoules* (hoods), yet another team of artists was also doing war service by the end of 1914. In September, following the Victory of the Marne, the painters Pierre Carrier-Belleuse and Auguste-François Gorguet, assisted by a team of twenty "elite artists", began work on a gigantic painting called the *Panthéon de la Guerre* in Carrier-Belleuse's studio in the boulevard Berthier. This work was to be a panorama, the kind of pictorial entertainment invented at the end of the eighteenth century and wildly popular during the nineteenth: a 360-degree view of a cityscape or a battle executed with painstakingly detailed realism on the inside of a large rotunda and viewed from a platform in the middle. Featuring battle scenes and hundreds of French war heroes, the *Panthéon de la Guerre* was to have, the press reported, a circumference of 115 meters.[65]

THERE WAS ONE more way in which French artists could serve their country: as shining beacons of the glories of French culture and civilization. The French newspapers had few doubts about what was at stake in 1914. The conflict was, they declared, *une guerre sainte*—a holy war. As *Le Matin* declared on August 4, France versus Germany amounted to a "holy war of civilization against barbarism." Less than a week into the conflict, France's most famous intellectual, the philosopher Henri Bergson, addressing its most august intellectual organization, the Institut de France, declared that the Germans in their "brutality and cynicism" had "regressed to the state of savagery."[66]

Such claims seemed hideously confirmed when at the end of August the Germans slaughtered hundreds of Belgian civilians and burned the city of Louvain—the "intellectual metropolis of the Low Countries," as *Le Matin* reminded its readers[67]—and its ancient library of more than 250,000 medieval books and manuscripts. Then two weeks later the Germans turned their guns on the cathedral of Reims, whose medieval sculpture had been celebrated by Rodin as the greatest of all masterpieces of European art and by France's foremost medieval scholar, Émile Mâle, as the height of human civilization. The Germans, wrote Mâle, "have turned their cannons on the beautiful statues that have spread peace about them, that speak only of charity, of gentleness, of forgetfulness of the self... The entire world has been moved by this crime: everyone feels that a star had paled, and that beauty had been diminished on the earth."[68]

Upholding French artistic and cultural values in the face of such barbarism was an important part of the war effort. "French art has to take revenge every bit as seriously as the French army!" declared Claude Debussy in September.[69] This enterprise became even more urgent a few weeks later, in the middle of October, when the first German salvo was fired on the cultural and literary front. On October 13, *Le Temps* carried a German manifesto (originally published in the *Berliner Tageblatt*) entitled "An Appeal to Civilized Nations." It had been composed and signed by a group of ninety-three German scientists, scholars, and intellectuals, including the biologist Paul Ehrlich, the physicist Max Planck, and Wilhelm Röntgen, the discoverer of X-rays. Their manifesto protested "the lies and calumnies" used to smear "the good and just cause of Germany in the terrible struggle that has been imposed upon us." What followed were a series of self-serving excuses and outright lies: that the French and English, not the Germans, had violated the neutrality of Belgium, that no French or Belgian works of art or architecture had been damaged, and that no Belgian citizen had been harmed by a German soldier except through the "hard necessity of self-defense." As for the French and British claim to represent European civilization: "Those who ally themselves with the Russians and Serbs, who are not afraid to excite the Mongols and Negroes against the white race, offering the civilized world the most shameful spectacle imaginable, certainly have no right to uphold themselves as the defenders of European civilization."

Such assertions were all the more shocking for having been composed and endorsed by intellectual titans—many revered by their French counterparts—supposedly dedicated to scrupulously truthful scholarly inquiry. What truly affronted many French intellectuals, however, was the invocation of German cultural luminaries at the end of the piece: "Believe that in this struggle we shall go on to the end as civilized people, as people in whom the inheritance of a Goethe, a Beethoven and a Kant is as sacred as our soil and our home."

The French began preparing their own responses, with risible efforts being made to prove that Beethoven was not German after all but, rather, Belgian.[70] The composer Camille Saint-Saëns had waded into the fray in the first weeks of the war. In an article for a daily newspaper, *L'Écho de Paris*, he acknowledged that it would be futile to deny the accomplishments of German artists and scholars ("That would be to imitate the Germans who say the French are a race of monkeys"). But he lamented the "absurd Germanophilia" that had corrupted public taste by, for example, foisting Wagner on French audiences. "Goethe and Schiller," he went on, "are great poets, but how overrated!" He ended with a nationalistic flourish: "It's sometimes said that art has no country. This is absolutely false. Art is directly inspired by the character of a people. In any case, if art has no country, artists do have one."[71]

The nation's artists and intellectuals responded with a publication of their own, one whose one hundred signatories combined France's intellectual and cultural might: the writers Octave Mirbeau, Anatole France, and André Gide, the composers Saint-Saëns and Debussy, and of course both Georges Clemenceau and Claude Monet. As the most famous painter in France—if not indeed the world—and as a sensitive and celebrated interpreter of French cathedrals, the very monuments being desecrated by German guns, Monet was essential to this cultural offensive. He had therefore quickly been recruited to lend his name and efforts. He responded to the publisher's overtures by saying that ordinarily he was not one for committees (which was true enough), but "things are not the same nowadays, and if you think that my name can be of some help in the work you're doing, feel free to make use of it."[72]

The response to which he readily added his name took the form of a book called *Les Allemands: destructeurs des cathédrales et de trésors du passé* (*The Germans: Destroyers of Cathedrals and the Treasures of the Past*). Addressed to foreign writers and artists, as well as "all lovers of beauty," it billed itself as a "memoir" of the bombardment of Reims, Arras, Louvain, and other cities. The volume was accompanied by photographs and other evidence for what Anatole France, writing in the appendix, called the "brutal and senseless destruction of monuments consecrated by both art and time."[73]

This would not be the last time Monet was called upon to lend his name and talents to the French war effort. In the meantime he could resume his investigations into color and form comfortable in the knowledge that by doing so he was, in a very important way, serving his country.

CHAPTER SIX

A GRANDE DÉCORATION

BY DECEMBER 1914, as Monet resumed work at his easel, Paris, too, resumed its more usual activities. The government returned from Bordeaux on the tenth. The Moulin Rouge reopened for matinees and evening spectaculars, while the Comédie-Française and the Opéra-Comique both staged plays and operas, topped off with stirring renditions of the "Marseillaise." Signs of the war were everywhere, it is true: the rehabilitation hospital for wounded soldiers in the Grand Palais; the ugly yellowish panes replacing the stained glass in the windows of Notre-Dame; the shaded lamps and darkened streets that caused visitors to rechristen the City of Light a "city of shadows."[1] But a cautious optimism was taking hold. "Toward the Final Success," declared *Le Matin* after printing official communiqués reporting the supposedly dismal failure of German assaults in Picardy and the Forest of Argonne.[2] "The year 1915 will bring us victory and peace," a French general, Pierre Cherfils, confidently announced.[3]

Georges Clemenceau was not quite so optimistic. "The war will last a good six months," he wrote to Monet from Bordeaux in the first week of December, "unless," he added grimly, "it takes three years."[4] A few days later, along with the politicians and diplomats, he was back in Paris, and within a day of his arrival he made his way to Giverny. The poor weather conditions, foul and gloomy with intervals of showers,[5] meant an inspection of Monet's garden—which was in any case bedded down for the winter and lacking the tender ministrations of the gardeners now at the front—would have been limited. However, the same gastronomical pleasures were to be enjoyed. Food was not yet in short supply in France for those who had money (although the French papers would soon be gleefully reporting on how the Germans were rioting over potatoes and choking down *les saucisses de chien*—dog-meat sausages—and bread made from straw).[6] Monet must have shown Clemenceau the new paintings, but by now the Tiger possessed other, more urgent priorities than encouraging the efforts of his friend. He was, instead, bucking up the entire nation, penning long rallying cries in his newspaper. Each day a thundering new editorial of more than two thousand words appeared on its front page. In one of them he praised the "superhuman energy" of the French soldiers but made a chilling appeal: "Today France cries that in order to survive she needs her children to give their lives."[7]

Clemenceau could not be accused of hypocrisy. His forty-one-year-old son Michel, a lieutenant in the Fourth Army, had very nearly given his own life a fortnight into the conflict when he was shot by a German lancer. Showing some of his father's famous dueling spirit, he managed to kill his antagonist before passing out. Still, Monet may not have wished to entertain arguments about the necessity of children laying down their lives for la Patrie. His own son Michel had finally been accepted into the army, in part because recruiting restrictions dropped following the deaths in battle of almost three hundred thousand French soldiers. How much Clemenceau discussed politics or the war with Monet is uncertain. Giverny was his sanctuary: he valued Monet's company, among other reasons, precisely because politics held so little interest for him.

Clemenceau was a sparkling conversationalist whose every witticism his acquaintances admiringly recorded in their diaries. Monet, on the other hand, was a man of few words. "Don't ask me anything," he once warned a visitor. "Don't try to make me talk. I have nothing interesting to say."[8] As Sacha Guitry observed: "Claude Monet did not have what is commonly called conversation. To the most important questions asked him on art, he would answer by a 'Yes' or a 'No'... You spoke to him: he listened to you."[9] Yes or no answers were, in fact, more than some people got out of Monet. A bystander once overheard him replying to friendly questions from Geffroy with a rough growl: "Rrrou...Rrou...Rrou..."[10] And he was laconically noncommittal even with Clemenceau. "One may have been the most intimate friend of Monet," he remarked to Guitry, "without ever having known the man's thoughts."[11]

Monet's friends never mistook his taciturn demeanor for a lack of intelligence. Guests moving from his dining room for the postprandial coffee in his living room passed through the "Salon Bleu," his eclectic and well-stocked library. According to Geffroy, Monet had loved books ever since he first arrived in Paris and met many writers and intellectuals at the Brasserie des Martyrs.[12] When he painted Monet's portrait in 1874, Renoir showed him not at the easel but, rather, hunched intently over a book, smoking a pipe and looking decidedly professorial. At Giverny, in his more sedate maturity, Monet used to read aloud in the evening as Alice sat beside him in the Salon Bleu, sewing and listening. Among his favorites, apart from Mirbeau and Geffroy, were authors such as Flaubert, Zola, Ibsen, Hardy, and Tolstoy. He also read the classics: Aristophanes, Tacitus, and Dante. He worked his way through nonfiction too: Montaigne, Hippolyte Taine, Jules Michelet's *History of France*, the *Memoirs* of Saint-Simon, the journal of Delacroix. Monet did not appear in the pages of the latter, although in his youth he used to spy on Delacroix's studio from the window of a neighboring building, hoping for a glimpse of the painter at work—thus demonstrating the same avid interest in the master that, decades later, others passing through Giverny would show in him.

MONET'S LITERARY INTERESTS, as well as the promise of a good meal, took him to Paris for a final time in 1914. The week before Christmas he attended the monthly luncheon of the Académie Goncourt, a literary society (more properly known as the Société littéraire des Goncourt) that had been founded with a legacy from Edmond de Goncourt. Geffroy and Mirbeau had been founder members of the Académie Goncourt in 1900, with Geffroy serving as president since 1912. It was a continuation, of sorts, of Mirbeau's Bons Cosaques (who broke bread together for the last time in 1888): the membership was broadly the same, as was the enthusiasm for both literature and food.

The ten members of the Académie Goncourt, known as Les Dix, met for lunch on the first Tuesday of each month, initially at the Grand Hôtel, then later at the Café de Paris. For the past few months, they had been gathering in a wood-paneled private dining room, the "Salon Louis XVI" (soon to be known as the "Salon Goncourt"), in the restaurant Drouant, a specialty seafood establishment near the Opéra much frequented by Clemenceau and other journalists. "They discuss various topics during the meal," a newspaper reported, "and then, as dessert is served, they begin to study the literary production of the year."[13] The upshot of these earnest deliberations over the *pêche Melba* was, each December since 1903, a five-thousand-franc literary prize: the Prix Goncourt.

Although not officially one of Les Dix, Monet was a regular fixture at the monthly Goncourt lunches. They were one of the few things that could lure him to Paris, the attraction being good food and good conversation in the company of his boon companions.

Monet's presence as a painter among a group of writers was not as incongruous as it might have seemed. He had long been on friendly terms with many writers besides Mirbeau and Geffroy. At the Bons Cosaques dinners in the 1880s he had met writers such as Henri Lavedan, Paul Hervieu, and J.-H. Rosny the Elder, whom he called "men of heart and talent."[14] He often seemed more comfortable with writers, in fact, than with painters. He had been close friends with Stéphane Mallarmé before the poet's death in 1898. One of his proudest possessions—on prominent display in his studio, among photographs of friends—was the yellowed envelope on which Mallarmé, a regular visitor to Giverny, had composed his address in verse:

Monsieur Monet que, l'hiver ni
L'été, sa vision ne leurre,
Habite, en peignant, Giverny,
Sis auprès de Vernon, dans l'Eure.

(Monsieur Monet who, neither winter nor
Summer his vision can blur,
Lives, painting, at Giverny,
Found at Vernon, in the l'Eure.)

The letter found its recipient, with Monet later marveling that the envelope had not been stolen by an "intelligent mailman."[15]

Monet was a painter uniquely admired by novelists, most enthusiastically, perhaps, by Marcel Proust, an unabashed Monet hero worshipper and would-be visitor to Giverny. Proust even hoped to write a book about Monet's garden.[16] However, the two men had never met. Visits arranged by mutual friends had failed to come off—possibly for the best, since the haze of pollens in Monet's garden might have distressed the severely asthmatic Proust, who was obliged to ask his visitors to forgo flowers in their buttonholes.

Proust had therefore to content himself with making pilgrimages to the places in Normandy painted by Monet "as though these were shrines."[17] He mentioned Monet many times in his writings: fifteen times in his notebooks, twenty-four times in his unfinished novel *Jean Santeuil*, a dozen times in *Contre Sainte-Beuve*, and at numerous points in his essays and letters. Monet's name was also destined to appear ten times in Proust's magnum opus, *Remembrance of Things Past*, the first volume of which, *Swann's Way*, had been published in December 1913.

Something of Monet's appeal for Proust was summed up in 1909 by the novelist and playwright Henri Ghéon, who outlined the difference between Monet and other painters, such as Degas and Cézanne: "They paint in space, he—if I may say—paints in time."[18] Monet was interested, like a novelist, in depicting and exploring the effects of time. By showing the natural world through different seasons and at all times of the day, his serial paintings of wheat stacks, for example, reveal how the viewer's impressions no less than the objects themselves are transformed by time's workings, giving a temporal perspective on people and places. The experience of these spaces and places, Monet believed, was affected by the particular moment in which we encounter them. Proust expressed the same philosophy in the last lines of *Swann's Way* when he wrote that "the places we have known do not belong only to the world of space" but are, rather, "contiguous impressions" experienced at particular points in our lives. Monet's paintings constituted a series of these contiguous impressions— of objects and spaces dissolving into time such that, as Proust wrote, the

Marcel Proust

"houses, roads, avenues are as fugitive, alas, as the years."

Swann's Way was eligible for the Prix Goncourt in 1914. There is no evidence that Monet ever read Proust or that Proust's admiration for Monet was in any way reciprocated. Monet did, however, act as an advocate for other writers. Besides tucking into the oysters and noisettes of lamb at the Goncourt dinners, he also participated informally in the decision making, occasionally trying to influence jurors. One year earlier the novelist Lucien Descaves, a member of Les Dix, had received a letter from Monet in which the painter frankly admitted he might be sticking his nose in where it did not belong—but "no matter," he shrugged, before urging Descaves to cast his vote for Léon Werth's novel *La Maison blanche.* Monet's advocacy of the novel had less to do with the novel's undoubted merits than the fact that Werth, a close friend of Mirbeau, had been serving as the ailing author's amanuensis, helping him to complete his novel *Dingo.* Monet explained to Descaves that Werth was a "man of real talent," that the prize would do him "a great good" and that his victory—and here was the nub of the matter—would "cheer poor Mirbeau."[19]

Werth did not win the prize that year despite Monet's backing. Nor did the novel that posterity would have garlanded, Alain-Fournier's *Le Grand Meaulnes.* Tragically, Alain-Fournier had been killed in battle in September, aged only twenty-seven, leaving his second novel unfinished. His death, announced in *Le Figaro* only a few weeks earlier,[20] must have hung heavily over the luncheon festivities that December afternoon, all the more so since Werth, at that moment, was in uniform at the front. The purpose of the meeting was, in fact, to decide whether or not to award the prize at all in 1914, given that many works announced for publication and eligible for consideration were still at the printers because of the mobilization of authors, editors, and publishers. In the end, Proust and all other hopefuls would have to wait: Les Dix decided against awarding the prize, announcing that, instead, two awards would be made in 1915.[21]

Much hope certainly rested on 1915. In August the Kaiser had assured his troops that they would be back home "before the leaves have fallen from the trees," while the chief of the general staff, Helmuth von Moltke, predicted that the war would be over by Christmas, a sentiment echoed by the British prime minister, Herbert Asquith, and quickly adopted as a popular saying in the first months of the war.[22] But there were, as the holidays arrived, no signs of peace breaking out. Christmas Day was observed, according to the official communiqués, by vigorous German attacks at Tête-de-Faux in the Vosges, north of Lens, and along the Aisne. "In the distance," wrote a French journalist in Alsace at sunset on Christmas Day, "the sound of cannons and machine guns still reaches us."[23] Only a heavy fog at last halted operations.

THREE DAYS AFTER Christmas, Monet wrote to a painter friend deploring the "terrible year" and expressing his hopes for a better state of affairs in 1915. He explained that, with Michel about to be mobilized, he and Blanche would soon be alone in the house. "I must admit," he wrote to Geneviève Hoschedé, "that I feel very hopeless and sad at this depressing end to the year, and fearful of the future."[24]

By early 1915, word of Monet's new project had begun to circulate. In January he received a letter from a friend in Paris, Raymond Koechlin. The fifty-four-year-old Koechlin was the sort of wealthy and cultured patron—albeit Protestant rather than Jewish—that Clemenceau originally had in mind for Monet's decorations. President of the Society of Friends of the Louvre and former editor of the highbrow *Journal des débats politiques et littéraires*, Koechlin was independently wealthy thanks to his father, an Alsatian textile manufacturer who relocated to Paris after the Franco-Prussian War and ultimately became mayor of the 8th arrondissement. Koechlin, a widower, filled his apartment overlooking

the Seine on the Île Saint-Louis with Japanese prints, Muslim ceram-
ics, Chinese pottery, and also modern paintings: Delacroix, Renoir,
Van Gogh, Gauguin, and of course Monet, whom he hailed as a fellow
"Japanese fanatic."[25]

Koechlin was anxious to hear how Monet was coping with the war.
He hoped that, despite everything, he had been able to carry through
on his water lilies project: "I hope you'll be able to describe to me a dining room encircled by water with the lilies on the walls floating up to
eye-level."[26] This vision of the paintings was very much in keeping with
Monet's hope, expressed in 1909, that he could install a "flowery aquarium" in a domestic setting to provide a tranquil oasis. However, Monet's
reply to Koechlin revealed a larger ambition. He explained that he had
recommenced work even though he felt ashamed to be painting when
so many people were suffering and dying. "But it's true that moping
changes nothing. Therefore," he told Koechlin, "I'm pursuing my idea
of a Grande Décoration."

This letter marks the first time Monet referred to his project by
this resounding name—one that indicated aspirations enhanced beyond
a set of dining room walls. "It's a big project to undertake," he admitted
to Koechlin, "especially at my age, but I don't despair of finishing as long
as my health holds. As you have guessed, it's the project I've had in mind
for a long time already: water, water lilies and plants spread across a very
large surface." He closed by inviting Koechlin to come to Giverny to
observe the state of his work.[27]

Monet's use of this new term, "Grande Décoration," which he
pointedly capitalized, was intended to pique the interest of Koechlin, a
respected art historian and administrator whose specialty happened to
be the decorative arts. He served on the council of the Union Centrale
des Arts Décoratifs, an association that supported and aimed to improve
France's industrial arts. He had been one of the prime movers behind the
Musée des Arts Décoratifs, founded in 1882 and relocated in 1905 to the
Pavillon de Marsan in the Louvre. This museum brought together for
public display the finest fruits of France's industrial arts: Sèvres porcelain, Gobelins tapestries, laces and bonnets once owned by the Empress

Marie-Louise, and books from defunct aristocratic libraries. There were also many exhibits from the East: ivories, goblets, and carpets, as well as a Japanese sword and prints by Hokusai and Hiroshige that had been donated by Koechlin himself. It staged an annual exhibition of Japanese prints, and before the war it had mounted a show of something else dear to Monet's heart: French gardens.[28]

Also on display in the museum were huge decorative murals by nineteenth-century French painters. All of them had originally been executed for prestigious locations such as the Tuileries, the Élysée Palace, and the grand salons of sundry spectacular châteaus. Two of the painters with work on conspicuous display in the Musée des Arts Décoratifs, Jules Chéret and P.-V. Galland, had executed murals for the Hôtel de Ville in Paris. It was a project that Monet knew all too well, because on two separate occasions, in 1879 and again in 1892, his name had gone forward for this very job—both times unsuccessfully.[29]

Furnishing important public buildings with *grandes décorations* had long been regarded as the most noble and illustrious role for painting. "Real painting," exclaimed Théodore Géricault a century earlier, "means painting with buckets of color on hundred foot walls."[30] His onetime protégé Eugène Delacroix had heartily concurred, deploring the artistic decline caused by small easel paintings and celebrating instead "the magnificent decorations of temples and palaces…in which the artist traces on the wall with the expectation that his expression will be eternal."[31] Delacroix was the most prolific muralist of the nineteenth century, having spent a good part of his career covering the walls and vaults of important public spaces with inspiring allegories and bloody battle scenes. The Palace of Versailles, the Palais-Bourbon, the Luxembourg Palace, the Gallery of Apollo in the Louvre, the Hall of Peace in the Hôtel de Ville – the politicians and potentates of France could scarcely raise their eyes to the heavens anywhere in Paris without encountering one of Delacroix's large-scale decorations. These commissions were not only tangible marks of the state's official favor—what the grateful Delacroix himself called its "flattering distinction"[32]—but also testimony to his vast ambition.

A generation later, Manet's friend Gustave Doré, an engraver, regarded muralists with little esteem. He used to insult his artistic opponents by saying: "Shut up, you're nothing but a decorator!"[33] Degas and Pissarro had been contemptuous of murals, but Manet and some of the other Impressionists—and then, as the century turned, Post-Impressionists such as Maurice Denis and Édouard Vuillard—were as enthusiastic as Delacroix. The Impressionists may have made their names with smallish canvases and portable easels that they carried into the fields and forests, but that did not mean none of them dreamed of painting with buckets of color on hundred-foot walls. In 1876, Renoir had lobbied the government's Fine Arts administration for a public mural commission, and in 1879 Manet had tried, like Monet, to secure the Hôtel de Ville commission. Neither met with success, and indeed none of the Impressionists made their marks with large murals in grand public spaces.* In 1912 the poet and critic Gustave Kahn pointed out in an article in a French newspaper the painful but undeniable fact that Impressionism had never been given the opportunity to express its decorative abilities "on the great walls of a palace of State."[34] Monet with his undoubted decorative abilities seemed the obvious choice for such a commission. In 1900 a curator at the Louvre had written: "If I were a millionaire—or a Minister of Fine Arts—I would ask Monsieur Claude Monet to decorate some huge festival gallery in a People's Palace for me."[35] But no millionaires or ministers had stepped forward.

Nonetheless, Monet's ambitions for his paintings were beginning to stretch beyond his and Clemenceau's original vision of a domestic setting. He was aiming instead, it appears, at a larger and more public venue—one that would allow his paintings, his Grande Décoration, to cover a "very large surface." The question was where and how a compliant millionaire or minister could be found in the dark days of 1915, and whose walls would be vast enough to hold these mighty decorations.

---

* The only exception—albeit in the United States rather than France—was Mary Cassatt's *Modern Woman* triptych created for the Women's Building at the 1893 World's Columbian Exhibition in Chicago.

*

THE FORLORN MOOD of the Monet home persisted through the winter. "We live here without seeing a living soul," he wrote in February. "It's not particularly cheerful."[36] Nonetheless, Blanche was still at his side, and Michel remained with him in Giverny, not yet having been mobilized—"which pleases me," Monet wrote, "because he'll avoid the cold days of winter."[37] The horrors of the trenches in winter were one of the many things provoking the wrath of Clemenceau. "Our soldiers are cold," he thundered in a letter, "and have not been given blankets or gloves or sweaters or warm underwear."[38]

Monet's mood was always closely related to the progress of his work, and the solitude of Giverny was at least conducive to painting. "I'm not creating miracles," he informed a friend in February, "and I'm wasting a lot of paint. But this absorbs me enough that I don't think too much about this ghastly, appalling war."[39] In fact, his work was sufficiently advanced by the end of the month for him to contact Maurice Joyant, a gallery owner in Paris, asking for the exact dimensions of his premises. The fifty-year-old Joyant, known as "Momo," had been a close friend of Henri de Toulouse-Lautrec, exhibiting his paintings (Joyant's gallery hosted a major Toulouse-Lautrec retrospective in 1914) and sharing with him an interest in food (he would later publish a cookery book with their joint collection of recipes). Momo ran a gallery on the Right Bank with his partner, an Italian printmaker named Michele Manzi. *Le Figaro* commended these two "men of taste" for taking such an active part "in the struggles of the modern schools."[40] In the summer of 1912 and again in 1913 they staged large Impressionist exhibitions, with Monet prolifically represented on both occasions.

Monet's reason for contacting Momo stemmed from the fact that two years earlier, in February 1913, the Galerie Manzi-Joyant had hosted an exhibition billed as "a large exhibition of decorative art, featuring all the artists who brought into modern art a note that was new and original."[41] The reviewer for *Le Figaro* rhapsodized over the sumptuous display; everything from ceramics and Lalique glassware to Gobelins textile designs and grand state-sponsored murals—a whole treasure trove, in other words, of belle époque decorations and furnishings. "Never have artists with greater skill," wrote the reviewer, "created such rich and beautiful objects for collectors both now and to come. Never has there been a greater preoccupation with creating for their homes such original and harmonious decorations."[42]

Among the artists whose paintings were featured in the exhibition was Monet, along with Degas and Renoir. The reviewer for *Le Figaro* expressed his regret, like Gustave Kahn a year earlier, at what might have been had these masters of Impressionism been used more productively as decorators. One of the great successes of the exhibition, it could not have escaped Monet's notice, was Gaston de La Touche, an old friend of Manet and Degas. La Touche had produced murals, in a timidly Impressionist style, for the Élysée Palace and the Ministry of Agriculture; and Raymond Poincaré and his wife "lingered for a long time" before these grand state-sponsored decorations during their visit to the exhibition.[43]

Joyant had been hoping to stage an even larger exhibition of decorative art in 1916, but the war had scuttled that plan. For Monet, however, an opportunity presented itself, hence the query to Momo regarding "the exact dimensions of your gallery, length and width. When I come to Paris," Monet tantalized him, "I shall tell you why."[44]

Monet's solo exhibitions ordinarily took place at the Galerie Durand-Ruel, whose proprietor, Paul Durand-Ruel, by now eighty-four years old, had faithfully supported and promoted the Impressionists since the 1870s, sometimes at great financial cost to himself. "He risked bankruptcy twenty times to support us," Monet later remembered.[45] Durand-Ruel's gallery was found in the rue Laffitte, which was known because of the proliferation of galleries as *la rue des tableaux* (street of pictures). It was, coincidentally, a few doors away from the house in which Monet had been born ("a possible sign of predestination," according to Clemenceau).[46] Here Monet had exhibited his wheat stack paintings in 1891, his poplars in 1892, his views of Rouen Cathedral in 1895, his paintings of the Thames in 1904, and his waterscapes in 1909. Durand-Ruel was, in addition, the man who financed Monet's move to Giverny in 1883

The art dealer Paul Durand-Ruel in his gallery.

and then, in 1890, his purchase of Le Pressoir. As Monet had told an interviewer at the end of 1913: "It would take a special study to explain the role played by this great merchant in the history of Impressionism."[47]

Yet Monet was anticipating a different venue for the unveiling of his latest paintings. Evidently the dimensions of the Galerie Durand-Ruel, which had only shown his smaller canvases, he judged inadequate for mounting a display of his Grande Décoration. He may also have found the lighting inadequate: Louis Vauxcelles, touring Monet's purpose-built studio in 1905, noted that "the light is so much better than in the dungeons of Durand-Ruel's gallery."[48]

Monet had plainly been making rapid progress since his foray into the cellar with Clemenceau only ten months earlier. Indeed, this new cycle of paintings appeared to be approaching some sort of completion. Even so, in February 1915 it was incredibly audacious, if not blatantly impractical, to envisage staging a solo exhibition of major new paintings—and paintings of a lily pond at that, ones that had been executed (as he told everyone) as a distraction from the anxieties of wartime at a time when, he acknowledged, other Frenchmen were suffering and dying. How ready the French public might be for poetic glimpses of a water feature in rural Normandy was surely open to doubt.

MONET MAY NOT have been planning to exhibit his Grande Décoration with Paul Durand-Ruel, but he did have another use for this self-sacrificing and indefatigably supportive businessman. Since the panicky days at the end of August, Monet had been dunning Durand-Ruel and his son Joseph for money: payment from their sales of his paintings. When his first request bore no results, he wrote more pointedly in November, asking Joseph to give him "at least a portion of what you have already owed me for some time already." The time might well come, he claimed, "when I'll be strapped for cash." Joseph no doubt could foresee a time when he, too, might be strapped for cash; nonetheless, he responded quickly, and before a week had passed Monet received a check for 5,000 francs. Monet duly thanked him but added meaningfully in a P.S.: "I took note of your promise to give me other payments when you can." Another payment arrived the following spring, at the beginning of April, when Durand-Ruel generously stumped up 30,000 francs.[49] This was a large sum, roughly equivalent to the annual salary and expenses of a senator. Durand-Ruel could ill afford such largesse at a time when the art market was depressed because of the war. But Monet, by the spring of 1915, had big plans for spending his money.

CHAPTER SEVEN

A GRAND ATELIER

ON THE MORNING of June 17, 1915, a Tuesday, two automobiles arrived at the station in Mantes-la-Jolie to collect a small party of passengers disembarking from the eight thirteen train from Paris. The vehicles then wound their way through the country lanes to where Monet was hosting at his house what was, in effect, a road trip for the Académie Goncourt. "I'm counting on you," he had written to Gustave Geffroy three days earlier, "to remind Descaves, Rosny, in fact everyone."[1]

Not all ten members could make the expedition, but at least five of Les Dix clambered into the automobiles to be conducted the fifteen miles to Giverny. Besides Geffroy and Mirbeau, the group included Lucien Descaves, Léon Hennique, and J.-H. Rosny the Elder. Also present was Mirbeau's wife Alice, a former actress and a novelist in her own right. It was to this cast of distinguished writers and friends that Monet was about to offer an early viewing of his Grande Décoration.

This audience was an appropriate one. Les Dix were a band of literary rebels committed to shaking up French literature and society in much the same way that, years earlier, the Impressionists had challenged France's conservative artistic tastes and institutions. They had come together as an alternative to the Académie Française, whose forty members (known as Les Immortels) had long been the arbiters of French literary taste in the same way that the Académie des Beaux-Arts — the bête noire of the Impressionists — had been the arbiters of French artistic taste. If Les Immortels were the guardians of tradition, Les Dix were determined to promote (according to the instructions in the will of Edmond de Goncourt) freshness, originality, and "new and venturesome leanings in thought and form."[2] These leanings were exemplified in the work of the Belgian-born Rosny, who once confessed to Edmond de

Goncourt that he was writing "a little bit in opposition to the currents of contemporary literature."[3] This was something of an understatement in light of his novels about aliens, mutants, vampires, parallel universes, life five hundred years in the future and, in his 1909 novel *La Guerre du Feu*, thousands of years in the past. "I read all of his books," Monet later reported, "which are admirable and full of substance."[4]

On that warm day in June, these writers were treated to the delights of Monet's table, followed by those of his garden; afterward they were conducted into the studio, which was accessed through a staircase in the garage where he kept, besides his automobiles, an aviary where parrots squawked and turtles "wandered around among the leaves of lettuce."[5] As Descaves later recollected: "A surprise lay in store for us." The walls of the spacious, high-ceilinged studio, which doubled as a showroom, were covered with paintings from throughout the course of Monet's long career. It was, however, the newest canvases—his impressions of the water lily pond—that naturally attracted their attention, in particular their size. "He set out these impressions," reported Descaves, "on huge canvases some two metres high and between three and five metres wide."[6] These paintings were therefore at least double the size of those in the 1909 *Paysages d'Eau* exhibition, with some of them (if Descaves's memory served) as much as fifteen feet wide. Monet's friends were suitably impressed, especially when they learned that more canvases were planned. Mirbeau asked Monet how much longer his ambitious new project would take. Another five years, Monet informed him. But Mirbeau, witnessing Monet's commitment and intensity, protested: "You exaggerate. Let's say two more years."[7]

From this estimate, Monet's friends could have been left in little doubt regarding the scale of his ambitions. Monet, they knew, was capable of covering a lot of canvas in a two- or three-year period. He was a painting machine who, when working at his customary pace, produced canvases at a terrific rate. A two-month stay in Venice in 1908 resulted in thirty-five paintings, or one canvas every two days, most of them two and a half by three feet. Three separate stays in London between 1899 and 1901, during which time he spent some six months in total in

Monet in his first studio, ca. 1914, after its transformation into
a sitting room. Rodin's sculpture of Monet is to the left.

the city, saw him produce a total of ninety-five canvases: once again, a
painting roughly every two days (although some of these London views
were, controversially, completed in Giverny—as indeed were some of
the Venice paintings). Mirbeau's prediction indicates his expectation
that the Grande Décoration would encompass as many as a hundred or
more large canvases.

Monet's guests must have wondered about the ultimate purpose
and final destination, and indeed the practicality during wartime, of this
series of huge canvases. How exactly he displayed the works for them
is not recorded, but he may have arranged them about the studio in
an oval or circle to offer a rough impression of the final effect. He no
doubt explained his old dream, expressed as early as 1897, to decorate
a circular room with paintings. Intriguingly, the wood-paneled Salon
Goncourt in the restaurant Drouant was oval in shape. Monet must
have been struck during his luncheons by the fact that here was exactly
the sort of space he had been coveting: an elegant salon populated by (as

Raymond Poincaré once called Les Dix) "a small number of men entirely devoted to the cult of beautiful things."[8] However, Monet's ambitions had grown along with the size of his canvases, and the visitors in his studio would have been hard pressed to envisage the intimate space of the Salon Goncourt hosting more than the merest fragment of these rapidly expanding decorations.

What room, indeed, could have been large enough to encompass Monet's Grande Décoration? For some of the guests, there may well have been a faint whiff of folly about the project: such a major undertaking in a time of war by a man on the cusp of his seventy-fifth birthday.

MONET REVEALED ANOTHER plan to his friends on that June day. Lucien Descaves reported that Monet was "having a studio constructed specifically for this series."[9] The need for more space no doubt struck Monet's visitors. Virtually every inch of the studio's walls was covered with canvases, while many others stood upright in ranks along the floor beneath. The studio already featured his two *grandes machines* from the mid-1860s, *Luncheon on the Grass* and *Women in the Garden*, both some eight feet high by seven feet wide. Now adding to the impressive square footage of Monet's painting career were these new, even larger canvases.

A large new studio was therefore required. Monet received a construction permit on July 5, several weeks after the visit of his friends. Soon afterward construction began on what would be his third studio in Giverny, with a builder and quarry owner from Vernon, Maurice Lanctuit, taking charge of the project. This new structure was to stand on the northwestern edge of the property, at a right angle to the house, and on a piece of land that Monet had recently acquired from a neighbor. After demolishing a dilapidated outbuilding that stood on the site, Lanctuit began raising an enormous building that would ultimately cost Monet 50,000 francs.[10]

In July 1915, the very month that ground for the new studio was broken, a French geologist expressed concerns about the scarcity of materials needed for rebuilding the country's war-ravaged fortresses, roads, and railways.[11] Lanctuit, however, seems to have experienced few if any difficulties acquiring materials, with the limestone for the walls coming directly from his nearby quarry. Construction proceeded through the summer on the structure that, once completed, would occupy a space seventy-six feet long by thirty-nine feet wide. The rakingly pitched roof, fitted with skylights, rose to a height of forty-nine feet; as such, it towered over Monet's house.

As the structure took shape over the course of the summer, Monet began to experience misgivings about its expense and—even more—its size and its frankly industrial-looking appearance. In August he confessed in a letter to Jean-Pierre Hoschedé, who by now was driving an ambulance at the front, that it had been unwise to involve himself in such a "gigantic" building project. "Yes, it's folly, sheer folly, especially since it's so expensive. Lanctuit built me such a monstrosity. I'm ashamed of it—I, who always shouted at those who try to uglify Giverny."[12] Twenty years earlier he had campaigned vigorously against a plan by the town council to sell a piece of land to a chemical company proposing to build a starch factory. His campaign against uglification even saw him responding with fury to the appearance in Giverny of telegraph poles.[13] Yet he was raising in the heart of Giverny a studio the size of an aircraft hangar, to which it bore an unfortunate resemblance.

Monet had another reason to be embarrassed about this large studio. There was a fine irony in the fact that a man who made his reputation by setting up his easel in the open air should construct one of the grandest ateliers in the history of art. Monet was keen to foster the myth that he did not use a studio and that he was, as Geffroy dutifully wrote in support of the legend, "the first artist to start and finish a painting in front of his chosen subject, refusing to reconstruct or repaint his canvas based on studies done in the atmosphere of the workshop."[14] When, in 1880, a journalist asked to see his studio in Vétheuil, Monet acted incredulous: "My studio? I have never had a studio…This is my studio!" he replied with an expansive gesture at the great outdoors.[15] In fact, at the time of the interview, Monet had both a studio in Vétheuil and a second in Paris in the rue de Vintimille, the rent for which was paid by his friend Gustave Caillebotte.

Eighteen years later, a journalist reported that Monet did not have a studio in Giverny because "the open-air painter works only out of doors." He concluded emphatically: "Nature is his studio."[16] These statements were likewise patently false. The paint was barely dry, at the time of this declaration, on the commodious two-story atelier that Monet, with input from the Art Nouveau architect Louis Bonnier, had constructed as a replacement for the converted barn he had previously used.

Working in the open air was still essential to Monet's project, even though he was tackling some of the largest canvases of his career. Three days after receiving the permit for his new studio, on July 8, he was photographed beside the lily pond, hard at work on a canvas five feet two inches wide by five feet ten inches high. This painting is an example of what Jean-Pierre Hoschedé later called Monet's *grandes études de nymphéas*—that is, large studies of water lilies.[17] Jean-Pierre claimed that Monet used these *grandes études*—most of which were some six feet across, and all of which were painted out of doors, beside the pond—as the basis for the even larger works that for logistical reasons he produced in the studio.

The photograph from that July day shows Monet sitting on a long-legged wooden chair beneath an enormous parasol, wearing a wide-brimmed straw hat. Blanche, likewise straw-hatted and dressed in white, sticks faithfully to his side. She no doubt helped arrange his canvas, easel, and paints. Besides wrestling with his easels, she also appears to have assisted with the preparation of his canvases. Clemenceau later said: "She worked on his canvases. She prepared the grounds for him."[18] Blanche firmly denied that she ever applied paint to his canvases: "It would have been a sacrilege."[19] However, it would have made sense for Blanche to help Monet to slather gesso (a chalk-based primer) across the expansive surfaces of the canvases before lightly sanding them and adding another coat—repetitive and unskilled work on which it would have been imprudent or unnecessary for a septuagenarian to expend his limited fund of physical resources. But Blanche's value to Monet extended far beyond her physical labors with his canvases. He had come to depend on her for solace and companionship, just as he had earlier depended on

Monet at work in July 1915
with Blanche beside him

her mother. She spent the first year of the war by his side, sitting with him in the library in the evenings or playing backgammon with him. She traveled with him wherever he went, she oversaw his finances, and she even shared his sometimes eccentric tastes in foods, such as a peppery salad oil that no one else would touch.[20] To Clemenceau, she was an angel: the Blue Angel, as he always called her, or sometimes the Queen of Angels, the Azure Angel, or the Angel with Azure Wings.

In the photograph taken that July day, one of Monet's stepgrand-children, six-year-old Nitia Salerou, occupies the foreground, her presence a reminder that, despite Monet's continual complaints about his solitude, his house was still the center of his extended family. In the painting itself, the mauve-shadowed blue of the sky is mirrored in tranquil water streaked green with the reflections of weeping willows and dotted with water lilies, their pads outlined in blue. Their flowers are bright sparks of red and yellow or, in the cluster beyond them, delicate shades of pale blue.

It is a stunningly beautiful painting. The photograph and canvas both suggest a pleasing summer idyll, a humming late afternoon shading into the mauves of a warm, tranquil evening. Yet appearances are deceiving. The day of the photograph was actually unseasonably cool, with a high of only 19.8 degrees Celsius recorded at the Eiffel Tower, and with clouds and spots of rain throughout the day.[21] Two days earlier a violent storm had struck Paris: lightning started a fire at a hospital and powerful winds toppled chimneys and trees. A tree in the Tuileries fell on a statue of a former prime minister, Pierre Waldeck-Rousseau, and—ominously—badly damaged the allegorical figure of France.[22] Monet was evidently making the most of a poor day, and the huge parasol was to protect him (and his canvas) from the rain rather than the sun.

So inclement was the weather across Western Europe that throughout the summer of 1915, despite the testimony of meteorologists, people began blaming the constant rainfall on gunfire on the western front.[23] "I have not stopped working despite the bad weather, which has severely hampered my studies," he wrote in the middle of August to the Bernheim-Jeune brothers, Gaston and Josse. They were gallery owners who had exhibited not only Monet's work but also that of his son-in-law, Theodore Earl Butler. During Monet's dark years following the death of Alice, they had given small dinners in his honor in Paris, sought out specialist eye doctors for him, and in the summer of 1913 hosted him at their neo-Gothic villa in Villers-sur-Mer, near Deauville.[24] They invited him back to Bois-Lurette in the summer of 1915, but Monet declined their offer. Any fine summer weather was to be spent at the easel, not enjoying refreshing breezes at a luxurious villa on the Normandy coast.

MONET'S DETERMINED EFFORTS before his canvas were captured once again that summer, by Sacha Guitry on a hand-cranked camera. The manifesto signed by the eminent German scholars and published the previous October in the *Berliner Tageblatt* had spurred Guitry into a cinematic response with the help of some of the French cultural luminaries who had put their names to *Les Allemands: destructeurs des cathédrales*. He began journeying around France with Charlotte Lysès and a camera, capturing these living monuments to French cultural excellence for a film to be called *Ceux de chez nous* (*Those from our Home*). The responses of his subjects varied, with Rodin, for one, unimpressed with both Guitry's camera and the concept of cinema: "Call it what you will, it's still nothing more than photography."[25] Nonetheless, Rodin acceded to Guitry's wishes, and the newfangled equipment captured the bearded sculptor chipping away at a statue, looking handsome and vigorous in a black beret, with a broad forehead and strong cheekbones that might have come from his own chisel.

Less impressive a physical specimen was the arthritic Renoir, whom Guitry filmed at Cagnes-sur-Mer in the middle of June, finding him in a wheelchair "bent double with pain" but utterly devoid of "melancholy and sadness."[26] By an unfortunate coincidence, Guitry and his camera arrived on the day that Renoir's wife, who had died a few days earlier, was to be buried. "It must be terribly painful, Monsieur Renoir," Guitry murmured sympathetically. "Painful?" retorted Renoir from his wheelchair. "You bet my foot is painful!"[27] In the film, Renoir appears gaunt, with a wispy beard and an enormous peaked beret. Assisted by his youngest son, fourteen-year-old Claude (known as Coco), he puffs on a cigarette, raising great clouds of smoke as—in an image of courageous determination—he dabs away at a canvas, his paintbrush tied to his gnarled hands with ribbons of cloth.

Guitry had more difficulties with the reclusive and miserable Degas, who refused to be filmed. Forced to skulk outside the painter's apartment on the boulevard de Clichy, he was finally rewarded with ten seconds of Degas walking obliviously along the pavement with his niece, Jeanne Levre: a figure with a white ruff of beard, wearing a bowler hat, and carrying a rolled umbrella.

Guitry was assured of a warmer reception when he and Charlotte arrived in Giverny. His footage opens with Monet wearing his straw hat and talking amiably with Guitry, sporting a boater, in the graveled path before the house. Nitia Salerou and two small dogs disport themselves in the background. The capering dogs were presumably Nitia's. Monet loved birds and animals, even leaving the windows of his dining room open so the sparrows could help themselves to bread crumbs from the table. Japanese chickens, a gift from Clemenceau, ranged freely through the gardens and

Still shot of Monet and Sacha Guitry from the film *Ceux de chez nous*

even in the studio, where the master fed them from his own hand. However, he refused to own dogs or cats for fear of the havoc they might cause with his flowers. Even Jean-Pierre's Irish water spaniel, Lassis, prizewinner at a 1913 dog show in Caen, was banned from the garden.[28]

The film cuts to a view of the wind-ruffled lily pond, the camera panning slowly right to left, capturing the irises, the archipelagoes of water lilies, and the Japanese bridge, all looking beautifully well-kept despite Monet's complaints about losing his gardeners to the trenches. Then, in the distance, the master appears at work beneath his giant parasol on the edge of the pond. The canvas—one of his *grandes études*—looms over him.

The film cuts again, this time to a close-up of a relaxed and genial Monet standing before the canvas, a cigarette with an inch of ash dangling from his mouth, followed by seventy-seven seconds of the master at work. He is looking not straight ahead, toward the bridge, but rather—because the canvas is so large—at a 90-degree angle to his right, toward the willow whose branches are draped over the water. He holds his brush by its end as he adds a few strokes to the canvas, constantly throwing appraising glances to his right. Then, as the branches stir in the wind, he selects another brush from the small bouquet in his hand. He cleans it with a rag, mixes paint on the giant palette—shaped like a lily pad—and dabs away again, the canvas wobbling slightly in the wind and under the pressure of his touch. It is a lively, self-assured performance, with Monet occasionally turning his face (brow and eyes shaded by his hat) to chat briefly at the camera.

Then the camera films a long view from the opposite bank. Monet steps back from the canvas and wipes his hands on a large handkerchief before walking away. Even allowing for the accelerated pace produced by Guitry's hand-cranked camera, his gait looks remarkably jaunty, almost a jig.

MONET'S NEW STUDIO was completed, after many "troubles and worries," in less than four months of work.[29] He wrote the Bernheim-Jeune brothers at the end of October to report that he had finally settled into "my beautiful studio."[30] His reservations about the structure had receded, in part because the grand new space, though physically unattractive from the outside, allowed him to appraise his work. "I'll finally be able to judge what I've done," he told Geffroy in the middle of October, eagerly anticipating being able to spread out his large canvases in the kind of cavernous space to which he hoped they were destined.[31] He placed them on large easels fitted with casters so they could be trundled around the wooden floor. These canvases were evidently multiplying. Monet worked "enormously hard" through the autumn of 1915 despite falling ill and being confined to bed for a time—"possibly due to a bit of overwork," he explained to Geffroy, "nothing serious, though it's a hassle if, like me, you're used to living outdoors."[32]

No sooner was the studio finished than, early in November, Monet made a long-delayed trip to Paris to visit friends, including Mirbeau, who had taken an apartment in the city for the winter, and Gaston and

Josse Bernheim-Jeune, with whom he had dinner. This second winter of the war saw the gastronomical pleasures of Paris beginning to dwindle. Seafood, Monet's particular delight, became a rare and expensive treat because of the mobilization of fishermen, the bad weather, and the perils of German U-boats in coastal waters. On the day of Monet's arrival in the city, an "indignant clamour" arose at Les Halles, Paris's central food market, over the price of fish, with several hundred outraged buyers running amok and overturning crates containing the daily catch. The disturbance was swiftly quelled, but the government began taking measures to provision the city with game and frozen meat, and to stockpile coal for the coming winter.[33]

Signs of the war were still all too evident. The racecourse at Longchamp had been turned into a pasture for cows to graze, while the courtyard of the Invalides displayed captured German cannons and airplanes. Bomb damage could also be seen: in March several Zeppelins had navigated down the Oise Valley and then, swinging into Paris's western suburbs, dropped their bombs over the "Pays des Impressionnistes." As Monet's train chugged toward the Gare Saint-Lazare he might have seen, had he looked the left, the house in the rue Amélie in Asnières destroyed by a Zeppelin, and a few minutes later, if he looked to the right, the shattered roof of the building in the rue Dulong in the Batignolles, hit that same evening. These places possessed artistic rather than any strategic value, leaving a French newspaper to joke bitterly that the Germans were attacking the "Fortress of Asnières" and the "Fortress of the Batignolles."[34] The Germans may even have made some sort of an attempt on the "Fortress of Giverny" since in May 1915, two months after the Zeppelin raids, the aerial war had come to Monet's village in the grisly shape of "an enormous spherical balloon" that, stained with blood and minus its gondola and aeronauts, crash-landed in Giverny; an uprooted cherry sapling was caught in its three-hundred-meter-long cables. Probably a German observation balloon shot down by "balloon buster" pilots, it was deflated and removed for inspection to Vernon.[35]

During Monet's two-day stay in Paris, Georges Clemenceau was elected president of the Senate's Foreign Affairs Committee, a position of considerable power. Clemenceau's outspoken attacks on the prosecution of the war—the inadequate munitions and medical services, the poor strategic planning of the generals—had been continuing unabated. His enemies accused him of "hateful and harmful politicking,"[36] and in August his newspaper was once again suspended. He was, however, forging himself a reputation as the champion of the *poilus*, or "hairy ones," as the supposedly unshaven and unkempt French soldiers were popularly known. At the end of September he made a trip to the trenches to see their conditions for himself. His report sought to allay criticism that he was "never happy" with the conduct of the military—and his report was, indeed, remarkably sanguine. He soon found himself "in the middle of the action" during a "great and happy offensive" by the French troops. He spoke to one and all, he claimed, and his experience left him with "something more than mere impressions" of the situation. His conclusion must have taken aback those who saw him as the voice of doom: "I feel a great joy to say that everything I've seen has given me a great satisfaction."[37]

A few weeks later, plagued by reports of munitions shortages and the lack of success at the front, René Viviani resigned as prime minister and Aristide Briand, a fifty-three-year-old socialist, formed a national unity coalition. He included politicians of every stripe, from Louis Malvy, a radical socialist, to a right-wing Catholic, Baron Denys Cochin, a collector of modern art who owned paintings by Monet, Manet, Van Gogh, Cézanne, and Paul Signac. Briand invited Clemenceau to join this disparate group, but Clemenceau replied that he would never enter a cabinet of which he was not the head.[38] The political battles and long hours of work began to take their toll on his health, and by 1915 he was suffering from diabetes.

MONET MADE A second trip to Paris in November, this time in the company of Blanche. "Try to find out in advance," he wrote to the Bernheim-Jeunes on the fifteenth, "if the première of the famous film will take place next Sunday."[39]

Sacha Guitry's *Ceux de chez nous* was to debut at the Théâtre des Variétés. During Monet's youth in Paris in the 1860s, this theater had been the venue for Jacques Offenbach's extraordinarily successful operas, such as *La Belle Hélène* and *La Grand-Duchess de Gérolstein*. It is, however, unlikely that Monet had ever settled down into one of its plush seats. Unlike Renoir and Degas—producers of beautiful paintings of dancers, orchestras, and opera boxes—he never displayed the slightest interest in either painting or participating in the nightlife of operas, ballets, or the new entertainment of cinema. "The cinema barely interested him," claimed Jean-Pierre. *Ceux de chez nous* would be, in fact, the only film he ever saw.[40] Monet's apparent lack of interest in technologies such as photography and film is curious and even paradoxical in someone otherwise so obsessed with the immediacy of the visual impression.

The film was screened at four fifteen P.M. and lasted for twenty-two minutes, giving the audience moving images in flickering black and white of France's greatest living cultural treasures. Among the illustrious cast dutifully playing themselves were Sarah Bernhardt, a vivacious figure reciting verses on a bench beside Guitry, and Camille Saint-Saëns, filmed tickling the ivories and then wielding his baton before an imaginary orchestra. An awkward-looking Mirbeau was interviewed in his garden, looking (as *Le Figaro* put it) "like he was sitting in a torture chamber," while Anatole France appeared at a desk in his study, writing industriously on a piece of paper and "trying hard not to smile."[41] Other cultural celebrities persuaded to pose for Guitry's camera were the theater director André Antoine and the playwright Edmond Rostand, whose *Cyrano de Bergerac* was providing competition at another theater.

"The name Sacha Guitry on a poster," declared *Le Gaulois*, "is a guarantee of originality, since this young man does not follow the beaten path."[42] It is safe to assume that the audience for *Ceux de chez nous* had never experienced anything quite like this production. "What makes this cinematograph so exciting for the public," *Le Gaulois* went on, "is Monsieur Guitry's commentary." Guitry and Charlotte concealed themselves in the wings of the theater and, as the film played, provided a live running commentary. "His life is the simplest in the world," Guitry intoned over the footage of Monet. "He watches, eats, walks, drinks and listens. The rest of the time, he works." The audience may have been startled to learn the dubious fact, aired by Guitry in his voice-over on his Renoir segment, that Monet and Renoir as young men once spent an entire year living on potatoes.

Guitry was most innovative in the production in his use of what *Le Figaro* called a "new and wonderful application of cinematography."[43] As the film played, he lip-synched the voices of his on-screen subjects and, in so doing, created one of cinema's earliest talkies. As *Le Petit Parisien* reported: "From the shade of the wings, Guitry and Madame Lysès, in flesh and blood, replicate the speech of their subjects by lending their voices to the figures projected onto the screen."[44] Thus the spectators at the Théâtre des Variétés witnessed a "conversation" between Monet and a boater-wearing Guitry, with Monet recounting the story of the American woman who asked him for one of his paintbrushes. "People have the strangest ideas, don't you think?" Monet asks. "No, not at all," replies Guitry. "And as proof I asked him for one myself." Guitry recounts how he examined a handful of used brushes, but Monet instructed him: "Take a new one, you can use it for something."

The film enjoyed an "enthusiastic reception" from the public and critics alike.[45] "Sudden emotions stir your heart," wrote Régis Gignoux, a critic in *Le Figaro*. He was entranced in particular by the footage of Monet and Renoir. "We see these masters at their easels, with Monet, out of doors, painting as he breathes, as he eats, and as he drinks—with gusto." Gignoux had reservations that the camera might expose the "secret of their genius", but took heart that the spectator was left with an insight into "the eye of the painter before the canvas, its possession of light, space, form—and the joy of painting!"[46]

Ceux de chez nous ran for the rest of the year and into early 1916, with both evening and matinee performances. When his latest play, *Il Faut l'Avoir*, opened in December at the Théâtre du Palais-Royale, Guitry spent a week bustling back and forth between the two venues before his film migrated to the Palais-Royale, giving him some slight respite. He was justifiably proud of his achievement—he would resurrect the film in 1939 and again in 1952—but he had no immediate further plans for cinema

The giant painting *Le Panthéon de la Guerre* in progress

work. He was, in fact, pessimistic about the future of the medium: "I consider," he declared, "that the cinema is already past its best."[47]

AS CINEMAGOERS FLOCKED to *Ceux de chez nous* throughout December, a smaller throng was discreetly making its way to the boulevard Berthier, to an obscure address in the northwest corner of the city. *Le Figaro* reported that the locals were intrigued by the comings and goings of military leaders and staff officers, "whose presence in this peaceful area was quite unusual." Rumors spread that a war council was meeting in the "mysterious little building" into which all of them quietly slipped. But the paper then enlightened its readers. For here, in the boulevard Berthier, another commemoration of France's glories was under way: a tribute to its men of war. "This rally of generals and officers of all arms," reported the newspaper, "was for the benefit of the artists Carrier-Belleuse and Gorguet."[48] The two painters were convening France's most distinguished soldiers in Carrier-Belleuse's workshop in order to include them in their giant panorama, the *Panthéon de la Guerre*.

The two men had accomplished much on their enormous project over the previous year. In June, a journalist from *Le Figaro* had visited the studio and reported that he had seen the fully completed sketch of the panorama. "Even in its limited dimensions," he wrote, "this sketch gives a good first impression of the work, which will present a painted surface of nearly two thousand square meters, exactly 115 metres in circumference and 15 metres in height." Carrier-Belleuse anticipated that it would cover, in total, some two thousand square meters of canvas. Thousands of portraits were planned, with the heroic figures to be grouped "in a splendid architecture beyond which appears, on the horizon, the whole theater of war, where we can distinguish the silhouettes of Ypres, Arras, Soissons, Reims, Nancy, Metz and Strasbourg." Despite the assistance of a large team of collaborators, Carrier-Belleuse predicted that the project would take another year of work.[49]

One of the visitors to Carrier-Belleuse's studio at this time was a French general, Louis de Maud'huy, one of the heroes of the Victory of the Marne. As the general sat for his portrait, a soldier arrived in the studio, a young lieutenant with his head bandaged and his arm in a sling. Maud'huy observed with emotion that the young man was injured. "Oh, a little bit, sir," the lieutenant replied. "I lost an eye and got a bullet through my arm." But it did not matter, he claimed, because he was off to the front again in a few days. After this brief exchange, General Maud'huy embraced him, his face wet with tears. "I've embraced so many children whom I shall never see again," he explained to Carrier-Belleuse.[50]

Claude Monet had been hoping to embrace his own soldier. At the end of November he made his way to Versailles to bid farewell to his son Michel, who, having finished his training, was on his way to the front. Alas, because of a mix-up, it proved a disappointing journey: Michel had departed the day before. Monet was left to return to Giverny "sheepish and sad. At my age," he wrote to Geffroy, "it's difficult." He had passed his seventy-fifth birthday two weeks earlier. As the year dragged to a close he wrote: "I've had enough of this horrible war."[51]

CHAPTER EIGHT

UNDER FIRE

A FEEBLE OPTIMISM stirred briefly in France in the first days of the New Year. On the Jour de l'An, a former prime minister, Louis Barthou, wrote that "1916 will see our liberation and victory."[1] It was a bold prediction. By this point, 50 percent of the French officers were either dead or wounded, and the German general Erich von Falkenhayn, chief of the general staff, had informed Kaiser Wilhelm: "France has been weakened almost to the limits of endurance."[2] Falkenhayn's plan for 1916 was to stage a massive attack that would force the French to defend and—in Falkenhayn's chilling phrase—to "bleed themselves white."[3] To that end, in early January, the Germans began excavating gun pits and tunnels and transporting to the front, on ten purpose-built railway tracks, hundreds of the heaviest guns ever used in land warfare.

As the massive artillery was maneuvered into position, Zeppelins took to the air. On the evening of January 29, people strolling the boulevards of Paris and enjoying the mild, springlike temperatures were surprised to see teams of men frantically extinguishing gas lamps and cutting the ignition on electric lights. Firefighters rushed through the streets in their vehicles, blowing bugles. For the past twelve months London and the English coast had been bombed by zeppelins, but a Paris newspaper had calmed its readers: "Rest assured, Parisians, you will not be hearing the hum of Zeppelin engines."[4] Of the four Zeppelins that lumbered through the clouds toward Paris in March 1915, two had turned back before reaching their destination, while the others haphazardly bombed suburban homes in the Pays des Impressionnistes. "The population of Paris was, as always, perfectly calm," a newspaper proudly reported.[5] Now, after a lull of ten months, the hum of a Zeppelin engine was again heard in the skies. Instead of dispersing at the alarm,

Spent shell casings at Verdun, with the ravaged woods in the background

the people on the boulevards looked to the skies—crisscrossed by search-lights—and chanted: "Death, death to the Huns!"[6] Soon the unmistak-able sounds of explosions could be heard. In total, eighteen bombs were dropped by the 536-foot-long cigar-shaped behemoth, leaving twenty-six dead and another thirty-two wounded.

Three weeks later a young German soldier outside the French fortified city of Verdun, 140 miles east of Paris, wrote a letter to his mother: "There's going to be a battle here, the likes of which the world has not yet seen."[7] His prediction was to prove appallingly accurate. On February 21, according to legend, the sword carried in the outstretched arm of the allegorical figure of the Republic in the *Marseillaise* relief on the Arc de Triomphe broke off—an ill omen if ever there was one. At seven o'clock that morning the ground along the western front began to tremble. Over the next few hours, hundreds of thousands of German shells rained down on the French lines at Verdun. After the bunkers and trenches collapsed under the relentless barrage, the German Fifth Army advanced through the wreckage of craters, wielding flamethrowers.

Verdun in ruins, 1916

A German aviator, having looked down on the scene of devastation, reported to his commanding officer: "It's done, we can pass, there's nothing living there anymore."[8]

Famously, the Germans did not pass: "*Ils ne passeront pas*" ("They shall not pass"), first uttered by General Nivelle, became the defiant French rallying cry. But the cost in human life was immense. "Our losses have been great," reported *Le Petit Parisien*.[9] This statement must have made for shocked and sober reflection among regular readers, coming as it did from a prowar newspaper that for the past eighteen months had been a tirelessly optimistic cheerleader, specializing in what became known as *bourrage de crâne* (brainwash). *Le Petit Parisien* had been reporting, for example, that the French soldiers "laugh at machine guns" and that they looked forward to battle "as to a holiday. They were so happy! They laughed! They joked!"[10] But now there was no laughing or joking. If Verdun fell, Paris would follow and France would be lost. As an American in Paris later remembered, the first days of the Battle of Verdun were "the darkest days of the war."[11]

*

A WEEK AFTER the Battle of Verdun started, Monet looked out his bedroom window to see his garden covered in snow. The sight put him in a wistful mood. Years earlier he had loved painting in the snow. In 1868, on a frigid day in Étretat, he had bundled himself into three overcoats and lit a brazier to warm himself as, hands protected by gloves, he painted a scene of snowbanks streaked in blue and mauve shadows. In Argenteuil in the winter months of 1874 to 1875—a season when snow fell in great quantities the week before Christmas, people sledded through the streets of Paris, and urchins threw snowballs at passersby[12]—Monet painted eighteen canvases of roads, houses, towpaths, and the railway line under blankets of snow. One of them showed people under wind-buffeted umbrellas fighting their way through snow flurries along a path beside the railway station toward where Monet was sitting with his easel, braving the elements. But by 1916, at seventy-five years of age, suffering from rheumatism and prone to chest problems, he was no longer fit for such wintry heroics. "Alas, by this time I am no longer of an age to paint outdoors," he wrote to the Bernheim-Jeunes, "and despite its beauty it would have been better had the snow not fallen and therefore spared our poor soldiers."[13]

Monet worried about several poor soldiers in particular, but when Michel arrived home on leave in March, having "seen some terrible sights," Monet peevishly complained that his son's presence "singularly upset my calm and regular way of life."[14] He continued to cope with the inconveniences and anxieties of wartime as he always did: by working frantically on his paintings. "I am so obsessed with my infernal work," he wrote to Jean-Pierre, "that as soon as I awaken I rush to my large workshop. I leave only to eat lunch and then work until the end of the day." He then discussed the newspapers with Blanche—"a great support to me"—before retiring to bed. "In this horrible war," he continued, "what is there to say but that is too long and odious, and that we need victory. It is a sad life that I lead in my solitude."[15]

As usual, Monet was exaggerating his solitude. He braved the Zeppelins in the early months of 1916 to make several trips to

Paris—although the primary motivation was medical rather than social: his teeth had overtaken his eyes as a source of bother. Since the completion of his new studio he had been suffering from "terrible sore teeth, abscesses and inflammations."[16] These problems necessitated multiple trips to the dentist. Nonetheless, Monet's painful teeth did little to curb his gourmandizing as he sought to coordinate his sessions in the dentist's chair with the dates of the Goncourt lunches. "If you're planning on inviting me to the next Goncourt lunch," he wrote to Geffroy in April, "I'd be very much obliged if you let me know the date as soon as you possibly can, since my poor teeth mean I shall have to come Paris frequently."[17]

One of Monet's other preoccupations at this time was with charities for wounded soldiers and their families. One year earlier, he donated several of his paintings to be won at raffles, purchasing 200 francs' worth of tickets himself.[18] In February 1916 he donated a painting to be raffled in aid of a charity providing clothing to French prisoners of war. He also began a correspondence with Madame Étienne Clémentel, wife of the minister of commerce and industry, regarding donations of his works for the benefit of an orphanage. Monet was eager to participate, but Madame Clémentel unfortunately wanted a drawing from him—"and I never do drawings," as Monet explained to her, "that's not my way of working." He therefore offered instead "a modest painted sketch," assuring her that it would "definitely be easy to sell for the benefit of the orphans." In the end, Madame Clémentel and the orphans were the beneficiaries of two pastels of the Thames, which Monet personally journeyed to Paris to deliver.[19]

Monet unquestionably did his bit for the war effort. However, he may not have been entirely altruistic with his donation to Madame Clémentel's charity. It would not have escaped his notice, one day before he offered the modest sketch, that Madame Clémentel's husband had persuaded Auguste Rodin to sign a document donating his works to France so that his Paris home, the Hôtel Biron, could be transformed, at state expense, into a museum dedicated to his honor. Rodin was in the process of consecrating himself in museums. He already

The sculptor Auguste Rodin

enjoyed dedicated museum space in London and New York. In the autumn of 1914 he had donated twenty of his sculptures, then on exhibition at South Kensington Museum (the present-day Victoria and Albert Museum), to the British nation "as a little token of my admiration for your heroes."[20] Two years earlier, the Rodin Gallery had opened at the Metropolitan Museum in New York, with forty of the master's works on display, including a twenty-seven-inch-high bronze cast of *The Thinker*. This large collection of works—bronzes, marbles, terra-cotta, plaster, drawings—had been donated to the museum by the French government, by the millionaire businessman Thomas F. Ryan, and by Rodin himself. Now Rodin was about to achieve further immortality through the creation of a museum in his name in a magnificent mansion in the heart of Paris, across the street from the golden dome of the Invalides.

Monet had been one of the supporters of the plan for a Rodin museum at the government-owned Hôtel Biron—where the sculptor had been renting space since 1908—as soon as it was first mooted.[21] He and Rodin were old friends, and his career had in some ways been closely linked to Rodin's. The two artists had been born in the same year—not on the same day, as was often claimed, but only two days apart. They found success around the same time, too: at a joint exhibition at the Galerie Georges Petit during the Exposition Universelle in 1889. Monet showed 145 works in the spacious rooms, which were interspersed with Rodin's massive sculptures—some of which, to Monet's irritation, Rodin placed directly in front of Monet's canvases, blotting them out. When Rodin caught wind of Monet's distress, he raged: "I don't give a damn about Monet, I don't give a damn about anyone, I only care about myself!"[22] The two men patched up their differences, and the exhibition was a wild success that set both men on the road to fame and riches. "The same sense of brotherhood," Rodin once wrote to Monet, "the same love of art, has made us friends forever."[23]

Not even Monet possessed the same grandiose sense of self-importance as Rodin, a man who, while in Rome a year earlier, informed the French ambassador that he, Rodin, "represented glory while the ambassador merely represented France."[24] Even so, Monet planned a similar sort of glorification for himself—and both Étienne Clémentel and the Hôtel Biron would become important parts of his plan.

MONET, IN THE spring and summer of 1916, was an old man in a hurry. "I'm getting old," he wrote. "I don't have a moment to waste."[25] In May he wrote an urgent letter to his supplier of canvases and paints: "I have discovered that I need more canvases, and that I shall need them as quickly as possible." He ordered six canvases that were to be 2 meters by 1.5 meters (6.5 feet by 4 feet 11 inches) and six more 2 meters by 1.3 meters (6.5 feet by 4 feet 3 inches) in size, "on condition that they be of exactly the same canvas." Speed was of the essence: he asked for them to be sent "in a sealed crate by the high-speed train to Giverny-Limetz"—though if the packaging and transportation costs should prove excessive, "it would perhaps be best for you to send your automobile again."[26]

Monet's supplier was a Paris firm called L. Besnard ("Canvases, Fine Colours, Panels"), near Place Pigalle. Monet dealt with an employee in the shop, a certain Madame Barillon. She was presumably accustomed to these frantic requests from Giverny, and there would certainly be more of them to come. Monet's enthusiasm for his "famous decorations," as he began calling them, remained intact through the winter and spring as he continued to "work hard" on them.[27] His vision remained good, but other things troubled him, in particular the poor weather—blamed by many, once again, on the heavy bombardment on the western front.[28]

Another problem was that, after more than eighteen months of war, France was facing certain privations. There was a tobacco shortage, with more than a million fewer cigarettes and cigars to be had compared with prewar years.[29] Monet therefore expressed his gratitude in April to Charlotte Lysès for the gift of cigarettes. "They saved my life at the very moment I'd run out," he told her.[30] Monet without a regular supply of cigarettes did not bear contemplation. He always lit up as he started painting but, preoccupied with his task, often tossed the cigarette away only half-smoked, leaving family members to gather up these butts and put them in a container through whose contents Monet, desperate for a puff, would later rummage "like a beggar."[31]

Besides tobacco, some foods were also more difficult to come by, and all cost considerably more. By the spring of 1916, cheese was 20 percent more expensive than its prewar price, butter 24 percent more, while beef had risen by 36 percent and sugar by an eyewatering 71 percent, forcing the government to set a maximum price in May (soon raised in October).[32] For the past year the French papers had been exulting in rumors that the Germans were reduced to eating bread made from straw, but in May the French government introduced "national bread" consisting of a third part wheat flour mixed with rice and rye, a coarse, crusty mixture that most people found inedible.

A newspaper declared that, since the needs of the army came first, it was "the duty of the civilian population to decrease consumption."[33] Monet was therefore reduced to eating what he called "a modest wartime lunch."[34] He offered Charlotte a harrowing view of domestic life with a tobacco-starved artist fretting because the weather was keeping him from his easel and the war from the pleasures of his table. He experienced, he told her, "moments of complete discouragement, causing great damage to those around me, like poor and devoted Blanche, who puts up with my bad moods."[35]

In July, Mirbeau arrived in Giverny for a visit. The deteriorating condition of his old friend was a cause of great concern to Monet. A visit in the spring—when Mirbeau had moved back to his house in Cheverchemont—was canceled because of the writer's poor health. His appearance in Giverny two months later did nothing to inspire confidence. "What a dreadful state he is in, our poor friend," Monet wrote sorrowfully to Geffroy at the end of July.[36] Indeed, the problems were no longer merely physical, since by 1916 Mirbeau was reduced to a state of semiconsciousness for months at a time, often unable to recognize friends.[37]

Monet may have received from the decrepit and disabled figure of his friend, eight years younger than himself, a haunting vision of his own looming future, a horrifying glimpse of what his life would be like if he, too, ever became incapable of work. Another friend was likewise struck down in similar fashion: Rodin suffered two strokes in quick succession—the second, on July 10, resulting in a fall down the stairs at his home in Meudon, outside Paris. He, like Mirbeau, was suddenly left unable to work, although he remained "quite happy—full of serenity and sweetness," according to his friend and biographer Judith Cladel. Like Mirbeau, he suffered serious cognitive deficits: "He thinks that he's in Belgium," reported Cladel.[38]

Another visitor that summer was Clemenceau, who came to Giverny before departing for a rest at Vichy. Yet at least Clemenceau, despite his diabetes and overwork, offered an inspiring picture of physical and mental vigor. He had been continuing his war on all fronts, journalistic and political. In February he had chaired a meeting of the Franco-British Committee, of which he was president, thrilling and moving friends and enemies alike with his resounding rhetoric. "Clemenceau took the floor," reported a newspaper, "and delivered one of the best speeches of his career—and we know Clemenceau has always been a good speaker." He condemned the Germans and their "prodigious convulsions of barbarism" and spoke of French sacrifices: "We give our children, we give everything we own—everything, everything—and the wonderful cause of independence and the dignity of man serves as its own reward, and despite the most painful sacrifices we never complain that it has been too much."[39]

A little more than a week later, at the beginning of March, one of Clemenceau's articles on the Battle of Verdun infringed censorship regulations, and once more his newspaper was suspended, this time for a week; a second newspaper, L'Oeuvre, was suspended for fifteen days for reprinting part of the offending article. Clemenceau was becoming an increasingly controversial and divisive figure. Though loved by the *poilus*, whose cause he vigorously championed, he received ten death threats per day, many from those on the religious right. The editor of *L'Action Française*, Charles Maurras, who regarded him as damaging to national morale, denounced him as a "disastrous mountebank" and as "the anarchist Clemenceau."[40] The charge of anarchism was baseless: Clemenceau's address to the Franco-British Committee spoke of the rule of law as the basis of civilization, while even a newspaper generally not in accord with his political philosophy, *Le Figaro*, praised his "elevated patriotism."[41] Equally absurd was the accusation of defeatism. To the Franco-British Committee he had used, for the first time, the phrase that would become his rallying cry: *"La guerre jusqu'au bout"* ("War until the end").

MONET HAD ONE other visitor late that summer: his son Michel, who returned to Giverny on a six-day leave after "three terrible weeks at Verdun."[42] The battle was beginning to define the horror and futility of the Grande Guerre. A newspaper pointed out in August that the Battle of Verdun had already lasted as long as the entirety of the Franco-Prussian War in 1870–71.[43] By the summer of 1916, however, the German offensive was failing amid catastrophic losses on both sides. General Falkenhayn had been partially successful in his stated ambition to bleed France white, since by September the French dead and wounded amounted to 315,000 men. But the German casualties were equally horrendous. Erich Ludendorff, in charge of his country's war effort, toured the battleground in early September, around the time Michel Monet was granted leave. Even the hardened Prussian general was stunned by the bloody devastation. "Verdun was hell," he said. "Verdun was a nightmare."[44]

And yet fewer than two hundred miles from the hell of Verdun was the paradise—as so many of Monet's guests called it—of the garden at Giverny. The contrast with Verdun could only have been *surréel*, a word that would be coined a few months later by Guillaume Apollinaire. Leaving the devastated landscape of Verdun, Michel Monet passed

Monet with (*left to right*) Blanche, Michel Monet, and
Jean-Pierre Hoschedé (*standing*) in 1916.

through Paris, with its perverse displays of normality. (Besides films,
plays, and musical performances, football games were played that summer, and a bicycle race was contested on the roads between Paris and
Houdan.) He then reached Giverny to find his father, the most famous
interpreter of the beauties of the French countryside, sitting before his
easel as in days of old, apparently as unperturbed by events as the lush
foliage and bright waters he was re-creating on his canvases.

It is doubtful that Michel ever tried to explain the horrors of Verdun to his father. Few soldiers of the Great War were able to speak of what they had seen: "We could no more make ourselves articulate," wrote one of them, "than those who would not return."[45] But the night-marishness of the war was made clear in the hellish summer of 1916 to readers of *L'Oeuvre*, the newspaper that had been suspended in March for printing Clemenceau's article on Verdun. In August the newspaper began serializing *Le Feu*, a war novel by Henri Barbusse, dedicated to "my comrades who fell beside me at Crouy and on Hill 119." Barbusse hoped to puncture romantic notions of warfare with an astonishingly frank description of its true horrors. As one soldier in the novel, the ironically named Paradis, says to the narrator: "War is frightful and unnatural weariness, water up to the belly, mud and dung and infamous filth. It is befouled faces and tattered flesh, it is the corpses that are no longer like corpses even, floating on the ravenous earth. It is that, that endless monotony of misery, broken by poignant tragedies; it is that, and not the bayonet glittering like silver, nor the bugle's chanticleer call to the sun!"[46]

Amazingly, *L'Oeuvre* somehow escaped the censors, and later in 1916 the novel was published in book form (and swiftly translated into English as *Under Fire*). Monet may not have read Barbusse's novel in either format, but the novel's harrowing portrait of the war was the subject of discussion at the Goncourt luncheons. Monet was still as active as ever in these meetings of the "Goncourtistes," as he called them, even advocating the postponement of one session until Mirbeau was well enough to attend: a gathering of Les Dix without Mirbeau was, Monet told Geffroy, "an impossible thing."[47] In 1916, Les Dix decided that the only novels eligible for the prize would be those written by men who had served in the war. In December, the Prix Goncourt was awarded to Barbusse.

ON THE SAME day that the Prix Goncourt was awarded, the Senate voted in favor of providing government funds to establish the "Musée Rodin" in the Hôtel Biron. That autumn the newspapers had been full of news of "*la donation Rodin*," with the Chamber of Deputies voting in favor of the bequest in September and the Senate then debating the issue throughout October and November. Acceptance of the donation—valued at 2.5 million francs and including Rodin's house at Meudon—was a close-run thing, since many senators were reluctant to spend government funds on the museum during a time of war. As one of them retorted: "I want to know what the *poilus* in the trenches think of such a debate." However, proponents of the scheme argued that Rodin was "the poet of marble" and the "great national artist." One senator argued that the war must not prevent the French from fostering "the cult of beauty."[48] At long last, on December 22, Rodin's donation to the state was, as the law emphatically declared, "definitively accepted."[49]

One powerful senator, however, declined to speak in favor of the Rodin donation. Clemenceau did not hold the esteemed sculptor in high regard: "He was stupid, vain, and cared too much about money," he once told his secretary.[50] That may have been so, but the discord between the two men had other roots. He and Rodin fell out over a bust the sculptor made of Clemenceau some years earlier at the request of the government of Argentina (to which Clemenceau had paid a visit in 1910). "He completely botched me," Clemenceau complained, "this sculptor whose busts recall the finest Roman portraits, and who captures features of which the model is unaware. I have no vanity, but if I have to survive, I do not wish it to be in the aspect that Rodin created."[51] He believed Rodin had made him look like a "Mongol general," to which Rodin retorted: "Well you see, Clemenceau, he is Tamerlane, he is Genghis Khan."[52] When Rodin refused to tweak the bust, Clemenceau denied him permission to exhibit it at the Salon of 1913. The two men never spoke again.

NOT FAR FROM the Hôtel Biron, on the other side of the Invalides, another project was taking shape with even greater enthusiasm and support from the authorities. Like Monet, the painters Pierre Carrier-Belleuse and Auguste-François Gorguet found themselves in urgent need of a more commodious space. In November they took possession of a temple-shaped exhibition hall that had been purpose-built—thanks to funds raised from sponsors and subscribers—for their massive panorama, *Le Panthéon de la Guerre*. The new building occupied land owned by the École Militaire that had been granted to the painters by General Joseph Gallieni, the military governor of Paris. They and their team of helpers moved all of their paintings and designs into the structure—not only the thousands of square feet of canvas but also the tons of metal armature that would be used to suspend the paintings.

Before his death in 1916, General Gallieni had been among the cast who posed for his portrait in the boulevard Berthier. *Le Gaulois*, one of the project's numerous sponsors, announced to its readers that Carrier-Belleuse and Gorguet "inform the families they are at their disposal to create portraits of decorated heroes both dead and surviving, either from nature or from photographs, in their workshop, for the purpose of glorifying these heroes."[53] Into the grand new building filed mourning women in black veils "crying while bringing their images, sacred relics of a dearly departed." From these dead heroes, Carrier-Belleuse claimed, "a living one was made."[54] There could be no shortage of these mourning women: by the time Carrier-Belleuse and Gorguet moved into their new building, French deaths were approaching one million.

Finding time in his busy schedule to stand for Carrier-Belleuse and Gorguet, with his arms crossed in a pose of steely determination, was Georges Clemenceau. He probably had scant regard for the old-fashioned artistic style of these painters, although he appears, at least, to have raised no complaints about his portrait having been botched. He was, in any case, highly sympathetic to the project of commemorating French heroism. In the autumn of 1916 he made another of his fact-finding visits to the front. Soon afterward, in November, he paid one of his regular visits to Giverny. "Clemenceau was just here," Monet wrote to Geffroy, "and he left enthusiastic for what I have done. I told him how badly I wanted your opinion on this formidable work, which is, to tell the truth, sheer madness."[55]

Monet was eager to show his work to friends such as Clemenceau and Geffroy, and to receive their opinions and encouragement. Despite the uncooperative weather, the problems with his teeth, and "all the anguish and worries of this war,"[56] his mood had been optimistic throughout much of the year. His greatest fear, he told Clemenceau— perhaps with the sorry fates of Mirbeau and Rodin in mind—was "never finishing this immense work."[57]

As his seventy-sixth birthday passed in November, Monet responded to good wishes from the Bernheim-Jeunes with a few lines of contented optimism: "I am happy to let you know that I am more and more passionate about my work, and that my greatest pleasure is to paint and to enjoy nature."[58]

CHAPTER NINE

A STATE OF IMPOSSIBLE ANXIETY

IN DECEMBER 1916, Monet prepared to receive an illustrious visitor. "Regarding Monsieur Matisse," he wrote to the Bernheim-Jeune brothers at the end of November, "you may tell him that I would be happy to receive him." However, he wished to delay Matisse's visit for several weeks because he needed, he said, "to add a few touches to the *grandes machines*."[1] Many others had been given a sneak preview of the paintings, from Clemenceau and the Goncourtistes to the beautiful American socialite Gladys Deacon, who had been welcomed in Giverny in the autumn of 1914. But Monet evidently believed they needed a bit of touching up before another painter should be allowed to see them.

And not just any painter. Henri Matisse was prominent and successful—"one of the most robustly talented painters of the day," according to the critic Louis Vauxcelles.[2] Over the past dozen years Matisse had gone from the leader of a shocking and controversial group of young painters dubbed the Fauves (wild beasts), whose paintings one critic attacked in 1908 as a "spectacle of unhealthy shams,"[3] to an acclaimed and respected artist who in 1910 had enjoyed a retrospective of his work at the Galerie Bernheim-Jeune and a solo exhibition in New York. "From morning to night it did not empty," Mirbeau had reported enviously to Monet on the triumph of the Bernheim-Jeune retrospective. "Russians, Germans, male and female, drooling in front of each canvas, drooling with joy and admiration, of course."[4]

At the end of 1916 Matisse was approaching his forty-seventh birthday. Dapper, bearded, and bespectacled, he looked like a professor, although he was still notorious enough for enraged art students in Chicago to have burned three of his paintings in effigy in 1913 and to have placed "Henry Hair Mattress" (as they mocked him) on trial for

The "robustly talented" Henri Matisse, photographed in 1913

"artistic murder" and "pictorial arson."[5] He and Monet had never met. For the most part Monet paid little attention to the younger generation of painters. In 1905 he told an interviewer that he did not understand Gauguin's painting: "I never took him seriously anyway."[6] Matisse, however, had been Monet's most talented artistic offspring, studying his works with the zeal of a devoted acolyte. He had first discovered Monet's works in the mid-1890s through his friend, the Australian painter John Peter Russell, for whom Monet was "the most original painter of our century."[7] Soon Matisse was setting up his easel in spots where Monet had once painted—before the rocks on Belle-Île-en-Mer, for example—and becoming such a dedicated admirer that, as a friend claimed, he "swears only by Claude Monet."[8]

Within a few years Matisse developed a bold new style of his own, forsaking the Impressionist palette and painting in the riots of unnatural, high-keyed colors that won him and his friends, such as André Derain and Maurice de Vlaminck, the nickname Fauves and the reputation as artistic *provocateurs*. Monet was, for the Fauves, a painter to learn from — and in 1905 Derain even went to London to paint the same subjects — but one ultimately to be superseded. They aimed to express something less fleeting and more substantial than what they claimed were the mere "impressions" put down on canvas by Monet. "As for Claude Monet," Derain wrote to Vlaminck in 1906, "in spite of everything I adore him… But finally, is he right to use his fleeting and insubstantial colour to render natural impressions that are nothing more than impressions and do not endure?… Personally I would look for something else: that which on the contrary is fixed, eternal and complex."[9]

The term "Impressionism," Matisse announced in 1908, "is not an appropriate designation for certain more recent painters" — himself and his friends — who "avoid the first impression, and consider it almost dishonest. A rapid rendering of a landscape represents only one moment of its existence." Matisse insisted that he wanted to depict the "essential character" of the landscape rather than the "superficial existence" brushed so rapidly by the Impressionists, whose canvases, he claimed, "all look alike." He wanted to give reality "a more lasting interpretation."[10] His windy afternoons at the easel by the sea on Belle-Île, struggling to capture the shifting effects of light, froth, and spindrift, were, at this point, clearly a thing of the past.

Monet was undoubtedly aware of Matisse's slighting comments, which had been published at the end of 1908 in *La Grande Revue*, a prestigious literary journal. They lie behind Mirbeau's savage assessment of Matisse's work in a letter to Monet in 1910: "You cannot believe such folly, such madness. Matisse is a paralytic."[11] But by 1916 the artistically restless Matisse had revised his position, and once more he was concerned with the more delicate nuances of light and atmosphere. "I felt that this was necessary for me right now," he told an interviewer.[12] In particular, he took a renewed interest in the work of Monet and Renoir, asking the Bernheim-Jeune brothers and other mutual acquaintances to arrange visits with both of them.

By this time Matisse was living in Issy-les-Moulineaux, a few miles southwest of Paris, his age having prevented him from joining the army in 1914 despite his efforts to volunteer. He had begun a *grande machine* of his own, a canvas some eight and a half feet high and almost thirteen feet wide. He had started this huge work, *Bathers by a River*, in 1909, working on it sporadically as he struggled to absorb and surpass Picasso's Cubism. He and Picasso were in the midst of an artistically productive game of tag, building on each other's styles to create, in the early years of the war, increasingly geometrical compositions with flat, fractured, and overlapping planes, broad passages of black, and rigid, angular human-oids with only the most schematic features. *Bathers by a River* would mark one of Matisse's closest encounters with Cubism.[13]

Yet Matisse's experimentation with a Cubist artistic vocabulary was rapidly running its course. In the summer of 1916 he showed works with Picasso at the Galerie Poiret in the rue d'Antin. The exhibition, *L'Art Moderne en France*, did not go down well with many critics, not least because Picasso elected to show *Les Demoiselles d'Avignon* in public for the first time. "The Cubists are not waiting until the end of the war to reopen hostilities," complained one critic, while another declared: "The time for tests and experiments is over."[14] The war years were difficult for artists in general, but for the modernists—especially ones who, like Matisse and Picasso, were not wearing uniforms—they were especially so. Matisse was in a tricky position. He was closely associated with Picasso, a foreign national and known pacifist. He was promoted by German dealers in Paris such as Wilhelm Uhde and Daniel-Henry Kahnweiler, both of whose collections were sequestered during the war as the property of enemy aliens. His works were bought by German collectors such as Karl Ernst Osthaus, who had been active in the Pan-German League. And by experimenting with Cubism he was identifying himself with a modern style of art that during the war years was castigated in France as *boche* (kraut). In the summer of 1916, for example, an illustrated weekly called *L'Anti-Boche* featured on its cover a cartoon, done in a faux Cubist style, of Kaiser Wilhelm; the caption screamed: "Kubism!!!"[15] Any taint of a German association was not to be taken lightly at a time when nationalism and xenophobia were such that the Académie Française was seriously debating how to eliminate the German letter *K* from the French alphabet.

It was during this period of political duress and artistic uncertainty, then, that Matisse approached Gaston and Josse Bernheim-Jeune about arranging a visit to Giverny. He may simply have been curious about Monet's new project, word of which was percolating through artistic circles. But he was also hoping to replenish his painting by abandoning his austere Cubist-inspired "foreign" style and returning to paintings that in their concern for color and atmosphere were much closer to Impressionism, and to "Frenchness."[16]

THE HISTORIC VISIT between Monet and Matisse failed to come off at the end of 1916. Early in December, Monet entertained the painter André Barbier, an unctuous young admirer, happily reporting to Geffroy (who arranged the visit) that he "seemed very enthusiastic about everything he saw." He even allowed Barbier to take away "a nice souvenir of his visit": one of his pastels.[17] But the obscure and fawning Barbier was one thing, Matisse quite another. Suddenly overcome with doubts about his paintings, Monet canceled the planned visit almost as soon as it was agreed on. "I am immersed in several changes in my large canvases," he informed the Bernheim-Jeunes in the middle of December, "and do not go out. I'm in a foul mood." He then added a P.S.: "If you should have occasion to see Matisse, explain to him that at the moment I'm all mixed up, and I'll alert you as soon as I emerge from this state of anxiety."[18]

Two days later, Sacha Guitry's offer of two free tickets to his new play at the Théâtre des Bouffes-Parisiens failed to tempt Monet to Paris. "I am going through a very bad period with my work," he explained. "I'm in a state of impossible anxiety. I've ruined the good pieces by trying to improve them, and now I have to try to fix it at all costs...For the time being, I can't leave here and I can't see anyone."[19]

For the previous two and a half years, Monet had worked happily and productively despite the anxieties and upheavals of the war, the periodic problems with his eyes and his teeth, his frustrations with the uncooperative weather, and the occasional bouts of discouragement that, nonetheless, always seemed to pass. He had delighted in showing the Grande Décoration to friends and gauging their reactions, which he always interpreted as positive; and he even sent out feelers to cultural entrepreneurs such as Raymond Koechlin and Maurice Joyant, planning (or at least dreaming of) a future exhibition or installation of his work. By November 1916, indeed, he appeared to think he was reaching the end of his labors. Yet uncertainty about his achievement suddenly took hold, apparently precipitated by the prospect of Matisse's scrutiny, which appears to have unnerved him or made him look at his paintings anew.

This crisis persisted through the Christmas period and into the New Year. Not even the highly successful sale of twenty-four of his works in New York, held over two days in mid-January, could lift his mood. This auction, conducted in the Grand Ballroom of the Plaza Hotel, was billed in the *New York Herald* as "the most notable sale of Monet paintings ever held in the world", and his paintings, all from James F. Sutton's collection, fetched what the *Herald* called record prices: a total of $161,600, or more than 800,000 francs. The sight of the paintings on the auctioneer's easel "elicited much applause from his admirers in the audience."[20] But the spectacle of wealthy Americans opening their checkbooks and applauding his paintings did little to cheer Monet, who once gracelessly complained that many of the people who bought his works were "idiots, snobs, and hucksters."[21] When the Bernheim-Jeune brothers excitedly gave him news of the auction, he sniffed: "The prices were a bit excessive, in my opinion," although he frankly admitted to them: "I'm in the state of mind to find everything absolutely wrong."[22] As he informed Geffroy a short time later, he was "saddened by this dreadful war, worried about my poor Michel, who risks his life at every moment, and…disgusted with everything I've done, which I now see I won't be able to finish. I feel that I'm at the end of my tether and no good for anything anymore."[23]

*

A FEW DAYS after penning these lines, Monet overcame his bad temper and began planning a trip to Paris to visit Geffroy. But at the last minute he canceled, citing the difficulties of the journey: the trains were running late, there were no waiting rooms on the Paris-bound platforms at Bonnières and Mantes-la-Jolie, and he would therefore have been forced to expose himself to the cold and wind, "which would be imprudent for an old man like myself."[24]

He was right about the cold. By the end of January, the weather was frigid, with the temperature in Paris failing to rise above minus 5 degrees Celsius (23 degrees Fahrenheit) for days on end, and dropping as low as minus 10 degrees Celsius (14 degrees Fahrenheit) during the night. The fountains in the Place de la Concorde froze solid; so did the canals and the narrow arm of the Seine on the south side of the Île de la Cité. Transport along the rest of the river was made treacherous by ice floes — indeed, all river traffic was halted between Paris and Rouen, where the ice closed the port. To add to the misery, coal was in desperately short supply, forcing some Parisians to chop up their furniture as firewood. "How long will it continue?" asked a newspaper in despair.[25] On that day, the first of February, a heavy snow fell across the region, and on the second, Candlemas, people nervously recited an old proverb: *"À la chandeleur, l'hiver se passe ou prend vigueur"* ("At Candlemas, winter either passes or takes hold"). On that day, ominously, the temperature at sunrise was minus 6 degrees Celsius (21 degrees Fahrenheit) and the weather (as *Le Matin* reported) "remained rigorously cold."[26]

At the Villa des Brillants, his house in Meudon, Auguste Rodin coped with the freezing weather and lack of coal by staying in bed all day with his longtime companion and onetime model, seventy two year-old Rose Beuret. The pair had wed only a few days earlier. Rose, feverish with bronchitis at the ceremony, soon fell ill with pneumonia; then Rodin himself was stricken. At the end of January, *Le Figaro* anxiously reported that "the master is very weak."[27] Rodin began a slow recovery, but Rose died on February 14, barely a fortnight after the nuptials for which she had waited more than fifty years.

Two days later, another death in Monet's circle affected him much more profoundly: that of Octave Mirbeau. On February 16 Monet wrote to Geffroy asking for the date of the next Goncourt dinner, "because the weather is improving and, having several important things to do in Paris, I intend to go there soon."[28] These urgent tasks had nothing to do with his paintings: he was still dismissive and despairing of his efforts, which he had not resumed in any force. Joseph Durand-Ruel had recently approached him regarding the possibility of selling some of these new works. He asked Monet for permission for his brother to send a photographer to Giverny: "He believes that he would have opportunities to sell them if he had photographs of the decorations and the prices that you would wish to have."[29] But Monet was having none of it: neither a photographer nor sales to Durand-Ruel's clients. "I will not have any photographs done until this work—which, incidentally, does not always go to my liking—is more or less finished," he curtly informed the dealer. He added: "Moreover, for the same reason I cannot think of selling, since I do not know if I will finish it."[30]

Monet did go to Paris, as he promised Geffroy, although not for the merriment of a Goncourt dinner. On February 16, Mirbeau died at his apartment in Paris, on his sixty-ninth birthday. The funeral was held on the afternoon of the nineteenth at the Cimetière de Passy. Geffroy, Clemenceau, the Goncourtistes, les Guitry—all were present along with Monet, who in his grief clung desperately to Charlotte Lysès as the distinguished band of mourners followed the wreath-laden funeral cart to the grave. One of the other mourners was struck by Monet's aged appearance and his unabashed distress at the loss of his old friend: "Bareheaded under the misty winter sky, this rough-mannered but sincere man stood and sobbed. From the depths of his eyes, red with grief, tears rolled into the thickets of his long beard, which was now quite white."[31] Such was Monet's grief, as he later explained to Geffroy, that he wandered away from the cemetery "without knowing what I was doing" and without bidding farewell to his friends.[32]

If Mirbeau's death was not unexpected, then what happened next certainly took some of his friends and readers by shocked surprise. On the day of his funeral, *Le Petit Parisien*, a newspaper with (as its banner proudly declared) "the largest print run in the entire world," published on its front page what it billed as Mirbeau's "political testament."[33] Despite his infirmity, Mirbeau had already written on the war for *Le Petit Parisien*, in a front-page article published eighteen months earlier in the summer of 1915. Entitled "To Our Soldiers," it had supposedly been coaxed out of him by "a woman of great heart" who asked him for "a few lines, a few sentences, even a word" for the men at the front. As someone who had condemned heroism in battle as absurd, "a dangerous and disturbing form of banditry and murder," Mirbeau might have been the last person expected to offer a few comforting lines to the men in the trenches. But he had duly produced, undoubtedly with the help of an amanuensis, a salute to the heroism and bravery of the young men fighting the war. He gave a poignant mention of a wounded young soldier whom he met by his garden gate in Cheverchemont. "He told me of the most incredible things and I felt moved to tears."[34]

These sentiments, with their eloquently expressed sympathy for the common soldier, caused no controversy. The article published on the day of his funeral was a different matter. The short introduction by the editor of *Le Petit Parisien* stated that Mirbeau had "yielded to the prayers of a compassionate woman"—that is, to Madame Mirbeau—and offered his "last thoughts" on France and the war: a testament that (so the editor assured his readers) expressed Mirbeau's patriotism, idealism, and confidence in the impending victory of France's "holy cause." In the article Mirbeau denounced "the greatest crime in the history of the world, the monstrous aggression by Germany," and advocated "sacrificing everything for France." He assured his "old and dear comrades" that France's preeminent moral position in the world offered the hope of a regenerated humanity.

Monet cannot have been especially perturbed by these sentiments, some of which he shared and some of which Clemenceau had already repeatedly voiced. But these words astounded and appalled some of Mirbeau's "old and dear comrades" on the left, who had known him as a committed pacifist and antimilitarist. Indeed, as *Le Petit Parisien* noted:

"Of all the detractors of war who, in times of peace, launched their anathemas against the dreaded goddess, Monsieur Octave Mirbeau was the most vehement."[35] Yet now the great detractor seemed to be worshipping at the goddess's shrine. Barely had he been laid into the ground than he was denounced as a worthless hypocrite, "the sum total of whose works amount to nothing."[36]

The testament was soon condemned as a forgery cooked up by his wife and a journalist named Gustave Hervé, a political turncoat (from socialist to ultranationalist) who formed part of "an abominable intrigue around the bedside of the dying man" and who delivered a rambling, reactionary eulogy at the graveside.[37] Mirbeau in his last days was incapable of recognizing his closest friends, let alone expostulating political and moral philosophy, and there can be little doubt that the article was composed by other hands.[38] But the damage done to his reputation was considerable. Monet was therefore left to mourn, not only the death of a friend whose physical and mental deterioration had caused him so much worry and grief, but also the fatal tarnishing of his name.

THE COLD WINTER turned slowly into spring. Still Monet did little or no work on his Grande Décoration. He made frequent trips to Paris ("which turns my life upside-down") in order to visit his dentist—although his dental problems did not prevent him from enjoying the occasional meal at the restaurant Drouant or the sweets sent to him by Gaston Bernheim-Jeune's wife. "She spoils me so much," he confessed to Gaston, "but she knows how greedy I am."[39] He also read books: Théophile Gautier's Le Capitaine Fracasse, a swashbuckling novel set in seventeenth-century France; and Sainte-Beuve's Galerie de femmes célèbres, with its biographies of illustrious Frenchwomen such as Marguerite of Navarre, Madame de Sévigné, and Madame de Maintenon. In despair over his work, Monet was losing himself in the rustling silk and clashing swords of France's ancien régime.

At some point he did pick up his brush and palette, but it was to paint something quite different from his lily pond: he began several self-portraits. The act was highly uncharacteristic. No painter was ever less interested in self-portraits than Monet, who was far more intrigued by the reflective surface of his pond than by his own image in the looking-glass. Occasionally he posed for his friends, such as Carolus-Duran in 1867 and, five years later, Renoir, who showed him hunched over a book, smoking a long-stemmed pipe. In 1886 he had painted his self-portrait wearing a black beret, looking serious and askance. His 1917 self-portraits were also uncompleted. Two of them he destroyed: they "perished on an unhappy day," according to Clemenceau, who managed to rescue the third before it, too, could suffer Monet's destructive wrath.[40]

Freely and even frantically painted, with slashing, stabbing brush-work, the surviving self-portrait shows Monet with ruddy cheeks and a large, yellowish beard. He would claim that a photograph taken of him later that year, though "very lifelike," made him "look a little like an escaped prisoner."[41] His self-portrait shows him to be nothing so desperate or sinister. Rather, he looks every inch the weather-beaten peasant—the same figure who, a year later, would impress a visitor for whom his vitality so belied his white beard that he seemed to be "a young father on Christmas Day wearing a false white beard to make his children believe in old Father Christmas."[42] For Clemenceau, this ruddy-cheeked self-portrait revealed Monet's "superhuman ambition."[43] However, as he worked in front of his mirror, Monet had in fact been drained of ambition and self-confidence.

A new opportunity, however, presented itself in the spring of 1917. On April 30, two important visitors arrived in Giverny for a visit: Étienne Clémentel and Albert Dalimier. Both men had been important members of Aristide Briand's government: Clémentel as the minister of commerce and industry, Dalimier as the undersecretary of state for the fine arts. When Briand's coalition government collapsed in the middle of March, replaced by one put together by Alexandre Ribot, both men kept their posts. There was still no place in government for Clemenceau. The British ambassador reported that the Tiger had been undermining his position with "continual but unreasoning attacks in his newspaper on Monsieur Briand and the authorities generally," and he concluded that Clemenceau had "rendered himself impossible."[44]

Étienne Clémentel, powerful politician
and welcome visitor to Giverny

The arrival for a personal visit of two important members of the government shook Monet out of his long torpor. They were most welcome guests, combining as they did an educated and sympathetic interest in the fine arts with sweeping financial powers. Clémentel was an energetic fifty-three-year-old with a large and important ministry under his control. Indeed, the name of his cabinet portfolio—minister of commerce, industry, posts and telegraphs, maritime transport, and the merchant marine—indicated his vast powers and responsibilities. He was famously busy, pursued by secretaries with documents awaiting his signature and pages bearing visiting cards from officials and captains of industry hoping for meetings. All were forced to compete for his time and attention with each other, with his mountains of paperwork, and with his young children, on whom he doted at his house in Versailles.[45]

Clémentel had long been a great supporter of the arts, in particular the Impressionists. He had even studied painting and sculpture before turning to politics. During long political meetings he often made swift pencil sketches of his colleagues, and his few periods of recreation were spent at an easel in the countryside, where he produced canvases, according to a friend, "in numbers that showed the painter's energy to be at least as tireless as the Minister's."[46] He was a friend of both Renoir and Rodin, and had been the one to persuade Rodin to donate his works to France so the Hôtel Biron could be transformed into a museum. He had even been the subject of Rodin's last work, a portrait bust that revealed him in a defiant pose: shoulders bare, chin up, moustache smartly bristling.

Clémentel and Dalimier were undoubtedly given a tour of the Grande Décoration in Monet's studio. However impressed they may have been with these efforts, they presented him with quite a different proposition. As Monet reported on the following day to Geffroy: "I agreed to go to Reims (at least when the shells stop falling) to paint the cathedral in its present state. This interests me a lot."[47] Monet had done his famous series of paintings of the cathedral in Rouen, and he seems to have entertained the idea, years earlier, of tackling a series of paintings of French cathedrals: one of his notes records his desire to paint "the cathedrals of France."[48] Now the opportunity presented itself to set up his easel in front of another cathedral—a state-sponsored commission, no less, arranged for him by the government's top cultural supremos.

Notre-Dame de Reims was not just any French cathedral. The critic Charles Morice, writing before the war started, called it "the national cathedral."[49] Twenty-six kings and queens of France had been crowned inside the cathedral, the latest version of which, begun early in the thirteenth century, was decorated with some of the most beautiful and innovative statuary in Europe, regarded by Rodin as superior to anything done in Italy. And yet Reims and its beautiful cathedral had become victims of German artillery, an obscene testimony, in the eyes of so many in France, to the barbarism of the "Huns." The Germans had bombarded the city for five straight days in September 1914, killing dozens of people and hitting the cathedral (which they claimed, by way of justification, was being used by artillery spotters) with more than two hundred shells. Stained-glass windows were destroyed, the roof caught fire, and a beatifically smiling angel on the façade—one of the masterpieces giving the cathedral its worldwide reputation—was decapitated, its head falling to the ground and breaking into pieces. The damage to such an important historical and religious monument gave the Allies, as a German journalist ruefully noted, "a convenient propaganda tool."[50]

To be sure, condemnation of the shelling of the cathedral had been widespread and immediate. The Académie Française denounced "the savage destruction of the noble monuments of the past," while the Académie des Beaux-Arts raged against the destruction "inflicted

Reims Cathedral under German bombardment, April 1917

on one of the most sublime productions of French genius."[51] A senator, Camille Pelletan, declared: "The cry of horror that has risen around the world shall be perpetual."[52] Photographs of the architectural carnage were widely distributed, showing the façade of the cathedral wreathed in smoke and the skeletal stonework rising above piles of rubble. The volume *Les Allemands: destructeurs des cathédrales* had been hastily produced, with Reims taking a starring role. Fragments from the building—glass, stone, a melted bronze crucifix—were conducted away like holy relics. A shell-damaged pilaster was incorporated into the pedestal of Anna Hyatt's statue of Joan of Arc, unveiled on Riverside Drive in New York in December 1915. Meanwhile, the shattered head of the smiling angel— henceforth known as *Le Sourire de Reims* (*The Smile of Reims*)—was dispatched on a tour of the United States, Canada, Argentina, and Chile.

The outrage did not stop the shelling. By the cold winter of 1917, Reims had suffered, according to one newspaper, "twenty-eight months of almost uninterrupted bombardment"; its population had shrunk from 120,000 people to 17,000.[53] In April, on the eve of Clémentel and Dalimier's visit to Giverny, the "Martyred City" (as it became known)

suffered another heavy shelling. Thousands of projectiles and "asphyxiation bombs" pummeled the city—some 65,000 shells in the first three
weeks alone.[54] The intensity was such that the remaining civilians were
evacuated to Paris and Troyes. "Ah, the bandits!" fumed an article in *Le
Matin*, noting that the Germans had recommenced their "abominable
vandalism" of the cathedral.[55] This time the towers were damaged and
the stone vaulting of the nave, left relatively unscathed in 1914, dramatically collapsed, leaving the battered structure without a roof. "The barbarians," reported *Le Matin* on the day of Clémentel and Dalimier's visit
to Giverny, "do not seem to want to leave a stone standing."[56]

THIS, THEN, WAS the assignment dangled before Monet: to paint the
war-ravaged cathedral "in its present state" as part of the propaganda
offensive against the German "barbarians." A series of paintings of the
half-destroyed cathedral, coming from the brush of Claude Monet,
would announce this dreadful vandalism to the wider world in a way that
no photograph could ever hope to.

Although Monet responded eagerly to the commission, it would
present a number of challenges. The most serious was, of course, that
unless the shells did indeed stop falling—which seemed unlikely in the
spring of 1917—he might be obliged to put himself in harm's way. A less
plausible war artist would be difficult to imagine than the seventy-six-
year-old Monet. A man who raged at the wind and rain as he painted
in his garden was unlikely to cope well with asphyxiation bombs and
collapsing rubble. Moreover, he would be obliged to travel the hundred
miles from Giverny to Reims.

Weighed against these considerable difficulties were some very
attractive rewards. Most important was the fact that Monet would
finally be working on a state commission—something he had coveted at
least since his failed attempt to secure the contract to decorate Paris's
Hôtel de Ville. In doing so, he would, moreover, be contributing to the
war effort. There were, besides, certain special dispensations, a few of
which he began collecting almost immediately. Barely had the two men
departed than Monet wrote to Geffroy: "I'm not sure what will be the

result of the two of them as regards my automobile."[57] At the end of 1914 the military authorities had conducted an automobile census in France, hoping to determine "the number of motor vehicles that may be used for the needs of the army."[58] All owners had been obliged to report to their local town hall with details of the vehicles, which were ripe for requisitioning for the war effort. Monet with his fleet of vehicles was particularly at risk, and indeed in April 1917, the month of Clémentel and Dalimier's visit, he received notice to report with one of them to Les Andelys, a town fifteen miles away. This notice was evidently presented by Monet to Clémentel for his special attention. Despite his massive workload, the minister wasted no time in intervening. One day after Clémentel's visit to Giverny, Monet was approached by a local government official bearing the happy news "that there is no need to present my automobile at Les Andelys and that I can keep it, which gives me great joy. I thank you a thousand times for your intervention," he wrote to Clémentel, "and also that of Monsieur Dalimier."[59]

Monet's automobile, while off-limits to the military authorities, was no good without petrol, which was in regrettably short supply, especially since a decree of April 16 had strictly regulated consumption by members of the public: only those with "real needs" were to be provided with fuel, and then only with "the strictest economy."[60] But a word in Clémentel's ear was all that it took for a supply of gasoline to make its way to Giverny from a fuel depot at Vernon.[61] These were only the first of many favors that Monet would extract from the minister as—theoretically at least—he went about his war work.

THE SPRING AND early summer of 1917 looked an unlikely time for an elderly civilian to make his way to the western front for some plein air sketching. Mutinies had broken out in the French army following the dismal failure in April of the offensive on the chemin des Dames, a few miles northwest of Reims, when massive casualties had been sustained (120,000 on April 17 alone) with no discernible gain in territory. The entire 21st Division, veterans of the atrocious combat at Verdun, refused to go into battle. Railway tracks were sabotaged to prevent troops reaching the front. The red flag was raised and revolutionary songs sung.

In Paris, prices continued to climb as food became ever scarcer. From the middle of May, in order to conserve supplies for the soldiers, buying and selling meat was banned on Thursdays and Fridays in all shops, hotels, restaurants, canteens, and bars. Fish, complained a restaurateur, was an "impossible hypothesis."[62] Patissiers could still make cakes with wheat flour, except on Mondays, while France's biscuitiers, according to a decree of May 3, were forced to make their wares from rice flour—a regulation that resulted in a protest from the Committee for the Defense of French Biscuits.[63]

Biscuit makers were not the only ones up in arms. May Day passed off peacefully apart from a few cries of "Long live peace!" and "Down with the war!" But the strikes began on May 11, first of all in the clothing industry and then, by June, spreading to companies making gas masks, helmets, and munitions. Soon 100,000 people in Paris were out on strike. In the middle of June, 5,000 workers at a gunpowder factory in Toulouse walked off the job, some carrying red banners and singing the "Internationale," whose opening lines—"Stand up, prisoners of hunger!"—resonated throughout France.[64]

Monet managed to get by in what he called "these times of austerity" with a little help from his friends, such as the Bernheim-Jeunes, who sent him a "superb package" of treats in the middle of May.[65] He also managed to produce a lunch for none other than Henri Matisse, whose invitation to Giverny—extended one day after Clémentel and Dalimier visited—clearly indicated how the Reims commission had enhanced his mood. "If Matisse and Marquet want to set a day next week to come and eat," he wrote to the Bernheim-Jeunes, "it will be my great pleasure."[66] Albert Marquet was an old friend of Matisse, a forty-two-year-old Fauve who, like Matisse, had cut his artistic teeth on Monet's works. He had also painted many canvases of Notre-Dame in Paris, and several of his works had been on display on the walls of Mirbeau's home in Cheverchemont.

Matisse and Marquet came to Giverny on May 10. After shunting along the tracks for nearly three hours on a stopping train—"There is

no other choice," Monet ruefully informed them—they arrived at the
station in Mantes-la-Jolie, where an automobile was waiting to collect
them.[67] Unlike the visitors who, if the weather was fine, found themselves rushed to the door as soon as the lunch plates were cleared from
the table, enabling the master to get back to work, the two painters
enjoyed an entire afternoon chez Monet. The automobile delivered
them back to Mantes-la-Jolie on time for the six P.M. train. By that time
the heavens had opened—contrary weather, to be sure, for the backdrop
to this springtime idyll of France's two great painters of sun-drenched
landscapes.[68]

  No record has been left of their conversation. However, Matisse's
memories of his afternoon in Monet's garden linger in a work he painted
only a few weeks later, *The Music Lesson*. The painting shows Matisse's
family gathered in the living room of their home in Issy-les-Moulineaux.
His daughter Marguerite instructs one son, Pierre, at the keyboard
while another—seventeen-year-old Jean, soon to be drafted into the
army—reads a book, cigarette in mouth, forelock adroop, adolescent
moustache proudly in evidence. Through the open window, in the background, beyond where Matisse's wife sits obliviously sewing on the balcony, we see the profuse greenery of a garden, complete with pond and
statue. The rich and savage vegetation—not to mention the nude statue
of a voluptuously reclining woman—provide a dramatic contrast to the
calm interior domestic space. In the center of the garden, gathered like
a bouquet, are a half-dozen heart- and teardrop-shaped leaves that look
unmistakably like the pads of water lilies.[69]

CHAPTER TEN

THE SMILE OF REIMS

THE HEAVY GERMAN bombardment of Reims continued throughout the summer of 1917. Indeed, REIMS BOMBARDED was an almost daily newspaper headline in the months after Monet received his commission to paint the cathedral. The papers kept a faithful grisly toll of the German onslaught—remorseless barrages of more than a thousand shells a day. An official communiqué on July 13 reported that "the Germans violently bombarded Reims. Sixteen hundred shells fell on the city." A few days later, on July 16, Reims was blasted by a further 2,537 shells.[1]

That month, *Le Matin* dispatched a special correspondent to Reims to view the ruins of the city. He poetically evoked the horrors of the bombardment, describing the "dishonoured towers" of the cathedral rising against a sunset in the midst of a thunderstorm. As the horizon kindled and flamed, the stones of the cathedral were cast in shades of red: not merely from the rays of the dying sun but also from "the red of the fires in the town…blazing like candles beside a dying man." Then, after the sun had set, "there began what, in Reims, passes for a normal night, one shaken by explosions and terror."[2]

"Everything changes," Monet had once written, "even stone." The reporter's vision of a beautiful cathedral bathed in a flickering reddish *enveloppe* evoked an Impressionist vision, one recalling Monet's paintings of Rouen Cathedral, some of which showed the façade blazing in the sunset with molten shades of red and orange. This depiction in *Le Matin* comes close to achieving in words what Clémentel and Dalimier expected Monet to produce in paint.

The critic Louix Vauxcelles, getting wind of the assignment, excitedly predicted that "the glorious leader of French Impressionism" would crown his career with his paintings of the ruined cathedral.[3] However,

Monet's talents did not readily lend themselves to a frank depiction of the horrors wreaked by the bombardment. He was always strictly faithful to the spirit—his impression—of the motif, but his stock-in-trade was not a nearsighted concern for accurately documenting the minute details of the physical objects he painted. He would have agreed with Édouard Manet, who once told a student, "You wouldn't dream of counting the scales on the salmon, would you?"[4] Monet occasionally took liberties with the visual facts for the sake of a better composition. In his paintings of the Manneporte at Étretat, for instance, he adjusted the position of the giant stone arch, while in some of his Argenteuil paintings he raised the height of the tollbooths on the bridge and even reduced the number of the bridge's arches from seven to five.[5] Faithfully depicting architectural features was less important to him than creating a striking composition. He once gave a visiting American painter a bit of advice: "When you go out to paint," he told her, "try to forget what objects you have before you, a tree, a house, a field, or whatever. Merely think, here is a little square of blue, here an oblong of pink, here a streak of yellow." He even told her that he wished he had been born blind and then suddenly regained his sight, "so that he could have begun to paint in this way without knowing what the objects were that he saw before him."[6]

This statement should not be taken to suggest that Monet played fast and loose with the visual evidence, or that his subjects, such as the wheat stacks and poplars, were chosen willy-nilly and bore no significance to him. However, the upshot of Monet's approach—concentrating as it did on the fuzzy *enveloppe* surrounding the objects—was that it was sometimes difficult for a viewer to know what his squares, oblongs, and streaks were meant to represent. As a friend of Monet wrote of his works: "The light becomes the most important thing in his paintings. Everything else is secondary. The subject doesn't matter."[7] This was to overstate the case, since the subject was, in fact, of great importance. But when the painter Wassily Kandinsky first saw one of Monet's wheat stack paintings in the mid-1890s, he struggled to identify what exactly he was looking at. He was disturbed at first, believing that "the painter had no right to paint so indistinctly. I had a dull feeling that the object was lacking in this picture." But Kandinsky believed that in a Monet painting the object was less important than how it was painted, since "objects were discredited as an essential element within the picture." Instead, Monet's paintings depended on the "power of the palette"—on the virtuoso use of color for its own sake, not the depiction in a lucid, recognizable way of objects in the natural world.[8]

Painting a canvas that was intended to document architectural destruction would therefore be something of a novel experience for Monet. In his previous paintings of a cathedral, that of Rouen, the fine architectural details had been elusive. A nineteenth-century guidebook described its façade as abounding with "niches and statues, and an almost endless variety of open and free tracery of the most beautiful description."[9] Yet Monet's canvases were decidedly short on this welter of architectural detail, emphasizing instead light, colors, shadows, and the day-to-day atmospheric effects. An architecture buff would examine them in vain for visual information about medieval statues. Indeed, someone studying Monet's canvases of the cathedral might well be surprised to learn that the façade is actually adorned with dozens of stone figures, from the Virgin Mary surrounded by angels to Salome dancing before Herod and then presenting the severed head of John the Baptist to her mother. For an English critic, he turned this masterpiece of Gothic architecture into "melting ice-creams."[10]

HOWEVER IMPROBABLE IT may have seemed, Monet remained enthusiastic about the Reims commission. Nonetheless, the evacuated populace and daily artillery barrages in the summer of 1917 hardly boded well for his plein air sketching. When he painted in peaceful Rouen more than two decades earlier, he had actually set up his easel not in the open air in front of the cathedral but, rather, inside a lingerie shop. War-ravaged Reims offered no shelters in which he could install himself so safely or commodiously. Louis Vauxcelles soon began to have second thoughts about Monet crowning his career with these paintings. "Perhaps Claude Monet will not create a masterpiece at Reims," he ruminated. "When he and Pissarro did their paintings of the cathedral at Rouen, they took their time, living for a long time in front of their stone model, in communion with it."[11] There would be precious little time for such leisurely communion in Reims.

Given the bombardment of Reims through the spring and summer, Clémentel may have been surprised to receive a letter from Monet at the end of July with some astonishing news. "Dear Minister and friend," Monet's letter began, before going on to express his fears about the cathedral commission, which was not yet official. Clémentel had failed to answer several previous letters, leaving Monet anxious that he was making a nuisance of himself, and indeed that the project had been scuppered—thereby bringing to an end not only the prestige of a state-sponsored commission but also his special supply of petrol and other concessions. "I feared you found me very annoying because I wrote of my troubles getting petrol, coal and so forth," he confessed. In one of his previous letters he had frankly asked if the commission was still standing, and Clémentel, much to his relief, finally affirmed that it was. Monet then dropped his surprise: "You may know that I went to see it."[12]

Did Monet truly go to Reims in the summer of 1917? On the day he wrote his letter to Clémentel, July 23, an official communiqué reported that 850 more shells had just fallen on the city.[13] It would have been either brave or foolhardy to undertake a painting expedition at such a time, and Monet, the septuagenarian homebody, was neither. No paintings or sketches of the cathedral record this casual claim of a visit. One could speculate that, fearful of losing the project, with all of its prestige and the happy privileges accruing to it, Monet was hoping to convince Clémentel of his enthusiasm and initiative with the help of some overstatement and even deceit.

Nonetheless, in the middle of September a journal carried a report on Monet's plans to paint the cathedral. The writer, Vauxcelles, added as an aside: "Thanks to his old friend Clemenceau…Monet got to go to Reims."[14] Vauxcelles was always well informed about Monet's plans and actions. It is therefore possible that Monet went to the western front in the company of Clemenceau, who made almost biweekly excursions to visit the men in the trenches. If so, it would have been a hair-raising adventure. Winston Churchill left behind an account of his visit to the front with Clemenceau, a white-knuckle ride across muddy roads, through desolate countryside scarred by trenches and cratered by shells. "The projectiles whined to and fro overhead…Rifle fire was now audible in the woods, and shells began to burst in front of us on the road and in the sopping meadows on either side." After twelve hours of "touring along the roads at frantic speed," the forty-three-year-old Churchill was exhausted, but "the iron frame of the Tiger appeared immune from fatigue of any kind or in any form." When Churchill protested that he must not expose himself to enemy fire, Clemenceau replied: *"C'est mon grand plaisir."*[15]

This kind of frantic, dangerous expedition was hardly the sort favored by Monet. But thanks to Vauxcelles's testimony, we can perhaps visualize the scenario—however unlikely and improbable—of Monet and Clemenceau setting off early one summer morning, their staff car barreling in a convoy over the rutted roads, passing snarls of barbed wire and the inevitable poppies that may have reminded Monet of the beautiful poppy fields outside Giverny that he had painted in the summer of 1890—a lifetime ago, before these flowers came to symbolize blood and death.

Whatever the case, Clémentel did little to put Monet's mind at ease about the commission. Two months later the official commission seemed no nearer, and so once again the unresponsive Minister received an anxious letter from Giverny. "Here I am, pretty worried about your silence," Monet wrote to him. "I know you must be overworked, but I wonder if you received my last letter. A word of response would make me happy, and I would like to reiterate that I would be delighted if you could take advantage of my modest invitation when you have a little leisure." The modest invitation was, of course, to enjoy lunch in Giverny. The letter ended on a pleading note: "At least send a little note to tell me if you received my letter."[16]

By the end of September, the bombardment subsided enough for the king of Italy, accompanied by Raymond Poincaré, to pay a visit to Reims on a special train, and some inhabitants began moving back to the city "despite the danger that threatens them every day."[17] But by October regular reports headlined REIMS BOMBARDED reappeared in the newspapers. Monet's plangent letter to Clémentel made no further mentions of visits to the martyred city.

ALTHOUGH THE REIMS commission may have looked in jeopardy, it appears to have kick-started Monet's interest in painting. By the summer of 1917 he had at last resumed work on the Grande Décoration following the long hiatus of uncertainty and despondency. Once again, work on the project began to consume him. At the end of May he had brushed aside the offer of theater tickets from Sacha Guitry, whose new play was opening at the Théâtre des Bouffes-Parisiens. "Bear in mind," he sternly informed Guitry, "that I must now work more than ever because each day I get closer to the end."[18] In a letter to Geffroy that summer he signed himself: "Your old, very old Claude Monet."[19]

Monet was bedeviled, as usual, by the uncooperative weather—what he called *temps de chien* (weather for dogs).[20] In August he reported that he was "working with more passion than ever, though I am furious at the changes in the weather"—which by this point included, besides constant heavy rains, damagingly ferocious winds that, in Paris, caused chimneys and cornices to topple and shatter in the street.

That same month, Monet's older brother Léon died at his home near Rouen. Léon, who had run a chemical factory, had been friendly with Camille Pissarro, whose paintings he sometimes bought, and for a time he had employed Monet's eldest son, Jean, who had trained as a chemist in England. But the two brothers had been estranged for many years, and Monet did not attend the funeral. However, the following month he did attend another funeral, that of Edgar Degas.

Monet and Degas had likewise been estranged for many years, although alienation from the obnoxious, obstreperous Degas was nothing unusual. "What a brute he was, that Degas!" Renoir once remarked. "What a sharp tongue and what *esprit*. All his friends felt obliged to desert him in the end: I was one of the last to stand by him, but I couldn't hold out."[21] Monet had fallen out with the anti-Semitic Degas during the

Dreyfus Affair, though they had a reconciliation of sorts a decade later when Monet's water lily paintings went on display in 1909. "For such an occasion," Degas told a mutual friend, "I'm reconciled."[22] Two years later he came to Giverny for the funeral of Alice, where he appeared as a poignant figure from another age, "groping around, almost blind."[23] Now, animosity evidently forgotten, Monet wrote a letter of condolence to Degas's brother René, reminiscing about their "youthful friendship and common battles" and expressing "the great admiration I have for the talent of your brother."[24]

A week after the funeral, Monet wrote to Geffroy to express his disappointment at having missed him in Paris. He also informed him of a rare event: he was going on vacation. "I have worked so hard," he told Geffroy, "that I'm exhausted and realize that a few weeks rest is called for, so I'm off to contemplate the sea."[25] Specifically, he was going with Blanche to his beloved Normandy coast. To the Bernheim-Jeunes he explained: "We plan to leave today via Honfleur–Le Havre and along the coast to Dieppe, an absence of 10 to 15 days. I shall be happy to see the sea again, since it's been a long time. I need the rest because I'm tired."[26]

MONET ADORED THE sea. He once told Geffroy: "I want always to be before the sea or on it, and when I die I want to be buried in a buoy." Geffroy added: "This idea seemed to please him, he laughed under his breath at the thought of being locked forever in this kind of invulnerable cork dancing among the waves, braving storms, resting gently in the harmonious movements of calm weather, in the light of the sun."[27] It is difficult to imagine Monet, with his furious rants about the *temps de chien*, bobbing calmly and passively on a tempest-tossed sea. Yet there is no doubting his attraction to the seaside, especially the Normandy coast. It had been the scene of numerous painting expeditions and family holidays, including his honeymoon at Trouville with Camille in the summer of 1870.

The Normandy coast had also been the scene of Monet's childhood and youth. "I remained faithful to this sea before which I grew up," he once told an interviewer.[28] The family home in the rue d'Eprémesnil in

Monet on holiday
in Honfleur,
October 1917

Le Havre had been only a few hundred yards from the pebbled beach where holidaymakers scrambled from beach huts to the tide line, and from where schooners and clipper ships put into port, their masts swaying and sails billowing. Monet painted some of them in 1872, when he produced *Impression, Sunrise*. Even more momentous, a short distance away, leading along the coast and toward the cliffs, was the road that, as an adolescent, he took one day with a local painter, Eugène Boudin. After Boudin had assembled his easel on a plateau overlooking the sea, Monet watched, transfixed, as he began painting the cliffs and sky. "As of that minute," wrote Geffroy, "he became a painter…To him the easel, colour box, paintbrushes and canvas; to him the immensity of the sea and sky!"[29]

On his vacation Monet stayed in both Le Havre and Honfleur. Then, blissfully unimpeded by the restrictions on petrol, he journeyed up the coast by automobile to Étretat, Fécamp, and Dieppe, places where, decades earlier, he had carried his canvases and easel along the paths both above and below the cliffs. He called it a "happy little trip," telling Joseph Durand-Ruel that he "relived so many memories and so much work."[30] Indeed, he could scarcely turn a corner in this part of the Normandy coast without encountering a view—a cluster of fisher-men's cottages, a contorted rock, waves breaking over strands of shin-gle—that he had painted at some point in the previous fifty years. But the war intruded even here along his beloved coast, with a field hospital in Étretat and, at Le Havre, a huge training camp that was preparing to receive thousands of American soldiers.

In Le Havre, Monet stayed not at the Hôtel de l'Amirauté—from one of whose windows he had painted *Impression, Sunrise* forty-five years earlier—but at another seafront hotel, the Continental. His friend Camille Pissarro had stayed at the Hôtel Continental a few months before his death in 1903, painting multiple views of the trawlers and sail-boats and visiting the origins and sources of Impressionism. Monet was now making a similar journey back into the realms of his artistic youth, an expedition possibly brought about by the death of his brother Léon as well as by the fact that, like Pissarro, who did indeed die within months of his visit, he believed his days were numbered. As he had written to Sacha Guitry a few months earlier: "Each day I get closer to the end."

But Monet was not yet ready to bob on the ocean's eternal swell. He told Joseph Durand-Ruel that he would return to Giverny "to work with more passion still."[31] The memories and familiar scenes, as well as the bracing sea air, clearly revived him. He was spotted beside the water by the painter Jacques-Émile Blanche, who found him "aged but handsome, stepping from a powerful motor-car and wrapped in a sump-tuous fur coat…He sat on the embankment in a bitter west wind that dishevelled his long white beard."[32] What was Monet thinking as he sat staring out to sea? "I saw once again," he told Georges Bernheim-Jeune, "beautiful things that stirred so many memories."[33]

MONET MAY HAVE been revivified by something more than the bracing sea air. By the time he reached the Normandy coast he had finally heard some reassuring words from Étienne Clémentel. One of his earlier letters to Clémentel had gone astray, or so Clémentel claimed—an ironic twist, given that he was minister of posts and telegraphs in addition to his other duties. And no sooner did Monet return to Giverny at the end of October than he officially received the Reims commission courtesy of the Beaux-Arts administration. "I want to tell you," he wrote to Albert Dalimier, "how flattered and honoured I am by this command."[34] He was to be paid 10,000 francs for the commission.[35] This was under the going rate for a Monet. He claimed a few weeks later that his "usual price" for a canvas was 15,000 francs,[36] and the paintings auctioned earlier that year from James Sutton's collection were hammered down for a price, on average, of more than 33,000 francs each. However, he was not undertaking the work for money, which he hardly needed: a few days later he received a check from Durand-Ruel for 51,780 francs, payment owing for sales of his works. But he knew that the commission would bring him certain things that money could not buy, such as coal, gasoline, and prestige.

Having received the commission at last, Monet's mood brightened such that he submitted to a longstanding request from the Bernheim-Jeunes. The brothers had commissioned a biography of Monet from the critic Félix Fénéon, and they were hoping to dispatch him to Giverny for an interview. Monet finally agreed, although he asked for a couple of weeks to set his studio in order and to "rework some things that I now see with a fresh eye." He was, however, uneasy with the idea of a biography. "For my part," he told Georges Bernheim-Jeune, "I think it would be enough simply to deliver my paintings to the public."[37] Monet's reluctance shows his sincere modesty, since a biography written by Fénéon—a highly regarded art critic, gallerist, friend of Matisse, promoter of Seurat, and editor of Rimbaud—would have been a great honor.

Monet also granted another appeal. The Durand-Ruels were still hoping to photograph some of Monet's new paintings in order to tantalize their clients. Back in the winter, Monet had declined their request in no uncertain terms. But he was now more amenable, and so a photographer arrived in the middle of November 1917, taking a series of photographs featuring not only the massive paintings but also the grand new studio. They offered privileged glimpses of Monet's commodious new working space. A large trestle table sat in the middle of the spartan room, the tools of the trade spread artfully across it: several jars holding dozens of brushes, a couple of palettes (one of them new), several dozen neatly stacked wooden paintboxes, and a corked bottle of wine. An old two-seater sofa faced one wall, flanked by a small end table and a wooden chair.

The real attraction of the photographs was, however, the paintings themselves, which lined the walls of the studio, riding for ease of movement on easels fitted with casters. The photographer took pictures of eight or nine canvases, ones standing more than six and a half feet high by almost fourteen feet wide. These colossal tableaux must have stunned Clémentel, Matisse, Marquet, and other visitors into an awed silence at the scale of the old man's vast ambitions and the scope of his abilities. Two of them showed weeping willows beside the pond, their thick trunks flanked by cascading curtains of branches; others showed the blurry, reflective surface of the water lily pond. All of them attested to his vigorous efforts and immense vision—and to the truth of his claims about having used up great quantities of pigment.

The photographs also hinted at the grounds of some of his anxieties about his work. Several of them show how he placed the canvases together at angles of perhaps 160 degrees. Two of the photographs reveal four of the fourteen-foot-wide canvases positioned end to end to create an immense, curving tableau, almost fifty-six feet in length, that would take its place, if all went well, in a large, circular room.

Monet had never before attempted anything either on this scale or presenting such complexity. He needed to concern himself not merely

Monet, with his ubiquitous cigarette, hard at work in his new studio. His large canvases rest on easels fitted with casters for ease of movement.

with the internal qualities of large-scale individual compositions themselves, but also with how they might work together as an ensemble to
form a continuous loop. Ensuring that the perspectives in all of them
remained consistent and convincing, and that the color and lighting in
one fourteen-foot-wide painting harmonized with the color and lighting
in the adjacent ones—portions of which were separated by more than
fifty feet and painted, presumably, many months apart—were unique and
troublesome challenges. Monet's obsession with capturing subtle, tran-
sitory effects had been (as his many rages confirmed) difficult enough
to achieve in paintings that were only three feet wide and that took,
perhaps, a few days to paint. Yet for the past three years he had been
attempting similar feats across compositions almost sixty feet wide and
on works that took, not days, but months or even years to complete.

MONET WAS NOT the only one showing energy and determination
that autumn. Several weeks after the photographer visited his studio
in November, Monet wrote to Joseph Durand-Ruel: "And now my old
Clemenceau comes to power. What a burden for him. Can he succeed
despite all the pitfalls that will be laid for him? What great energy all
the same!"[38]

Momentous events had unfolded in Paris. French politics was
becoming increasingly fractious and disordered, with opposing forces on
the left and right making it virtually impossible for the prime minister
and his cabinet to govern. After a duration of less than six months, the
government of Alexandre Ribot collapsed in September, to be replaced
by one headed by Paul Painlevé, which in turn lasted only two months.
Two days after Painlevé was forced from office on November 13, the
president of the republic, Raymond Poincaré, summoned Georges
Clemenceau to the Élysée Palace. The fifty-seven-year-old Poincaré was
famously cold and calculating. "He has a stone for a heart," remarked
another politician.[39] Poincaré's heart was, in fact, reserved for animals,
an endless succession of beloved Siamese cats, collies, and sheepdogs on
whom he lavished tender affections, claiming these "mysterious creatures" were in no way inferior to humans.[40] His faith in dumb creatures

Raymond Poincaré

had not even been punctured by a bizarre recent event in which his wife, Henriette, while relaxing in the gardens of the Élysée Palace, was attacked and dragged into a lime tree by an escaped chimpanzee. The episode seemed to characterize the president's tragicomic ineptitude.[41]

As president of the republic, Poincaré was far from the most powerful or important man in French politics. He was elected by the Chamber of Deputies, who usually chose politicians posing little threat to their various agendas. "I am criticized for doing nothing," Félix Faure had declared during his term as president, "but what do you expect? I am the equivalent of the Queen of England."[42] It was not a bad analogy, since the president enjoyed many of the powers and restrictions of a constitutional monarch. Clemenceau used a different comparison: "In the end," he quipped, "there are only two useless organs: the prostate and the Presidency of the Republic."[43]

The president did have one important duty, which was to appoint the prime minister, the man who put together a cabinet and formed the government. But prime ministers were likewise not always the most impressive political specimens. Just as the deputies elected a weak politician who posed little challenge to them, the president for the same reason was prone to selecting a mediocre politician as prime minister. But the collapse of three successive governments in 1917 — not to mention the failure of the French military offensives, mutinies in the army, and shortages of food and coal — convinced Poincaré that a firm hand was needed at the tiller. He was therefore prepared to think the unthinkable.

The decision was not an easy one for Poincaré. He and Clemenceau cordially loathed one another. "Madman," Poincaré fumed about Clemenceau in his diary. "Old, moronic, vain man." Clemenceau, meanwhile, skewered Poincaré with one of his famous insults, once again making an unflattering reference to a redundant organ: "There are only two perfectly useless things in the world. One is an appendix and the other is Poincaré." He also called him "a somewhat unpleasant animal… of which, luckily, only one specimen is known."[44]

On this occasion, relations between the two men proved surprisingly affable. "The Tiger arrives," Poincaré wrote in his diary. "He is fatter, and his deafness has increased. His intelligence is intact. But what about his health, and his will-power? I fear that one or the other may have changed for the worse."[45] Poincaré knew nothing of Clemenceau's diabetes, but he was aware that only a few weeks earlier the Tiger had celebrated his seventy-sixth birthday. He debated with himself, and then with fellow politicians, about whether to risk calling on this *diable d'homme*, as he called him, to lead the government. "I see the terrible defects of Clemenceau," he wrote in his diary. "His immense pride, his instability, his frivolity. But have I the right to rule him out when I can find no one else who meets the requirements of the situation?"[46] Moreover, Poincaré knew that failing to allow Clemenceau to form a government would undoubtedly mean that this *tombeur de ministères* would claim the scalp of yet another prime minister.

On the day following the meeting the headline of *L'Homme Libre* therefore declared: CLEMENCEAU AGREES TO FORM A CABINET. There would be many pitfalls laid for Clemenceau, as Monet noted, but for the moment even some of his most hateful critics were prepared to accept his appointment. As an editorial in *La Croix* declared, making reference to Clemenceau's medical training: "The situation is critical, and we require an energetic doctor. To do the necessary work, he will need to perform surgery."[47] Another newspaper noted that this new government at least had one thing going for it: Clemenceau would not be campaigning against it.[48]

Any doubts that Clemenceau would take a firm hand in conducting the faltering war effort were dispelled when he took for himself the

post of minister of war and, on November 19, in a speech before the
Chamber of Deputies, stated his policy in three words: *"Faire la guerre"*
("Make war"). A day later he vowed "to make war, nothing but war…
One day, from Paris to the most humble village, bursts of great cheers
shall greet our victorious standards, twisted and bloodied, covered in
tears, torn by shells—the magnificent apparition of our great dead. It
is within our power to bring about this day, the most beautiful of our
people."[49]

An English politician present in the Chamber that day, Winston
Churchill, then Great Britain's minister of munitions, was highly
impressed by the sight of Clemenceau in action: "He looked like a wild
animal pacing to and fro behind bars, growling and glaring…France had
resolved to unbar the cage and let her tiger loose upon all foes…With
snarls and growls, the ferocious, aged, dauntless beast of prey went into
action."[50]

MONET MAY HAVE been concerned for the political battles soon to
be faced by "my old Clemenceau," but he could hardly have failed to
recognize how the appointment of his friend boded well for the Grande
Décoration. After all, Clemenceau during his previous stint as prime
minister had arranged, in the autumn of 1907, for the purchase by the
government of one of Monet's paintings of Rouen cathedral; the work
was promptly placed on display in the Musée du Luxembourg. Also,
he would have been relieved to see that, although Albert Dalimier was
removed as undersecretary of state for the fine arts, Étienne Clémentel
remained safely in the cabinet as minister of commerce and industry.

If Clemenceau was pledging *"la guerre, rien que la guerre"* (war,
nothing but war), for Monet the slogan was *"La peinture, rien que la peinture."* The photographs taken in November showed a massive amount
of work—a body of painting that, once placed together, would cover
well over one hundred feet of wall space. That vast expanse did not
even include his numerous studies, including the six-foot-wide *grandes
études*. But still Monet continued to paint. In January 1918 he wrote to
Madame Barillon, asking for her to send a dozen high-quality large, flat

paintbrushes "as quickly as possible," along with the dimensions of further canvases she was also shipping.[51]

The scale of Monet's ambitions were divulged to an art critic, François Thiébault-Sisson, who came to Giverny on a springlike day early in 1918 and wrote up an account of his visit some years later.[52] Monet began by describing his project as a "series of overall impressions" of his water lily pond that he hoped—as he humbly told Thiébault-Sisson—"would not be devoid of interest." These modest intentions were at odds, as the critic soon learned, with the scale of the work. Monet's plan, he revealed, was to paint a total of twelve large canvases, of which eight had already been completed, while the other four were "under way." That is, he claimed to have completed eight canvases six feet seven inches by fourteen feet in size, a statement certainly borne out by the photographs taken in November 1917. Meanwhile four other paintings of similar size were in various stages of progress. The finished ensemble would therefore stretch for 168 feet, or 56 yards, around the perimeter of the desired room, which would need to be at least 60 yards in circumference and almost 20 yards across. With these dimensions, Monet's canvases were capable of extending halfway around a room as vast as the Chamber of Deputies, which sat six hundred people. Monet was not envisaging this particular site for his work, but these dimensions prove how anything other than a room of state or a dedicated museum would have been inadequate. The "very rich Jew" imagined by Clemenceau a few years earlier was no longer a viable option. Only a large public space would suffice.

Thiébault-Sisson found Monet lively and robust, with "a smile on his lips, a cheerful light in his eye, and a most honest and cordial handshake. His seventy eight years weighed lightly upon him… The only sign of his age was his beard, totally white." He struck the critic as optimistic about his task, believing the end of his gargantuan labors was in sight. "In a year," he told the critic, "I shall have completed the work to my satisfaction, unless my eyes play new tricks on me."

Rather than his eyes, Monet found himself grappling with other irritating difficulties in the early months of 1918—ones caused by the war. Labor shortages meant he had problems finding a carpenter to

build large stretchers for his canvases. Once he finally got the stretchers built, he had trouble getting them shipped to Giverny because coal
shortages and lack of rolling stock meant that fewer and fewer trains
were running. And because of restrictions imposed on civilians, the
rare trains that did come steaming down the track refused to carry his
large stretchers either as luggage or mail. To top it off, his color merchant soon had trouble meeting his demand for oil paint.[53]

The shortage of paint may well have been due to the efforts of
Guirand de Scévola's camouflage unit. Along fifteen miles of front, from
Rouvroy to Bois des Loges, the *camoufleurs* had recently installed 2.7 million square feet of raphia (a straw-like material) and 1.4 million square
feet of canvas, all painted and used to disguise roads, canals, airfields, and
trenches, and otherwise to deceive the Germans. In June 1917 a studio
of *camoufleurs* had painted a huge trompe-l'oeil of an attacking army that
was raised dramatically above the trenches at Messines, intended to sim-
ulate a wave of three hundred soldiers "going over the top." Meanwhile,
a "fake Paris" was being created along the Seine near Maisons-Laffitte,
fifteen miles downstream from the real thing, complete with sham factories and railways, and even a dummy Champs-Élysées—all done to
draw the German bombers away from Paris.[54] A report prepared by none
other than Clémentel himself stated that for camouflage the French
military required ten thousand tons of jute each month.[55]

Paint, canvas, transport vehicles—all were desperately needed for
the war effort. But of course Monet, too, was doing war work. In January
he had received a letter from Clémentel, who claimed to be looking forward to "the consecration to the entire world of your splendid war work.
I hope that this spring you will continue raising a corner of the veil,
exposing the wonders that to this day only friends have been allowed
to admire."[56] The "war work" (*oeuvre de guerre*) to which the minister
referred was evidently not the recent Reims commission but instead the
Grande Décoration.

So began the transfer from Reims to the Grande Décoration. These
great canvases of water lilies and weeping willows were "war work" insofar as they had been painted during the war, but they were not done as

part of the war effort, and indeed they had been begun before the first guns were fired. By the beginning of 1918, however, Clémentel appears to have been entertaining the possibility that the Grande Décoration, like the ill-fated Reims commission, might serve as a powerful propaganda tool, announcing the glory of French culture. Not unreasonably, having seen the yards of painted canvas, he believed Monet's work was nearing completion and might be ready for a more public unveiling by the spring of 1918. Clémentel may have had in mind something similar to the official visits paid by visiting dignitaries to the work in progress that was the *Panthéon de la Guerre*. Viewings of the giant panorama in the rue de l'Université had become almost mandatory stops for delegations visiting Paris. Tours were likewise conducted for interested private citizens, such that the panorama was rarely out of the news, with distinguished visitors gushing to the newspapers about the "noble and patriotic inspiration" of the Carrier-Belleuse and his team of painters.[57]

Monet did nothing to disabuse Clémentel of the notions of an imminent unveiling while making no further mention of expeditions to Reims. He did, however, continue using the commission to gain certain privileges. By the beginning of 1918, coal was extremely expensive and strictly rationed. Gendarmes were obliged to guard the Bois de Boulogne to stop freezing Parisians from chopping down its trees to use as firewood.[58] Even Clemenceau's ex-wife, Mary, living in Sèvres, was forced to send her maid into the street to forage for wood chips and rubbish to burn as fuel.[59] Monet had no such difficulties. "I finally received the coal," he wrote to Clémentel in January, "which I greatly appreciate."[60]

As one resident wrote of the first months of 1918: "All over Paris, it was *faire la queue* for everything, even for tobacco and matches."[61] Many queued in the bitter cold in vain. A report prepared by Clémentel stated that in early 1918 the troops in the trenches could be provided with two thousand tons of tobacco per month, "but on the condition that supplies for the civilian population are almost completely removed."[62] A tobacco-starved journalist for *Le Gaulois* humorously described his frantic attempts to buy a pack of cigarettes in Paris following "a sleepless night, crossed by the wildest hallucinations, where I saw a packet of tobacco again and again escape my greedy clutches and vanish into thin air." In every shop he tried—including a tobacconist in the boulevard Poissonnière outside of which a hopeful and desperate crowd had gathered—he was given the same reply: "None left."[63]

Yet one civilian was not forced to *faire la queue* for cigarettes or rebuffed with the dreaded phrase *Il n'y a plus*. Inside his well-heated studio, Monet was able to smoke to his heart's content. He sent a letter of thanks to Clémentel for taking "so much trouble" in getting him a supply of cigarettes. "You know very well," he told the minister, "how much I love to smoke."[64]

CHAPTER ELEVEN

THE WEEPING WILLOW

———

THE GERMAN PILOTS, in the end, had not been deceived by the acres of canvas and paint with which the *camoufleurs* were creating their fake Paris. As midnight approached on January 30, four squadrons of Gotha bombers zeroed in on the real thing. For the next two hours sirens wailed, antiaircraft guns barked, and French warplanes buzzed through the skies. Many Parisians gathered outside in the crisp night air to watch a spectacle that Marcel Proust, observing from a balcony in the Ritz, called the "admirable Apocalypse."[1] By morning, 36 people were dead and 190 wounded, while the wreckage of a French airplane occupied the place de la Concorde. As in the terrible days at the end of August in 1914, the train stations were suddenly besieged with would-be evacuees.

In December 1917, Georges Clemenceau had warned the Army Committee: "I believe the Germans will make their greatest effort since the beginning of the war, greater than at Verdun. There is no doubt of it."[2] This alarming claim may have come as a surprise to those who heard it. Following more than three years of gory stalemate, the idea that the war might actually end was almost unfathomable. One British officer even calculated that, based on the average gains at the Somme, Vimy Ridge, and Messines, the Allies could not expect to reach the banks of the Rhine for another 180 years.[3] Moreover, by 1918 the Germans, having made a separate peace with Russia, were free to concentrate their efforts on the western front, attempting to crush the Allies with a rapid offensive.

The attacks on Paris increased with the coming of spring. At seven o'clock in the morning of March 21, a massive artillery shell exploded in Paris. It was followed by twenty-one more over the course of the day, all of them fired from a wooded hillside seventy-five miles away. This was

The ruins of a Paris shoe store destroyed by Le Supercanon

the work of a fearsome new weapon, the Paris-Geschütz, or the Paris Gun, a 138-ton cannon with a barrel almost 40 yards long. The biggest piece of artillery used in the entire war, the huge cannon (soon named Le Supercanon and La Grosse Bertha by the Parisians) was capable of propelling a 234-pound shell into the stratosphere, 25 miles above the ground. For days on end its shells pounded Paris, killing scores of people and causing more panicked evacuations. In the deadliest incident, at four twenty in the afternoon of March 29, a shell struck the church of Saint-Gervais, causing the roof to collapse on the congregation attending a Good Friday service. "The miserable wretches," cried the archbishop of Paris. "They chose the date and time of Christ's death to commit their crime!"[4] A total of eighty-eight people were killed and sixty-eight wounded.

Clemenceau remained optimistic and defiant. "I am delighted," a newspaper quoted him as saying. "Things are going well."[5] To David Lloyd George, his opposite number in London, he sent a telegram: "We are calm, strong and confident about tomorrow."[6] He made weekly trips to the front and toured Paris to witness the ravages of the Paris Gun. Seeing the Tiger covered in mud following a visit to the front line or standing amid the bombed-out buildings inspired those who remained

in the city. Soon he began reminding them of one of the greatest figures in French history: "We believed in Clemenceau rather in the way
that our ancestors believed in Joan of Arc," claimed Maurice Barrès,
the novelist and right-wing deputy. Another writer, the Goncourtiste
Léon Daudet, claimed that one constantly heard the same thing in the
Métro and on the omnibuses: "The old man's there. We'll beat them!"[7]
Winston Churchill, who toured the front with Clemenceau at the end of
March, was awestruck by Clemenceau's energy, courage, and unflappa-
ble determination. "He is an extraordinary character," he wrote home to
his wife. "Every word he says—particularly general observations on life
& morals—is worth listening to. His spirit & energy are indomitable. 15
hours yesterday over rough roads at high speed in motor cars. I was tired
out—& he is 76!"[8]

The German onslaught continued. At the end of May, following the
most intense artillery bombardment of the entire war—when two million shells were fired by the Germans in the span of four hours on the
morning of the twenty-seventh—the Allied line finally broke. The western front suddenly bulged inward along almost one hundred miles of
trenches, from Quéant to Reims, as the Germans swept across the Aisne
and reached the Marne at Château-Thierry, less than forty miles from
Paris. Once more the city was threatened with invasion. Churchill later
admiringly recorded the combative words Clemenceau spoke before
the Chamber of Deputies in those terrible days: "I will fight in front of
Paris. I will fight in Paris. I will fight behind Paris."[9]

MONET ANXIOUSLY FOLLOWED events from Giverny. He briefly
considered the possibility that he might be forced to flee, leaving house,
garden, and paintings behind. "I sometimes ask myself," he wrote to
Georges Durand-Ruel, one of Paul's four sons, "what I would do if the
enemy launched another attack. I suppose then, like so many others, I
would have to abandon everything." He admitted that "it would be hard
to surrender everything to the dirty Krauts."[10]

The bombardment and the threat of invasion made Monet nervous
about the fate of his paintings in Paris as well as those in Giverny. In

the middle of March a German airplane bombed the rue Laffitte, across the street from Durand-Ruel's premises, which held as many as a hundred of his canvases. A month later a strike by Le Supercanon destroyed several banks in the street.[11] Joseph Durand-Ruel began evacuating his firm's store of paintings, while Gaston Bernheim-Jeune offered to collect Monet's canvases from Giverny and take them for safekeeping to the museum in Rouen, used to shelter many of Paris's treasures. But Monet declined the offer, striking a defiant pose. Both he and his paintings would stay to face down the invaders. "I don't believe I shall ever leave Giverny," he told Gaston. "As I've said, I would still prefer to perish here in the midst of all I have done."[12]

Monet continued to endure the inconveniences of wartime. Having evidently depleted his supply of tobacco from Clémentel, he began trying to cadge cigarettes from his friends. "Now, if you can get any Bastos cigarettes," he wrote to the Bernheim-Jeunes in March, "think of me." Sacha Guitry's chauffeur did manage to furnish him with cigarettes, but Monet wrote back requesting not the cheap and nasty ones that came in blue packets but rather a "much better" variety, Scaferlati, which he called "elegant cigarettes of superior tobacco."[13] It is unclear if the chauffeur managed to lay hold of any of these elegant cigarettes. In January a magazine claimed Scaferlati tobacco was so expensive that the poor were forced to go without its "pungent sweetness," and so rare that to flourish a packet in a café was "testimony of ingenuity without equal."[14]

If Monet was not in the least uneasy about making these demands, he felt somewhat sheepish about continuing to paint. "I confess to feeling a little embarrassed about working," he told Joseph Durand-Ruel in the middle of June.[15] As always, however, he worked best in a crisis, throwing himself into his work to escape the calamities that were virtually within earshot of his garden. He was therefore extremely busy with his paints and canvases throughout the frantic and perilous spring of 1918. In April he placed an order for twenty canvases and two new palettes, which he asked to be wrapped well and delivered "as soon as possible" to the train station in Limetz.[16]

Monet kept busy in his garden throughout the spring and into the summer, raging against old age and the bad weather. "I haven't long to live," he told Gaston Bernheim-Jeune, "and must dedicate all my time to painting, with the hope of finally achieving something good—something that, if possible, might satisfy me."[17] What he achieved during those months was a number of remarkable canvases that reveal a combination of artistic experimentation, mental disturbance, and defiant resolution in the face of age and death. Most striking were a series of paintings of his Japanese bridge, virtually all of them painted on canvases only three feet high—much smaller, that is, than either the *grandes études* or the panels making up the Grande Décoration. All of them were painted only at certain times of the day. In February he had explained to Thiébault-Sisson that in order to preserve his eyesight he painted outdoors only in the early morning and late afternoon. Most of these paintings are therefore depictions of dawn and dusk, of gauzily lit mornings and fierce, sulfurous sunsets. Many he would later rework, but all were painted with wildly undulating forms added in flickering tongues of tropical color. In some, the Japanese bridge is outlined with bloodred accents; other times it dissolves into a sea-green reverie with calm sapphire highlights; while in other canvases (probably retouched later) the bridge is a multicolored arch twisting across a lake of fire and blood, with a conflagration raging in the background—an apocalypse devouring a fairyland. Monet might not have made it to Reims to paint its ruined cathedral by the harsh light of artillery barrages, but in his garden he had imaginatively reconstructed a scene of devastation.

Monet once speculated that his paintings might calm strained nerves and offer "an asylum of peaceful meditation." The vertiginous paintings of the Japanese bridge could hardly serve that pacifying function. Nor could another series of works begun that summer, some ten paintings of the weeping willows beside his pond. The motif was an interesting one to choose after almost four years of war and more than a million French dead. The weeping willow had been a symbol of death and mourning ever since its introduction to Europe early in the eighteenth century. It was often either personified as a woman or used to

symbolize female mourning in particular. A prose poem in the illustrator J. J. Grandville's *Les Fleurs animées* (*Flowers Personified*), published in
1847, was typical: "Come into my shade, all you who suffer, for I am the
Weeping Willow. I conceal in my foliage a woman with a gentle face. Her
blond hair hangs over her brow and veils her tearful eye. She is the muse
of all those who have loved...She comforts those touched by death."[18]
More to the point for Monet, in 1877 his friend Maurice Rollinat wrote
a poem describing weeping willows "that look like mourning women /
Bowing painfully into the wind."[19]

Such associations meant that weeping willows were a common
sight in French cemeteries. The image of a willow shading a grave,
famously made by Desdemona in Gioachino Rossini's 1816 opera *Otello*
("Willow...prepare a merciful shade for my woeful tomb"), was picked
up by the poet Alfred de Musset in his 1835 poem "Lucie":

> *My dear friends, when I die,*
> *Plant a willow in the cemetery.*
> *I love its weeping foliage;*
> *Its pallor is so dear to me,*
> *And its shadow will be gentle*
> *Upon the ground where I shall sleep.*[20]

A weeping willow was duly planted beside Musset's grave in the
cemetery of Père-Lachaise following his death in 1857, although a
nineteenth-century guidebook reported that this "famous willow" (once
upon a time arguably the most celebrated tree in France) was often
stripped of leaves and branches by souvenir hunters.[21]

Monet's paintings of his weeping willows have something of these
traditional elegaic qualities, alluding to sorrow and loss. But he added
a new twist—literally—to the motif. In his weeping willows we find no
merciful shadows, gentle female faces, and pallid, outstretched limbs.
Rather, the weeping willows of Giverny, with their contorted branches
and Monet's darker palette, suggest torture and suffering. The images
are fraught and disturbing, echoing lines from one of his letters in June:

"What anguished lives we lead."²² Monet may have been painting in order to distract himself from the Grande Guerre, but the war infuses every inch of these canvases. They are a firm riposte to anyone who regards Monet simply as the "great anti-depressant."

Grandville and many others personified the weeping willow as female, but it is possible to see a different kind of figure in Monet's anthropomorphized trees: the vivid image, as Paul Hayes Tucker intriguingly suggests, of "a weathered landscape painter." The willow is, he proposes, the "ideal metaphor" for Monet himself, a kind of emblem of the artist heroically struggling during the war years.²³ In one of the weeping willow paintings the canvas is divided between a shower of mustard-colored light and an inky darkness. The willow stands in between, its gnarled branches stretching toward the iridescent glow. A similar canvas depicts the same tree at closer range, its slender trunk ablaze and its limbs forcefully aloft, clutching at the lurid phosphorescence of its sunlit canopy—an image recalling Rollinat's description in his poem of the "fantastic" branches of the willow looking like rays thrown by a sorcerer.

Monet had earlier turned an old oak in the Creuse valley, which he called "my tree" and painted more than a dozen times in 1889, into what Tucker has called "a kind of personal symbol" of his rages and suffering.²⁴ It is not difficult to read, with Tucker, an autobiographical element into Monet's renderings of these trees beside his pond—these bent willows that are partially engulfed in darkness but defiantly thrusting their crooked boughs outward as if raging against the dying of the light.

MONET WAS VISITED in August by an art dealer, René Gimpel, who faithfully recorded his impressions in his diary. Gimpel and another dealer, Georges Bernheim—no relation to Josse and Gaston Bernheim-Jeune—took their bicycles on the train to Vernon and then cycled the three miles from the station to Monet's house.

The thirty-six-year-old Gimpel was one of Paris's up-and-coming art dealers, a junior partner in Gimpel & Wildenstein, a firm cofounded by his father, Ernest. René was enviably well connected, since his family tree included not only Louis Vuitton (his great-uncle) but also the art dealers Nathan Wildenstein (his grandmother's cousin and his father's business partner) and Joseph Duveen (his brother-in-law). With premises in the rue La Boétie in Paris and on Fifth Avenue in New York, Gimpel & Wildenstein primarily specialized in Old Masters and eighteenth-century painters such as Jean-Honoré Fragonard—what an American publication, describing their wares, called "high class old paintings."[25] However, since his father's premature death from diphtheria in 1907, René had begun expanding the collection to cover what might have been called "high class new paintings," in particular the Impressionists. Earlier in 1918 he paid court in the South of France to both Renoir and Mary Cassatt. Now he had his eye on another, even bigger prize.

The visit marked Gimpel's first meeting with Monet, whose appearance and manner left a vivid impression on him.[26] He appeared before his guests wearing a "big pointed straw peasant's hat" and then, without further ado, launched into a long monologue that—if Gimpel recorded it faithfully—amounted to an artistic manifesto tinctured with personal eccentricities. "Ah, gentlemen," he greeted them, "I don't receive when I'm working, no, I don't receive. When I'm working, if I'm interrupted, it just finishes me, I'm lost. You'll understand, I'm sure, that I'm chasing the merest sliver of color. It's my own fault, I want to grasp the intangible. It's terrible how the light runs out, taking color with it. Color, any color, lasts a second, sometimes three or four minutes at most. What to do, what to paint in three or four minutes? They're gone, you have to stop. Ah, how I suffer, how painting makes me suffer! It tortures me. The pain it causes me!"

Despite these dramatic protestations, Monet invited to the two men to join him for lunch. For Gimpel, the painter's supposed distress about his impossible task was offset by his jaunty vigor. "I've never seen a man of that age look so young," he confessed. "He can't be taller than about five foot five, but he is absolutely erect." Gimpel was also favorably impressed by Monet's garden, but even more—once he and Bernheim were finally conducted into the sanctum sanctorum of the large studio—by his paintings. Monet staged a special exhibition for the two men, arranging series of a dozen canvases in a unique way. He placed them not upright on their easels but rather in a circle on the floor. He therefore created a simulacrum of the lily pond in his studio, or what Gimpel called "a panorama of water and water lilies, of light and sky." He found the effect almost overwhelming. "In its infinity, the water and the sky had neither beginning nor end," he wrote. "It was as though we were present at one of the first hours of the birth of the world. It was mysterious, poetic, deliciously unreal."

Gimpel estimated the size of these canvases at "about six feet wide by four feet high." These dimensions indicate that Monet showed his two guests not the Grande Décoration—whose individual canvases, at six feet six and a half inches by fourteen feet, were much larger—but, rather, works painted in the spring and summer of 1918, many of them on a smaller set of canvases ordered at the end of April. Though only a dozen of these smaller canvases were put on display, Gimpel guessed that Monet had completed as many as thirty of them. If Gimpel's estimates can be accepted, Monet had produced 180 feet of canvas in addition to the approximately 112 feet photographed nine months earlier and then seen by Thiébault-Sisson in February.

Gimpel was puzzled by what would become of all of this paint and canvas. He believed that even the smaller canvases, each some six feet wide, were still too large for one of Monet's most reliable markets: the homes of affluent Americans. Most of the Monets decorating American homes were roughly half that size, although it would surely not have been difficult to imagine his six-foot-wide canvases gracing the salons of Manhattan town houses or Newport mansions. However, Gimpel had another use for them: he believed they would make great decorations for swimming pools.

ON AUGUST 3 a newspaper headline triumphantly declared: COM-PLETE SUCCESS ON THE AISNE AT REIMS.[27] At four A.M. on August 8, a combined force of British, Canadian, and Australian troops launched a massive attack on the German Second Army near Amiens, striking with such speed and intensity that Canadian troops, bursting out of the morning mists, captured virtually the entire 117th Division. It was the greatest defeat yet sustained by the Germans—"the black day of the German Army," as General Ludendorff famously wrote in his diary. Kaiser Wilhelm, despairingly appraising the situation, declared to his generals three days later: "We have nearly reached the limit of our powers of resistance. The war must be ended."[28]

Clemenceau continued making his trips to the front to confer with the generals and inspire the troops. On September 1, a photographer captured him having lunch among the ruins at Roye, southeast of Amiens, complete with a table draped in white linen. He was also photographed on the shattered ruins of a battlefield, sitting on a stack of two-by-fours and eating lunch from a wicker picnic basket with his son, Michel. On one such visit to the front his motorcar came under heavy artillery fire. When officers tut-tutted his imprudence in putting himself at risk, he retorted: "These damned generals are always scared about something."[29]

On another of these visits, Clemenceau was presented with a garland of flowers plucked from the roadside by a young soldier, "frail, dried-up stalks" that he promised the young soldier he would take to his grave.[30] By this time the soldiers began calling him by the name that would soon spread quickly from the trenches to the towns and villages all over France: Père-la-Victoire (Father Victory). The name was an allusion to a military song, "Le Père la Victoire," popular in the cafés concerts of the 1880s and 1890s. The lyrics tell the story of a one-hundred-year-old veteran of the Napoleonic Wars who urges France's youth to follow his valorous example. After running through highlights of the old man's career—in which a fondness for wine, women, and song feature along with battlefield heroics—the song ends with a passionate exhortation: "*Marchez à la gloire, mes chers enfants / Revenez triomphants*" ("March to glory, my dear children / Return triumphant"). The song was revived in 1917 for a two-minute-fifty-four-second film by Paul Franck called *Le Père la Victoire*, which included two of the original six verses—and which no doubt inspired the soldiers who watched it in the cinemas to think of Clemenceau, their own feisty old warrior.

George Clemenceau with French officers on one
of his many expeditions to the front

Yet even Clemenceau, whom Ludendorff ruefully called "the most energetic man in France," was beginning to show the strain.[31] In September the British ambassador to France, the Earl of Derby, wrote: "I had a talk with Clemenceau this morning and for the first time in my life thought him tired, but it is hardly to be wondered at when I tell you that yesterday he was 14 hours in his motor and that at the age of 77!"[32] Clemenceau was, of course, suffering from diabetes. "No one knows," he later said, "that I made war with forty grammes of sugar in my urine."[33] He was also suffering from eczema, which had worsened to the point that he wore gray gloves to conceal and protect the painful rash. He enthusiastically self-medicated, and one friend was amazed that he did not accidentally poison himself: "He has remedies in his drawer and helps himself by the handful." He once downed an entire bottle of a sleep aid when the prescribed dose was a single spoonful.[34]

During these months, Clemenceau led a hectic but solitary life. He rose at five or six A.M., performed calisthenics, fenced with an instructor, and then had a massage. He rushed back and forth between the Ministry of War—where, in contrast to his predecessors, he occupied one of the smallest offices—and the Palais-Bourbon. He almost never accepted invitations, and his social life was reduced to occasional visits from his brother Albert, his sister Sophie, and his grandchildren. There were numerous trips to the front—sometimes as many as two or three a week—but no time for relaxing lunches in Giverny.

As when he served as prime minister between 1906 and 1909, Clemenceau chose not to occupy an official residence but instead stayed in the apartment in the rue Franklin into which he moved more than twenty years earlier. The rue Franklin was in Passy, an upscale district across the Seine from the Eiffel Tower, but Clemenceau's lodgings were extremely modest: a three-room apartment featuring dirty woodwork, a threadbare carpet, and "almost lodging-house furniture."[35] However, the small apartment was adorned with his library of five thousand books and, equally dear to him, his various Japanese artifacts. These treasures included vases, tea bowls, prints by Utamaro, incense burners, an ivory-inlaid scabbard, and "a Japanese mask of terrifying and wonderful expression."[36] He also had a number of *kogo*, or incense boxes, that he liked to handle while reading or talking with someone. These precious artifacts were the remnants of a much larger collection of *japonerie* that financial problems had forced him to sell with much regret in 1894. The sale catalogue listed 356 illustrated books, 528 drawings and fans, and an incredible 1,869 Japanese prints. His admiration for the Japanese was such that in the first days of the war he wrote (in block letters) to an English friend: "IF ONLY THE JAPANESE WOULD COME."[37]

Now, four years after those terrible first days of invasion, the end was almost in sight. On September 5, shortly after one of his visits to the front, Clemenceau rose to the podium to address the Chamber of Deputies. The magnificent chamber must have made a sobering sight as he gazed at the men fanned out before him. More than a dozen deputies had been killed on the western front, and their red-velvet seats remained shrouded in black crêpe and adorned with a tricolor scarf. One of them still serving, thirty-six-year-old Gaston Dumesnil, a veteran of Verdun and a holder of both the Croix de Guerre and the Légion d'Honneur, would be killed by a shell three days later.

Clemenceau's theme, as he spoke, had not changed in four years. "Our soldiers, our great soldiers," he declared, "the soldiers of civilization, to give them their true name, are victoriously beating down the hordes of barbarism. This work will continue until it reaches the full completion that we owe to the great cause for which the best French blood has been so magnificently shed. Our soldiers shall give us this great day—the triumphant day of release—which is so long overdue."[38]

CHAPTER TWELVE

THIS TERRIBLE, GRAND, AND BEAUTIFUL HOUR

NOVEMBER 11 DAWNED foggy in Paris. It was, as the brutal daily tally in *Le Figaro* reminded its readers, the 1,561st day of the war. By nine o'clock people feverishly awaiting news filtered into the streets. One day before, the radio station at the top of the Eiffel Tower had received a message that the German command had agreed to the conditions of an imposed armistice. The morning newspapers in the kiosks were optimistic, announcing the imminent signing of the ceasefire and the abdication of the Kaiser. "The war is won," proclaimed *Le Matin*. "Glory to the soldiers!" declared *L'Homme Libre*. "*Vive la France!*"

Even so, people were cautious of celebration. Four days earlier, false news of an armistice had turned the boulevards prematurely jubilant. Moreover, the newspapers and public health officials had been warning against "the agglomeration of crowds."[1] During the previous month, thousands of Parisians had died from influenza, including, two days earlier, Guillaume Apollinaire. Early on the morning of the eleventh a series of dilapidated hearses, requisitioned to carry the bodies of the victims of the Spanish flu, had made their somber procession along the Champs-Élysées.[2] Rumors and alarms were spreading as rapidly as the disease. Was the epidemic the result of a summer heat wave that left germs lingering in the stagnant air? Or was it the work of German bacteriologists infecting French food with deadly bacilli? Whatever the cause, the deaths steadily mounted. A Parisian housewife lamented: "This scourge is more terrible than the war or the Berthas and Gothas"—and it was, to be sure, quickly claiming more lives in Paris than the German bombs.[3] There were calls for Paris's theaters and concert halls to be closed to prevent the contagion from spreading. Schools were frantically aired and disinfected, assemblies and awards ceremonies banned, religious celebrations curtailed. The only crowds in the anxious first week of November had been the ones in front of pharmacies, where Parisians, some wearing antiseptic-soaked protective face masks, fought each other for dwindling supplies of quinine, castor oil, aspirin, and rum—none of which did any good.

There was yet another reason why people were chary of celebration: not everyone wanted the war to end. Many people were skeptical of German requests for a cease-fire, believing that no peace should be signed until the enemy had been driven back across the Rhine and comprehensively defeated—a goal that, after four years, was suddenly within reach. A report prepared for the police, who took soundings outside a butcher's shop, concluded that the great majority of people favored continuing the war.[4]

Their opinion was shared by, among others, Raymond Poincaré. But Ferdinand Foch, commander in chief of the Allied armies, believed the Allied goals had been met. "Enough blood has flowed," he protested.[5] Indeed, French deaths were approaching 1.4 million; almost 4 million more had been wounded. A quarter of all French men born in the 1890s—the children of the belle époque—had been wiped out. Although his policy had been to *faire la guerre*, Clemenceau agreed with Marshal Foch, instructing him to draw up the technical military and territorial conditions on which an armistice should be based. Thus, at ten forty-five A.M. on the eleventh, Foch arrived back from the forest of Compiègne by train bearing the document that had been signed in his railway carriage at five eighteen that morning. He made his way to the Ministry of War in the boulevard Saint-Germain. Handing the signed armistice to Clemenceau, he told him: "My work is finished. Your work begins."[6]

At eleven o'clock precisely—the moment when the armistice was to take effect—cannons were fired in the Champ de Mars and by the submarine *Montgolfier*, moored in the Seine by the Pont de la Concorde. "Bombs," speculated the pupils in one Latin Quarter school.[7] Then the bells of Notre-Dame began to ring. Suddenly there could be no doubt—and suddenly no one was worried about the agglomeration of crowds. People poured into the place de la Concorde, the Tuileries, the

Armistice celebrated in the place de l'Opéra, November 11, 1918

Champs-Elysées. Jubilant Parisians clambered over captured German tanks and airplanes, laid flowers on the statue of Strasbourg in the place de la Concorde, and stripped away the sandbags and scaffolding protecting the statues on the Arc de Triomphe. Flags appeared in windows, bunting on buildings. Airplanes swooped overhead, dropping not bombs but paper cutouts—"butterflies of joy"—that fluttered into the streets. Students in the Latin Quarter poured out of their schools, forming an immense human serpent that writhed along the boulevard Saint-Michel. Singing the "Marseillaise" and led by beribboned soldiers, another serpent wound its way toward the Ministry of War, with everyone shouting "*Vive la France!*" and "*Vive Clemenceau!*"[8]

The Ministry of War had been bombed in March; its façade was still pockmarked, its courtyard strewn with rubble. Clemenceau briefly appeared in a window. "He was frenetically cheered," reported *Le Petit Parisien*. Visibly moved, he gestured for silence, then shouted: "*Vive la France! Say it with me: Vive la France!*" The crowd obediently roared back. Later he was taken by motorcar the five hundred yards to the Palais-Bourbon, which had been invaded by a huge multitude hoping to pay tribute to him. "Who of those present," asked a reporter in *Le Figaro*, "can ever forget the arrival of Clemenceau in the Chamber of

Deputies?" At four P.M. he rose to the podium and, after reading aloud the terms of the armistice, announced that "it seems that at this hour, at this terrible, grand and beautiful hour, my duty is done."⁹ The reporter for *Le Figaro* saw tears fall from his eyes. The session ended with all of the Deputies singing the "Marseillaise."

That night, more wild celebrations, more stirring renditions of the "Marseillaise," more drinking of champagne in cafés that the prefect of police allowed to keep their doors open to accommodate the thousands of revelers arriving in Paris from the suburbs and countryside, "many of them already drunk," as a journalist churlishly observed. The Eiffel Tower was lit for the first time in more than four years. Red, white, and blue searchlights beamed across the sky. It was left for a writer on Clemenceau's newspaper to see in this heedless revelry the beatific auguries of a better future. "It was a breath of universal delirium," wrote Jacques Barty in *L'Homme Libre*, "that portended the birth of a new world, the sublime resurrection of all the great heroes who died for their country, for civilization." These dead heroes were, he wrote, like "the marvellous and beneficent divinity of a liberated humanity, united for greater destinies."

Clemenceau strolled the exuberant boulevards arm in arm with his sister Sophie. "I've been kissed by more than five hundred girls since this morning," he later boasted to Poincaré. A bitter Poincaré angrily confided to his diary: "To everyone he is the liberator of the occupied territory, the organizer of victory. He alone personifies France...And for myself, naturally I don't exist."¹⁰ But the cool, aloof Poincaré could not possibly compete with the articulate, avuncular, and absolutely ferocious Père-la-Victoire. Winston Churchill, who heard Big Ben toll the peace that morning in London, later wrote: "Clemenceau embodied and expressed France. As much as any single human being, miraculously magnified, can ever be a nation, he was France."¹¹

Clemenceau may have claimed that afternoon, as he stood before the cheering deputies, that his duty was done, but the feeling was only temporary. Back in the terrible days of June he had announced to the Chamber of Deputies: "It remains for the living to complete the magnificent work of the dead."[12] He would stay in office to complete his task. On the evening of November 11, as he returned to the rue Franklin, he was under no illusions about the almost insuperable difficulties. He suddenly appeared withdrawn and even depressed. Contrary to what he had said in the chamber, his duties, he knew, were far from finished. The words of Marshal Foch no doubt rang in his ears. "We have won the war," he told one of his generals. "Now we have to win the peace, and it may be more difficult."[13]

"**THE GREAT CLEMENCEAU** came to have lunch with me," Monet wrote to the Bernheim-Jeunes on November 24. "It was his first day off and I'm the one he came to visit, which makes me very proud."[14]

Clemenceau went to Giverny on November 18, exactly a week after the armistice was signed. Monet had written to him on November 12, a day when newspapers such as *Le Petit Parisien* were hailing Clemenceau as the "liberator" of France. "Great and dear friend," Monet wrote, "I am on the verge of finishing two decorative paintings that I want to sign on the day of Victory and have you offer to the State on my behalf. It's not much, but it's the only way I can take part in the Victory. I want the two panels placed in the Musée des Arts Décoratifs and would be happy if you chose them. I admire you and embrace you with all my heart."[15]

Clemenceau was eager to see the works, but even more eager to visit Monet, of whom he had seen little if anything during the previous year. What's more, the "great Clemenceau" needed some respite from all of the acclaim and applause. A few days earlier he had tried to travel incognito through the crowds to take part in the victory celebrations by listening to the soprano Marthe Chenal, wearing a black Alsatian cap, sing in the place de l'Opéra. "But Monsieur Clemenceau cannot remain incognito for long," reported a newspaper. The crowd, soon spotting him, tried to carry him in triumph through the streets, forcing him to take cover in a nearby house from whose window overlooking the place de l'Opéra he watched the performance. The day before traveling to Giverny he appeared with Poincaré and other dignitaries before the statues of Strasbourg and Lille in the place de la Concorde—only

to have the crowd repeatedly chant *"Vive Clemenceau! Vive Clemenceau!"*
It must have been disconcerting for a man who thrived on controversy
and invective, and who believed that life was a battle, suddenly to find
himself almost universally adulated.[16]

So, on Monday the eighteenth, relieved of official obligations for
the day, Clemenceau telephoned Gustave Geffroy at his home in the
grounds of the Gobelins: "I shall pick you up," he announced.[17] A short
time later he and Geffroy were speeding west, traveling with two cars
and four chauffeurs, the extra vehicle and spare drivers accompanying
them in case of a mechanical breakdown.[18] No mishap was going to prevent Clemenceau from keeping his appointment with Monet.

Monet had been expecting to find his old friend aged, "but I think
I can say," he told René Gimpel a few days later, "that he has taken off
ten years." After an embrace, Monet told Clemenceau that he had saved
France, but Clemenceau, ever the champion of the humble French soldier, replied: "No, it was the infantry."[19] Clemenceau then paid Monet
a compliment of his own, telling him he was proud that Monet was a
Frenchman.[20] Monet's paintings had long been for Clemenceau among
the highest expressions of French art and civilization, feats of supreme
beauty that were evidence of French cultural and moral superiority—
the kinds of values that for the past four years had been defended by the
heroic *poilus* against the terrible threat of German "barbarism."

The visit must have followed the familiar routine of what another
visitor called Monet's "fraternal hospitalities,"[21] starting with a long
lunch on white porcelain in the yellow dining room, perhaps a belated
celebration of Monet's seventy-eighth birthday, which fell four days earlier. Then a tour of the gardens and a visit to the large studio. "War talk
was taboo," Clemenceau later told Sacha Guitry regarding this visit. "I
went there to rest."[22] A journal would report on the encounter in its gossip column, relishing the image of the fearsome Clemenceau among the
profuse greenery of Monet's garden: "On that day, the Tiger inhabited
the jungle, and he was perfectly happy."[23]

However, there was business to discuss—in particular, the donation of the two paintings. Geffroy was, as usual, poetic in his account,

describing how Monet with this donation offered to France "a bouquet of flowers in tribute to the victorious war and triumphant peace."[24] Yet how this process of donation might have worked is unclear. Monet's letter of November 12, with its invitation to Clemenceau, was slightly puzzling. The letter claimed that Monet had almost finished two canvases that he would sign and donate, via Clemenceau, to the state. This seemed to indicate that Monet had two specific paintings in mind, that the choice was fait accompli, and that they would be placed in the Musée des Arts Décoratifs. Yet the letter then went on to say that Monet wanted Clemenceau to select the two paintings. Which two paintings Monet originally envisaged is unknown. Clemenceau duly chose two paintings on November 18, although these were quite possibly not the ones Monet had considered: he selected a water lily painting and a weeping willow.

Exactly which canvases Clemenceau selected is not known, either. However, the latter subject, with its connotations of grief, suffering, and defiance, was certainly appropriate for a work signed on the day of the armistice and donated to the nation. With the Grande Guerre finally over, the commemoration of the legions of French dead was a cultural priority—along with somehow making sense of the grotesque and almost inconceivable magnitude of these losses. Already debates were being held and plans mooted about how best to honor the dead. One project already floated in November was to place at the summit of Mont-Valérien, west of Paris, a gigantic monument with the words *À nos Morts* (To our Dead). The names of Paris's dead soldiers would be inscribed on the marble, with their remains interred beneath. The exercise, it was hoped, would be duplicated in cities all over France.[25] Monet's two canvases, placed in the Musée des Arts Décoratifs, were intended to make their own commemoration of France's sacrifice and loss as well as of the Victory—with both of them selected by Father Victory himself.

THE MUSÉE DES ARTS DÉCORATIFS, housed in the Louvre and overseen by Monet's friend Raymond Koechlin, might once have seemed a logical choice to install some of the new paintings. Monet had courted Koechlin during the war years, inviting him to Giverny and giving him

lunches and private viewings of the Grande Décoration. Yet on that
November afternoon Clemenceau must have realized, after seeing so
many yards of painted canvas adorning Monet's large studio, that there
was scope for a larger donation than merely two paintings—and also,
perhaps, the chance for a more conspicuous location than the Musée
des Arts Décoratifs. Monet surely explained to his two friends what
he had told Thiébault-Sisson a few months earlier: that he planned an
ensemble of twelve canvases, each fourteen feet wide, of which at least
eight were completed. To donate two canvases in honor of the French
victory seemed a modest benefaction when these artistic riches would
soon become available.

More grandiose plans were quickly proposed. The witness to the
proceedings that afternoon, Geffroy, later wrote that Clemenceau came
to Giverny "to choose some canvases from the new series of water lilies." His use of the indefinite pronoun *quelques-uns* (some, a few) leaves
open the possibility that either Monet or Clemenceau already had plans
of expanding the donation beyond two canvases.[26] Another of Geffroy's
accounts, published in 1920, was even more explicit about the expanding donation. "On that day," he wrote of the November visit, "the gift
to the State of a series of water lily paintings was decided, with the
paintings to be selected by Clemenceau and accepted as a tribute to
victorious France." The donation, therefore, was no longer to consist
of two paintings but rather an entire series. Geffroy went on to claim
that these "immense decorations" produced by Monet during the war
years were to be "kept together in this way, on the walls of quiet rooms
where visitors could come to seek distraction from the social world, to
ease their fatigues, to indulge their love of eternal nature. That is the
vow," he claimed, "that Monet formulated during the visit in November
1918, when I accompanied Clemenceau."[27] Geffroy therefore attributed
the concept of an expanded donation to Monet himself, and these
"immense decorations" were to be housed, he claimed, in several rooms.
However, in another article, also published a few years later, Monet
gave the credit for enlarging the donation to Clemenceau.[28] Naturally
Clemenceau would have had a great deal of sympathy for the plan, as his

decades-old dream of keeping together an ensemble of Monet's paintings as a national monument was revived.

These were retrospective constructions, to be sure, composed at a time when the donation had certainly assumed a greater magnitude. How much of this new plan was actually discussed on November 18 is debatable. However, since the late 1890s Monet had dreamed of installing a series of his works on permanent exhibition in, as he always stipulated, a circular room. The time must have seemed right in November 1918, with Monet having completed so much "war work" and with Clemenceau in a position of such power and influence.

THERE WERE CERTAINLY some recent precedents for such an ambitious plan. Monet and Clemenceau may have regarded with some envy the events unfolding in the rue de l'Université in Paris. Here the huge circular room had been inaugurated only a month earlier, on October 19, when the *Panthéon de la Guerre* was unveiled in its purpose-built panorama. The finished creation was 45 feet high, 128 feet across, and 402 feet in circumference. It incorporated five thousand full-length portraits of French and Allied leaders and soldiers, including the defiant-looking Clemenceau. The Tiger had not been present at the inauguration; Poincaré did the honors. Clemenceau seems not to have been a booster of Carrier-Belleuse's great enterprise, and his portrait was conspicuously absent from the preliminary studies exhibited alongside the panorama.[29]

Nonetheless, the *Panthéon de la Guerre* offered a model of how such an artistic enterprise, linked to the Grande Guerre and offering an "immersive" experience to the public, could become a popular success. Archbishops, generals, visiting monarchs, numerous dignitaries and out-of-towners, celebrities such as Sarah Bernhardt—all of them were making their way to the rue de l'Université. Here they scuttled through a narrow passageway before emerging on an elevated viewing platform from which they thrilled at the 360-degree view. There was even a guestbook to which they added their signatures "accompanied by the warmest praise."[30]

The other precedent, even more germane, was the new Rodin museum, the driving force behind which was, of course, Étienne

Clémentel. Rodin had died a year earlier, in November 1917, but prepa-
rations for the museum dedicated to his work in the Hôtel Biron were
steadily progressing. The statues and busts had been tastefully arranged
on pedestals in the capacious rooms, his casts placed in the chapel built
by nuns a century earlier. A curator at the Luxembourg Museum wrote
in eager anticipation of how pilgrims would "come from all intellectual
centres of the world to admire in these rooms the creative power of the
greatest poet of form in modern times."[31]

Monet had gone to Meudon for Rodin's funeral, which featured
Poincaré, most members of the government, an enormous crowd, and
an honor guard from a nearby garrison—pomp and circumstance surely
befitting the grandiose pretensions of the deceased, above whose tomb
loomed a cast of *The Thinker*. The funeral oration was delivered by the
sculptor Albert Bartholomé, who had linked Rodin to the young soldiers
dying in the field of battle. Just as these young men were making their
"sublime sacrifice," so, too, Bartholomé declared, "must go those magnificent elders who stood behind the flag of France."[32]

Monet was one of the few magnificent elders who remained. He
and Rodin had come a long way together. They were artistic twins—
"friends forever," as Rodin had declared.[33] Their fame and fortunes had
been forged in tandem. Rodin had gone before him, but the great sculptor now had his own museum, his shrine for pilgrims. It remained for
Monet to follow with his own hostage to posterity.

A FEW DAYS after Clemenceau and Geffroy departed, Monet keeled
over while at work in his studio: "Some sort of fainting fit," he later
explained, "no doubt brought on by the cold weather." His sudden collapse caused much alarm. He was forced to cancel a visit from René
Gimpel and Georges Bernheim, sending a telegram to Paris: "Am sick.
Don't come." But an apparent recovery meant a second telegram was
soon winging its way over the wires: "False alarm. Come."[34]

Even so, Monet was still unwell when the two picture dealers arrived
a week later. Gimpel, who had been so impressed by the painter's robust
appearance in August, was taken aback by his weakened state. He was

also alarmed by Monet's despondency. "I am unhappy," the painter told his guests, "very unhappy." Surprised, they asked him why, to which he replied with his customary lecture about the mental horrors of a man's reach exceeding his grasp—how painting made him suffer, how he was unsatisfied with all his previous works, how "each time I begin a canvas I hope to produce a masterpiece, I have every intention of it, and nothing comes out that way. Never to be satisfied—it's frightful. I suffer greatly." He told them that he was much happier in the days when he sold his canvases for only 300 francs: "How I miss those days."[35] This nostalgic recollection of his supposedly impecunious but happy youth conveniently overlooked his frequent episodes of anger and despair in those days.

Although Monet soon recovered from his fainting fit, in the middle of December he complained of "sharp rheumatic pains."[36] These health problems became the nominal source of yet another request to Étienne Clémentel. The minister had recently pulled strings in the case of Michel, who was not yet demobilized, and who had faced—until Clémentel's timely intervention—an unappealing change in duties. Now a ministerial decree taking effect at the beginning December made it necessary for anyone wishing to travel by road or rail to seek a safe-conduct pass from the civil authorities.[37] Such a restriction seriously cramped Monet's style. He disliked traveling to Paris or more distant environs but loved pootling along the lanes near Giverny with his chauffeur Sylvain at the wheel. "I have another service to ask of you," he therefore wrote to Clémentel. "It would be nice of you to recommend me to the Prefect of the Eure to see if he could give me a permit to travel, not throughout the country—I don't ask for such a favour at the moment—but only to Vernon and Bonnières, to see my doctor, and as far as Mantes, from where I can catch the train to Paris." Monet's letter also reminded the minister about a shipment of coal that was due to him: he had received "a portion, half of it, only the anthracite, but the coal for the house has not arrived." Perhaps Clémentel could have a word with Louis Loucheur, the new minister of Industrial Reconstruction?

Monet's other concern, as the year wound down, was money. He wrote to Georges Durand-Ruel on the day after Christmas, noting that

Georges had mentioned sending him "a little money." He therefore took him up on the offer, asking him "to send me a cheque, if you are able, for 30,000 francs."[38] He explained that he had some big bills to pay, which may well have been the case, though he could hardly have been strapped for cash. A check from the faithful Durand-Ruels was with him in less than forty-eight hours.

Monet duly penned a letter of thanks to which he appended yet another request. As if the other shortages of coal and tobacco were not bad enough, France now faced what a newspaper called a "crisis of wine."[39] Much of the supply had been requisitioned for the military (the 1917 mutinies had been suppressed, in part, by the troops receiving better and more generous rations of wine as well as tobacco), along with the *wagons-foudres*, the giant barrels in which wine was transported by rail throughout the country. The wine merchants were therefore able to command, as a newspaper deplored, "very high prices, the demand greatly exceeding the supply."[40] This shortage was drastic for Monet, a man who liked to start his day with a glass of white wine and to wash down his lunch with great swigs of a fine vintage. He therefore found himself wondering what treasures might be lurking in the Durand-Ruel cellars. Could they possibly part with some of their wine, letting him know the price and the quality? "The wine merchants rob us blind," he complained. If the Durand-Ruels could therefore send a shipment to the station at Vernonnet "*as soon as possible,*" he would be much obliged.[41]

AT THE END of the year, Monet entertained a most welcome visitor, a young man whom he proudly called his grandson. The twenty-five-year-old Jacques Jean Philip Butler, better known as James or Jimmy, had come to Giverny for Christmas, on leave from service in the United States Army.

Jimmy was the son of Theodore Earl Butler and Monet's stepdaughter Suzanne Hoschedé. After Suzanne died in 1899, Butler had married her older sister, Marthe, who helped him raise Jimmy and his other child, Lili. Over the years Theodore painted many landscapes in and around Giverny, frequently exhibiting in Paris, sometimes in the same salons as his sister-in-law, Blanche. Among the most talented of all the American Impressionists, he nonetheless suffered because of his perceived imitation of Monet. One critic claimed that Butler "clings to the example of Claude Monet like a remora, with a conviction and literal obedience that raises painful comparisons."[42] Everyone was a critic: when Butler and Marthe arrived in New York for a visit, bringing with them thirty of his paintings, the customs inspector carefully scrutinized these masterpieces of American Impressionism before asking: "Are these finished?"[43]

The Butler family had lived a stone's throw from Monet's house, down the street and around the corner, in the rue du Colombier. In 1914 they joined the American exodus, crossing the ocean and eventually taking up residence in Washington Square in New York. Butler eked out a living painting murals for public buildings, and once America entered the war he designed recruitment posters for the United States Signal Corps. Butler clearly brought his Impressionist lessons to bear on these posters, painting them, according to the *New York Sun*, "in vibratory tones of violet and purple, harmonizing with the olive drab of the uniforms and the yellow glow of the lamp."[44] By the spring of 1918, he was busy painting targets for the United States Army, creating landscapes and cityscapes for the recruits to practice firing at. Here, it seems, hard-won Impressionist techniques were frowned upon: "A house must be a house in this kind of art," sniffed an observing journalist, "and not look like a scrambled egg going up a stepladder, as it might if some disciple of the New Impressionism were thumbing the palette."[45]

Jimmy Butler, whose bath times had been immortalized by his father in dozens of canvases, continued the family tradition. He painted Giverny landscapes, exhibiting them as early as 1911 in the Salon d'Automne before crossing to New York with his father and stepmother. In 1917 he volunteered for the U.S. Army, and in September 1918 Monet proudly reported to Georges Durand-Ruel that "the young Butler" was back in France.[46] He became the fourth member of Monet's extended family—along with Michel, Jean-Pierre, and Albert Salerou—to serve on the western front. Miraculously, all of them survived, something for which Monet frequently expressed gratitude and relief. A commemorative plaque in the church down the street would later be inscribed with the names of the thirteen men from Giverny who died in the war—a wretched toll in a village of fewer than three hundred people.

Jimmy Butler spent the Christmas of 1918 with Monet and Blanche. Monet greatly enjoyed reacquainting himself with his grandson. "He's a nice boy and we have been very lucky to have him with us for a few days," he wrote to Georges Durand-Ruel. While in Giverny, Jimmy received orders to report back to his company within twenty-four hours and prepare for a return to the United States. As ever, Monet tried to pull some strings. "I immediately tried to see if he could be demobilized in France, as some of his comrades have been, but I don't know if it will succeed."[47] His pessimism was well warranted. The United States Army was one of the few places where the name Claude Monet did not carry much clout.

CHAPTER THIRTEEN

AN OLD MAN MAD ABOUT PAINTING

———————

HEAVY RAINS FELL throughout the Christmas period, causing the rivers to swell and the meadows to fill. In Paris, the Seine burst its banks, inundating the quays and preventing barges from unloading their precious cargoes of coal. Bread ran short as bakeries were engulfed by the floods. Beside the Pont National, a barge sank with a load of wine, which the resourceful and the desperate managed to salvage. Downstream in the suburbs, floodwaters flowed through the Pays des Impressionnistes, turning the streets into rivers, the squares into lakes. In Asnières, people boated through the streets; others were evacuated from their homes.[1]

Giverny was soon cut off from the outside world. "We are surrounded by water," Monet wrote on January 10.[2] Fortunately, the inundation was not as severe as the legendary flood of January 1910, when Monet's Japanese bridge was partly submerged and the floodwaters crept halfway up the garden toward his house before receding weeks later, leaving behind a stinking horticultural wreckage. On that occasion Monet had been predictably distraught; now, however, he was resigned to his losses. "My pond has become part of the Seine," he wrote to the Bernheim-Jeunes. "It is very beautiful, but very annoying and sad. We had no need of this."[3]

Monet may have been wistfully reconciled to his swamped garden because he was doing very little painting. He had neither the morale nor the physical health for much hard work. In January he confessed to Clémentel that he had been unwell for a while, by which he probably meant as far back as his collapse in November.[4] He may have been suffering from a milder bout of what he took to calling "this nasty flu."[5] The epidemic was still raging throughout France despite experimental new treatments such as injections of colloidal gold, silver, and rhodium.

It temporarily felled members of both the Durand-Ruel and Bernheim-Jeune households.

Monet's poor health led to a low morale, and soon he claimed to be suffering from "the most complete discouragement and disgust." As he explained to Josse Bernheim-Jeune: "I feel that everything is breaking down, my sight and all else, and that I'm no longer capable of doing anything worthwhile."[6] Bernheim-Jeune gently challenged this pessimism: "You are still in such good shape that many young people envy you your health, and yet you let yourself be invaded by dark thoughts!" His prescription for the painter was the same one that Mirbeau had given so many times in the past: "My dear Sir, I think you isolate yourself too much, and a stay of about a week in Paris, in the midst of friends who love you, would dispel your little troubles."[7]

Monet took courage, however, from news of Renoir, who was continuing to paint despite his infirmities. "How I pity him," he explained to Josse Bernheim-Jeune, "and yet how I admire him for being able to overcome his sufferings in order to paint."[8] He could also take courage from another example of fortitude in trying times: that of Clemenceau. The Tiger had survived not only the Spanish flu but also, in February, an assassination attempt.

IN EARLY DECEMBER, Clemenceau had gone to London to meet with Lloyd George. Received at Buckingham Palace, he enjoyed "an extraordinary demonstration of popular enthusiasm," not the least of which was, courtesy of the Royal Horticultural Society, a mauve and yellow orchid named in his honor. Reporters noticed that he was suffering from a slight indisposition that left him with a bad cough, but a new serenity had come over him. Asked by reporters what was left for him to do, he replied jovially: "Oh, the Tiger has now no teeth or claws. He has nothing but smiles left."[9]

Yet in the months ahead there would be plenty of need and opportunity for the Tiger to show his teeth and claws. The Earl of Derby wrote in his diary that Lloyd George "is very much anti-Clemenceau and it is not to be surprised at as both of them are men who like to be top dog."¹⁰ Meanwhile, Woodrow Wilson arrived in France for peace talks in the middle of December, to be greeted with a rapturous welcome by Parisians: cheering crowds, a horse-drawn procession along the Champs-Élysées, signs declaring *VIVE WILSON*. He was received with a dose of skepticism from Clemenceau, who believed the American president had little grasp of the scale of the destruction in France. According to the Earl of Derby, Clemenceau called him an idiot.¹¹ In the Chamber of Deputies he spoke of the *noble candeur* of Wilson's mind, which much of the French press—and, consequently, Wilson himself—took to mean that Clemenceau thought him naïve and ingenuous.¹² Wilson for his part had not wanted to come to Paris: he had favored holding the peace talks in Switzerland. Paris was, his advisors informed him, a "belligerent capital."¹³ Only fears of a Bolshevik-style revolution in Switzerland persuaded him to make his way to Paris, and when in Paris he declined the opportunity—pressed on him by Clemenceau and Poincaré—to visit the war-devastated French towns and cities. "I could not," he shrugged to an advisor, "despise the Germans more than I do already."¹⁴

Despite his bad cough, Clemenceau was working as hard as ever, attending celebrations in the December cold in Metz, Strasbourg, and Liège, and only taking a short break in the rainswept Vendée in early January. An English correspondent was astonished by his "marvellous vigour of mind and body," watching in awe as he remained at the Palais-Bourbon until one o'clock in the morning and then returned at eight thirty A.M. The Tiger's friends, noted the reporter, were anxious for him to economize his strength in view of the inevitable strain that awaited when the Peace Conference opened.¹⁵ An English newspaper dubbed him "The Grand Young Man of Europe."¹⁶

The peace talks had barely begun when, on the morning of February 19, Clemenceau left his apartment in the rue Franklin and climbed into a Rolls-Royce driven by his faithful chauffeur, Albert Brabant.¹⁷ The limousine headed south before turning left into the boulevard Delessert. Suddenly a young man, tall and blond, with long hair and baggy velvet trousers, rushed out from behind a public urinal and discharged seven shots, two while standing in the boulevard and five more as he ran after the fleeing vehicle. The Rolls-Royce accelerated away but then, as policemen seized the shooter, wheeled around and headed back to the rue Franklin. "Go easy," Clemenceau remarked as he was assisted from the automobile by Brabant. "I must have been hit in the shoulder." He then proceeded to walk at a steady pace into his apartment.

Over the next few hours a succession of physicians, surgeons, and military men, and even President Poincaré, rushed to his small apartment. They found Clemenceau sitting peaceably in an armchair, saying, "It's nothing, it's nothing," and protesting that he had urgent business to attend to. The first official bulletin was issued at eleven thirty A.M., as a huge crowd gathered outside in the rue Franklin: "Penetrating wound to the back of right shoulder blade without visceral injury. General and local condition perfect." By one o'clock he was eating soup, drinking mineral water, and smoking cigarettes. He told Marshal Foch when he came to visit: "I have dodged bigger ones than that at the front." In fact, he had been struck by three bullets. Two simply caused abrasions on his hand and arm, but a third, more serious, had struck his shoulder blade and lodged near his lung. Two more had passed through his clothing, while another two missed entirely. Clemenceau pretended to be disgusted at such poor marksmanship at point-blank range.

A nun, Sister Théoneste, was summoned from the *maison de santé* at the convent of Très-Saint-Sauveur in the rue Bizet, where Clemenceau had recuperated from his prostate operation in 1912. On that occasion his political enemies had taken much delight in learning how the recovery of this rabid anti-Catholic had been superintended by nuns. Clemenceau was typically unmoved by their criticism: "I don't care," he retorted. "I want to be well cared for."[18] He had a huge respect and affection for Sister Théoneste, an Alsatian whom he called "a brave soul and a gentle heart."[19] He had personally delivered a bouquet of flowers to her on the day following the armistice. "On the day when you reenter your country," he told her, "I want you to be on my arm."[20] She was perhaps the only person in France capable of handling such a stubborn patient.

Another person to whom Clemenceau turned was Monet, who received a telegram from officials at the Ministry of War: "The President sends you his affectionate greetings," it read. "The state of his health is satisfactory and all danger seems to have passed."[21] The bullet, however, was judged by doctors to be too close to his heart to permit removal: he would go through the rest of his life with a souvenir of the incident embedded in his chest.

The attempt had been what *L'Homme Libre* called "the isolated act of a madman." The gunman, a twenty-two-year-old anarchist named Émile Cottin, was protesting what he regarded as Clemenceau's suppression of anarchists, and in particular the violent strike-breaking at an aviation factory in May 1918. He would be condemned to death four weeks later. Clemenceau took a more charitable view. "I suggest he should be locked up for about eight years, with intensive training in a shooting gallery."[22] In fact, Cottin would be reprieved by Clemenceau and serve, in the end, only five years in prison.

DIPLOMATS AND DELEGATES arriving in Paris for the peace conference had been greeted by posters plastered on kiosks and buildings: *QUE L'ALLEMAGNE PAYE D'ABORD* (LET GERMANY PAY FIRST).[23] Among Clemenceau's greatest ambitions for the peace talks was for Germany to pay reparations to France for the four years of unprecedented destruction. "A most terrible account between peoples has been opened," he had told the Chamber of Deputies back in December. "It shall be settled."[24]

The Germans had occupied almost an eighth of France: some 25,000 square miles, equivalent to the areas of Connecticut and Massachusetts combined. Almost 300,000 French homes had been completely destroyed, another 435,000 badly damaged. More than 6,000 churches, town halls and schools were destroyed; 10,000 more were seriously damaged. Some 1,500 rail stations and railway bridges needed repairs, as did more than 3,000 miles of railway lines and 30,000 miles of roads.[25] Entire French villages had been wiped off the face of the earth; others, such as Douai, with their missing façades and still, deserted houses, had been turned into what the historian Gregor Dallas has poetically described as "little Vermeers of ruin."[26] The countryside was scarred by shells, poisoned by gas, and crossed by hundreds of miles of trenches and barbed wire. Meanwhile, Germany's factories, fields, railways, roads, and urban infrastructures remained intact and untouched. It was Clemenceau's fear that Germany would emerge from the peace talks economically and militarily stronger than France, ready to strike again. The economist John Maynard Keynes, in Paris with the British delegation, summed up his position (with which he strongly disagreed): "Clemenceau's aim was to weaken and destroy Germany in every possible way... He had no intention of leaving Germany in a position to practise a vast commercial activity."[27]

Clemenceau, back at work within weeks of the assassination attempt, faced a battle with France's own commercial activity. The wartime strikes in 1917 and 1918, which began with Paris seamstresses and workers at a Renault factory, led to a rebirth of industrial militancy. In 1919, two thousand separate strikes in France involved hundreds of thousands of people demanding higher wages as a response to inflation: steelworkers, coalworkers, construction workers, and mechanical engineers. On the Métro, workers blocked and sometimes set fire to trams. Even bank employees went on strike in Paris, congregating in their bowler hats and milling politely together in the street. When waiters walked off the job in Paris's cafés, they were attacked by enraged patrons.

Labor problems were not confined to Paris. In Giverny, Monet was experiencing difficulties of his own. "Seeking a very good cook between 30 and 40 years of age, for the country," read an advertisement in *Le Figaro* that spring. "Good wages. Good references required. Write to Claude Monet at Giverny, near Vernon."[28] But a good cook proved hard to find, since a few months later he wrote despairingly that he had "no cook, no housemaid, in fact, absolutely no staff whatsoever."[29] By the beginning of summer he had lost every one of his gardeners, including men who had served him for twenty years. His head gardener, Félix Breuil, went back whence he had come: to Rémalard, eighty miles southwest of Giverny, where he had once worked for Octave Mirbeau's father. "I'm in complete disarray," Monet wrote. "I thought for a moment I would have to abandon the garden and Giverny."[30] Help was at hand, however, and soon afterward he acquired the services of a gardener named Léon Lebret.

Meanwhile the wine he ordered from the Durand-Ruels finally arrived, several months after he ordered it. To his extreme disappointment the cask was "virtually empty": it contained only thirty liters of wine, forcing him to refuse the delivery and then spend time trying to get to the bottom of "this unfortunate affair." He suspected someone of having siphoned off the precious liquid, "an evil that comes about because of our great drought."[31]

IF MOST OF France seemed to be on strike by the summer of 1919, Monet at least was hard at work. As in 1917, several months of discouragement were followed by frantic and enthusiastic labors at the easel. At the end of August he reported that he was working "in a state of euphoria, favoured by the splendid weather."[32] In fact, the weather had been blisteringly hot for weeks on end, with France registering its highest temperatures in forty years. In the middle of the August, Paris reached 33 degrees Celsius (92 degrees Fahrenheit) in the shade. People took to sleeping in the open air, and Paris was so hot and empty of people that *Le Figaro* dubbed it "Paris-Sahara."[33]

Undaunted by the heat wave, Monet declined an invitation to enjoy cooling breezes at the Bernheim-Jeunes' seaside villa. He donned his hat, opened his parasol, and sat painting beside his pond for hours on end. "I've started a series of landscapes that I love and that I hope will interest you," he told the Bernheim-Jeunes, explaining that he had "postponed" further work on the Grande Décoration until winter.[34] These new paintings were done in a smaller format, most on canvases some three feet wide by six and a half feet high. Similar in theme to the Grande Décoration insofar as they showed the reflective surface of the pond dotted with water lilies, they were intended to be sold on the art market. Monet felt the need to raise money, no doubt because his donation to the state—especially if expanded to include a good part of the Grande Décoration—meant he would earn nothing from his time-consuming labors of the previous five years. He therefore sent four of these new paintings to the Galerie Bernheim-Jeune.

Ominously, none of the four works managed to find a buyer, an indication of how artistic tastes were changing in the aftermath of the war. The decade before the Grande Guerre had been the heroic age of modern art, with the scandalous successes of Fauvism, Cubism, Expressionism, Futurism, and Vorticism. But appetites, attitudes, and artistic practices had shifted dramatically by the time the war ended. More than 350 French artists had died in battle.[35] Among the dead on both sides had been many apostles of modern art: Umberto Boccioni, Henri Gaudier-Brzeska, August Macke, Franz Marc, Isaac Rosenberg, and Raymond Duchamp-Villon (brother of the more famous Marcel). Others, such as Gustav Klimt, Egon Schiele, and Guillaume Apollinaire, had perished from the Spanish flu.

"The war has not killed Cubism," a literary magazine declared in the summer of 1918.[36] But in fact the horrors of the Grande Guerre meant that, as the art historian Kenneth Silver has amply demonstrated, both the public and the painters themselves turned their backs on daring innovations in a process that Jean Cocteau, in a lecture at the Collège de France, would soon call *le rappel à l'ordre* (the call to order).[37] As the derogatory references to "Kubism" revealed, the wilder artistic experiments and adventures of the prewar years were seen by many in France as specifically German and, therefore, abhorrent. In 1919 a commission in Paris tasked with erecting triumphal arches and other "great monuments to the glorious dead" appealed to French artists for their help. But a particularly conservative and patriotic kind of art was preferred. As one city councillor thundered: "France must not produce or celebrate any art except French art."[38]

Monet's art was certainly French. Indeed, many of his landscapes had captured quintessentially French scenes. However, Impressionism was still a controversial movement in some quarters. At the height of the war in 1916, the art critic and ardent French nationalist Marius Vachon condemned what he saw as the widespread idea that Impressionism was France's "official art"—that it was patriotic and in some way symbolic of France as a whole. Vachon complained that Impressionism was, on the contrary, "essentially international," with adherents scattered all over the world. Worse still, it was a "combat organization" whose followers were "violent, aggressive, revolutionary, demagogic, and even anarchist," bent on "attacking and destroying all artistic traditions."[39] Vachon was an extreme case, but his virulent criticism revealed that opposition to Impressionism was still very much alive in the second decade of the twentieth century, its antipathy suddenly nourished by the xenophobic forces unshackled by the war.

It would have been difficult to construe the Claude Monet of 1919 — the well-fed and well-upholstered *bourgeois gentilhomme* presiding over his grand and beautiful domain — as a dangerous anarchist. However, his hazy visions were not the kind of art beloved of either artistic conservatives or a youthful avant-garde. What Louis Gillet called Monet's "upside-down paintings" offered few certainties in a confused and traumatized postwar world in search of steady assurances. His canvases of water lilies may not have been as outrageous or controversial as the Cubist or Futurist visions of the world, but they left the viewer uneasily adrift, with no clear footholds. As Gillet and Kandinsky recognized, Monet's works verged on a kind of abstraction in which the brushstrokes seemed to liberate themselves from the duty of representing a stable and recognizable natural world in any obviously realistic fashion.[40] Moreover, his views of his pond were not typically or even discernibly French, failing to evoke the soil and toil of the countryside in the way that his wheat stacks, poplars and views of the Seine unquestionably did.

If Monet was disappointed by his failure to find buyers, his new paintings left him with an even more disagreeable legacy. For the previous five years he suffered very few problems with his cataracts, partly because of the precautions he took: his hat, his parasol, his habit of working only early in the morning or later in the afternoon. Moreover, his enthusiasm for work left him determined to overcome or ignore any physical disabilities. However, the good weather in the summer of 1919 had coaxed him out of the shadows and into the bright light, and the many hours of staring at the sparkling surface of his pond exacerbated his eye condition. During a visit to Giverny in November, Clemenceau advised an operation, but Monet was wary of submitting himself so readily to the surgeon's knife. "I'm very worried that an operation might be fatal," he wrote to Clemenceau, "and that once the bad eye has been cured the other eye will follow. So I prefer to make the best of my bad sight, such as it is, and give up painting if necessary, but at least be able to see something of the things I love, the sky, water and trees, not to mention my nearest and dearest."[41]

The thought of a Monet who was blind and unable to paint must have horrified Clemenceau, who could well imagine the madness and mayhem such a state of affairs would unleash. But he could do little to convince his friend of the benefits of an operation. And so began what Clemenceau called the "unspeakable drama" of the cataracts.[42]

ONE REASON WHY Monet painted a new series of canvases in the summer of 1919 was that he had, for all intents and purposes, completed the Grande Décoration. Little remained to be done, beyond touch-ups and tinkerings, on these vast surfaces the obsessive covering of which had seen him through the terrible years of the war. Their completion, together with the loss of so many contemporaries and the steady approach of his eightieth birthday, enhanced his feeling that the shadows were lengthening. Two further events at the end of 1919 only served to amplify the impression.

First came the ghost of an old friend. In November, Gustave Geffroy sent him an edition of the poet Maurice Rollinat's final writings, entitled *Fin d'Oeuvre* (*Last Work*), for which Geffroy had composed the preface. For Monet, the volume made poignant reading. He had been good friends with Rollinat, whose letters he carefully preserved in a folder marked, in violet ink, "Lettres de Rollinat."[43] "While it brought me great pain," he wrote to Geffroy, "it has been a great pleasure to read your beautiful preface, and to relive the wonderful hours spent with such a lovely but unfortunate man. What a sad end!"[44]

Maurice Rollinat had been one of those figures whose doomed life of tormented brilliance stood out even in the absinthe-soaked, syphilis-infected world of nineteenth-century Paris. A disciple of Baudelaire and Edgar Allan Poe, he had entranced Oscar Wilde, who eagerly scribbled down his maxims and emulated his flamboyant coiffure. He was a star turn at Le Chat Noir, the celebrated cabaret in Montmartre where his songs about death, hallucination, and disease mesmerized audiences in performances that featured him crashing violently away on the piano and imitating the wild gesticulations of the inmates he had carefully studied in the local insane asylum. "Day and night, through all the earth," ran a typical poem,

He dragged his lonely heart
In fright and mystery
In anguish and remorse.
Long live death! Long live death![45]

One critic exulted that Rollinat exceeded Baudelaire "by the sincerity and depth of his diabolism," while another champion, Mirbeau, found in his poetry "an explosion of masturbatory joy."[46]

Perhaps surprisingly, Monet had enjoyed the company of this morbid, exotic creature. In 1889, when he painted his series of canvases of the Creuse valley, he spent much time at the remote cottage in Fresselines, two hundred miles south of Paris, to which Rollinat had repaired with his partner, an actress named Cécile Pouettre. Here the poet known for his macabre visions happily fished, walked in the hills, kept animals, sang in the local church, and clattered around in wooden shoes—all (except for the churchgoing) equally congenial pastimes for Monet, who was full of admiration for his host. "What a true artist," he wrote. "At times he is thoroughly discouraged, full of bitterness and sadness precisely because he is an artist and therefore never content and always unhappy."[47] As such Rollinat was, as the Monet scholar Steven Z. Levine has noted, "the perfect masochistic double of Monet's perpetually anxious artistic self."[48]

Rollinat's removal to Fresselines had been aimed at protecting his "ultra-sensitive temperament" from the anxieties, neuroses and overwork of Paris.[49] He could not escape the demons, however, and his life followed an all too predictable pattern as he became addicted to both

Maurice Rollinat: "What a sad end!"

absinthe and opium. However, the true cause of his downfall was the agonizing death from rabies of Cécile, who had become a nurse in Fresselines. The horrendous spectacle of her suffering unhinged Rollinat. After several suicide attempts, the grief-stricken poet died in a clinic at Ivry-sur-Seine in 1903 at the age of fifty-six.

Rollinat's death was not the only sad end that Monet forlornly contemplated as 1919 drew to a close. "As for me, my poor friend, I live in complete distress," he wrote to Geffroy in the same letter in which he acknowledged the receipt of *Fin d'Oeuvre*. "Once again my sight is altered and I shall have to give up painting, and leave half-finished the work I have begun. What a sad end for me."[50]

MONET WAS SOON confronted with a more immediate death: that of Pierre-Auguste Renoir. Having suffered respiratory problems ever since catching pneumonia while painting outdoors with Paul Cézanne in the winter of 1881–82, Renoir came down with pneumonia again in December 1919. On December 3, in bed at his home in Cagnes-sur-Mer, he called for a pencil so he could sketch some flowers at his bedside. Legend has him finishing the drawing (or sometimes a painting) and handing the pencil (or brush) back to his nurse while uttering his last words: "I think I am beginning to understand something about it."[51] He passed away soon afterward, at the age of seventy-eight.

The story is an appealing one that accords well with the image of the decrepit Renoir courageously continuing to paint despite his infirmities. It also appeals because of its implication that becoming a great artist takes time and patience—that it takes, indeed, an entire lifetime.

Still shot of Sacha Guitry and Pierre-Auguste Renoir from Guitry's film *Ceux de chez nous*

The anecdote probably derived from the story about the French painter J.-A.-D. Ingres, who, a few days before his death in 1867 at the age of eighty-seven, took up a pencil and began making a sketch of a Holbein portrait. Asked what he was doing, he replied: "I'm learning."[52] The story may also have drawn on comments by the Japanese artist Hokusai, who in old age (he lived to eighty-nine) signed his works "The Old Man Mad About Painting." "I have drawn things since I was six," Hokusai supposedly reported. "All that I made before the age of sixty-five is not worth counting. At seventy-three I began to understand the true constructions of animals, plants, trees, birds, fishes and insects. At ninety I will enter into the secret of things. At a hundred I shall certainly have reached a magnificent level. And when I am a hundred and ten, everything—every dot, every dash—will live."[53]

Renoir, like Monet, was an old man mad about painting. However, reliable accounts of his death fail to confirm the story that he was finally beginning to understand his art. Paul Durand-Ruel reported that the painter muttered *"Je suis foutu"* ("I'm done for")—once the refrain of the ailing Mirbeau—and then smoked a cigarette. He hoped to sketch a vase of flowers but failed because—alas for the legend—a pencil could not be found.[54] Another account comes from Renoir's eldest son, Pierre, in a letter to Monet a few days after his father's death. There is no mention

of flowers, sketches or pencils, only a gentle quietus. "The consolation
we can have is that he died without suffering," Pierre wrote, "carried
away in two days by pulmonary congestion from which he was recov-
ering when his heart stopped. His last moments were agitated, and he
talked a lot in a semi-conscious delirium, but when direct questions were
put to him, he replied that he felt fine. He then dozed off and about an
hour afterward his breathing stopped."[55]

Although hardly unexpected, Renoir's death was a terrible blow
to Monet. "You can imagine how sad the death of Renoir has been for
me," he wrote to a mutual friend. "He takes with him a part of my life.
In these past three days I've constantly been reliving our younger years
of struggle and hope." To Geffroy he wrote sorrowfully: "It's very hard.
There's only me left, the sole survivor of the group."[56] Monet did indeed
become, with the death of Renoir, the last of the Impressionists. As a
newspaper reminded its readers, Renoir had been part of a "unique generation that revived French painting…He was, with Monet, the sole
survivor of this heroic epoch."[57]

Adding to Monet's foreboding, perhaps, was the end of a decade:
one that had encompassed the deaths of his wife and eldest son, the loss
of many close friends, the periodic failing of his own health, as well as
the inconceivable horrors of the Grande Guerre.

Claude Monet, *Women in the Garden*, 1866 (Musée d'Orsay, Paris)

Édouard Manet,
*Claude Monet Painting in
His Studio Boat*, 1874
(Neue Pinakothek, Munich)

Claude Monet, *Rouen Cathedral: The Portal and the Saint-Romain Tower, Full Sunlight: Harmony in Blue and Gold*, 1894 (Musée d'Orsay, Paris)

Monet, *Wheat Stacks, End of Summer*, 1891 (Musée d'Orsay, Paris)

Monet, *The Gare Saint-Lazare: Arrival of a Train*, 1877
(Fogg Art Museum, Harvard University)

Paul Cézanne,
Bathers, 1890–92
(Saint Louis Art Museum)
One of the fourteen
Cézannes owned
by Monet.

Monet's dining room at Giverny, faithfully maintained in the original "Monet yellow"

Monet, *Waterlilies*, 1908 (National Museum Wales, Cardiff)
One of the "upside-down" paintings from Monet's landmark 1909 exhibition
at the Galerie Durand-Ruel.

Monet, *Water Lilies*, 1916 (National Museum of Western Art, Tokyo)
The painting for which Kojiro Matsukata paid a record 800,000 francs.

Monet, *Weeping Willow*, 1918–19 (Kimbell Art Museum, Fort Worth)

TOP: Monet, *Nymphéas*, 1907 (Museum of Modern and Contemporary Art, Saint-Étienne Métropole) The object of Chaumier and Le Griel's 1925 pilgrimage to Giverny.

BOTTOM: Monet, *The Rose Path, Giverny*, 1920–22 (Musée Marmottan Monet)

Autochrome of Monet in his flower garden, c. 1921

Monet at work in his large studio, 1920

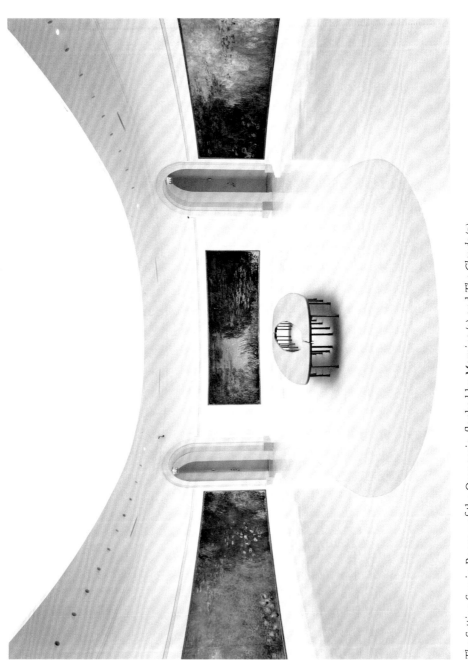

The Setting Sun in Room 1 of the Orangerie, flanked by *Morning* (L) and *The Clouds* (R)

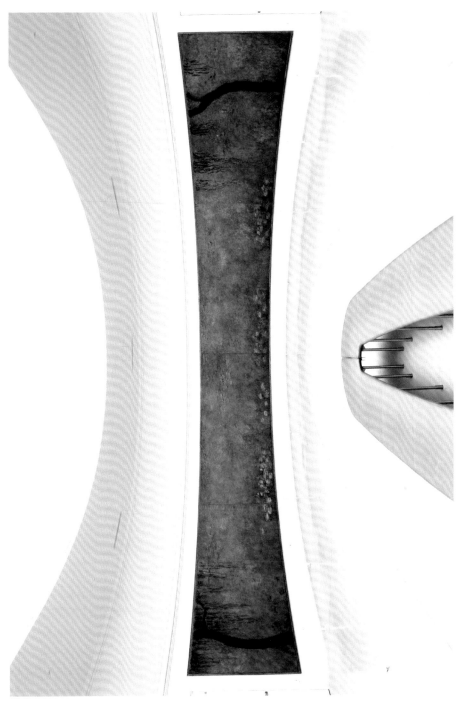

The Two Willows in Room 2 of the Orangerie

Claude Monet's house in Giverny today

MEN OF IMPECCABLE TASTE

ON SUNDAY MORNING, January 18, 1920, Georges Clemenceau arrived by motorcar at the Élysée Palace. His ministers and undersecretaries of state, by prior arrangement, were awaiting his arrival. All of them had added their signatures to the letter he was carrying. Addressed to Raymond Poincaré, it read simply: "Mr President: We have the honour of offering you our resignations. Please accept, Mr President, the tribute of our respectful devotion."[1] With those laconic words, Clemenceau's government was dissolved and his long political career finished. "What a trick they played on him!" fumed Monet.[2]

Clemenceau had been right to worry that winning the peace would be almost as difficult as winning the war. The Treaty of Versailles, after much negotiation, had finally been signed at the end of June 1919. Among its hundreds of clauses were ones calling for German disarmament, the return to France of Alsace-Lorraine, a fifteen-year occupation of the Rhineland, the payment of reparations, and the establishment of the League of Nations. In order to take effect, the treaty needed to be ratified by the Germans and three of the Allied powers. The German government ratified it almost immediately, the British a few weeks later, and then the Chamber of Deputies in October. On that same day Woodrow Wilson suffered a massive stroke in the White House, having just returned from a 9,500-mile cross-country tour in which he tried to sell the treaty to the skeptical American people. In November, the United States Senate—whose irreconcilable members, led by Henry Cabot Lodge, Wilson had unwisely dismissed as "contemptible… narrow…selfish…poor little minds that never get anywhere but run round in a circle and think they are going somewhere"[3]—rejected the treaty. *Le Temps* reported hopefully that this setback "did not deal any irreparable blow to the treaty,"⁴ but Clemenceau hurried across the channel to London to confer with the British.

How much political capital Clemenceau had lost was starkly revealed in January when his name was put forward to become president of the republic to replace Poincaré, whose seven-year term was coming to an end. Ironically, Clemenceau had little desire to occupy the office—which he had joked was as useless as the prostate gland—but allowed himself to be persuaded by friends as well as by Lloyd George.⁵ His rival was sixty-four-year-old Paul Deschanel, an old adversary against whom, in 1894, he had fought a duel with swords. Deschanel came off worse on that occasion, quitting the field of honor with his head swathed in bandages. More than two decades later he avenged his loss, polling 408 votes as opposed to 389 for Clemenceau. As a newspaper reported, Clemenceau was "opposed by the Socialists, who found him too conservative, and by a large number of Conservatives, who found him too progressive."⁶ Clemenceau immediately withdrew his candidacy, and on the following day Deschanel was elected with 734 votes. Sensing he had lost the faith and support of the chamber, Clemenceau made his journey to the Élysée Palace, letter of resignation in hand. Two English visitors to Paris at this time were shocked by his treatment. "This time it's the French who are burning Joan of Arc," remarked Lloyd George, while the ambassador to Paris, Lord Derby, wrote to King George V: "I think the general feeling—and it is one I must say that one feels oneself—is that he has been treated with base ingratitude."⁷

ONE OF CLEMENCEAU'S first acts, two days after his resignation, was to visit Giverny for a consoling lunch. Clemenceau's resignation did not bode well for the donation of the paintings, for which, more than a year on, nothing had yet been signed or made official. Equally inauspicious was the fact that Étienne Clémentel was no longer in government, having left the Ministry of Commerce and Industry at the end of 1919 to become the founding president of the International Chamber of Commerce. Monet had, however, managed to extract from him, before he left office, an ample supply of coal for the winter.⁸

In January, the Grande Décoration piqued the interest of an important collector. Jacques Zoubaloff was an industrialist from the Caucasus who, years before, had staked his small fortune—including his wife's modest jewelry collection—on an oil well in Bibi-Eybat (in present-day Azerbaijan). Just at the point when he was on the verge of ruin and contemplating suicide, his well began to gush, making him "a millionaire a hundred times over."[9] Zoubaloff fetched up in Paris, and by the outbreak of the Grande Guerre he was the most insatiable and generous collector in France. By 1920 he had amassed an unparalleled collection of French painting and sculpture, including works by Monet, Degas, Matisse, and Derain. When not even his capacious mansion in the rue Émile-Ménier, in Passy, could contain his collection, he began showering his works on the Louvre, on the Musée des Arts Décoratifs, on the Petit-Palais, as well as on provincial museums such as the one in Nantes. In the Louvre alone, his inexhaustible munificence filled two entire rooms with bronzes. Early in 1920 the newspapers reported that for "services to national museums," Zoubaloff, "as discreet as he is generous," had been promoted to Officer of the Legion of Honour.[10]

This fabulously wealthy philanthropist visited Giverny toward the end of January, agreeing to purchase one of Monet's *Poplars* for 25,000 francs. Back in his stately mansion, Zoubaloff seems to have been overtaken by second thoughts. His lawyer wrote to Monet explaining that he wished to exchange the *Poplars* for a *Palace of Westminster* that he had seen during his visit. The lawyer reported that "*Poplars* is a wonderful canvas but does not harmonize very well with the two other masterpieces of yours that he owns already." Zoubaloff therefore offered to bump up his payment to 35,000 or even 40,000 francs so long as he could acquire the Westminster painting. Somewhat perversely, Monet turned down the offer, apologizing to the lawyer, Adrien Hébrard, but explaining that he wished to keep the *Palace of Westminster*, which was not for sale at any price. But Hébrard had another request from Zoubaloff, casually expressed in a postscript: "What is the price of the *grandes décorations* that you are working on at the moment?"[11] Once again Monet failed to oblige the collector. "As for the decorative panels that I am in the process of painting," he airily informed Hébrard, "it is impossible to fix a price before they are completed."[12]

The timing of Zoubaloff's inquiry might have been significant, coming so soon after the ousting of Clemenceau and the potential faltering of Monet's donation to the state. It is tempting to see the hand of Clemenceau steering Zoubaloff toward Giverny and the Grande Décoration.[13] A sale to Zoubaloff would have ensured that Monet received a handsome sum for his years of work on the Grande Décoration. Moreover, given Zoubaloff's spectacular record as a benefactor, the panels would undoubtedly have found their way into a public collection in France. However, if such a plan had been hatched, Monet knew nothing about it. His abrupt dismissal of Zoubaloff's query was curious in light of how the Russian was precisely the sort of generous and discriminating patron about whom he and his friends had once dreamed: someone who would keep a series of water lily paintings together in order to create a "flowery aquarium."

In Monet's reticence about the Grande Décoration—his insistence that it was not finished and his reluctance to part with any of the panels—lay the first disquieting hints of another crisis: what could be called the "unspeakable drama" of the water lilies.

IF MONET WAS reluctant to offer the Grande Décoration for sale, he was only too happy to sell another work taking up a large amount of space. In February he learned that the Society of Friends of the Louvre, headed by Raymond Koechlin, was proposing to purchase *Women in the Garden*.[14] This huge canvas, rejected by the jury for the 1867 Paris Salon, had been in Monet's possession for more than fifty years, existing as a proud trophy of his embattled and at times impoverished youth. It was the angry exclamation mark to what he called his "younger years of struggle and hope." To a visiting journalist he once pointed to the shadow across the path in the foreground, cast by a tree. "It's impossible to imagine," he said, "the howls of outrage caused by this blue shadow."[15]

Monet was not being exactly truthful: *Women in the Garden* had never been exhibited in public and therefore, unlike Manet's *Déjeuner sur l'herbe* or *Olympia*, had never been exposed to the ridicule of the masses and the barbs of the critics. Even so, to have this symbol of his earlier rejection enter the Louvre would mark an important moment for Impressionism in general and Monet in particular: the consecration of a movement that had once been so savagely scorned. But the purchase probably had another, more practical element. Koechlin no doubt arranged it as a quid pro quo for Monet's donation of his paintings, the original venue for which had of course been the Musée des Arts Décoratifs, another institution with which Koechlin was closely involved.

Monet's four paintings of his pond may have been languishing in the salesroom in Paris, but throughout the spring of 1920 would-be buyers of his other canvases were beating a path to Giverny. In March he complained to Paul Durand-Ruel: "I have nothing to complain about except the incessant visits of buyers, who bother and often bore me." He claimed that among them were some "men of taste," although these were the only visitors, he claimed, who could not afford his works.[16] This comment reveals Monet's discourteous attitude toward some of his patrons. Always eager for money, he scrutinized his accounts with the Bernheim-Jeunes and Durand-Ruel with a rigorous precision that belied his failing eyesight. At the same time he was contemptuous of those who lavished huge sums of money on his paintings. When in the spring of 1920 his works once again achieved high prices at a sale in New York, he churlishly claimed that "this does nothing except prove the stupidity of the public."[17] Some of this contempt for well-heeled collectors may have been behind his refusal to sell one of his London paintings to Jacques Zoubaloff or to consider an offer from him for the Grande Décoration. If so, the disdain was unfair and badly misplaced, for Zoubaloff, as a journalist rightly noted, sought out his works with "zeal and passion" and selected them with impeccable taste.[18]

One of the would-be buyers visiting Giverny in the spring of 1920 was Marc Elder, a novelist who had won the Prix Goncourt in 1913 for *The People of the Sea*. A friend of Mirbeau, on whom he published a long essay in 1914, he came to Giverny in his capacity as president of the Society of Friends of the Museum of Nantes. This group of art lovers could not help but notice that the "tumults of Impressionism" had left no trace in Nantes, and so they came together, wrote Elder, to procure "a collection of new painters"—including, they hoped, a Monet.[19] The painter was happy to requite them by donating one of his water lily paintings.

A few weeks later Elder published a description of his visit *chez* Monet. He had arrived in Giverny on a lovely day, "gray but soft, exalted by the brightness of early spring."[20] Monet took him outside, where several gardeners—evidently new recruits—were toiling in the flower beds "under the eye of voracious finches" as the pear trees shook their snowy blossoms. Elder had grown up in Nantes, facing the Atlantic, and as the two men sat on a bench beside the water lily pond their conversation turned to the sea and, in particular, to seafood. "Forgive me, my dear master," Elder later wrote in his account of the visit, "if I reveal that our words touched upon gluttony!" The two men discussed in lip-smacking detail "pike with white butter, grilled red mullet under vine leaves, and the fresh saltiness of Breton oysters in their grey shells." When Monet expressed disappointment at a dish of lampreys he was once served, Elder replied: "You must come eat them with us!"

Monet's robust appetite and pleasure in food were evidently as strong as ever. But he revealed to Elder the loss of one of his other pleasures. As they sat beside the pond, he lamented his hearing loss and of not being able to hear "the faint fluting of toads." "O gourmand of nature," wrote Elder, "there was such melancholy in your voice!"

THESE "INCESSANT VISITS" of would-be buyers continued into the summer when, in early June, a small group of distinguished Americans came to Giverny. A map of the Monet paintings in the United States would have shown dense clusters in New York, Boston, and Connecticut; others were scattered as far afield as Denver and New Orleans. All offered testimony of the "rapacity of the Yankees" when it came to collecting Monet. But the densest agglomeration would have been in Chicago, where the 1893 World's Columbian Exposition had brought the Impressionists to the attention of well-heeled local collectors. Framed Monets could be found in elegant mansions all along Chicago's Gold

Coast. The poppy fields of Giverny adorned the château-style mansion of Evaline Kimball, widow of the piano maker William W. Kimball, and snow-covered wheat stacks hung in the home of Annie Swan Coburn, widow of a prominent attorney. By far the greatest collection, however, had been on the red-velvet walls of the picture gallery in "The Castle," Bertha Palmer's turreted mansion on Lake Shore Drive. Over the years she had purchased ninety Monet paintings.[21]

When Bertha Palmer died on her Florida estate in 1918, one of her pallbearers was Martin A. Ryerson, another Gold Coast resident who owned more than forty Monet paintings. Ryerson was an American version of Jacques Zoubaloff: someone who happily combined enormous wealth with discerning tastes and an extraordinarily generous philanthropy. The son of a wealthy lumber baron from Michigan, he had studied in Paris and Geneva before going to Harvard Law School and then taking over the family business. He had been one of the founders and benefactors of the University of Chicago, serving as president of the board of trustees and funding both a physics laboratory and library. However, perhaps his most generous benefactions had been reserved for the Art Institute of Chicago, to which he began donating paintings in 1892, and for which, in 1900, he had endowed an art library. His philanthropy was guided in part by his friend, the wealthy financier Charles L. Hutchinson, founding president of the Art Institute and a relative of Ryerson's wife, Caroline. The two men and their wives often toured Europe together in search of paintings and other objects for the museum. France was a particularly favored destination for Ryerson, who was fluent in French. Thanks to their efforts, the Art Institute became, in 1903, with the purchase for $2,900 of *Bad Weather, Pourville*, the first museum in the United States to acquire a Monet.

Many of Ryerson's Monet paintings were already on loan to the Art Institute (and most would eventually be donated to the collection), while Bertha Palmer's bequest to the museum included nine Monets. This generosity made Léonce Bénédite, director of the Luxembourg Museum, exult over the French treasures in American museums during a tour of Boston, Philadelphia, and Chicago in 1920. "Their museums!

Such wonderful collections!" he exclaimed in an interview with a French paper on his return, noting that Ryerson had donated two entire rooms of Impressionist paintings to the Art Institute. By 1920 these museums surpassed the Impressionist collection of the Luxembourg: it held a total of ten Monet paintings, plus a paltry two by Édouard Manet, three by Cézanne, five by Degas, seven by Pissarro, and eleven by Renoir. Bénédite was humbled by the "noble and generous friends of French culture" in the United States, a land where the people cherished France as "the great source of ideas, a civilizing agent."[22]

Ryerson and Hutchinson had plans for an even greater opportunity to celebrate French culture. In the summer of 1920, the sixty-four-year-old Ryerson came to France and, accompanied by Caroline and Hutchinson's wife, Frances, made his way to Giverny. Also present were a curator from the Art Institute and an architect.[23] This small but high-powered delegation was determined to purchase for the Art Institute no fewer than thirty of Monet's large paintings of his lily pond for installation in the museum in a space specially prepared to display them. A Chicago newspaper later reported that Monet was offered $3 million—the equivalent of 45 million francs—for thirty paintings.[24] This figure was certainly mistaken, for it dwarfed the total amount, $1.15 million, that Ryerson had donated to the University of Chicago for the construction of its laboratory and other facilities.[25] It would have meant he intended to pay $100,000 (1.5 million francs) per panel, a sum vastly in excess of what Monet's paintings went for. (A few months earlier, Monet informed a would-be buyer that his canvases went for "around 25,000 francs.")[26] A more likely sum was 3 million francs ($200,000) for thirty large-scale paintings, meaning that Ryerson was offering 100,000 francs ($6,666) for each. This was a large but plausible sum given the sheer size of the canvases as well as the tremendous wealth of Ryerson.

Monet had yards aplenty of painted canvas by the summer of 1920. He could quite easily have satisfied Ryerson's wishes, banked the heftiest paycheck of his entire career, and still retained enough work to make a sizable donation to the State. By this point, his Grande Décoration comprised, in the estimate of Lucien Descaves, a total of 170 meters

The American collector and philanthropist Martin Ryerson at Giverny in the summer of 1920

(186 yards) of canvas, while the journalist Arsène Alexandre speculated that he had done enough work to decorate fifteen rooms.[27] In a moment of sober reflection that summer Monet had asked another visitor as together they surveyed the immense expanses of canvas: "Do you not think that I was completely mad to paint all of this, because what the devil can be done with it all?"[28]

However, Monet once again flatly refused to entertain thoughts of parting with any of the Grande Décoration. The Chicago newspaper later attributed this demurral to what it regarded as the painter's baffling and contrary personality, rehashing the story about how in 1908 he had destroyed $100,000 worth of his own paintings. It also claimed by way of explanation that he had few friends and "led a hermitlike existence, barring his beautiful home to journalists, critics, and photographers."[29]

In fact, journalists, critics and photographers were regular visitors to Giverny, and Monet had no shortage of friends despite the recent predations of the Grim Reaper. But the rebuff to Ryerson is perplexing nonetheless. He may have been reluctant for even more of his paintings to cross the Atlantic to grace the walls of homes and museums in the United States. As early as 1885, before enjoying any international success, he had expressed regret at his paintings leaving France "for the land of the Yankees," saying that he would rather have them remain in Paris, "because there and only there is there still a little taste."[30] Undoubtedly, Monet entertained a disagreeable streak of anti-Americanism. His dislike of the prewar American residents of Giverny—among whom his reputation for boorishness was well-known—stretched across the ocean to include their compatriots at home. Unlike Bénédite with his affectionate view of Americans as noble and generous friends of French culture, Monet believed his popularity in the United States merely proved "the stupidity of the public."

In fairness to Monet, he wished the Grande Décoration to remain in France—above all, in Paris—for reasons that were patriotic as much as they were snobbish. As he explained to a visitor that summer: "It bothered me to think that all my work might leave my country…I need a location within Paris itself."[31] But in his deflection of this delegation from Chicago there can also be seen a further symptom of his extreme reluctance to part with these works on which he had spent so much time and exhausted so much energy.

AN EVEN CLEARER indication of Monet's reluctance to part with his latest paintings came later that month. With Clemenceau no longer in government, informal negotiations for the donation were being handled by the art critic François Thiébault-Sisson, a friend of the new prime minister, Alexandre Millerand. Monet informed him that he would donate his paintings to the state only if two conditions were met. The first was that he would be allowed to keep his canvases "until the end," ensuring they would not be removed from his studio until he died. Second, he would need to see and approve the place where they were to hang and how they would be displayed. "This is for me," he told Thiébault-Sisson, "an unalterable decision."[32]

Negotiations soon began to falter, especially when Thiébault-Sisson moved into the Hôtel Baudy in Giverny and became a constant pestering presence. Not only did Monet resist handing over any of his paintings, he was also wary of having his donation publicized. "Please do not talk to anyone about what I've written to you regarding my decorations," he wrote to Thiébault-Sisson in July. "Don't give any more publicity to this matter, since this bothers me beyond imagining and I have no desire to hear about it. I want to be calm in order to work…I have no time to waste right now."[33] Monet clearly did not wish to be pressurized by having the attentions of the press turned on his donation.

Clearly the gift to the nation had gone well beyond the two paintings selected by Clemenceau in November 1918. What had yet to be determined was exactly which and how many canvases would constitute this donation. There was no shortage of candidates, and so it must have come as a surprise to those, such as Thiébault-Sisson, who had seen some six thousand square feet of painted canvas in Monet's studio, to learn that the Grande Décoration was not yet finished and that, incredibly, even more canvases were being produced in a seemingly unstoppable tide of color. Monet wrote to Geffroy in June complaining of problems with his eyesight but claiming that he was conserving his forces and "working constantly" on the Grande Décoration. To Thiébault-Sisson he wrote that "at this time I think of nothing but work...I'm at an age where I can't afford to lose a minute."[34] Like a shark that would drown if it stopped swimming, Monet seemed to believe that he would die if he stopped painting. By the summer of 1920 it was clear that he would be painting the Grande Décoration "until the end."

Although not eager to part with his paintings or have his donation publicized, Monet was still keen to enjoy the perks of working for the state. In the muggy heat of July he penned a letter to Étienne Clémentel to safeguard a supply of coal for the winter. "If the State wishes me to work for it," he informed Clémentel, "it must provide me the means, and you, my dear friend, are the only one I can count on." He asked for the coal to be supplied, as before, by a collier in Rouen—and he informed Clémentel that he would need ten tons.[35]

MONET'S TRIPS INTO Paris were becoming ever more infrequent. By the summer of 1920 more than three years had passed since he visited the city. At the end of 1919 he confessed: "I don't think I shall ever go back." To Geffroy he wrote in the summer of 1920: "Naturally, I don't budge from here, and surely I never shall."[36] In fact, since his visit to the Normandy coast in the autumn of 1917, he traveled no further than the occasional jaunt to Versailles to have lunch with Clémentel and visit a plant nursery.

Clemenceau, on the other hand, was traveling the world. In February, barely a fortnight after his ouster, he had departed on a twelve-week trip to Egypt, visiting Cairo, Alexandria, the Nile valley, and Egyptian Sudan. From Luxor he wrote jauntily: "Claude Monet, my good friend, what are you doing on the Seine when here, with each passing moment, the Nile plays with the sky and the mountains of Thebes an opera of light that would make you perfectly crazy."[37] There was no chance that Monet would ever set sail for Egypt, but Clemenceau, on his return to France, had hopes of luring Monet from Giverny. "It's not good to retreat into your shell," he told him.[38] To that end, in August he sent Monet a railway timetable for the journey between Giverny and the far-distant village of Saint-Vincent-sur-Jard, near the coastal resort of Les Sables-d'Olonne, on France's Atlantic coast, 280 miles southwest of Paris.

Clemenceau had put his weekend cottage in Bernouville up for sale. At the end of 1919, on a holiday in the Vendée, near where his childhood had been spent, he happened upon a little beachfront house that he came to call (with no false modesty) *la bicoque* (the shack). Known as Belébat, the house was owned by the local squire, Amedée Luce de Trémont, who lived nearby in a more stately pile, the Château de la Guignardière. An ardent Catholic and royalist, Trémont nonetheless greatly admired Clemenceau, offering to give him use of the property for free. When Clemenceau insisted on paying, they agreed on a rent of 150 francs per year, which was to be donated to the poor.[39]

Clemenceau moved into Belébat in August, taking possession of what he called "my sky, my sea, and my sand."[40] He quickly wrote to Monet, sending him the timetable and encouraging him to visit. Knowing that the best way to his friend's heart was through his stomach, he tried to tempt him with some of the local cuisine, a cabbage soup: "Consider that if you don't come you will never taste *le bouillon des choux-rèbes*."[41] But Monet showed no signs of stirring from Giverny. "I'm at war with nature and time," he wrote that August, "and I'd like to finish some paintings I've started."[42] Soon afterward, Clemenceau once again set off for foreign parts, this time to Singapore, the Dutch East Indies, and India. The latter visit was at the behest of the maharajah of Bikaner, who had invited him to hunt his namesakes in the jungles of Rajasthan.

CHAPTER FIFTEEN

A GRAND DONATION

ON SEPTEMBER 27, 1920, Paul Léon, the newly appointed director-general of fine arts, traveled to Giverny in the company of Raymond Koechlin. The forty-six-year-old Léon described himself as "a kind of jack-of-all trades" whose new job gave him responsibility not only for purchases of paintings by the state but also for the construction and upkeep of concert halls and museums, and for the restoration of historic buildings.[1] He was an expert on France's historic monuments— especially those damaged or destroyed during the war—and the author of a recent article on the reconstruction of Reims. For several years he had been vigorously promoting his restoration work in Reims as a propaganda tool against what he called the ravages of German barbarism.[2]

However, discussions that afternoon did not, apparently, touch on Monet's erstwhile commission to paint the cathedral of Reims, a project in which Léon appears to have had no involvement.[3] Instead, over a lunch of roast chicken and veal risotto served by a butler dressed all in white, the three men reached a decision regarding Monet's donation to the state of canvases from his Grande Décoration "I'm going to give the Hôtel Biron twelve of my last decorative canvases," Monet explained to René Gimpel a short time later. However, there was an important stipulation: "They'll have to build the room as I want it, according to my plan," Monet stressed, "and the pictures will leave my house only when I am satisfied with the arrangements."[4]

Plans for the donation had therefore been finalized at last. The gift had swollen from a pair of paintings to a dozen, complete with a purpose-built venue, to be constructed according to Monet's specifications in the grounds of the Hôtel Biron, which for the past year had housed the museum devoted to the work of Rodin. It is not clear when the Hôtel Biron was decided as an appropriate location or who first suggested it, but Monet had no doubt been contemplating such a site for himself ever since Rodin first signed the papers for his own donation in 1916. France's greatest sculptor and her greatest painter—the two men whose glorious paths through the artistic firmament had followed such similar trajectories—would therefore come together in a single, magnificent space: the Musée Rodin side by side with a Musée Monet.

One day after this momentous lunch at Giverny, an architect named Louis Bonnier, at his home in the rue de Liège, near the Gare Saint-Lazare, took a telephone call from Paul Léon. The sixty-four-year-old Bonnier was, like Léon, a busy and important man. He was architect in chief of civil buildings and national palaces, surveyor in chief of the city of Paris, and director of architectural services for the prefect of the Seine. Bald and with a white ruff of beard, he was an arbiter of architectural tastes and the author of numerous municipal reports on public hygiene, urban renewal, and cultural heritage. He had been the force behind a new set of building regulations—allowing for greater height and variety—that made possible the construction of some of Paris's most stylish Art Nouveau buildings. "The people have as much right to beauty," he once famously declared, "as they do to hygiene."[5]

Bonnier was, besides, a practicing architect of no little distinction. He had built the town hall at Issy-les-Moulineaux as well as various elegant villas, including one in Auteuil for the writer André Gide. His only defect, according to a newspaper, was the unfortunate one shared by all architects, namely that "when they build a monument, they do not care in the slightest degree about the people for whom the building is done."[6] Gide would have agreed: his house in Auteuil, though grand and emphatically à la mode, was ruinously expensive, poorly lit, and so cold that in winter he took to swaddling himself in multiple pullovers and wearing a woollen hat and mittens.[7]

Bonnier had another notable building to his credit. Almost a quarter of a century earlier he had been the consulting architect on Claude Monet's light-filled second studio at Giverny. He had come to know Monet thanks to his wife, Isabelle, whose brother, the landscapist

Monet's
beleaguered
architect
Louis Bonnier

Ferdinand Deconchy, was an old friend of Monet's who lived in the village of Gasny, only four miles from Giverny. Monet had expressly asked
for Bonnier to serve as architect on the Hôtel Biron project, not only
because they knew one another, but also, no doubt, because of Bonnier's
eminent reputation and his connections at the highest levels of government. Bonnier accepted the job and immediately made plans to visit
Giverny to discuss matters with his client.

Bonnier arrived in Giverny in early October accompanied by
Ferdinand Deconchy. He listened carefully to Monet's instructions,
studied his canvases, took their measurements, and afterward, back at
his office, made an ominous memo: "Foresee great expense for the pavilion."[8] Ordinarily Bonnier did not trouble himself with such trifling matters as the cost of a project. The cost overruns on the house in Auteuil
had driven Gide to despair: "I scarcely know how I shall pay for it—or
how, after paying for it, we shall live."[9] But the cost of Monet's pavilion

did concern Bonnier, mainly because the project needed governmental approval. "The State would be very embarrassed to refuse a gift that could cost it a million francs," he wrote.[10] In particular, Monet's specifications were problematic. Monet was adamant that the pavilion should be built to his own instructions, and his main instruction was that it should be oval in shape—a design that would, he believed, allow for the best display of his twelve canvases. However, Bonnier calculated that the construction of an elliptical room, with its elongated axis and variable curvature, would cost 790,000 francs, a sum that he feared would struggle to gain government approval. On the other hand a circular room, which he advised instead, would only cost 626,000 francs.[11]

When Monet remained inflexible, Bonnier duly set to work designing an oval shape, sending the first rough plan to his client within two days of their meeting. However, Monet was not happy and suggested certain revisions. "Monet has a new idea each day," Bonnier lamented.[12] And so was to begin yet another unspeakable drama: that of the pavilion.

MONET'S DONATION WAS at last something much more substantial than a vague promise made in the aftermath of the armistice. As Louis Bonnier toiled late into the night on his various plans for the pavilion, word of the project reached the ears of the press. THE PAINTER CLAUDE MONET DONATES TWELVE OF HIS FINEST CANVASES TO THE STATE, declared a headline in *Le Petit Parisien* in the middle of October.[13] Another newspaper reported, with no undue awe, the sheer scale of this gift to the nation: 163 meters (178 yards) of painting.[14] This figure was an exaggeration, and Monet wrote to the author to correct him, good-humoredly pointing out that such an expanse "would have been too cumbersome for the State."[15] However, in its totality the Grande Décoration would actually encompass this prodigious swath and then some. In December he would report that his Grande Décoration consisted of forty-five to fifty panels making up fourteen separate series. All of these panels, he claimed, measured 4.25 meters wide by 2 meters high (14 feet by 6.5 feet) except for three that had been done on single canvases measuring 2 meters high by 6 meters (almost 20 feet) wide.[16] The

Grande Décoration at the time of this accounting therefore stretched for more than 200 meters. Barely a quarter of these canvases formed the donation to the state arranged in 1920.

In fact, Monet's twelve panels consisted of 51 meters (56 yards) of canvas, covering a total area of just over a 100 meters. François Thiébault-Sisson wrote his own more accurate account of the donation in *Le Temps*, describing how the canvases would be arranged end to end along the walls of the new glass-ceilinged pavilion.[17] His article allowed readers to envisage the display: a dozen panels, each 2 meters by 4.25 meters (6.5 feet by 14 feet), arranged around an elliptical room to form four separate large-scale compositions separated by narrow breaks and giving the impression of one continuous scene. The dozen canvases would form four compositions: *Green Reflections* (made up of two panels), *The Clouds* (three panels), *Agapanthus* (three panels), and *The Three Willows*, a work that encompassed four panels and therefore stretched to 17 meters (almost 56 feet) in length.

But that was not all. Thiébault-Sisson reported that the skylight in the pavilion would be high enough to allow Monet to "introduce decorative motifs" at intervals in the spaces above the dozen canvases. He was planning, in fact, a series of panels showing the wisteria festooning his Japanese bridge. He would ultimately produce nine of these "garlands," as he called them.[18] Since these panels ranged between 2 and 3 meters across, he was adding some 20 more meters (more than 60 feet) of canvas to his donation.

The munificence of the donation, with these vast reaches of canvas, appears to have made Monet regard any fuss about the project's funding as petty and ungrateful. Thiébault-Sisson noted that Monet's gift was especially generous given that in the last six months he had received offers to purchase "all or part of this work"—an allusion to the overtures of Zoubaloff and Ryerson. Thiébault-Sisson was careful to imply that the door had not been definitively closed on these would-be patrons and that one of them came from faraway Chicago. "All these offers," he pointedly declared, "flattering as they were, have been provisionally declined."[19] A sale to Ryerson was a convenient threat to use against those who might object to the tremendous expense to the state of the donation—those who, like the journalist for the socialist weekly *Le Populaire*, complained: "Will the Chamber of Deputies really grant funds for the construction of a pavilion for the installation of the paintings donated by Claude Monet to the State? Does the donation really require a new building?"[20]

The many debates around Rodin's donation could have left Monet and his allies in no doubt about the upcoming fights on the floor of the chamber and in the pages of the newspapers. Ryerson's offer to whisk the paintings away to Chicago—an offer that had only been "provisionally declined"—would therefore be an important bargaining chip. Further pressure was exerted by a journalist for *L'Humanité*, a onetime newspaper colleague of Clemenceau's named François Crucy, who argued that Monet was a prophet without honor in his own land. He noted that for the past thirty years Monet's work had been celebrated in America, Britain, and Germany, that his paintings were well represented in foreign museums, but that French museums, by contrast, possessed only a few scattered canvases. Such "prolonged negligence," he wrote, made for an obligation to support Monet's donation, which was all the more valuable given the institutional neglect of his work.[21]

The critic Arsène Alexandre, writing in *Le Figaro*, took another tack, praising the quality of the paintings and anticipating the incomparable splendor of the display. Few of his readers could have objected to the cost, so lip-smacking was his description of this new series of paintings—not one of which, of course, had ever been put on public display. These latest paintings, Alexandre declared, showed not only the continued strength of Monet's pictorial power "but also a new breadth of vision, an abundance of lyricism that both summarizes and goes beyond anything we knew of him." He wrote that the exhibition of Monet's enormous paintings in a specially adapted oval room of the "Musée Monet" would be "a feast for the eyes that is unprecedented in any school and in any age." The visitor to this unique museum would be "plunged into the passion of color and the hundredfold dream of the great artist." Striking a patriotic note, he wrote that the paintings "will go all around the world to sing, in their suave and intoxicating harmonies of color, the inexhaustible richness of French art."[22]

Alexandre had one further announcement for readers of *Le Figaro*: "The State, wishing to recognize Monet's generosity, has acquired for our museums an excellent work of his youth, *Women in the Garden*, a painting from the epoch of Manet that was refused at the 1867 Salon." This painting would be placed in the Luxembourg Museum, where it would join Manet's *Olympia*, "a work of equivalent importance and signification." Alexandre did not give the price paid for this painting of Monet's youth, but another newspaper soon provided details: "The purchase price, which would have terrified the jury of 1867, as well as the public, is, today, relatively modest: 200,000 francs."[23] There was, in fact, nothing modest about this price, even for such a large work, especially since Monet had noted that the going rate for one of his paintings was 25,000 francs.

Hearing the amount that Monet was to receive for this work, René Gimpel exclaimed: "Monet is a true Norman!"[24] The most common synonyms for Norman were *malin* (shrewd, cunning), *futé* (crafty), and *roublard* (wily).[25] It was indeed a wily maneuver. In reaping such a large sum for a work once derided by officialdom, Monet had extracted a brutal, satisfying, and lucrative revenge on history.

IN THE MIDDLE of November, a further cause for celebration presented itself. "Today," declared an article on the front page of *Le Figaro* on November 14, "the illustrious founder and lone survivor of 'Impressionism' reaches the age of eighty. Still active in his studios in Giverny, he receives only on Sunday. His friends take the opportunity to bring him their good wishes in private."

A small group gathered in Giverny for the celebrations. Two figures were conspicuous by their absence: Clemenceau, who was in Singapore; and Thiébault-Sisson, who "bothered me so much during his stay in Giverny," as Monet told Joseph Durand-Ruel, "that I fear I've come to pray that he will refrain from coming here on the 14th."[26] A senator and the new prime minister, Georges Leygues, were likewise dissuaded in

Claude Monet on his eightieth birthday, typically
attired in English herringbone tweed

order to keep the occasion intimate and unofficial for a man who disliked crowds and ceremonies.

Certain formalities were nonetheless observed. A friend, the duc de Trévise, a descendant of one of Napoleon's generals and a noted art collector, recited a poem in Monet's honor. "You paint, what's more to say?" his poem began—and then ran to some twenty stanzas.[27] A photographer, Pierre Choumoff, was on hand to snap photographs. One of them showed Monet looking relaxed in tweeds and pleated cuffs, a handkerchief peeping out of his breast pocket. Everyone was agreed that the master looked energetic and youthful—sixty rather than eighty. "He provides striking evidence," wrote Alexandre, "of the inanity of what used to be called the age limit."[28] Another friend christened him "the old oak of Giverny," pointing out that, although his beard was white, his dark eyes were "acute and profound" and his body unbowed.[29] To Trévise he had "the appearance of a leader, full of vigour, simplicity and authority," and his lively, robust physique reminded him of a wrestler—which was appropriate, he noted, since Monet wrestled with his paintings and with nature.[30]

Soon after Monet's eightieth birthday, the socialist newspaper *Le Populaire* carried a mischievous report: "Several members of the Académie des Beaux-Arts have suggested that Claude Monet could take the seat left vacant by the departure for the hereafter of Luc-Olivier Merson. We don't know the names of these courageous men who would dare to introduce the great painter into the Academy of so-called Fine Arts. But we would love to know who they are."[31]

The official consecration of Monet therefore looked set to continue. The Académie des Beaux-Arts was one of the sections of the Institut de France, the official guardian of French art, science, and literature. Members of the institute, the "Immortals," wore green coats embroidered with laurels and occupied plush green seats, the famous *fauteuils*, in the domed building on the Left Bank of the Seine. The Académie des Beaux-Arts consisted of forty members, including fourteen painters and eight sculptors. For someone to be admitted into this august company at the age of eighty would have been unprecedented. The average age of members of the Académie des Beaux-Arts in 1920 was sixty-nine. Only two members were older than Monet: Jean-Paul Laurens at eighty-two and Léon Bonnat at eighty-seven, but both had been elected as much younger men. In 1920, the average age of the members at their election had been fifty-five—an indication of just how overdue the honor was in the case of Monet.

Indeed, this talk of belatedly elevating Monet into the ranks of the Immortals starkly revealed how for many decades both he and the other Impressionists had been deliberately ignored by officialdom. "Claude Monet is 80 years old," *Le Populaire* pointed out. "To think it took that long for him to be deemed worthy of a place among the illustrious official painters." But of course the Académie des Beaux-Arts was the staunch defender of conservative artistic values. Merson had been typical, a specialist in the kind of mythological, historical, and religious scenes— complete with dewy-eyed sentiments and valiant, gratuitous nudity— against which the Impressionists had rebelled in the 1860s and 1870s. In 1911 a critic named Émile Bayard, proclaiming *"Haro les impression-nistes!"* ("Down with the Impressionists!"), had celebrated Merson, along with Laurens and Bonnat, as staunch defenders of a "classical tradition" against the encroachments of Impressionism.[32] Bonnat had served on the 1869 Salon jury that rejected Monet's two offerings, *Fishing Boats at Sea* and *The Magpie*. "He detested my painting," Monet later explained, "and I never thought much of his."[33] Bonnat had been a close friend of Jean-Léon Gérôme, the archnemesis of the Impressionists who, famously, had hastily conducted visiting dignitaries away from a room exhibiting Impressionist paintings at the 1900 Exposition Universelle—a room that included fourteen Monets—with the words: "Pass by, gentleman, here we have the disgrace of French art."[34] Gérôme had, of course, been a stalwart member of the Académie des Beaux-Arts until his death in 1904.

Would Monet wish to become a member of such a club? *Le Populaire* ended its report by noting that if Monet were to refuse their offer, "what a blow to the Institut!" Unlike his friend Manet, who had been eager for medals ("In this bitch of a life," Manet once claimed, "one can never be too well-armed"),[35] Monet scorned official honors. Jean-Pierre Hoschedé claimed that he had turned down the Legion of Honor because he regarded such recognition as "a medal for well-behaved children."[36] Clemenceau was equally contemptuous. Although unanimously elected to another section of the Institut de France, the Académie Française, in November 1918, he once said: "Give me forty assholes and I give you an Académie Française."[37]

Over the next few months, gossip about Monet and the vacant seat in the Académie des Beaux-Arts was sprinkled through the newspapers. "Will the master Claude Monet consent to enter the Institut?" a newspaper breathlessly asked.[38] Despite talk of a seat being "offered" to Monet, membership actually required an election by secret ballot after candidates, approached by sitting members, allowed their names to go forward. There was no shortage of candidates to replace Merson, with Le Figaro reporting that six men had been approached. "They then thought—a little tardily—of Claude Monet."[39] If this report was true, Monet might have been miffed at the fact that he was apparently not one of the first people approached. In any case, he soon made it clear that he had no wish to join the ranks of the Immortals. In December, one of his friends, who went unnamed, told Le Figaro: "He was afraid that if he became a member of the Académie, people would ask him why, and he'd prefer people asking him why he was not." The newspaper then observed: "Such high disdain is sweet revenge for forty years of stupidity and anxious, scrupulous hatred."[40]

Monet may well have enjoyed exacting sweet revenge. However, to snub the artistic establishment, and to risk appearing surly and ungrateful, was hardly politically wise at a time when he needed hundreds of thousands of francs of public money to make his gift to the nation possible. Had Clemenceau not been, as a newspaper reported, "shooting his namesakes in India," he may have counseled Monet to accept.[41]

PLANS FOR THE oval pavilion did not progress happily. Louis Bonnier made a second trip to Giverny at the end of November 1920, along with Paul Léon and Raymond Koechlin. That evening Bonnier wrote glumly in his diary: "The whole project has to be rethought."[42] He quickly produced yet another plan. According to this latest design, the pavilion was to be made from reinforced concrete; it would feature a polygonal exterior and a brick façade painted white in order, as Bonnier wrote, to give an impression of "great simplicity" and "quiet neutrality." Entered through a wrought-iron door, the interior would be twenty-five meters in diameter, featuring a "distinctive shape...true to the instructions provided by the program of Monsieur Claude Monet."[43] Illumination was to be obtained by means of a glass ceiling through which a vellum blind would gently diffuse sunlight.

At the end of the year, Bonnier's plan was submitted for approval to the General Council for Public Buildings. "For the exterior," Bonnier had emphasized, "we have not sought any effect for the planned building that might be detrimental to the architecture of the Hôtel Biron."[44] Alas, the architects on the committee did not see things in the same light, unanimously turning down the design, which they found too modern in comparison with the stately grace of the eighteenth-century Hôtel Biron, in whose grounds it was to sit. The rejection of Bonnier's modernist pavilion was not, perhaps, surprising, given both the historic location and the artistic temperament of the time, embodied in recent legislation to do with rebuilding after the war. This new law stipulated that architects should "ensure, to the greatest extent possible, the preservation of historical and archaeological memories, maintaining the special architectural style of the region and a respect for landscapes, sites and scenic aspects, which are an important part of the artistic heritage and morale of our people."[45]

Bonnier hastily assured Monet that the General Council's decision could be overturned, but Monet disliked the plan in any case. His unhappiness stemmed from the fact that the "distinctive shape" designed by Bonnier was not elliptical but, for reasons of cost, circular. "I confess to be a little disappointed in the way the room, with its regular shape, looks like it's been designed for a circus," he wrote cuttingly to Paul Léon. "I fear such a shape will not produce a good effect." He then told Léon that to reduce costs he was willing to accept a smaller building so long as it was elliptical—but this reduction in space meant, regrettably, that his donation would shrink accordingly, from a dozen panels to only eight or ten.[46] To Camille Pissarro's son Lucien he bitterly complained that the donation had become more trouble than it was worth.[47]

There was, at least, progress with *Women in the Garden*. In early February 1921 he was able to report that the painting was "en route to Paris."[48] The massive canvas had been removed from the wall and carried down the stairs, where Monet carefully superintended its placement in the truck sent by Paul Léon. He confessed that the departure of the painting was heartbreaking because of "the many memories it holds for me."[49] He had painted the work in the year he had met nineteen-year-old Camille Doncieux, who posed for three of the figures, most spectacularly as the young woman of fashion seated in the grass in a voluminous Worth dress, a bouquet of flowers on her lap. For many decades, young, pale, and beautiful, shaded by her parasol from the light of a long-ago sun, she had gazed sightlessly down on the life at Giverny that she had never known.

IF SISTER THÉONESTE was the only person in France who could manage Clemenceau, then Clemenceau was the only person in France who could manage Monet. Heavy sighs of relief must therefore have been heaved in Paul Léon's office when, on March 21, 1921, the Tiger returned from his six-month expedition to the Far East. As Léon later recalled: "Monet, aged, anxious and menaced with blindness, was prey to fits of discouragement. Each day we had to stop him putting his foot through his paintings. He constantly changed plans and dimensions, putting us in an awkward situation. It was often necessary to appeal to Clemenceau for arbitration."[50]

Clemenceau's tour had been wildly successful. "He went everywhere, saw everything, and talked to everybody," wrote Sir Laurence Guillemard, the governor of the Straits Settlements, on the Malay Peninsula. "The charm of his manner was irresistible; his gay humour was infectious; his courtesy won all hearts, and in two days he was the idol of Singapore. He never seemed tired. Every morning he came down to breakfast in high spirits."[51] At the invitation of the sultan of Johor he went on a tiger-hunting expedition but returned empty-handed from the humid jungle. He had better luck when he moved on to India and, wearing a pith helmet, a bow tie, and his ubiquitous gray gloves, set off on a three-day hunt with the maharajah of Gwalior, with whom he bagged several specimens. He also enjoyed less predatory delights, writing to Monet from Varanasi in Uttar Pradesh: "Let it not be said that I came to Bénarès [Varanasi] to enjoy the most prodigious bath of light and that I did not find a word to say to the man called Claude Monet." Just as he had described the beauty of sunlight of the Nile, so, too, he sent a description of the Ganges, "a great, clear river with a grand sweep of white palaces that fade in the powdery light of dawn. In the splendour of their clarity and simplicity the river and sky enfold the whole life of things. If I were Claude Monet I should not wish to die without seeing it."[52] Monet had taught Clemenceau a sensitivity to the special quality of the effects of light, especially over water. As he would later write to Monet: "I love you because of who you are, and because you taught me to see light. In this way you've enriched my life."[53]

By the time Clemenceau returned to Paris, several possible alternative venues for Monet's donation had been proposed. At the end of March, Clemenceau, Léon, Bonnier, and Geffroy—though not Monet, who was still not budging from Giverny—went to view two buildings at the west end of the Tuileries, by the place de la Concorde. One of them was the Jeu de Paume, built in 1861 to house the courts for *jeu de paume*, a precursor to tennis, and since 1909 a venue for art exhibitions. (A show of Dutch art featuring "incomparable Rembrandts" was upcoming.)[54] The other was the Orangerie, a greenhouse built in 1852. Clemenceau immediately reported the results of the mission to Monet, telling him that the Jeu de Paume, with a width of only eleven meters, would probably not be sufficient, but the Orangerie, somewhat wider at more than thirteen meters, "seems to me very adequate...It will cost more than the Jeu de Paume, but Paul Léon makes his case for it. I suggest you call it a deal."[55]

A week later, on April 6, Monet finally stirred from Giverny, paying his first visit to Paris in more than four years in order to view the

Orangerie "with my own eyes."[56] It was a rather undistinguished building about which Monet probably knew very little. Known as the Orangerie des Tuileries to distinguish it from the more famous Orangerie at Versailles, it had been built for the Emperor Napoleon III to replace a sixteenth-century greenhouse erected in the Tuileries by King Henri IV, a lover of oranges. The structure was used to overwinter the orange trees from the Tuileries, and the stately emergence of these trees onto its terrace had long been one of the first signs of spring in Paris. It still housed orange trees in winter but also had a varied career as what today might be called a "multipurpose space." At various times it served as a studio for the sculptor Jean-Baptiste Carpeaux, who gave lessons to Napoleon III's son; as an assembly room for school awards ceremonies; and, in the summer of 1878, as the venue for a series of benefit concerts in aid of victims of an explosion in a toy shop in the rue Béranger. By the 1880s it boasted a champagne bar overlooking the Seine, and over the next few decades it hosted operettas, dog shows, a display of insects sponsored by the Société Centrale d'Agriculture et d'Insectologie, and exhibitions of wheat and flour. Its grounds served as a combination of parade ground, fairground, and athletics track: there were footraces and, by 1898, displays of automobiles. The Orangerie narrowly escaped demolition in 1913, and during the Grande Guerre the charity L'Algérienne took over the premises, serving couscous, *méchoui* (spit-roasted sheep or lamb), and other Algerian foods to wounded North African soldiers.

Within two days of Monet's visit, a newspaper was reporting that Paul Léon's administration was dreaming of "expelling the orange trees in order to install an exhibition of the works of Claude Monet."[57] The situation was, however, not so simple or straightforward. Monet had enjoyed his brief foray into Paris, having "a very full and pleasant day," taking in a lunch with Clemenceau and then a visit to the Louvre, "where I feasted my eyes on everything."[58] But he was, quite understandably, anxious about this new plan. In the middle of April he wrote a long letter to Léon explaining that he was still hoping to sign a deed of donation (thus far, nothing had been made official or legally binding). "But a formal assurance is necessary, and a guarantee also that the necessary work will be carried out quickly." As he pointed out, seven months had already passed, "and if it takes as many to decide what to do in the Orangerie, plus a year and a half for the execution, where will that lead us?" He therefore asked for the entire process to be expedited, "and only then shall I agree to sign the protocol of donation"—which, he said, would be null and void if he died before the premises were properly prepared.[59]

By the end of April, after further consideration, Monet was much less pleased with the Orangerie as a venue. He wrote to Georges Durand-Ruel that things were not going well with the donation "and I'm extremely annoyed."[60] The new space, radically different from that of Bonnier's pavilion, called for a reconsideration of how many canvases he would donate, how they would relate to one another, and, crucially, how they could be seen to their best advantage in what he was rapidly coming to believe was an unsuitable environment. The new setting was, as Clemenceau pointed out, some thirteen meters wide, but it was also a good deal longer, at just over forty meters, than the pavilion planned for the Hôtel Biron, requiring his canvases to be adapted to the confines of the existing space.

The Orangerie presented, in Monet's view, three specific drawbacks. First of all, its ceiling was lower than that planned for the pavilion at the Hôtel Biron, ruling out the possibility of the decorative frieze of wisteria panels. He was also concerned that its walls were not rounded, as per his repeated insistence, and that his paintings would therefore be shown on a "completely straight" surface rather than a curved one.[61] Finally, the narrowness of the available space—barely half the width of the pavilion planned for the Hôtel Biron—meant that viewers would not be able to stand back from the paintings.[62]

Monet therefore came to a momentous decision. On April 25, he wrote to Paul Léon explaining how one of the formal conditions of his donation had been his satisfaction with the room in which the paintings would be shown. The narrow, rectangular space of the Orangerie did not fit the bill. "As you may imagine," he wrote, "I have thought carefully about the Orangerie and I am, regrettably, obliged to waive the donation that I had wished to make to the State."[63]

Monet may well have been bluffing at this point, threatening to withdraw his donation in order to win vital concessions. Léon did not seem overly concerned at this point. Indeed, biding his time, perhaps waiting for the storm to pass or for Clemenceau to take charge of the situation, he failed to respond to Monet's letter. However, Monet's hand was soon strengthened when, a few months later, another buyer for the Grande Décoration arrived in Giverny.

CHAPTER SIXTEEN

A MOST ARDENT ADMIRER

ON THE FIRST of June 1921, a distinguished visitor arrived in Paris: the twenty-year-old crown prince of Japan, Hirohito. The young man was treated to a grueling round of Paris's sights. He was given a tour of the Louvre, a visit to Versailles, and a lunch at Chantilly hosted by the Société Franco-Japonaise. He watched horse races from the presidential box at Longchamp, went on trips to Compiègne and Pierrefonds, saw the battlefield at Verdun, and at Fontainebleau ate dinner in the company of Clemenceau and Poincaré. At some point the schedule permitted His Imperial Highness to spend an hour enjoying the view from the top of the Eiffel Tower.

Crown Prince Hirohito was not treated to that rare and sought-after delight, a visit to Monet's garden. However, during this visit, Clemenceau brought two other distinguished Japanese guests to Giverny: Baron Sanji Kuroki and his wife, Takeko. For the previous two years the couple had resided in France, in elegant rooms in the Hôtel Édouard VII. Baron Kuroki, the son of a famous admiral, had met Clemenceau when he arrived at the Paris Peace Conference as part of the Japanese delegation. Clemenceau's admiration for Japanese culture was attested to by everything from his collections of netsuke and *kogo* to the bonsai tree that sat on the steps of his apartment, tended by a Japanese gardener.[1]

Baron Kuroki and his wife had already visited Giverny some months earlier, purchasing a painting—a 1907 panel from the *Paysages d'Eau* series—for the hefty price of 45,000 francs.[2] The baron and his wife were part of a steady procession of Japanese artists and collectors welcomed in Giverny in 1921. The wives delighted Monet by wearing kimonos, and Clemenceau, whenever possible, insisted on the honor of ferrying these delegations to and from Paris in his automobile.[3] Then,

Takeko Kuroki, Monet, Lili Butler, Blanche, and Clemenceau, ca. 1921

in June, Clemenceau's chauffeur-driven Rolls-Royce (on loan from the Greek-born financier Basil Zaharoff) brought its most important Japanese visitor to Giverny: Kojiro Matsukata.

As a French journal reported, Matsukata was "an illustrious man of state."[4] The uncle of Takeko Kuroki, he was the son of a former prime minister of Japan and a personal friend of the emperor. As *L'Homme Libre* reported, Matsukata was also "a great friend" of Clemenceau, and he never came to France without paying a visit to the Tiger.[5] A debonair fifty-six-year-old tycoon with wingtip collars, a fob watch, and a ubiquitous cigar, he described himself "a captain of industry."[6] As the president of Kawasaki Shipyards, he was a man of astounding wealth. He had become, in the years immediately after the war, possibly the world's greatest patron of art. The Kawasaki Shipyards constructed massive dreadnoughts thanks to a large crane that Matsukata had bought in England, then dismantled and shipped to Japan. This majestic crane made Matsukata's fortune during the war, when he supplied the Allies with battleships, but it also led to his interest in modern art: one day in the window of an art gallery

The Japanese collector Kojiro Matsukata

in London he spotted a painting of a shipyard with a crane. The work was by Sir Frank Brangwyn, who henceforth became a trusted friend. His interest in Western art thus strangely piqued, Matsukata, during a visit to Paris in 1916, asked Paul Durand-Ruel, with advice from Léonce Bénédite, curator of the Luxembourg Museum, to put together a collection of modern art for him. "I know nothing about art," Matsukata explained, "but I consider the contemplation of masterpieces of art a great way to educate the workers."[7]

Matsukata's collection would soon swell to hundreds of paintings that he planned to ship to Japan to form a museum of modern Western art, built to the designs of Brangwyn on a site overlooking Mount Fuji.[8] In the meantime the canvases were being stored in the Hôtel Biron, in galleries not open to the public, where they were tended by Bénédite. This museum was to be called Kyoraku Bijutsu Kwan, or the Art Pavilion of Pure Pleasure. A selection of Monets was naturally required, and so in 1921, accompanied by Clemenceau, Matsukata paid a visit to Giverny. Monet had previously advised Matsukata to visit the galleries of Durand-Ruel and the Bernheim-Jeunes, where he would find a greater selection than in his studio.[9] But Matsukata did not, understandably, wish to be denied the pleasures of a trip to Giverny. Moreover, he was no doubt intrigued by what he must have heard from Clemenceau about the Grande Décoration.

All of this Japanese interest in Monet was welcome, fitting, and happily reciprocated. Like Clemenceau, Monet had been a devotee of Japanese art and culture for many decades, ever since the "magical day" (in the words of Mirbeau) when, visiting Holland in 1871, he went into a grocery store in Zaandam and afterward, opening his purchases, discovered that the fat man behind the counter had wrapped his pepper and coffee in a Japanese woodblock print. Full of "infinite admiration," he bought the rest of these exotic wrapping papers, which had come from the Far East in the hold of a ship carrying spices. Among them, supposedly, were works by Utamaro and Hokusai.[10]

This story may well be apocryphal, but there could be no doubting Monet's genuine enthusiasm for Japanese art, in particular the work of Utamaro, Hokusai, and Hiroshige, the latter of whom he called a "Japanese Impressionist."[11] In 1909, Monet was quoted in an interview as saying: "If you absolutely insist on affiliating me to others, let it be to the old Japanese"[12]—by which, presumably, he meant Hokusai and his contemporaries in the first half of the nineteenth century. In 1921, around the time of the visits by Kuroji and Matsukata, Monet told another journalist: "I'm especially flattered that the Japanese understand me, since they are the masters who have felt and represented nature so profoundly."[13]

This statement—like any artist's statement about "nature"—is virtually meaningless. So what was it that Monet actually admired and sometimes, perhaps, emulated in Japanese art? He told another interlocutor, the duc de Trévise, that what Western artists valued in Japanese art was the "bold manner in which the subjects are outlined."[14] That may well have been so in the case of painters such as Van Gogh or Toulouse-Lautrec, but the fact is that one looks in vain for a bold outline in any of Monet's paintings. Nor does one find the large areas of unmodulated colour that many Western painters took from Japanese art. The shock of recognition and feeling of infinite admiration in that Zaandam spice shop came, rather, from the fact that Hiroshige and his contemporaries depicted scenes of modern Japanese life in beautiful but modest surroundings: beside rivers, on bridges, in busy streets, during local festivals, and in teahouses or flowering lakeside gardens. These were, of course, exactly the sort of places that the Impressionists, with a French twist, had been busily depicting in their own work since the early 1860s. The Utamaro, Hokusai, and Hiroshige prints collected by Monet were known as *ukiyo-e* (Pictures of the Floating World). The "floating world" was a Japanese-style bohemia of Kabuki theaters and licensed broth-els populated by actors, prostitutes, and the emerging class of wealthy merchants: a milieu not entirely different from that of Paris of the belle époque.

Japanese prints therefore gave Monet and his friends permission to see beauty in the simple and analogous vistas in their own world: city streets, riversides, women's fashions, sailboats, bridges, theaters, and opera houses. Pleasure and leisure, rather than myth and history, became the preferred subject matter of the Impressionists. Japanese depictions of gardens and the landscape were particularly important for Monet. Various prints from Hiroshige's series *One Hundred Famous Views of Edo*, published in the 1850s, include weeping willows draped over lakes, irises sprouting by the water, and festoons of cherry blossoms by a Japanese bridge. Many of these subjects and the radical ways of com-posing them—strong diagonals, asymmetrical compositions, and unex-pected angles of vision, such as slanting or downward-looking points of view—had become second nature to Monet.

Monet also took away something else: a Japanese practice that none of his fellow enthusiasts except for Cézanne applied to their work. Japanese artists often did multiple views of a single motif. Hokusai and Hiroshige, for example, each did a series called *Thirty-six Views of Mount Fuji* showing vistas of the holy mountain from various angles and dis-tances, in different weather, seasons, and times of the day, and with numerous different scenes occupying the foreground. The most famous of them, Hiroshige's *The Great Wave off Kanagawa*, featured Mount Fuji in the distance with a giant wave rearing menacingly in the fore-ground. These series of landscapes, in which a single motif was picked out dozens of times under differing viewing conditions, may have influ-enced Monet's approach in his wheat stack paintings and led him into his decades-long experiment with series painting. They also influenced Cézanne, who painted, not coincidentally, thirty-six views of Mont Sainte-Victoire.[15]

*

THERE WAS ONE further Japanese influence on Monet. In 1904 a journalist observed that Monet's garden with its peonies, irises, and little green bridge looked distinctively Japanese—a point, he noted, likewise made by Tadamasa Hayashi, the man from whose Paris gallery Monet bought many of his Japanese prints.[16]

In France, Monet was far from alone in creating a garden inspired by those of Japan. The exotic specimens of plants and flowers on display at the Japanese pavilion at the Exposition Universelle in Paris in 1878 had caused a horticultural sensation matched only by that created eleven years later in 1889, when a Japanese garden designed by Wasuke Hata, featuring bonsai trees and miniature cypresses, was created at the Trocadéro. By that time the traveler and photographer Hugues Krafft had already designed a Japanese garden at Loges-en-Josas, near Versailles, where his twelve-hectare wooded park, complete with a pavilion constructed by carpenters specially imported from Japan, was christened Midori-no-sato (Hill of Fresh Greenery). Krafft hired Hata, after his Trocadéro triumph, to tend Midori-no-Sato. Hata also designed a much smaller space for the aristocratic dandy Robert de Montesquiou, a friend of Mirbeau, at his home in the rue Franklin. This same apartment came to be occupied, a few years later, by Clemenceau, who shared Montesquiou's enthusiasm for all things Japanese.

Another of Wasuke Hata's creations had been the garden for Edmond de Rothschild's château at Boulogne-Billancourt, a few miles outside Paris. In the spring of 1913, Clemenceau took Monet to see this garden, which boasted a pagoda and a tearoom, in order to cheer him during his long depression following the death of Alice and the diagnosis of cataracts. Afterward, Edmond's wife, Adelaide, wrote to Clemenceau: "We are delighted that Monsieur Claude Monet had a pleasant impression of his walk in Boulogne. If his magic palette could capture a corner of our Japanese garden, we would have great joy in seeing this reflection."[17]

But the only garden whose reflection Monet was interested in capturing on canvas was his own. He once denied that he had attempted to create a Japanese garden at Giverny.[18] That may sound at first like one of his perverse misdirections. He had, after all, planted bamboo, Japanese apple and cherry trees, and Japanese tree peonies, some of which had been given to him by Japanese friends. The edge of his pond, meanwhile, was graced by a Japanese-style bridge straight out of a Hiroshige print. However, his garden included none of the features of a traditional Japanese garden: stepping-stones, waterfalls, bonsai trees, pagodas, Buddha statues, or areas of raked sand. Moreover, his bridge had been painted green, whereas the more authentic color (such as the bridge at Midori-no-sato) was crimson. Monet was inspired less by actual Japanese gardens, with which his acquaintance was slight, and more by the appealing motifs of ponds, bridges, and trailing willow branches that he had seen in his collection of Japanese prints. By a happy coincidence, five days before he purchased the parcel of land for his water garden in 1893, he had attended an exhibition of Utamaro and Hiroshige prints at the Galerie Durand-Ruel. On display were three hundred prints depicting bamboo forests, Japanese bridges, cherry blossoms, and weeping willows.[19]

KOJIRO MATSUKATA, ON his visit to Giverny in 1921, found Claude Monet to be "a delightful gentleman."[20] His ambition to fill the Art Pavilion of Pure Pleasure with the finest specimens of modern painting meant his trip with Clemenceau—who introduced Matsukata to Monet as "one of your most ardent admirers"[21]—had ended in a buying spree: some fifteen paintings. He was treated to lunch, naturally, and was then given a tour of the studio. Clemenceau told Monet: "Show him your best work and give him, as my friend, a good price." But Matsukata made it clear that he did not expect any special favors: "Go ahead and ask high prices," he instructed Monet, "because I'm used to treating my friends well and I would blush to make a profit from a friendship." Monet then showed some of his finest canvases to Matsukata, who "made his choice and handed the artist a check for a million francs."[22]

This vast sum, stated in *L'Homme Libre*, was also reported in another reliable source, *Le Bulletin de la vie artistique*, a publication of the Bernheim-Jeune brothers.[23] Matsukata's purchases included wheat stacks, poplars, snowscapes, views of London, and the cliffs of

Belle-Île—a fairly comprehensive range of Monet's periods and series.[24] If the figure of a million francs is correct, Matsukata was paying almost 70,000 francs for each canvas. When he went to New York in early 1922 to buy a selection of American paintings, the *New York Herald* reported with awe at how this "mysterious Japanese" was paying "extravagant prices" for all kinds of works of art.[25] One of Brangwyn's assistants suspected that Matsukata was being unduly exploited by avaricious dealers,[26] and, to be sure, if the reports of a million francs can be credited, he had certainly paid beyond the market price for Monet's paintings.

Matsukata, on his visit to Giverny, seems to have fixed his eye on another prize. In the middle of June, Monet wrote to Arsène Alexandre: "I have received a serious offer on a particular part of the decorations."[27] Having seen the Grande Décoration in Monet's studio, Matsukata expressed an interest in acquiring at least some of these large decorative panels. Monet had already rejected similar offers from Zoubaloff and Ryerson, but by the summer of 1921, frustrated with the difficult logistics of his donation to the state, he was willing to entertain Matsukata's overtures. As the door of the Orangerie closed, that of the Art Pavilion of Pure Pleasure creaked invitingly open.

Matsukata was therefore able to purchase part of the Grande Décoration, one of Monet's 4.25-meter-wide canvases, *The Water Lily Pond, Willow Reflections*. Matsukata proudly told a journalist that one of the canvases he had purchased in Giverny was "fourteen feet in length... It is a scene of his garden. What did it cost? I don't remember."[28] If the story about the check for a million francs is correct, *The Water Lily Pond* was presumably, along with the canvases of poplars, cliffs, wheat stacks, and London, part of this remarkable purchase. No price, it seemed, was beyond the abilities of Matsukata's checkbook. But he had also done something even more remarkable than spend a million francs on paintings: he had pried loose from Monet's studio part of the Grande Décoration.

BY JUNE 1921, Paul Léon had still not responded to Monet's letter announcing the retraction of his gift to the nation. His bluff called, Monet reopened negotiations through the art critic Arsène Alexandre, who had recently served as inspector general of France's museums and who was in the midst of composing Monet's biography. Monet confessed to Alexandre that not being able to keep his promise to the state had been a "great pain" and that the purchase of *Women in the Garden*—for which he received a check for 200,000 francs—had put him in a position of acute embarrassment. How could he refuse to deliver his paintings after banking the check from the government?

He therefore told Alexandre: "If the Ministry of Fine Arts can broaden by three or four meters that part of the Orangerie reserved for my paintings, I am still committed to donating them, and moreover, donating enough for two rooms. I think I cannot say better than that. If this is possible, I should be very happy."[29] But the offer was met with further silence from Léon. Monet fretted anxiously for two weeks before writing again to Alexandre: "Have you communicated my last letter to Paul Léon? Has he said if the enlargement of the Orangerie will be possible?"[30]

Still no answer came. Monet therefore—perhaps unexpectedly for all concerned—put the difficulties from his mind and calmly went back to work in his garden. In the spring he had been experiencing more troubles with his eyesight: "My poor sight," he wrote in May. "I feel it diminish each day, almost by the hour."[31] But either his eyesight or, more likely, his mood had improved by the end of June, perhaps due to the lucrative attentions of Matsukata, and he spent the next few months "working flat out with great enthusiasm."[32] So content was he with his work that as autumn approached he began contemplating a trip to the seaside—not to his beloved Normandy coast, but to the far-off Vendée in order to visit Clemenceau. The Tiger was surprised but delighted that Monet had finally taken him up on his offer. "What? Claude Monet enters circulation like an ancient coin from Merovingian times that has come out of hiding to impress our counterfeit banknotes. Hallelujah in the highest!"[33]

If 1920 had been a year of Monet celebrations, the following year—with Clemenceau's eightieth birthday due to fall on September 28—belonged to the Tiger. After escorting Matsukata to Giverny, Clemenceau had gone to England to collect an honorary degree from the University of Oxford, whose public orator declared, amid a "burst of enthusiasm," that no one else's name would live longer in history.[34] Then, following a trip to Corsica, he had gone to his house in Saint-Vincent-sur-Jard. Nearby, in his childhood village of Sainte-Hermine, a statue in his honor was due to be unveiled amid much celebration on October 2. "This will be, I think, a pretty good fair with dances and fireworks as in the old days," he wrote to Monet a fortnight before the event. "We shall eat out of our hats, and sleep in the trees or in ditches. See if you feel like coming. My car will transport you."[35] Monet passed on these festivities but agreed to come the following week, when things would be more peaceful.

Sainte-Hermine turned out in force to celebrate Clemenceau. The tiny village's two streets were decorated with banners and its houses painted red, white, and blue. People arrived from all over the countryside by train, automobile, truck, horse cart, and bicycle—so many of them, reported a newspaper, that the crowds were thicker than on the boulevards of Paris.[36] A village band played the "Marseillaise," then the monument was unveiled: a massive sculpture commemorating one of Clemenceau's visits to the front, showing him on the parapet of a trench, staring determinedly forward with six soldiers at his feet. For many of those present, the flesh and blood Clemenceau was even more impressive than the effigy carved from stone. *"Victoire de la France!"* he declared in an extemporaneous address. *"Victoire de la civilisation! Victoire d'humanité!"* According to the press reports, the "grand old man" looked younger than ever: "He looks suntanned," reported *Le Petit Parisien*, "bronzed by the sea breezes and the bright ocean sun."[37]

Life in the Vendée certainly agreed with Clemenceau. A few days earlier he had written to Monet: "As for me, my hands are burning from eczema and my shoulder is knackered, but I forget my woes as soon as the waves tickle the soles of my feet. I would not be surprised if you got on with some painting here. The sky and the sea are a palette of blues and greens."[38] Clemenceau's house was only forty yards from the Atlantic, from which it was separated by a stretch of sandy ground on which he was cultivating a garden. To Monet he called his small patch of the Vendée "my fairyland of earth, sky and birds."[39]

Clemenceau in his
garden at Belébat

Clemenceau explained to one visitor that the name of his house, Belébat, was old French for *beaux ébats*, meaning happy entertainment.[40] Happy entertainments were certainly planned for Monet, who, two days after the festivities at Sainte-Hermine, arrived in the chauffeur-driven Rolls-Royce. He was accompanied by Blanche and Michel. "I have two small rooms for you and the Blue Angel, where she will be able to spread her wings," Clemenceau had promised. "Your son will be lodged in a nice house with a car and a makeshift garage next to mine."[41]

Clemenceau was happily domesticated in this corner of the world where he was spending summers and holidays.[42] He was tended by an elderly cook named Clothilde and a manservant, Pierre, who addressed him as "Monsieur le Président." He had a donkey named Léonie, housed in a stable at one end of the house, and a little dog named Bif, an animal with "the brains of a sardine," as he apologized to his guests; he frequently chastised the creature for barking by shouting in American-accented English: "Cut it out!" The kitchen where Clothilde prepared the meals had a flagstone floor, whitewashed walls, and exposed beams. Outside the door was a rustic bench on which, after meals, Clemenceau often sat staring at his humble stretch of garden and the mighty ocean beyond. When in residence he raised his standard on a flagpole: a twenty-foot-long windsock in the shape of a carp, given to him a few months earlier by Matsui Keishiro, the Japanese ambassador to France.

Gardening, painting, food: Clemenceau had tempted Monet to the Vendée with all three of these great loves. All three, no doubt, were suitably indulged during the eight-day visit. As with Sacha Guitry and Charlotte Lysès at Les Zoaques eight years earlier, so, too, with Clemenceau at Belébat: Monet offered advice on Clemenceau's little stretch of dunes, bringing some plants with him, including ones that Clemenceau called *boules d'azur*—blue flowering plants that reminded him, apparently, of Blanche's eyes.[43] (Clemenceau frequently made reference to Blanche's blue eyes, and indeed this seemed to be why—in combination with her endless patience with the turbulent curmudgeon who was her stepfather—he called her the Blue Angel.) This blue plant, evidently some sort of thistle, was one of the few things that would survive the winter in Clemenceau's garden, which was buffeted by the harsh and salty Atlantic gales. Monet would also give Clemenceau roses, aubrietas, daffodils, and gladioli.[44]

"Paintings await you," Clemenceau had promised Monet.[45] Monet did indeed do some painting during his visit—not of the sea (as Clemenceau clearly expected) nor of the modest patch of garden, but rather a watercolor of Belébat itself, as if commemorating for himself his friend's seaside abode.[46]

Thanks to Clothilde, meals had become almost as much of a ritual at Belébat as at Giverny. A visitor who arrived a few days before Monet was treated to sardines and Clothilde's ragoût of mutton.[47] Monet was presumably served the cabbage soup with which he had been tempted a year earlier, but Clothilde's specialty was poulet Soubise, a dish named after the prince de Soubise, a seventeenth-century marshal from the Vendée. Roasted, chopped up, and cooked in a thick onion sauce, this chicken dish took forty-eight hours to prepare. Clemenceau once proclaimed: "I like the sauce even better than the marshal did."[48]

One of Clemenceau's great pleasures was making the ninety-minute-long expedition to Les Sables-d'Olonne to purchase ingredients from the market, including shrimps from a woman named Mathilde, whom he cheerily observed charged him double. Another visitor that October described Clemenceau's flirtatious banter with the "vast and radiant Mathilde," who tried to make him purchase more, "but he replied that he wanted nothing else, except Mathilde herself. She replied that she was too big to be taken away. Clemenceau pointed to the enormous waiting automobile and stated that he liked his women plump." In the market he also purchased pears, prunes, cake, and newspapers. As soon as he arrived, a cry went up: "*Voilà le Tigre!*" At the patisserie a young woman in a butterfly-shaped headdress thanked him for doing her the honor and offered to carry his purchases to the automobile.[49]

Then it was back along the lanes to Belébat, with Clemenceau urging his chauffeur, the faithful Albert, to drive ever faster. (Several years later, with Albert at the wheel, Clemenceau's motorcar would accidentally run down and kill a woman, a Madame Charrier, while returning from Les Sables-d'Olonne—although Clemenceau insisted that on that occasion the Rolls-Royce had not been speeding.)[50] The carp would be run up the flagpole, fluttering and snapping in the breeze. It is possible to imagine Clemenceau and his guests listening to the sighing of the pines and the rumble of waves crawling across the strand of beach, and watching, as dusk crept over the ocean, the pulses of light from the great lighthouse eighty miles away in the Gironde estuary. "Eight small suns shall fade during your stay," Clemenceau had written to Monet, "but our friendship never will."[51]

After the eight suns extinguished themselves in the ocean, Monet returned to Giverny. Barely had he disappeared down the lane than Clemenceau, in his study overlooking the ocean, composed a letter to him. "Philosophy teaches us," he wrote, "that the greatest pleasures are short. Your visit has been particularly vivid since passed in a flash. You especially deserve credit for having undertaken the visit since you're as lively as a tortoise…As for me, I shall continue to be whirled around like a top whose strings are pulled one by one by all the devils in Paradise."[52]

THE MATTER OF Monet's donation to the state must have been one of the topics of conversation during the visit to Belébat. The situation was still unresolved, and so Monet wrote to Clemenceau at the end of October to reiterate his conditions. He would accept the Orangerie as a venue as long as the administration undertook "to do the work that I judge necessary." Back in June he had informed Arsène Alexandre that he was willing to donate more than a dozen works, and now he restated the offer: he told Clemenceau that he was willing to offer eighteen works to the state. He enclosed a plan showing how the space in the Orangerie could be separated into two separate rooms, both elliptical. "If the administration accepts this proposal and undertakes to do the necessary work," he repeated, "the affair will be settled."[53]

Clemenceau, who had returned to Paris on October 22, swung into action. He met with Paul Léon at the beginning of November, then reported happily to Monet: "Everything is arranged according to the conditions you set."[54] He arranged for Léon and Louis Bonnier to visit Giverny, which they did a week later, with the upshot that, as Monet pointedly reminded Léon one day later, he agreed to donate eighteen canvases making up eight compositions; these panels would be "destined for two rooms arranged as ovals."[55] All that was needed now was a new architectural plan from Bonnier as well as a notarized contract making the donation official and legally binding on both parties.

Negotiations had therefore reached more or less the same point they were at exactly a year earlier: the paintings and a venue had been determined, and now Bonnier was at work on a design. Predictably, exactly the same difficulties presented themselves. Within weeks Monet was complaining to Clemenceau that Bonnier's plan for the Orangerie was unsuitable and that, as before, the architect was trying to cut costs.[56] Once more an intervention from Clemenceau was required. In the middle of December, after a meeting with Paul Léon, he was able to reassure Monet: "He will do everything you want...There will be no difficulties."[57] The result of these negotiations was that Bonnier was removed from the project and another architect, forty-five-year-old Camille Lefèvre, architect in chief of the Louvre and the Tuileries, appointed in his place. The only problem was that no one seemed to have informed Bonnier of this change, and so Monet was taken aback when his latest set of plans arrived. "I don't know how to respond to him," Monet complained to Léon.[58]

Bonnier may well have been relieved to be rid of the project. Within weeks Lefèvre, too, found himself mired in design difficulties, in particular with how to provide adequate natural light despite the fact that for structural reasons the roof beams in the Orangerie could not be altered or moved. Yet again Monet complained to Clemenceau, who by this point was becoming thoroughly fed up with the constant wrangling between the artist and his long-suffering architects. In early January he wrote a blunt and impatient letter to Monet, declaring: "It must be settled."[59]

Lefèvre produced three different plans over the next few months, all of them providing ovoid rooms, while Clemenceau worked on the wording of the terms of the agreement, which went back and forth between him and Léon. Meanwhile, Monet sent anxious telegrams to Clemenceau, who was beginning to find him, as he readily confessed, "a pain in the backside."[60] Monet's mood darkened. In a rare moment of self-scrutiny, observing the difficulties his tempers were causing Blanche, he admitted to Clemenceau: "What a bastard I am."[61]

Léon and the architects may have agreed with this assessment. However, by the spring of 1922 matters were finally shunting along toward their conclusion. In March, Monet informed Léon that he was expanding his donation to twenty-two panels making up twelve compositions, though he noted that the compositions "may be modified during installation."[62] In other words, the number of paintings depended on the actual space they would inhabit, with room for flexibility. The documents were prepared and ready to sign by early April, although Monet still found it necessary to complain about the "sluggishness" of Léon and his legal representative in making their way to Giverny.[63] At long last, on April 22, in the offices in Vernon of Maître Baudrez, Monet's lawyer, the artist and Léon put their signatures to the deed of donation. Monet undertook to deliver nineteen (rather than twenty-two) panels to a "Claude Monet Museum" within two years—that is, by April of 1924.

Monet's plan for the donation, as outlined in the contract, was for nineteen panels making up eight compositions, to be distributed across the curving walls of two oval rooms in the Orangerie. Three of the compositions from the earlier plan for the ill-fated pavilion at the Hôtel Biron were maintained: *The Clouds*, *Green Reflections*, and *The Three Willows*. However, the *Agapanthus* triptych was dropped, along with the decorative frieze of wisteria panels. Five new compositions from the Grande Décoration were added to this latest scheme. In the first room, *The Setting Sun*, made up from a single panel 6 meters (20 feet) wide, would be displayed with another new entry, *Morning* (three panels), along with the *Clouds* triptych and *Green Reflections*. In the second room, the massive, 17-meter-wide *Three Willows* composition (destined for the end wall) would share space with *Reflections of Trees* (two panels), to be placed on the entrance wall. The other walls would feature a pair of other compositions, both encompassing two 6-meter-wide panels and both, at this stage, simply entitled *Morning*.

Many more meters of canvas had obviously been added to the donation since the agreement made with Paul Léon eighteen months earlier. Indeed, the donation had expanded to 83.5 meters of canvas, or just shy of 274 feet. However, most of these compositions were, by the spring of 1922, presumably well on their way to completion. For instance, the largest of the compositions, *Three Willows*, had been virtually finished when its four panels were captured in a photograph in Monet's studio almost five years earlier, in November 1917.

Monet lay down what he called a number of "inviolable conditions" attached to his donation of the nineteen panels.[64] He was donating them, he pointed out, to "a Musée Claude-Monet," and once in place the works were never to be removed from the Orangerie, nor could other works of art be placed in the two rooms. Anxious to avoid the dull veneer of so many Old Masters, he further stipulated that his paintings should never be varnished. Ominously, he included the proviso that since his eyesight might deteriorate, he would not be able to guarantee the aesthetic quality of the panels.

Clemenceau was delighted at the news of the signed contract, the difficulties and intricacies of whose negotiation must have brought back unpleasant memories of working on the Treaty of Versailles. From Belébat, on the eve of the signing of the contract, he wrote a long letter of encouragement to Monet: "You know very well that with your brush and your brain you have reached the limit of everything that can be achieved. At the same time, if you were not pushed by an eternal search for the unattainable, you would not be the author of so many masterpieces…You will strive until the last minute of your life, thereby achieving the most beautiful body of work." He ended with an exhortation: "Paint, paint until the canvas bursts."[65]

There was, in truth, very little painting that remained to be done. Monet had two years to deliver canvases that in the spring of 1922—with the possible exception of *The Setting Sun*—were virtually finished. He should have been relaxed and contented, relieved that his masterpieces had found their home, as he had wished, in the very heart of Paris. But the real problems were only just beginning.

CHAPTER SEVENTEEN

THE LUMINOUS ABYSS

ON JUNE 25, 1922, after a Sunday lunch with Clemenceau at Giverny, Monet sat down and wrote a letter to Gustave Geffroy: "No need to tell you how much I have been excited, modesty aside, by the good things you say about my work and myself, and I'm deeply moved...I thank you from the bottom of my heart...With my love and thanks once again for all that is beautiful in this book."[1]

The book in question was hot off the press: Geffroy's *Claude Monet: Sa vie, son temps, son oeuvre* (*Claude Monet: His Life, His Times, His Work*). *Le Figaro* called it a "magnificent monument, a great, definitive book,"[2] and Monet did indeed have much for which to thank his friend. In writing the book, Geffroy hoped to perform a number of services for both Monet and Impressionism. In particular, he was at pains to counter the criticism of those, such as the Post-Impressionists and their supporters, who believed that Monet did not capture an underlying essence (as the Fauves and Cubists claimed to do) but only the shimmering surface of things. Instead, he repeatedly stated that Monet's paintings captured nature's mix of the ephemeral and the eternal, its magnitude and its minutiae, its glittering appearances and its dizzyingly fathomless depths. His text was peppered with references to "the complex life of things"—to mystery, universality, truth, eternity and (as its final line stated) "the dream of infinity."

Geffroy was eager to prove, in other words, that Monet's paintings went beyond pretty pictures of women strolling under parasols or sunlight dancing on the Seine. As a stern riposte to anyone who believed Monet's paintings were simply about shadows, ripples, and reflections, he wrote that, *au contraire*, Monet inserted himself at the point "where there blossom without ceasing the phenomena that last both an instant and an eternity." And to anyone who thought Impressionism a pleasant recreation involving little more than setting up an easel beside a river on a sunny afternoon and slopping bright colors onto a canvas, he memorably described Monet as a tortured, obsessive artist who pursued his dream of form and color "almost to the point of self-annihilation."[3] It was certainly an account all-too-familiar to those who had made the artist's close acquaintance.

Geffroy was not the first writer to make these points about the hidden depths of Monet's paintings. As far back as 1891, Octave Mirbeau wrote that Monet did not "limit himself to translating nature" and that his paintings revealed "the states of unconsciousness of the planet, and the suprasensible forms of our thoughts."[4] A year later, Camille Mauclair enthused that Monet's paintings were "made from a dream and a magical breath…leaving for the eyes only a mad enchantment that convulses vision, reveals an unsuspected nature, lifts it up unto the symbol by way of this unreal and vertiginous execution." Monet, he claimed, skimmed over "the philosophy of appearances" in order to show "eternal nature in all her fleeting aspects."[5]

Monet was, in these views, a tormented genius who possessed both an intellectual bedrock and a spiritual essence: someone whose paintings plumbed the ineffable mysteries of life rather than merely catching superficial glints. Geffroy's proof of this intellectual and spiritual power rested above all on works that had not yet been created when Mirbeau and Mauclair celebrated Monet's "mad enchantment" thirty years earlier: the waterscapes Monet painted beside his pond. All of these canvases were, Geffroy claimed, part of "a measureless dream of life" that Monet "expressed, reprised and ceaselessly expressed anew in his frenzied vision before the luminous abyss of the water lily pond."[6]

Mirbeau, Geffroy, Clemenceau—all were familiar with Monet's volatile temperament and feverish obsessions. However, this talk of anguish, annihilation and the abyss, of frenzied visions and mad enchantments, may have surprised some of Monet's other admirers. For those travelers who, as they passed through Giverny, paused by the roadside to peer at the beautiful blossoms through the gap in Monet's fence, or who craned their necks as their train puffed along the tracks, eager for a sight of the pond and its bright constellations of water lilies, Monet's garden was a vision of Paradise. "Here is the Eden" was the typical response of one visitor, "here is the Paradise where, under the shade of some airy trees, bright flowers play on the sun-dappled grass."[7] But this place of beauty was also a place where Monet, struggling with his canvases, contemplated what Geffroy called the "unfathomable nothingness." This unfathomable nothingness was represented for Geffroy by the shifting, reflective surface of the pond and also by the aquatic foliage that had been Monet's decades-long obsession: the water lilies, which were "more silent and esoteric than any other flower."[8]

MONET'S OBSESSION WITH water lilies had begun when he glimpsed Latour-Marliac's hybrids at the 1889 Exposition Universelle. By that time the water lily—like the weeping willow with its allusions to grief and loss—possessed special associations and symbolic values. The plant and its flowers went beyond horticulture and botany, inhabiting the realms of art, myth, literature, and religion. Water lilies (and related members of the Nymphaeaceae family, such as the lotus) held an important place in numerous cultures and religions. The word "lotus" comes from the name of a nymph, Lotis, who, as Ovid writes, turned into a water lily "while fleeing from Priapus' vile pursuit"[9]—for which reason water lilies were a symbol of chastity for the ancient Romans, who laid before them the cropped tresses of the Vestal Virgins. For the ancient Egyptians, they were an image of rebirth and immortality because of how their flowers opened in the dawn and closed at dusk, while their circularity made them a symbol of eternity and perfection. In India, the sun god, Surya, was known as "Lord of the Lotus," and Hindu legend maintained that Brahma was born from a lotus flower placed in the navel of Vishnu as he reclined on the cosmic serpent.[10] In Buddhist mythology, Gautama Buddha was nourished as a child by a lotus when his mother was unable to nurse him. The Aztec rain god, Tlaloc, was likewise represented with a water lily in his mouth, while both North African "lotus-eaters" (described in book nine of Homer's *Odyssey*) and the Mayans of Mesoamerica used water lilies, which contain opiate-like alkaloids, as psychotropic drugs.[11]

Monet probably knew little or nothing of this rich cultural freight, but water lilies also had a very distinctive cluster of meanings and associations in nineteenth-century France with which he would have been familiar. Appearing by the dozen in poems and paintings, they evoked the mysterious and the unknown, the feminine, the oriental, the exotic, the voluptuous, and often, at the same time, the sinister, deathly, and gruesome.

The botanical characteristics of the water lily were helpfully explained by Jean-Pierre Hoschedé, a stickler for horticultural detail. "Everyone thinks that Monet *sowed* his water lilies," he wrote, "when in fact they were *planted*. Many have said that these plants *floated*. This is an error: water lilies root in the mud at the bottom of the water, producing long petioles and peduncles, which rise to the air at the surface, the petioles giving birth to leaves that spread in a circle on the water, and the peduncles to the large flowers." He pointed out that water lilies lived in stagnant water, such as bogs and ponds.[12]

Anchored in the mud, their beautiful blossoms floating on stagnant waters—such characteristics were bound to attract symbolic meanings. For the poet and playwright Maurice Maeterlinck, water lilies were primordial plants, "the inhabitants of the original ooze and mud."[13] For the novelist George Sand, they were an emblem of fragile innocence blooming in a foul and dank environment. In her preface to *François le Champi*, first serialized in 1848, she described how her inspiration for the novel came from seeing (in a city she does not identify) a poor boy in a street known as the chemin aux Napes, an ugly and dangerous dead end bordered by a ditch "where in the muddy water, amid salamanders and snakes, grow the most beautiful water lilies in the world, whiter than camellias, more fragrant than lilies, purer than a virgin's dress." These plants were, she wrote, "the wild and admirable vegetation of the sewer."[14] The image of virgins and sewers was repeated a few years later by a French theologian who argued that the water lily, with its white flower rooted in the mud, symbolized the Virgin Mary because of her obscure origins in the hinterlands of Nazareth.[15]

For other writers, the muddy ponds in which water lilies flourished gave them more ominous connotations. For Monet's doomed, demented friend Maurice Rollinat, a stagnant pond was always a source of suspicion and anxiety. One of his poems evoked a "black bog, sinister and fearful," lit by hobgoblins, in which the moon's reflection looked like a skull and crossbones.[16] The murky waters in which they thrived therefore gave water lilies not a miraculous purity and chaste innocence but, rather, more than a hint of menace. One of his prose pieces, "The Red Pond," described "monstrous water lilies" with blossoms of "mortuary white" masking "the perfidy of the deep" and floating on "the dark water like decomposing hearts."[17]

An even more ghastly image of water lilies was to be found in Mirbeau's *The Torture Garden*. This horrifying novel of sex, death, and horticulture was first serialized in *Le Journal* in 1898 and then published in book form the next year, followed in 1902 by a deluxe edition featuring gruesomely voluptuous illustrations by Rodin. Mirbeau described a garden in the middle of a prison in China, constructed for the emperor in a previous century at the cost of the lives of thirty thousand laborers, whose corpses, along with the excrement of the present-day prisoners and the blood of the torture victims, were used to nourish the soil. Thanks to this uniquely fertile environment, the garden was home to "the rarest and most delicate species of flowers,"[18] among which were interspersed dead and dying bodies, as well as the instruments of torture and death from which the exotic plants and flowers took their sustenance. Torture and water lilies came together as the narrator stood on a wooden bridge and gazed down into a pond: "The water lilies…with their big blooming flowers ranged across the golden water," he observed, "made me think of severed, floating heads."[19]

Mirbeau's dark parable was nourished in the rotten humus of the Dreyfus Affair: "To priests, soldiers, judges, to the men who raise, lead or govern men," he wrote, "I dedicate these pages of murder and blood." His image of flowers thriving in excrement may have come in part from the fact that at Carrières-sous-Poissy, to which he had moved in 1893, the sanitation department spread human excrement on the

One of Rodin's illustrations for a 1902 edition of Octave Mirbeau's *The Torture Garden*

fields as fertilizer. But his image of the wooden bridge, the pond, and its water lilies all come from his visits to Giverny. Mirbeau gave the first ever description of Monet's garden following a visit in 1891. His write-up used words such as *dégringolée* (tumbled), *mêlée, orgie*, and *inépuisable floraison* (inexhaustible flowering)[20] — not words normally used to describe nineteenth-century French gardens. A visiting poet, Émile Verhaeren, described Monet's garden in a similar fashion a decade later, writing of "the beautiful vegetal violence, the mad abundance, the tightly woven enlacement of colors and lights! One would say a congestion of flowers, of grasses, of shoots, and of branches."[21]

Whether or not Monet's garden was truly an orgiastic melee of vegetal violence, it certainly inspired something in Mirbeau's imagination. Indeed, in 1903 the writer Edmond Pilon, after describing a visit by Mirbeau to Giverny, asked a rhetorical question: "Who knows if it is not the dear memory of these flowers that one day exhaled over the mass grave of *The Torture Garden* its scent of lotus and mangroves."[22] In the novel, the wooden bridge spanning the pond is painted green, like the Japanese bridge in Monet's garden, and the surrounding garden features irises, canopies of artfully pruned wisteria, and water lilies. As the literary scholar Emily Apter has noted, Monet's garden at Giverny and Mirbeau's fictional torture garden "exhibit a disturbing similarity," with Mirbeau's brutal garden mirroring Monet's layout "virtually element for element."[23]

None of this suggests, of course, that Monet should have glimpsed in his pond or shrubbery the same deathly specters that his friends

Mirbeau and Rollinat, with their brilliantly depraved imaginations, were able to conjure from the sight of lily ponds. But it does indicate that the garden in fin de siècle France could be more complicated and disturbing than merely a blissful reflection of Paradise. Even Monet's beautiful pond of water lilies could become, as Geffroy suggested, a place for tormented meditations on annihilation and the abyss. Such, certainly, was all too often the case—as his frequent references to suffering and torture suggest—when Monet confronted his garden with his paints and palette: "Ah, how I suffer, how painting makes me suffer! It tortures me. The pain it causes me!"[24]

ANOTHER FRIEND OF Monet's, Stéphane Mallarmé, likewise wrote evocatively about water lilies. In 1885 he published a prose poem called "The White Water Lily," later collected into an anthology that he sent to Monet in 1891. His strange little story describes a man rowing a skiff along a stream in search of both water flowers and the property of an unnamed woman to whom he plans to pay his respects. As the river widens into a pond, the rower recognizes the bridge, hedges, and lawns as belonging to the park of the mysterious woman. As he bends over his oars, daydreaming about her, he hears a noise that may or may not be her—although he does not look up to confirm her presence, and instead turns his skiff and rows stealthily away. Mallarmé ends with one of his dazzling metaphors: the rower will gather up the woman's "virginal absence   just as, in memory of a special site, we pick one of those magical, still unopened water lilies which suddenly spring up there and enclose, in their deep white, a nameless nothingness made of unbroken reveries, of happiness never to be."[25]

The water lily became, in Mallarmé's vision, a substitution or replacement for the hidden or absent woman. Mallarmé died in 1898, just as Monet was beginning to paint his water lily pond, but the hidden or absent woman features in many interpretations of Monet's paintings of his pond. Emily Apter goes so far as to say that Monet's water lilies are "an evident sign of the feminine" serving as substitutes for the female models denied to Monet by the jealous Alice.[26] ("If a model comes in

here," Alice once declared, "I walk out of the house.")[27] The French poet
and critic Christian Limousin has likewise argued that Monet's water
lilies take the place in his paintings of the female figure, "prohibited by
the sick jealousy" of Alice: "Behind every flower is a woman—or, rather,
her absence, her hollow—a corpus of inaccessible woman, forbidden,
blocked. Cézanne and Renoir worked on their bathers, Monet on his
water lilies, which are at the same time both flowers and women."[28] Art
historian Steven Z. Levine, meanwhile, has claimed to see in three of
Monet's paintings of his pond "a human figure or face floating in a nim-
bus of reflections."[29]

These modern critics were not the first to glimpse women hidden behind or beneath Monet's water lilies. When he went to Monet's
landmark 1909 exhibition, Lucien Descaves thought he glimpsed happy
female faces and disrobing bodies. "I leave your exhibition dazzled and
amazed!" he wrote to Monet. "I can say that I have seen in painting, in
the living water, mobile like the face of happy young woman, water whose
mysteries are revealed to me, water that the shadows drape and the sun
unclothes, water on which all hours of the day are inscribed, like the
age on a human face."[30] Descaves was not alone. A female critic at the same
exhibition, as she stared at the paintings, felt herself turning into a water
nymph: "One has a sensation of being in the water, of being an inhabitant
of the ponds, the lakes, and pools, of being a nixie with glaucous hair, a
naiad with fluid arms, a nymph with fresh legs."[31] Another writer was confident that, if he kept painting them, Monet's water lilies would ultimately
assume human form, mutating into "deities and nymphs."[32] Women, it
seemed, were never far below the surface of the pond.

Nymphs lurked in Monet's pond for these viewers not least, perhaps,
because the most common French name for a water lily was *nymphéa*.
Jean-Pierre Hoschedé told the story that a "complete ignoramus" once
came and asked to fish in the pond at Giverny, asking if this was the
spot "where Claude Monet painted his nymphs."[33] The ignoramus may
have spoken truer than either he or Jean-Pierre knew. The word *nymphéa*
obviously evokes nymphs (*nymphes* in French), the female deities of place,
always represented as young girls, graceful and naked, who personify

the forces of nature, haunting the waters, woods, and mountains. The word comes from the Latin *nympha*, meaning a bride, mistress, or young woman; it is etymologically linked to the Latin verb *nubere*, to marry or wed, from which we get the words "nubile" and "nuptial." *Nymphes* also had another meaning, as a nineteenth-century French textbook on anatomy carefully explained: the *nymphes* were the membranous folds lining "the upper half of the vulva inside the labia majora."[34] A link between water lilies and the female sexual organs was graphically spelled out by J.-K. Huysmans in his 1884 novel *À Rebours*, which described how when the ancient Egyptians mummified a woman they placed her on a slab of jasper and inserted into her sexual parts, as a purification ritual, "the chaste petals of the divine flower"—that is, the lotus blossom.[35]

The critic Louis Gillet, a friend of Monet, made a metaphorical link between nymphs and water lilies at Giverny, writing that his lily pond was "the nymph with whom Monet was in love."[36] He also wrote regarding Monet's water lily paintings: "It is always the same fairy, the same fleeing ondine whom he attempts to seize."[37] An ondine was a water nymph, and so Monet's act of painting was akin, in Gillet's reckoning, to trying to catch a fleeing maiden. But chasing after water nymphs was a dangerous business, as mythology attested. "To see them," a nineteenth-century French encyclopedia soberly reported, "was to risk madness."[38] The perils of water nymphs were spelled out in the story of one of the Argonauts, Hercules's beautiful and beloved page, Hylas. Many ancient writers told the story of how the golden-haired youth, sent in search of freshwater, came upon a grotto filled with nymphs. In the version of Apollonius of Rhodes, one of them, admiring his beauty, "raised her left arm over his neck in her longing to kiss his tender mouth, while with her right hand she pulled on his elbow and plunged him into the midst of the swirling water."[39]

The story of the capture and drowning of Hylas was a favorite of painters, the most famous example being John William Waterhouse's *Hylas and the Nymphs*, painted in 1896: it shows bare-breasted young lovelies lurking among the lily pads, drawing the youth into the water. But before Waterhouse came French artists such as Jules-Eugène

Jules-Eugène Lenepveu, *Hylas Lured by the Nymphs* (1865)

Lenepveu, whose *Hylas Lured by the Nymphs* was exhibited at the Paris Salon in 1865, winning praise (in the year of the scandal over Manet's *Olympia*) for its sensual depiction of pearly flesh and lascivious poses.[40] It showed Hylas bending over a pool filled with come-hither beauties and, of course, water lilies. But Hylas was not always needed by artists, and clean-limbed nymphs disporting themselves in ponds, among the water lilies, were a mainstay of the Paris Salon. They were the kind of soft-focus mythological scenes against which, ironically, Monet and his friends had been rebelling. These nymphs lingered in the waters of Giverny, if not in Monet's imagination, then at least in those of the spectators and critics. Meanwhile, Monet, with his obsession, forever risked being drawn by them into the luminous abyss.

CHAPTER EIGHTEEN

THE FATAL PROTUBERANCE

"YOUR STEELY GAZE breaks through the husk of appearances," Clemenceau once told Monet, "and you penetrate the deep substances."[1] He sincerely believed that Monet with his preternaturally good vision marked an important moment in human evolution. Others were of a similar mind, with the poet Jules Laforgue declaring in 1883 that the Impressionists enjoyed the benefit of "the most advanced eye in human evolution."[2]

Opponents of Impressionism allowed that painters such as Monet did indeed possess an eye different from that of a normal person: they had the defective vision of madmen and hysterics. In 1892 a German writer named Max Nordau had published a work called *Degeneration* in which he pointed to "the craziest fashions in art and literature" in France as evidence that the nation had become hopelessly degenerate.[3] The style of the Impressionists (or "stipplers," as he called them) could be understood, he claimed, in light of research into the visual derangements of lunatics and hysterics, whose optic nerves were weak or disordered, and whose eyeballs trembled. "The painters who assure us that they are sincere, and reproduce nature as they see it, speak the truth," he declared. "The degenerate artist who suffers from *nystagmus*, or trembling of the eyeball, will, in fact, perceive the phenomena of nature trembling, restless, devoid of firm outline."[4] J.-K. Huysmans used this same research (conducted on hysterics by the neurologist Jean-Martin Charcot and the Pitié-Salpêtrière Hospital in Paris) as proof that the Impressionists suffered from degenerating optic nerves and a "malady of the retina." Monet, he believed, provided ample evidence: he was "a man off his rocker, someone who rams his finger into his eye up to the elbow."[5]

Those looking to explain the supposed perversities of the Impressionists could point to their all-too-real real eye afflictions. Pissarro suffered numerous eye infections that badly disturbed his vision, while Edgar Degas had experienced sensitivity to light since the early 1870s, when he was in his late thirties. By his fifties, suffering from a blind spot in his field of vision, he could no longer read the newspaper, and by his seventies he found drawing difficult. His condition baffled the ophthalmologists, whose remedial measures included what Degas called his "lugubrious instrument": a pair of spectacles with the right lens completed blacked out and the left occluded but for a small, oblique slit.[6] None of their correctives provided any improvement, and by the end of his life he was virtually blind.

Although periodically disturbed by cataracts since 1912, Monet's eyesight had not caused him serious problems throughout his work on the Grande Décoration. However, ten years after his initial diagnosis, his vision began deteriorating. His stipulations for his donation, signed in April 1922, had raised the specter of his failing eyesight, and no sooner had the ink dried on the contract than his vision seemed to worsen, making work on his canvases difficult and even inadvisable. In May he confessed to Marc Elder that working on his panels in his present state of visual impairment had been a big mistake. "Right now I'm almost blind and so must stop all work," he told him.[7] He had ruined several canvases, with the result that he felt compelled to destroy them, as in the old days. Visiting Giverny a short time later, Elder spotted canvases slashed by an "angry hand." "The trace of the knife was visible, and the painting bled like a wound," he wrote of one of the victims.[8] Monet had instructed the servants to burn other canvases—a jumble of shredded pinks, blues, and yellows heaped beneath a table. None of these works seems to have been among those destined for the Orangerie, but the dismemberments and conflagrations were an ominous development.

Working on the Grande Décoration under such circumstances must clearly have seemed imprudent. Yet Monet continued to paint through the summer. In July he wrote to Joseph Durand-Ruel that he was hoping "to paint everything before my sight goes altogether."[9] Joseph was, however, unimpressed with the results, finding Monet's latest works "atrocious and violent."[10]

Much of Monet's work in the summer of 1922 was indeed arresting. He recommenced the paintings of his Japanese bridge—the subject of a few blazing canvases from the anxious, tortured summer of 1918—along with some of the rose-festooned pathway leading to his house, a vista he had painted more than two decades earlier.[11] These paintings are truly some of the most remarkable canvases he ever produced, but they would indeed have been difficult for Durand-Ruel to market. Monet dramatically and unrecognizably transformed the beautiful alley of roses into a giddy chaos of oranges, yellows, and purples, all added to the canvas in pyrotechnic swoops and squiggles. In one of the canvases, the alley of well-tended roses leading to his beloved house almost seems to become the maw of some satanic, ravening beast. These dazzling eruptions of color were due, no doubt in part, to his failing eyesight: he complained, that August, about how he saw everything in "a complete fog."[12] But the arresting disintegration of solid form into pure color was the result, too, of a frantic intensity of vision that had less to do with his retinas and photoreceptors and everything to do with his determination to push the boundaries of painting. Some, it is true, were artistic failures, but others were magical, adventurous compositions of light and color that reveal the Old Man Mad About Painting to be, despite everything, still at the top of his game.

Unsympathetically surveying these latest works, Joseph Durand-Ruel believed that Monet's "great success with the Japanese [had] gone to his head."[13] The Japanese in question was Kojiro Matsukata, who was still busily stocking up on Monet canvases. By 1922 he owned twenty-five of his paintings, and in May a Paris newspaper reported that the great industrialist had handed Monet a check for 800,000 francs and asked him to select a work for him.[14] If the report was true, this handpicked painting not only exceeded the price of the entire auction of the twenty-five Monets sold from James F. Sutton's collection in New York in 1917, but it also became the most expensive work of art by a living artist ever purchased, almost doubling the previous record of 478,500 francs for Degas's *Dancers at the Barre*, bought by Louisine Havemeyer in 1912. Monet could certainly drive a hard bargain, as indicated by the 200,000 francs he pocketed for *Women in the Garden*. Moreover, having contracted to give to the state the fruits of almost ten years of unrelenting labor, he was no doubt determined to recompense himself from other sources.

The identity of this 800,000-franc painting is unclear, although it was almost certainly—like the work purchased by Matsukata in Giverny in 1921—part of the Grande Décoration. The most likely candidate was *Water Lilies*, one of the *grandes études*, painted in 1916: a six-and-a-half-foot square canvas purchased by Matsukata in 1922 and now in the National Museum of Western Art in Tokyo. As Tucker has pointed out, this painting was unparalleled among Monet's surviving studies, virtually unique in its level of finish, with a brilliance of color, touch, and composition that made it stand out from among the other *grandes études*. It was no doubt dear to Monet's heart, and it was a canvas, he must have known, that would worthily represent him among the masterpieces in the Art Pavilion of Pure Pleasure.[15]

BY SEPTEMBER 1922, Monet's eyesight was bad enough that he overcame his strong aversion to Paris, and his even stronger aversion to doctors, to consult an ophthalmologist. His doctor was Charles Coutela, an eminent ophthalmologist and friend of Clemenceau's whose office was found in the rue La Boétie. The forty-six-year-old Dr. Coutela confirmed the drastic worsening of Monet's vision: he was legally blind in his right eye—always the worse of the two—and enjoyed only 10 percent vision in his left. As Monet informed Clemenceau a day later: "Result: one eye completely gone, with an operation necessary and even unavoidable in the near future. Meanwhile, a course of treatment might improve the other eye and permit me to paint."[16]

Coutela hoped to operate on Monet's right eye, but he found his patient timid and reluctant. He therefore prescribed mydriatic eyedrops for the left eye in order to dilate the pupil. The results, at first, were encouraging. The following week Monet wrote a jubilant letter to Coutela, telling him that the effect of the eyedrops was "simply wonderful," that he could see better than he had in a long time and that he regretted not consulting him sooner. "That would have allowed me to do some good work rather than the awful smears I did when everything was a fog."[17]

Nothing short of an operation could, however, rejuvenate the vision in Monet's right eye, which was becoming "even more warped."[18] He soon became resigned to the inevitability of going under the knife, no doubt thanks to some gentle pressure exerted by Clemenceau. Plans were arranged for him to submit to what he called "the dreaded operation"[19] in early November, with a follow-up procedure scheduled for a few weeks later. However, on the eve of the first operation, feeling physically unwell, he suffered a failure of nerve, asking Clemenceau to cancel his appointment with Dr. Coutela. He claimed that he was in "too unfortunate a condition" to risk an operation, and that he was "too afraid of the result."[20]

Having helped resolve the problem with the pavilion, Clemenceau was now asked to manage yet another crisis involving his friend. However, he would not be available to chastise and encourage. The day after he received Monet's letter, he boarded an ocean liner in Le Havre, bound for the United States. As the *New York Times* reported, Clemenceau was "ready again to take up political life…in a fashion which is altogether new."[21]

BY 1922, CLEMENCEAU had become increasingly discouraged by international politics. In particular, he was troubled by the American withdrawal from Europe, by the various conferences that weakened the Treaty of Versailles, and by the fact that the Germans had failed to pay any reparations to France, while the Americans were insisting on full repayment of monies loaned to the Allies. Unless the Germans were forced to fulfill their obligations under the Treaty of Versailles, and unless the measures to protect France against German aggression were taken, "everything," he portentously declared, "would begin all over again."[22]

Clemenceau quickly became embroiled in an international controversy. The catalyst was an interview with Rudyard Kipling published on

September 10 in the *New York World*. Some months earlier, Kipling had hosted the English sculptor Clare Sheridan, Winston Churchill's cousin, at his home in Sussex. Since she did not reveal that she was working for a newspaper (she arrived for tea in the company of her children), Kipling was duped into voicing intemperate anti-American opinions. He supposedly claimed that the war had not been fought to a finish, that the Americans had entered the war "two years, seven months, and four days too late," and that they had quit on the day of the armistice, forcing the Allies into making peace at the first opportunity rather than marching on Berlin.

Kipling denied having made any such statements, but the topic of America's role and responsibility was suddenly open for debate.[23] Many in France shared Kipling's opinion, if not necessarily about America's evasion of responsibility, then at least regarding the necessity of pressing the Germans to pay reparations. Indeed, on the same day that Kipling's interview appeared, Raymond Poincaré was in the ancient cathedral city of Meaux to observe the anniversary of the Battle of the Marne. He gave an impassioned speech about the need to hold Germany to account: "It is…necessary to make it clear, before all, that we mean to recover our credits on Germany. If we are reproached with insisting on our rights, we repeat that we cannot renounce our claims without ruining France, and the ruin of France will be for Europe the most terrible of catastrophes."[24]

Clemenceau was, however, the most forceful and articulate prophet of doom, and it was to him that the *World* immediately turned for a quote. Did Clemenceau, the newspaper wondered, believe that America had fulfilled its duty of solidarity to the Allies? The Tiger announced via a telegram from Belébat that he would sail to the United States in November, at his own expense, to provide a response to the American people in person, in order, as the *New York Times* reported, "to restore the prestige which France has lost in the United States."[25]

Some French newspapers celebrated the return of Clemenceau to the world stage. "Whatever may be the results of the voyage we must acknowledge the grandeur of the gesture," one reported. "Friends and adversaries will render homage to the old man, who, withdrawn from the ardent battle of ideas, now voluntarily reenters the arena, not to indulge in vain polemics, but to speak to the world once more the clear language of France."[26] But not everyone was eager or pleased to have the Tiger once more on the prowl and possibly straining Franco-American relations by reproaching the Americans for not ratifying the Treaty of Versailles or living up to their part of the bargain. Clemenceau did little to allay their fears, dramatically announcing: "I am going to talk squarely to America."[27] A journalist for an English newspaper, interviewing him on the eve of his departure, found that he had lost none of his intimidating manner. He could "growl as ominously as in the old days. He can snap formidably." Wearing his omnipresent gray gloves, he beat the table with his fists and offered opinions—"impetuous, scathing, devastating"—that were "not for publication."[28] The editor of Le Matin, writing in an American paper, sighed that "France knows that not much good can result from this trip and France fears that very much evil may come of it."[29]

Clemenceau's enemies had not counted on his fame and charisma as a conquering hero. He arrived in New York on November 18, aboard the French liner Paris, to a rapturous welcome as the "hero of the World War" (the New York Times) and "the chief artisan of Allied victory" (the New York Tribune). Sirens blared in the harbor and the band of New York's Street Cleaning Department serenaded him from a tugboat. Blizzards of tickertape and torn-up telephone directories fell across the streets of Manhattan as he made his way to City Hall. The appropriate dignitaries turned out to greet him, and from Washington came a telegram from Woodrow Wilson. Clemenceau stayed at the home on East Seventy-Third Street of Charles Dana Gibson, the owner of Life magazine, whose wife, Irene, found him "a darling old man and not the least bit difficult to please."[30] He toured the American Museum of Natural History and addressed the masses at City Hall and the Metropolitan Opera House. He dined with Ralph Pulitzer at the Ritz-Carlton and, rising at four A.M., went out to Oyster Bay to doff his hat and lay a wreath at Teddy Roosevelt's grave. Journalists were impressed at how his fluency in English allowed him to express his caustic witticisms "with a sort

Clemenceau
in New York,
November 1922

of grim delight and sly malice."³¹ But not all his comments were grim or
sly: he gallantly observed that American women were even more beautiful than fifty years ago.³²

Not everyone, to be sure, was seduced by Clemenceau. He had
some harsh words for his American hosts, announcing that he would
have pressed on to Berlin in 1918 had he known what little effect the
Treaty of Versailles would have on Germany. On the floor of the Senate
he was condemned by William Borah of Idaho; other isolationists feared
he was trying to lure American soldiers back to France to enforce the
Treaty of Versailles. They also feared that he wished to impoverish the
Germans by forcing them to pay reparations—an act that, Senator
Gilbert Hitchcock argued, would drive Germany "into the arms of the
Bolsheviki."³³

From New York, Clemenceau went to Boston, where the mayor presented him with a safety razor as a gift. ("He is sorely puzzled.")[34] Then came Chicago, St. Louis, Washington, Philadelphia, and Baltimore. "I am going back to France in a very few days now," he told a newspaper in December, as the tour approached its end, "to tell my countrymen that we need have no fear, America still is with us, her heart has not changed." But he was still as pessimistic as ever: "Pray the Lord that war will not have broken out by the time I get back."[35]

ON THE DAY after Clemenceau arrived in New York, *Le Figaro* carried an article celebrating Monet as having "a miraculous eye."[36] This familiar statement about his preternatural vision was becoming ever more ironic. By December his eyesight had become so impossibly dim that he finally overcame his trepidations about an operation. His wish, he told the returning Clemenceau, was that surgery should take place as soon as possible, "around the 8th or 10th of January, because I can no longer see very much."[37] The operation, performed on his right eye by Dr. Coutela, duly took place on January 10, at the Clinique Ambroise Paré in the Paris suburb of Neuilly-sur-Seine. The first of the two planned procedures was an iridectomy: the removal of part of the iris in his right eye. A follow-up procedure, an extracapsular cataract extraction, was scheduled for a few weeks later.

The operation was relatively straightforward but inevitably involved high levels of discomfort and a lengthy and delicate convalescence. The local anesthetic consisted of injections of cocaine into the optic nerve to numb the cornea.[38] Following the operation, Monet would be required to lie still in bed in the clinic for ten days, in complete darkness, with both eyes shaded and without a pillow. Since the hardiest and most patient soul would have been challenged by this regime, it is hardly surprising that Monet did not cope well. Dr. Coutela's notes reported that the operation went according to plan even though the patient became nauseous and even vomited, "exceptional and unforeseeable reactions, caused by his emotion, and extremely awkward and alarming."[39] Immediately following the operation, Monet saw colors with great intensity

Monet in bed after his cataract operation

and saturation, relishing "the most beautiful rainbow one could imagine."[40] But these glorious effects did not last. He was forced to undergo the strict and prolonged regimen of lying absolutely still with both eyes bandaged, subsisting on a diet of vegetable broth, lime tea, and a mysterious meat, variously labeled "duck" or "pigeon," that a nurse spoon-fed into his mouth.[41]

The bandages were occasionally removed for the application of eyedrops and further doses of cocaine. A 1906 treatise on the use of cocaine in eye operations reported that the drug's toxicity caused "many accidents and alarms" and that it therefore needed to be used with caution.[42] A guard was usually stationed beside patients following these injections to ensure they did not become delirious from the cocaine and remove the dressing or otherwise cause problems. Monet was certainly a high-risk patient. Another ophthalmological treatise claimed elderly patients, especially heavy drinkers, were prone to delirium when both eyes were bandaged.[43] Hoschedé claimed that no guard was stationed beside Monet, with the predictable result that, in a fit of pique or panic, he one day ripped off his bandages, potentially jeopardizing his eyesight.[44]

The devoted Blanche was at his bedside at the clinic in Neuilly for much of this disagreeable recuperation. "He was so nervous and overexcited," she reported, "that he was moving all the time."[45] He rose from his bed on several occasions, ranting that blindness would be preferable to lying still. He eventually calmed down, she wrote, but his fits of exasperation impaired his recovery such that his stay in the clinic needed to be extended. He was in fact not discharged before he underwent the second procedure, the extracapsulary cataract extraction that took place on the last day of the month. Once more the anxious, querulous patient was prescribed a course of complete immobility.

MONET WAS FINALLY discharged in the middle of February, having spent a total of thirty-eight days in the clinic. The state of his vision was still uncertain, but he celebrated his freedom by going with Clemenceau and Paul Léon to see the Orangerie. He had been disappointed the previous September when he stopped by the building following his first consultation with Dr. Coutela. On that occasion his poor eyesight did not conceal from him the fact that work was by no means progressing expeditiously. "No workers at all. Absolute silence," he had complained to Clemenceau. "Only a little pile of rubble by the door."[46]

Three months later, in December 1922, the refurbishment of the Orangerie had received legislative approval, with the state pledging 600,000 francs toward the project. In the meantime, as construction progressed, the Orangerie continued to be used as an exhibition space. A month after Monet signed the contract for his donation, the annual "Exposition Canine" took place at the Orangerie as usual, with a thousand dogs on show, the small ones "yapping in their cages," the large ones "growling and howling like wolves."[47] Also, a "Canadian Exhibition Train" was being planned for 1923. Thirty carriages of a railway train filled with displays of hundreds of Canadian products and artifacts—canoes, furs, paintings, along with dioramas of forests and trappers—were due to be arranged in the Tuileries, including some on the terrace of the Orangerie. *Le Bulletin de la vie artistique* protested that, with the Orangerie undergoing its extensive renovation for Monet's donation, the venue should be off-limits to such temporary exhibitions. However, the minister of commerce and industry, Lucien Dior, defending the Canadian exposition, responded that the high cost of the renovations meant that Léon had agreed "the same facilities could be used for both events." The display of Canadian beaver pelts and canoes might impede construction, but on the other hand they would provide some much-needed revenue.[48]

The Orangerie des Tuileries

Monet's concerns about the Orangerie during the visit in February 1923 involved how his canvases should be fixed to the walls. Wooden stretchers and frames were obviously out of the question, because the paintings needed to be placed on curving walls. He therefore opted for a technique called marouflage in which the backs of the canvases were coated with glue and then fixed directly to the wall, rather like sticking an advertising poster on a billboard. The process was tried and trusted, having been used prolifically in the nineteenth century to fix many of the large canvases to the walls and ceilings of the Panthéon, the Sorbonne, the Hôtel de Ville, and the vault of the foyer in the Théâtre-Français, which featured a canvas mural that was eight meters (twenty-six feet) wide. However, Monet wished to meet the *maroufleur* personally, and he exacted from Léon a promise to bring both Camille Lefèvre and the *maroufleur* to Giverny for a consultation at the earliest possible opportunity "in order to allay any anxiety about the process."[49] One of his inviolable rules for the donation had been that the paintings would never be removed from the Orangerie, and his keen interest in making sure the technique was carried out properly surely demonstrated his fear that his canvases, unless permanently fixed to the walls, might, after his death, end up languishing in a dark and dusty basement.[50]

Léon and Clemenceau were, at this point, more anxious about Monet's eyesight than anything else. Clemenceau was keeping in close touch with Dr. Coutela. "I cordially thank you for your valuable information," he wrote to the ophthalmologist a week after Monet's release from the clinic. "Like you, I think that the morale of our friend must be carefully managed, because he could resist a second intervention."[51] Another intervention began to look increasingly likely as the weeks passed and Monet's vision did not significantly improve. By April, as Clemenceau explained to him, "a kind of vascularization caused by the devil knows what has caused an opacity that restricts your vision."[52]

In fact, the opacity was caused by a secondary cataract developing in his right eye, a not uncommon complication of the surgery but one causing the reluctant patient a great deal of distress. Monet suffered from "bad days of pain and sensitivity," which forced him to don dark glasses, remain indoors, and dictate his letters to Blanche. "Today," he recited on April 9, in a long letter to Coutela, "I have had sharp electrical pains shooting up the centre of the eye itself, and, in addition, my eyes water all the time." Coutela made his way to Giverny on several occasions in the months following the surgery, although he irritated Monet by postponing several consultations and then, at Easter, leaving for a holiday in Morocco. "I await your visit," Monet seethed in the letter dictated on Palm Sunday, "which, this time, will not be postponed."[53]

By the spring of 1923, Monet was entering what Jean-Pierre, another witness to these frustrations, called the "dark days": a period of "discouragement, despair and panic."[54] Clemenceau, as usual, did his best to stiffen the sinews. "Whether it rains or shines," he wrote to Monet in April, "my rule is to accommodate myself."[55] Such, alas, was not Monet's approach. As he had done in the dark days of 1913, Clemenceau took him for what he called "a visit to Japan,"[56] a trip to see Edmond de Rothschild's Japanese garden at Boulogne-Billancourt. He also brought several beautiful and glamorous women to Giverny: Charles Dana Gibson's wife, Irene (a Southern beauty whose sister was Nancy Astor), and the Duchess of Marchena, "a great lady and a humble millionairess," as Clemenceau explained, "who loves flowers and paintings, especially those of Monet. She has asked me with irresistible insistence if I could drive her to your house."[57] The estranged wife of the brutal and feeble-minded Francisco María de Borbón y Borbón, a cousin of the king of Spain, the duchess had for many years been the mistress of Clemenceau's fabulously wealthy friend Basil ("Zed") Zaharoff, who loaned him the Rolls-Royce.

But Monet remained, as he informed Dr. Coutela, "absolutely discouraged." By the middle of June he was able to read with the help of glasses—fifteen or twenty pages a day, he claimed—but his distance vision remained poor, especially outdoors. Soon black dots began appearing before his eyes. Perhaps worst of all, five months after his surgery he had begun to lose faith in Coutela. He regretted having undergone "this fatal operation" and bluntly told the doctor that "it is criminal to have me put in this situation." Coutela made an appointment for him in Paris for June 22, but on the day Monet—despite his frequent appeals to the doctor for help—failed to show. The consultation was rescheduled for the following week, and this time the secondary cataract was diagnosed and surgery scheduled for the middle of July. Monet was glumly reconciled to the procedure. "Since I know the truth about my fate," he wrote to Coutela, "I await the day when I am delivered from the fatal protuberance and I need not tell you of my regret that this did not take place earlier."[58]

This time, the surgery was performed in Giverny. On Wednesday, July 18, Dr. Coutela arrived at the station in Vernon at nine twenty A.M. "My visit to Giverny was satisfactory," he later reported to Clemenceau, who was at Belébat. "Excellent morale…Everything is for the best." He noted, however, that Monet once again had difficulties with faintness, nausea, and vomiting.[59] The patient was well enough on the day following the operation to walk in his garden with Blanche, and a return visit from Coutela two days after the surgery confirmed that matters had gone well. Before setting off for an August holiday in Brittany, the doctor decided that on his return he would prescribe Monet a pair of remedial spectacles.

"Now you're done with it," Clemenceau wrote to Monet a few days later, gently chastising him for being "a nervous man who, in spite of himself, creates complications." He signed off the letter by calling Monet a "*mauvais petit gamin*"—a bad little boy.[60]

"**NOW YOU'RE DONE** with it": Clemenceau himself probably did not dare believe these words even as he wrote them. Nonetheless, he continued to encourage Monet and to urge patience. Monet was initially optimistic. Once more dictating to Blanche, he informed the Bernheim-Jeunes that this latest operation had been more painful than the previous two, having left him in "some suffering and distress," but he eagerly awaited the arrival of the "lifesaver spectacles" on which he was pinning his hopes for improved vision.[61] An examination in the third week of August led Dr. Coutela to pronounce, in a letter to Clemenceau, the satisfactory outcome of this latest surgery, although both men recognized that an operation on the left eye was inevitable if Monet were truly to have his vision restored. Clemenceau gently broached the topic, telling Monet that he wanted "to make sure that, like everyone else, you can see with both eyes."[62]

The odds of Monet submitting to another operation suffered a blow when, at the end of August, the "lifesaver spectacles" finally arrived. "What a disappointment," he declared to Clemenceau, while to Coutela he dictated: "I am absolutely devastated because, despite all my good intentions, I feel that, if I took a step, I would fall on my face. Whether near or far, everything is distorted, I see double, and it's intolerable to keep wearing them. To continue with them seems to me to be dangerous. What shall I do? I look forward to your response. And I am most unhappy."[63] Coutela instructed him to persist, and two days later a slightly cheerier letter arrived reporting that, "my goodness, I have been able to read, a little bit at first...with a little fatigue, naturally. Distortion as before, but I endured courageously." He took to liberally dosing his left eye with drops and covering it with a patch while wearing the glasses.[64]

At the end of August, Monet received a telegram from Clemenceau offering yet another pep talk. "The fact that you can see is absolute proof that your sight is returning…Success is assured."[65] Such optimistic reports and opinions were reminiscent of the pronouncements—such as "Things are going well"—that he confidently issued in March 1918 when the Allied line collapsed, German soldiers swarmed toward Paris, and Le Supercanon began bombarding the city. The energies that had once inspired a nation were now turned on Monet, albeit so far with somewhat limited success.

Although the glasses allowed Monet to read, the latest problem was a severe disturbance of his color perception. It was an alarming development for a connoisseur of nature and an artist whose works expressed the most subtle nuances of color and light. On August 30 he reported to Clemenceau, via Blanche, that "the distortion and exaggerated colors that I see absolutely terrify me." So lurid and off-key were these colors that he claimed (not without a certain self-dramatization) that he would prefer to go blind in order to keep unsullied his memories of the beauty of nature. Clemenceau dismissed this pose as absurd ("Is there any more room in the madhouse?"), but the serious fact was that, as Monet pointed out, "both nature and my paintings look hideous to me."[66] Compounding matters was the fact that his left eye had now deteriorated to the extent that he could see nothing without eyedrops, which Coutela, much to Monet's annoyance, had strictly rationed. After this catalogue of visual disturbances, his statement to Clemenceau that he had several canvases in need of retouching must have sounded alarm bells.[67] These efforts could only have ended, it seemed clear, with the slashing of knives and the crackling of bonfires.

Dr. Coutela made a trip to Giverny in early September.[68] He tested Monet's vision by making him read him a letter from Clemenceau, which, Coutela remarked in his report to Clemenceau, he himself had difficulty deciphering ("You don't mind me saying that your handwriting is small and difficult to read"). But Monet read the letter without hesitation. Coutela confided a touching detail: "He is very pleased with the letters that you write to him." He noted, however, that Monet's distance vision was poor, although it would, he surmised, improve with time and habituation. In the meantime he worried about Monet doing such things as climbing the ill-lit stairs to his bedroom.

Monet was less concerned about flights of stairs than by the fact that poor distance vision meant he could no longer appraise his work by stepping back from the canvas. Even more, he was panicked by what he called his "upheavals" in color balance: he told Clemenceau that he no longer saw thirty-six colors but only two: yellow and blue.[69] Coutela reassured Clemenceau that such distortion was not uncommon following cataract surgery, causing little alarm to patients who did not possess Monet's "marvellous gift of color analysis." To rectify the situation, he proposed a selection of tinted lenses, although Monet, after the letdown with the lifesaver spectacles, was staunchly pessimistic about the odds of their working. He was also irked by the fact that Coutela seemed "to care very little" about his problem with color.[70]

Making Coutela's task difficult was the fact that Monet's claims about his disordered color perception were ambiguous and sometimes contradictory. "He sees everything in yellow tones," observed Coutela following this consultation. He therefore diagnosed xanthopsia, a condition caused by the ageing of the lens and often exacerbated by cataracts (and, in a posthumous diagnosis of Vincent van Gogh, possibly by substance abuse).[71] However, Monet's statement to Clemenceau about seeing only two colors, yellow and blue, had originally read "yellow and green" before Monet struck out "green" and wrote "blue," while a few days later he wrote to Coutela that he saw "yellow as green and everything else more or less blue."[72] This predominance of blue sounds more like cyanopsia, often the temporary side-effect of a cataract operation. Meanwhile, Sacha Guitry arrived at Giverny during this time of troubles, finding Monet in a dreadful state, sitting alone in his studio "with the look of a man overwhelmed by misfortune." Guitry kissed his cheek and Monet lamented: "My poor Sacha! I can't see yellow anymore."[73]

Clemenceau continued to send letters and telegrams to Giverny, offering his usual combination of morale-boosting optimism and gentle

Dr. Charles Coutela, Monet's eye doctor

reproof. "Stay calm, my sweet, furious brother," he urged. Or again: "Have a bit of patience, little baby."[74] He had become increasingly concerned about the fate of the donation of the Grande Décoration. For the past year Monet had been able to do little if any meaningful work on his canvases; meanwhile the April 1924 deadline was little more than six months hence. He therefore wrote to Coutela two days after the consultation in Giverny, pointing out that Monet needed to be "in fine fettle" for the inauguration. Would it be possible, he asked Coutela, for Monet to make the necessary corrections to his panels with vision in only one eye? If not, an operation on the left eye would be necessary. But would Monet recover from this procedure on time to work on the panels? And would he even consent to a further operation? There was, as Clemenceau tactfully pointed out, the "psychology of the patient" to consider. "The ball," he told Coutela, "is in your court."[75]

Coutela had been placed in an extremely difficult situation, and he was increasingly reluctant to play ball. He composed a long reply to Clemenceau from a "noisy café" in Saint-Flour. (This location, in the beautiful and remote Auvergne, more than three hundred miles south of Paris, was probably best kept from Monet, who already felt that the doctor's leisurely peregrinations kept him from being at his beck and call.) Coutela was fast becoming exhausted by his celebrity patient with his special demands and perhaps unrealistic expectations: a replay of the experiences of the unfortunate Louis Bonnier. "For the life of an ordinary man," Coutela wrote to Clemenceau, "the result, it seems to me, is sufficient. But Monsieur Monet needs vision for something more than ordinary life…His distance vision is good enough for the everyday citizen but not for such a man as him." In other words, the operation had been a success, but unfortunately the painter had died. In answer to Clemenceau's question, he believed an intervention on the left eye was absolutely necessary. However, Coutela had little relish for tackling the job himself. "Personally, Monsieur Monet has made me go through such agony that I decided to pass on this second eye." Yet he was willing to reconsider, he told Clemenceau, because Monet is "such a brave man" and because he liked him "despite his flashes of anger."[76]

Clemenceau therefore wrote to Monet in the middle of September, telling him bluntly: "You will not be able to finish the panels without the second operation."[77] Monet was equally blunt in return: "I want to tell you frankly and after mature reflection," he wrote on September 22, "that I absolutely refuse (for the moment at least) to undergo an operation on my left eye."[78]

THE ONE THING that could have persuaded Monet to undergo an operation on his left eye was the testimony of an artist successfully delivered from a similar plight. So it was that he wrote to the painter Paul-Albert Besnard. The seventy-four-year-old Besnard was one of the Immortals, a much-decorated artist who had served as director of both the Académie Française in Rome and the École des Beaux-Arts in Paris. Extremely well connected both socially and professionally, Besnard was known to both his fellow Immortals and, as the organizer of a recent exhibition, the Salon des Tuileries, to many of the younger generation of painters as well, many of whom had been his students in Rome and Paris. It was this social omniscience, it seems, that solicited the letter from Monet, who appealed to an "old friendship" with Besnard.[79]

"My dear Besnard," Monet began. "I have a favour to ask of you." After outlining his recent medical history—three cataract operations since January, their less-than-satisfactory outcomes, the possibility of another—he asked if Besnard knew of an artist who had successfully undergone a cataract operation to regain his color perception. He was asking Besnard, he said, because he could not trust the doctors, with their conspiracy of silence, to be candid: "The oculists close ranks and keep secret anything that suggests a failure."[80]

Besnard failed to produce evidence of a successful operation. However, Monet knew the plight of Mary Cassatt, whose eyesight began to fail around the turn of the century, when she was in her mid-fifties. She had been diagnosed with cataracts in both eyes in 1912, the same year that Monet received his own diagnosis. By 1923 she had undergone five operations, all without the slightest improvement. René Gimpel, who visited her in the spring of 1918, following her first three operations, observed: "Alas, the great devotee of light is now almost blind." He reported her sorry condition to Monet a few months later "and I sensed an old man's indifference."[81] Monet's indifference might have been explained by the fact that in 1918 his eyesight was causing him fewer problems. In the event, he appears not to have approached Cassatt for advice, despite mutual friends such as Gimpel and the Durand-Ruels. The failure of her operations would have done little for his confidence, and she certainly could not be counted among the success stories that he was desperately hoping to find. In the absence of such evidence, he was more determined than ever not to submit himself yet again to Dr. Coutela's knife.

By the end of September, fearing for the fate of the panels and losing all patience, Clemenceau started exerting pressure on Monet to undergo another operation. Letters flew back and forth between Belébat and Giverny, with Clemenceau advocating further surgery and Monet replying with letters that were, in Clemenceau's words, "nothing but one long groan."[82] In the midst of this impasse, Monet did what he always did when he reached the deepest fathoms of a crisis: he took up his brushes and began painting. He was assisted by a new pair of German spectacles that arrived in October. "To my great surprise," he informed Coutela, "the results are very good. I can see green and red again and, finally, a feeble blue."[83] As he began working frantically toward his April deadline, determined to finish the panels on time, Clemenceau was relieved and delighted. "How happy I am, my dear friend, to know that you are hard at work! That's the best possible news... Your good ship sails again. Navigate well. It's foggy here, but the important thing is to have the sun in your heart."[84]

Two weeks later, in the middle of December, Clemenceau and Coutela made their way to Giverny to present Monet with yet another pair of spectacles. On their return to Paris they were injured in a road accident when the Rolls-Royce, swerving to avoid an automobile braking ahead of them, collided with a tree. Clemenceau, who always sat in the front seat, suffered lacerations to his face, lost a lot of blood, and was taken with Coutela, likewise injured, to the hospital in Saint-Germain-en-Laye. They were released that evening after receiving stitches. Clemenceau wrote jovially to Monet that it was a "poor excuse for an accident" and that he would try to do better next time. A day later he signed off another letter—unwisely tempting fate—"Until the next catastrophe."[85]

CHAPTER NINETEEN

THE SOUL'S DARK COTTAGE

AT ELEVEN FIFTY-EIGHT A.M. on September 1, 1923, a deadly earthquake struck the Kanto region around Tokyo. It was followed by raging fires that turned the imperial capital into, in the words of an eyewitness, "a sea of flame."[1] As many as 140,000 people perished in the disaster. Among the dead, according to French newspaper reports, was Kojiro Matsukata.[2]

Rumors of the tycoon's death turned out to be greatly exaggerated, but the dreadful scale of the destruction wreaked on one of France's allies—a nation "that was by our side in our days of struggle," as the Chamber of Deputies somberly declared[3]—spurred the French into sympathetic and charitable actions. Prime Minister Millerand sent his condolences to Emperor Yoshihito, while the mayor of Verdun, hitherto the world's most famous devastated city, sent his condolences to the Japanese ambassador. A "*gala japonais*" was held at the Hôtel Claridge, aid parcels were collected for shipment to Japan courtesy of a women's group headed by Madame Poincaré, and box office receipts from art exhibitions and cinematographic performances were allocated to disaster relief. The Théâtre du Colisée showed a series of documentary films on the principal sights of Japan, with the receipts of its matinee performances earmarked for the many thousands of injured and homeless.

Few could have been surprised, then, when early in January 1924 an exhibition for the benefit of the victims of the earthquake opened at the Galerie Georges Petit in Paris. Curated by Matsukata's friend and advisor Léonce Bénédite, it was entitled *Claude Monet: Exhibition Organized for the Benefit of the Victims of the Catastrophe in Japan*. The exhibition featured some sixty of Monet's paintings, including *Women in the Garden* as well as all of those owned by Matsukata and destined for the

Art Pavilion of Pure Pleasure. The exhibition was certainly a timely and appropriate gesture, as a reviewer for *Le Rappel* commented: "Claude Monet has many admirers throughout the world, but especially among Japanese artists. Was he not one of those who revealed to us the beauty and originality of the painters and engravers of the Far East, of whom he was a devoted worshipper?"[4]

The only person surprised by the exhibition, it turned out, was Monet himself. "Just think," he fumed to Geffroy, "this Bénédite said nothing to me about this exhibition, he didn't even consult me, as if I no longer mattered. What an oaf."[5] Learning of the exhibition only a few days before the opening, he immediately appealed to Clemenceau, who in turn appealed to Paul Léon. Monet was outraged by the fact that, in loaning the paintings from Matsukata's collection, of which he was custodian, Bénédite proposed to put on public display two large decorative panels, examples of the Grande Décoration. "The plain fact is," Monet wrote to Bénédite, "that you failed in your duty as soon as you decided to stage this exhibition without first informing me. Not that I would have refused, of course, but above all I would have begged you, for the reasons that you know, not to exhibit the two decorative panels."[6]

Monet's reaction was quite understandable. One of the decorative panels in question was the fourteen-foot-wide wide canvas that Matsukata had purchased on his visit to Giverny in 1921, the other the six-and-a-half-foot-square *grande étude*, *Water Lilies*, for which he reportedly paid 800,000 francs a year later. A showing of such paintings would preempt the opening of the Musée Claude-Monet, which, if all went well, would take place in the spring. Monet was no doubt especially anxious for the removal of the larger of the two paintings because it was a study for (even perhaps a version of) the massive composition, *Reflections of Trees*, destined for the second room of the Musée Claude-Monet: a dark and even disturbing vision whose unsettling impact at the Orangerie would be offset by this rather casual preview. Adding insult to injury was the fact that this large canvas had been hung upside down—a gesture that, however unintentional, may have brought back bitter memories of how, when the bankrupt Ernest Hoschedé's collection was auctioned in

1878, some of the Impressionist paintings were deliberately hung upside down to emphasize their supposed unintelligibility.[7] Intervention by Paul Léon, Bénédite's superior, saw the removal of the fourteen-foot-wide painting from the exhibition, but the other work, the 1916 *grande étude*, remained on show.

Readers of the journal *Revue des Deux Mondes* were likewise offered a sneak preview of the Grande Décoration. In the middle of January, the art historian Louis Gillet came to Giverny to visit Monet and see his paintings. Two weeks later, he whetted his readers' appetites for "*la grande décoration* on which Claude Monet has been working in secret for eight years."[8] It would be, he claimed, Monet's major work, more spectacular even than the landmark waterscape exhibition. "It had seemed," he declared with reference to this 1909 show, "that the art of painting could go no farther." But of course Monet had dared to go even farther. During the war, Gillet informed his readers, the master "resolved to risk more than ever, and to pit his Impressionism against the great monumental art of Delacroix and Puvis de Chavannes." He described Monet's increasingly solitary life, his shredded canvases, and how, in order not to lose a minute, he summoned the local barber to cut his hair as he worked at his easel. Gillet then dramatically announced that the massively ambitious project had been completed and soon could be seen in all its glory: a "vast circle of dreams" that would "encompass with its magic touch the halls of the Orangerie."

THE APRIL OPENING date of this "vast circle of dreams" was, however, still very much in doubt. Before Christmas, Léon had asked Clemenceau how Monet was progressing. "I told him that you were at work and that I had reason to believe that all was going well," Clemenceau informed Monet. "I added that I would resume my conversation with you in a month. He seemed satisfied." As the annus horribilis of 1923 ended, Clemenceau therefore appeared to believe that all was going well: Monet was painting again, the panels would be ready for delivery in April, and the Orangerie, as Léon had assured him, would be prepared to receive them. The day after Christmas, Clemenceau had written to

Monet that the pair of them would have a talk at the end of January or early in February "in which you'll let me know your state of mind and what you've done."[9]

Clemenceau duly arrived in Giverny in early February, eager to have Monet specify a date for the delivery of the panels. The results of the meeting were inconclusive and no date was set. A month later, as the deadline loomed, Clemenceau became ever more frustrated. Monet was once more becoming discouraged after "slaving away" for months on end and, in his opinion, achieving nothing worthwhile due to the poor state of his vision. "Life is a torture to me," he wrote in his familiar refrain to Coutela. He added forlornly: "I am Bernique."[10] The reference was to a song from his youth, Gustave Nadaud's "Mon ami Bernique," a popular song that described a man whose hopes and plans—to practice law, seduce women, make a fortune from wine, travel to America, inherit money—all come to nothing.

Clemenceau was treading a delicate line, impatient for Monet to relinquish his canvases but conscious that, in his present condition, he must not be placed under too much pressure. He wrote him an affectionate letter at the beginning of March, addressing him as "my dear old nutcase" and praising his decorations, "la Création Monétique," as "the most prodigious assembly of observation and imagination." He tried to buck up his spirits by pointing out, quite rightly, that Monet had always thrived under adversity: "Your life has been spent between successive crises and dealing with hostile reactions to your work. These are the very conditions that have made your triumphs possible." These same adversities now came to him in the form of an "overworked retina." And indeed, despite his impaired sight, he had managed to create, Clemenceau assured him, "a consummate masterpiece,"[11] yet another example of his triumph over disaster and misfortune. Monet, however, could not agree that his recent work was any good, and it became increasingly obvious that the panels would not be delivered by April.

At this point, Monet's stress and frustration at his impaired vision and inability to paint made him unbearable for those around him. As the deadline for delivery approached, Monet seems, not for the first time, to have made Blanche's life a misery. His frequent tempers had caused her great distress over the years. Two years earlier Monet confessed to Clemenceau: "The poor Blue Angel has a hard time with me."[12] As Clemenceau wearily explained to a friend: "Monet writes me black letters…His stepdaughter weeps."[13] The weeping and the black moods seem to have reached their peak in the spring of 1924. Distraught at his impossible eyesight and failed task, and with the deadline lurching ever closer, Monet became insufferable, leading Clemenceau to write several letters gently urging him to—as he put it in one of them—stop ruffling and plucking the feathers of the Blue Angel.[14]

Clemenceau adored Blanche, constantly flirting with her through his letters to Monet, referring to himself as her "chubby little love."[15] Even more, he admired her because of her complete devotion to Monet, which was even more valuable than his own support and encouragement. "She was admirable in every way," he later noted. "She took care of him, pampered him. She watched over him as if he had been her child."[16] As Clemenceau knew, without Blanche's saintly support there could have been no Grande Décoration.

BY THE END of March, the work at the Orangerie had more or less been finished. "Work on the terrace beside the water seems to have stopped," Clemenceau reported to Monet. "I think it's done." The dogs that each spring for the past few decades had invaded the Orangerie for the Exposition Canine Internationale de Paris were exiled, in 1924, to the Grand Palais. The two oval rooms, designed to Monet's specifications, now awaited the canvases. But of course no panels were delivered. Clemenceau's request for an extension was met by prolonged silence from Paul Léon before, some months later, a postponement was agreed on. Having done everything he could, Clemenceau prepared to step back from the affair. "I think that the best service I can do for you at this point," he wrote to Monet, "is to leave you to your own devices so that you're on your own whenever you have a fit."[17]

Only a few years earlier, Clemenceau had written that the sun would never set on his friendship with Monet. However, Monet's refusal to undergo another operation, and his failure to deliver the panels to the Orangerie, put a serious strain on their relationship. Clemenceau's leisurely lunches at Giverny looked in danger of becoming a thing of the past. On April 22, two days after Easter Sunday, Clemenceau wrote a letter that revealed his frustration and disappointment, although he was as understanding and encouraging as ever. He was reluctant to come to Giverny, he said, because what Monet needed most of all was tranquillity. "So don't take for a snub what is really done out of friendship." He also dissuaded Coutela from visiting because, as he pointed out, Monet was suffering from problems other than ones with his eyesight. "You're having a moral crisis in which a crazy fear robs you of confidence in yourself. I see no other remedy than a self-examination. Criticism from others only makes you more obstinate." He ended with his usual words of exhortation: "Work patiently or angrily—but go to work. You know better than anyone the value of what you have done."[18]

But Monet could not be convinced that his recent work had any value, or that he was capable of finishing the paintings. "Clemenceau may say my last works are masterpieces," he wrote to Coutela in May, "but either he is wrong or I am." He had lost faith in Coutela, too, telling him, "I need to see you, although I'm not convinced there's anything you can do."[19] He continued to experience exaggerated colors, especially blues and yellows, although by the summer of 1924 he was complaining that he could not see yellow at all. At the beginning of June he wrote a curt letter to Paul Léon putting off his proposed visit and informing him that "at the moment it is impossible to dream of transporting the panels in question."[20]

Hope sprung eternal, however, and soon Monet's expectations were raised by the prospect of a new type of spectacles. He already possessed quite a collection, none of which he ever persisted with long enough to allow his eyes to adjust. But during a visit to Giverny in May, Coutela told him about a new development in optics, a special cataract lens made by the German firm Zeiss, a leading manufacturer of optical instruments. Since 1912, Zeiss had begun making nonspherical (or aspherical) lenses known as Katral lenses, in which the glass became progressively flatter toward its periphery, where the magnification was reduced. In 1923, Zeiss went to market with a special Katral lens specifically designed for those who had undergone cataract surgery. The lenses were difficult to manufacture and enormously expensive, but Coutela promised to acquire a pair for Monet.

Coutela was preempted, however, by the painter André Barbier, "the most enthusiastic of Monet's admirers," according to Jean-Pierre.[21] By his own account, having learned of the new development, the eager Barbier likewise informed Monet of the corrective Katral lenses, then went on his own initiative to a Zeiss representative in Paris, who referred him to Professor Jacques Mawas, an ophthalmic pathologist at the Institut Pasteur qualified to take the precise measurements necessary for prescribing the lenses. Barbier went to see Dr. Mawas, telling him that he needed the special Zeiss lenses "for an aged painter with cataracts who didn't live in Paris." Mawas responded: "It's Claude Monet." Barbier admitted that it was. Mawas then explained that he was the oculist to the painter Maurice Denis, that he was very interested in painters' vision, and that he would be pleased to visit Giverny.[22]

Accompanied by Barbier, Dr. Mawas arrived in Giverny for a lunch with Monet and Clemenceau in early July. "The Tiger gave me an icy reception," Mawas claimed.[23] Clemenceau was irritated that his friend, Coutela, had been elbowed aside by another doctor and that Barbier had taken upon himself the task of trying to revive Monet's failing eyes. Monet, however, was in a cheerful mood. Following lunch, Mawas "took the famous measurements," Barbier later wrote, "and I saw how it was a complicated affair requiring an experienced practitioner."[24]

The latest scientific advances were being brought to bear on France's most famously acute pair of eyes. The measurements included making allowances for the asymmetry of the eyes and ensuring that the lenses were centered on the pupils with their posterior faces at a defined distance from the top of the cornea. A recently invented instrument called a keratometer, a tube with a lens likewise made by Zeiss, was used to measure the diameter of the cornea and pupil.[25] Mawas would have gazed down this slender tube into Monet's eyes like an astronomer peering at the heavens through a telescope. After having the topography of his eyeballs carefully mapped, Monet showed Mawas into his studio, giving him a tour of the Grande Décoration. Mawas was by no means a disinterested observer: Maurice Denis claimed that the oculist "prefers payment in paintings,"[26] although he left Giverny empty-handed as far as canvases were concerned.

The manufacture of the Katral lenses would take several months, but in the meantime Mawas went into action, adding to Monet's growing collection of eyewear by ordering a new pair of spectacles for him from E. B. Meyrowitz, a dispensing optician in the rue de Castiglione, an upmarket street of expensive jewelers, couturiers, and wine and lingerie shops. According to a 1923 report on France's trade in luxury goods, E. B. Meyrowitz had made myopia fashionable through its selection of elegant tortoiseshell frames adorned with enamel and precious stones. "How," asked the report, "with such pretty glasses, can one not see life in tints of rose?"[27]

When Monet's new glasses arrived a few weeks later, they did help him to see much better. However, he then promptly lapsed into a depression, because—suddenly able to see properly—he was unhappily confirmed in his opinion regarding his blundering efforts with the paintbrush. He received scant sympathy when he wrote to Clemenceau, who replied sarcastically: "It's irritating for you not to be able to complain about your sight after all of your wild lamentations. Fortunately, your work 'gives poor results,' and therefore you can whine about that instead, because complaining gives you the greatest joy of your life." However, Clemenceau glimpsed signs of the painter of old stirring beneath these lamentations. He recognized that Monet's art was bound up with these sorts of complaints, and with a tortured state of perpetual self-doubt. "Keep up this howling," the Tiger exhorted, "because it is what you need to paint."[28] Or, as he wrote a few weeks later: "If you were happy, you would not be a true artist since it's necessary for your reach to exceed your grasp...Keep putting yourself in a rage every five minutes, because it stirs up the blood."[29]

Monet needed little encouragement, at least, to throw furious temper tantrums. He continued to howl and rage—though not to paint—throughout the summer and autumn of 1924. When Louis Gillet announced in September that he was coming for a visit, Monet gloomily informed him he would find "a very discouraged man" awaiting him.[30] He did not exaggerate, and Gillet became so alarmed at Monet's emotional state that he feared for what he might do to the Grande Décoration. "I am greatly frightened lest you burn those beautiful, grandiose, mysterious and savage things that you showed me," he wrote after returning to Paris.[31] There was good cause for alarm, since that autumn Monet had set fire to six canvases along with the dead leaves from his garden.[32]

Gillet's concern for both Monet's state of mind and the fate of his donation led him to write a worried letter to Clemenceau, who was fast reaching the end of his patience. "With old people as with children," he wrote sternly to Monet from Belébat, "we forgive everything we can. However, there are limits." He then catalogued the oddities, inconsistencies, and self-inflicted difficulties of Monet's approach in the years since the contract had been signed. "First you wanted to complete the unfinished parts. Though not really necessary, it was understandable. Then you got the absurd idea of improving the others." Next, with his sight rapidly deteriorating, he began painting new works, "most of which were and still are masterpieces, if you haven't ruined them. Then you wanted to make super-masterpieces—with vision that you yourself wished to keep imperfect."

Enough, finally, was enough. Clemenceau was done with cajoling. He angrily pointed out what was at stake: "At your request, a contract was drawn up between you and France in which the State has fulfilled its commitments. You asked for the postponement of yours and, with my intervention, you obtained one. I acted in good faith, and I don't want you to take me for a lackey who performed a disservice to art and to France by bowing to the whims of his friend. Not only did you oblige the State to make significant expenditures, but you have required and granted your approval for the site. You must therefore bring things to a conclusion, for the sake of both art and honour."[33]

But Monet was forsaking both art and honor. Late in 1924, or perhaps in the first days of 1925, he wrote to Paul Léon, without first informing Clemenceau, that he was canceling his donation.[34]

*

MONET HAD CLEARLY reached a point of crisis surpassing the one precipitated by the terrible struggle with his waterscape paintings almost two decades earlier. Back then, he had been infuriated by the difficulties of painting vegetation such as water lilies, shadows, and reflections on the surface of the water, as well as the bleary fathoms, all unified by the fugitive effects of light glimpsed at particular hours of the day. He was dissolving the visible and materializing the invisible, and placing his vision of this "luminous abyss" before the spectator without perspective or frame, in what Gillet called "upside-down paintings." Now, with the Grande Décoration, he was attempting all of these same feats, but on a much more ambitious scale. The size and logistics of the donation had been complicated by its dramatic enlargement from a pair of panels to nineteen, by the change of venue, and by the modification of the single room to a pair. His paintings needed to be site-specific and mindful of spatial dynamics and viewing angles—a complex yet coherent program of a sort that he had never before attempted. And he had set himself this difficult task at a time of life, what was more, when his normally robust health was faltering and his eyesight failing.

By his eighty-fourth birthday, Monet appeared to believe that he had failed at his prodigious endeavor, and that he was no longer capable of painting anything worthwhile. However, no one who saw his panels during those dark years of anguish and doubt could agree with him. Clemenceau, of course, believed he was still painting masterpieces, singling out as evidence the massive composition called *The Clouds*. This composition—a triptych that would ultimately stretch to a width of 12.75 meters (41 feet 10 inches)—must have been largely completed by 1920 because it had featured in Monet's plans for the pavilion at the Hôtel Biron. However, he must have extensively reworked the canvases over the next few years, even as his sight failed, because in the spring of 1924 Clemenceau spoke of "the panel of the cloud" as one of Monet's new creations.

Monet disagreed with Clemenceau's assessment, but the Tiger was far from alone in his opinion. Various other visitors to Giverny in

1924 were astounded by his work, including the recent efforts done while he was in the throes of despair and semi-blindness. The painter Maurice Denis, who came to Giverny in February, wrote in his journal: "Astonishing series of large water-lilies. This little man of eighty-four pulling on the wires of his window blinds, shifting his easels…And he can only see through one eye with a lens, the other is closed up. Yet his tones are more exact and more true than ever."[35] The artist and illustrator Henri Saulnier-Ciolkowski saw the paintings in 1922 and then again in October 1924, the very moment when Monet was hopelessly floundering in his slough of despond and starting to light bonfires. He wrote in amazement: "Far from having spoiled them, the old master… has developed them further."[36]

Indeed, successive photographs reveal that in these worst years of visual disturbance Monet somehow managed not only to harmonize his colors but also to create ever more subtle effects of shadow and light. The Monet scholar Virginia Spate notes that in one of the works destined for the Orangerie, *Clear Morning with Willows*, largely repainted following cataract surgery, he "created luminous sparkling shadows across the base of the three panels, aerated the water, softened and diminished the far-off lily islands so that they suggest infinite distance…and added delicate accents of clear color so that the whole painting seems to vibrate with light."[37] The three large canvases making up the *Agapanthus* composition were likewise extensively reworked (even though they had been dropped from the Orangerie scheme): forms became more abstract, depth and detail disappeared, and the colors—blues, lavenders, yellows, and pinks—became ever more subtle and nuanced.[38] Evidence that Monet was painting and repainting his canvases comes from the fact that in places he applied no fewer than fifteen layers of paint.[39]

Monet's evident aplomb with his paintbrush despite his dimming eyes and faltering body raises the question—which was, as it happens, about to be raised by a German professor named Albert Brinckmann—of what happens to a great artist as he gets old and infirm but continues to paint. In a slim volume called *Spätwerke großer Meister (Late Works by*

Great Masters), published in 1925, Brinckmann would argue that certain artists achieved powerful and distinctive styles as they grew old,
creating works markedly different from, and arguably more adventurous than, those of their youth or middle age. Donatello, Michelangelo,
Titian, Poussin, Rubens, and Rembrandt—all developed in the last years
of their lives, according to another German professor, "a sublime style"
that displayed "a deepening and broadening in form and idea" that compensated for "the natural uncertainty of vision caused by the decay of
bodily forces."[40] Characteristics of this sublime style included an increasing abstraction and an exuberantly expressive handling of paint, combined, however, with what an English critic, Kenneth Clark, has called
an "astonishing vitality of touch."[41] These innovating visions—often
scenes of turmoil and even torture—were not always appreciated during
the artists' lifetimes: J. M. W. Turner's late works were described by a
critic as the "outbreaks of a madman,"[42] while Rembrandt's enormous
Conspiracy of Claudius Civilis, painted for the town hall in Amsterdam,
was regarded as far too uncouth and disturbing to hang in such an august
setting: it was promptly returned to the artist.

Over the previous decade, Monet's paintings were undoubtedly
affected by his deteriorating vision as well as by his fierce rage and gathering gloom. Larger, bolder, more experimental, visionary, and abstract,
these canvases were manifestly different from the work of his youth
and middle age, which had already been revolutionary. Arguably, only
Michelangelo and Titian ever achieved as much, or developed as forcefully, as they worked in their ninth decades.

Where did this renewed artistic power come from? The last poem
of Edmund Waller, composed in 1686, when he was over eighty and
nearly blind, contains a couplet about wisdom and vision in old age:
"The soul's dark cottage, batter'd and decay'd, / Lets-in new light, thro'
chinks that time hath made." As the body falls apart, in other words, an
eternal light pours through. It is difficult to separate discussions of an
artist's "late work" from romantic associations of blind seers offering
up unutterable visions from beyond the threshold, or of old men raging
against the dying of the light. But it is undeniable that as his eye filmed

over and his vision slowly dimmed, Monet, "who caught and sang the sun in flight," focused ever more intently on the fleeting rays of light that he had always chased and cherished.

AS CLEMENCEAU RECOGNIZED, Monet was plagued by a moral crisis that went beyond the problems with his eyesight. His vision cannot have been so bad that he did not appreciate the quality of his new work. On some level he must have recognized that, as Clemenceau put it, "all your masterpieces were created in the midst of your complaints about them" and that the wild lamentations were necessary to his creative process.[43] His steady stream of visitors in 1924 indicates that he was certainly not shy about showing the Grande Décoration to all and sundry. Indeed, this hospitality belied his claims that he had ruined his work. Important critics like Gillet, artists such as Barbier, Denis, and Saulnier-Ciolkowski—all were freely admitted into the grand atelier to see what the master had been creating, and all were duly and sincerely impressed with the results. At the beginning of June, on the very day he informed Paul Léon in no uncertain terms that it would be impossible to ship the panels to the Orangerie, he had enthusiastically welcomed into his studio the painter Paul César Helleu and the Comtesse de Béarn. The countess was yet another example of the exotic and glamorous women who beat a path to Giverny: a fifty-five-year-old named Martine Marie-Pol de Béhague, scion of an aristocratic family and ex-wife of the Comte de Béarn. A traveler and collector, she owned paintings by Watteau, Fragonard, and Titian. She had placed the poet Paul Valéry in charge of her library, and in her home in rue Saint-Dominique she hosted concerts and salons, entertaining her guests while wearing a green wig and sprawled on a sofa covered in animal skins. Monet's doubts and fears about the quality of his work cannot have been too vivid if he was willing to invite this erudite and cultured visitor into his studio.

A large part of Monet's crisis was that he simply did not wish to relinquish his canvases while he still drew breath. Indeed, he had told Thiébault-Sisson as early as 1920 that he wished to keep these works in his studio "to the end." For the past ten years the Grande Décoration had given him a purpose in life. It had carried him through the bleak years following Alice's death, through the terrible years of the war, and through the endless difficulties with his eyesight. Without his "vast circle of dreams" awaiting his obsessive attentions, he would no longer have any function or motivation. Tellingly, the lower right-hand corner of one of the huge canvases on which he had worked for at least two years, the twenty-foot-wide panel *The Setting Sun*, remained untouched by his brush: a bare triangle of blank canvas that he could have filled in a few minutes of work but evidently chose not to. Like Scheherazade's stories or Penelope's everlasting shroud, the Grande Décoration was something that must never reach its end.

EVEN SO, MONET'S decision to cancel his donation had been a drastic step. At first he gave no hints to Clemenceau of this dramatic resolution, and in the last months of 1924 their letters were lighthearted and affectionate, with Clemenceau ribbing Monet as a "frightful old hedgehog" and Monet sending dahlias and willow herb for the garden at Belébat.[44] The week before Christmas, Monet informed Clemenceau that his sight had improved thanks to his latest pairs of spectacles, which had been prescribed by Dr. Mawas and once again dispensed by Meyrowitz. These were not yet the special Katral lenses for which he had been waiting almost six months, but in early December he reported to both Mawas and Barbier that, thanks to these new, untinted lenses, he saw colors "much better" and therefore worked with more certainty.[45] Clemenceau was much heartened. "I received your letter, which warmed my heart...I'd like to give a few kicks to the stars."[46]

His heart was not warmed by Monet's next letter, which arrived a few weeks later and undoubtedly made him wish to aim his kicks elsewhere. Early in the New Year, Monet belatedly related to Clemenceau what he had told Paul Léon: that he was retracting his donation. The letter has not survived, and it is easy to imagine the Tiger angrily tearing it to shreds. Predictably, he was furious. He wrote first to Blanche, telling her that he had received the "abominable letter" and that Monet would receive his answer by the same post. "If he does not alter his decision," he told her, "I shall never see him again."[47]

Monet was one of the few people in France in whom Clemenceau did not inspire a perpetual terror, but even he must have quailed before the anger and disappointment in the Tiger's reply. Addressing his "unhappy friend," Clemenceau made plain that he felt deeply insulted and disrespected by Monet's "foolish whim," but that by cynically going back on his word Monet had damaged himself more than anyone else. "No one, no matter how old or feeble, whether an artist or not, has a right to go back on his word—above all, when he gave his word to France." He then revisited familiar territory, emphasizing the "grandeur and beauty" of the Grande Décoration ("Everyone who has seen the panels declares them incomparable masterpieces") and how Monet's troubles were stubbornly self-inflicted because, "like a bad child," he refused to have an operation on his left eye. He concluded with the same harsh but heavyhearted ultimatum he had delivered to Blanche: "If I love you, it's because I gave myself to the person I believed you to be. If you are no longer this person, I shall continue to admire your paintings, but we will no longer be friends."[48]

CHAPTER TWENTY

"SEND YOUR SLIPPER TO THE STARS"

WHILE CLEMENCEAU, ANGRY and hurt, kept his distance in the first months of 1925, other visitors continued to arrive in Giverny. On the last Saturday in January, an automobile appeared in the village after following the meanders of the Seine from Paris. Along the journey, the two passengers had been offered through their windows brief but startling glimpses of Impressionist landscapes: beautiful parks enclosed by walls, charming country inns that looked like stage sets, barges and tugboats plying the rain-stippled waters. But so modest was the pink and green house in the rue de Haut that for a moment the men, as they climbed from the automobile, doubted they had found the right place.[1]

The two men, Sébastien Chaumier and Jacques Le Griel, were municipal councillors from the city of Saint-Étienne. They had made the 350-mile journey north in hopes of purchasing one of Monet's paintings for their museum. Like Kojiro Matsukata, they had asked Monet to make a selection for them. Unlike Matsukata, they did not have deep pockets. However, they had managed to scrape together 30,000 francs to purchase a painting from what they called "the last survivor of the masters who, seduced by divine light, wished to capture its dazzling radiance for the eyes of others."

The prospect of this visit had thrown Monet into a dreadful panic. "These people are coming in a mob," he raged, as if a swaggering band of marauders were advancing on Giverny, rather than a pair of provincial worthies. "They'll get everything dirty, they'll pillage everything." Four days earlier he had sent an urgent telegram to Saint-Étienne urging them not to come. Either it had failed to arrive on time or the two eager delegates had chosen to ignore it.

After knocking on the narrow door, Chaumier and Le Griel were greeted by Blanche, who told them in a "sweet and friendly voice" that Monet was afraid of them, that he never received visitors, and that he worked all day on his decorations for the Orangerie. "But since there are only the two of you, and since you don't look wicked, I shall search him out. I think he'll be glad you came anyway."

The two men were conducted into Monet's studio, whose walls, they noted, were covered with half-finished paintings hung closely together without frames, including ones of the banks of the Seine at Vétheuil, through which they had passed barely a half hour earlier. The furniture was modest except for a mahogany bureau on which sat an india ink drawing of Monet by Édouard Manet, a portrait of Manet by Edgar Degas, a photograph of Clemenceau, and a reproduction of a Corot painting. In the center of the room, on an easel, there sat for their appraisal the canvas with which Monet would be (as he wrote on the label in his own hand) "worthily represented in the museum of Saint-Étienne." It was a water lily painting from 1907, done on a circular canvas some two and a half feet in diameter.

Presently the master appeared on the threshold, looking as youthful, Le Griel later claimed, as in his decades-old portrait on the bureau. "Gentlemen," he greeted them, "you are welcome here. I was afraid of not being able to receive you, and I'm pleased you didn't receive my telegram." After Chaumier and Le Griel politely deplored the telegraph service, Monet peppered them with questions. Was their journey difficult? By what means did they travel? Was Saint-Étienne far away? Did their museum possess an interesting collection?

The councillors explained that Saint-Étienne could boast 200,000 inhabitants. Coal was mined in the vicinity. Ribbons and weapons were manufactured. "How curious!" exclaimed the master. Their museum, they further elucidated, was poor; however, it would greatly be enriched by Monet's canvas. They proceeded to rattle off some of the painters in their collection: Henri Martin, Hippolyte Flandrin, Dubois-Pillet ("at whose name Claude Monet nodded and smiled"), and a series of works by Alexandre Séon (at whose mention

Monet intervened: "Séon?...I don't know him"). Monet asked why the councillors had come to purchase a painting directly from the artist rather than going to a dealer but, before they could reply, proceeded to answer his own question. "The merchants sell my work at very high prices," he noted, adding: "For far more than they're worth."

The two councillors respectfully disputed this point but acknowledged that the works in the galleries in the rue La Boétie, which they had visited the day before, came with eye-watering price tags. Monet declared that he had not set foot in Paris for four years (which was not quite true). Had they seen any nice pictures there? Of course, they replied: some beautiful Monets in the Galerie Rosenberg. In that case, he declared, they must have seen Corot's *La Femme à la Mandoline* in the same gallery. "I have a reproduction," Monet told them (and, indeed, the two men had already spied it on the mahogany table). "It's one of the best paintings of the nineteenth century. It's bloody beautiful. Here is my canvas," he abruptly announced, turning to the easel. "Do you like it?"

They did indeed approve. "Who, master, could better choose than you?"

"Well, then, take it away."

"But we have no packaging," they pointed out, "and the proper administrative forms must be filled out."

"How curious," remarked Monet, "but I suppose that must be the case." He then pointed out that they could not take the circular frame, which he was keeping because it was old. The councillors protested that they would happily have it restored. "But then I would be obliged to charge you for it," Monet explained, "because it's very expensive." So they agreed on a price: 200 francs. "Ah, master," they murmured, "such a bargain."

The two men were then treated to a tour of the gardens. In the bleak depths of winter, there was little more to see than the naked branches of the rose trellises and the shriveled remnants of the water lilies tracing their black initials on the gray surface of the pond. "Ah! gentlemen, if only you knew," Monet enthused, "in summer I have such beautiful flowers! Come back this summer and you will see my garden. It's my pride and joy!"

But in their circular painting on the easel, the councillors from Saint-Étienne had already caught a glimpse of Giverny in all its vibrant glory. "On the canvas by Monet that will leave for our museum," wrote Le Griel, "it is and always will remain, despite the winters outside, an eternal feast of an ideal and dream-like springtime."

OTHER MORE CUSTOMARY visitors—André Barbier, Gustave Geffroy—also made their way to Giverny that grim winter. Then, in February, a huge automobile roared through the narrow streets. At the wheel was the painter Maurice de Vlaminck, accompanied by the critic Florent Fels. The forty-eight-year-old Vlaminck, one of the Fauves, was paying homage to the master in the same way that his friend Matisse had done eight years earlier. Like Matisse, he had regarded Monet as his guiding star, once declaring: "I owe the first great enthusiasms and the first revolutionary certitudes of my twenties to Monet."[2] His career as a painter had begun one morning in June 1900 when he and André Derain, who had met only one day earlier, took themselves off to paint at La Grenouillère, on the spot that today the Musée de la Grenouillère in Croissy calls, not without justification, the "birthplace of Impressionism." On that bright June day at the beginning of a fresh new century, Vlaminck and Derain, setting up their easels by the Seine, had been following, quite literally, in the footsteps of Monet and Renoir, and those same few square yards of riverbank might equally be called "the birthplace of Fauvism."

Monet left a memorable impression on his two visitors. Fels described him as "a proud, small old man, who dodged the obstacles in his path uncertainly. Behind the thick lenses of his spectacles, his eyes appeared enormous, like those of an insect searching for the last light." Monet told his two visitors—possibly exaggerating somewhat—that he could not see them at all. His eyesight was still poor despite his latest pair of Meyrowitz spectacles, for which, as usual, his initial burst of enthusiasm had rapidly dwindled into fits of frustration and impatience.

"For two years now, since my operation," he told them, "I have been able to see only a sort of fog in which, from time to time, certain details appear more precisely... With my eyes as they are, it is useless for me to continue painting."³

Yet Monet continued to paint. Chaumier and Le Griel had been informed that the master was toiling nonstop on his canvases for the Orangerie, and, around the time of their visit, Monet informed Louis Gillet that despite a "crisis of profound discouragement" he was struggling to bring his Grande Décoration to completion.⁴ To Pierre Bonnard he wrote that he was obsessed with his panels, that the date on which he had to deliver them was fast approaching, and that he cursed his idea of donating them to the state. He lamented to Bonnard that he would be forced to hand them over "in a deplorable state, which truly makes me sad. I make every effort to pull myself together a bit, but without much hope."⁵ He made no mention to either of them, nor to Vlaminck and Fels, that he had canceled his donation. The absence of his letters to both Léon and Clemenceau—neither of which has been located—raises the question of whether he was entirely serious about abandoning the donation or whether his threatened cancelation was simply (like so many of his letters) a plea for help, understanding, and yet more time.

A VISIT THAT spring caused Monet even more anxiety than that of the municipal councillors from Saint-Étienne. On March 22, a cool day with showers and sleet, Clemenceau made his first trip to Giverny since the breach. He had preserved a long silence throughout January before writing to Blanche in the middle of February to report that he would have nothing more to do with "this unhappy affair."⁶ A few days later he wrote to Monet himself, more in sorrow than in anger: "It's true, my dear friend," he told him, "that I hold against you the fact that you've harmed yourself and thereby hurt your friends. But I did not stop admiring and loving you as always. Even in the state of distress into which you've put yourself, I wanted to help you, and I would continue to do so if you had made it possible. I respect your scruples, but I see the effect of an unhealthy state of mind which I cannot change."⁷ A few days later another letter, this one fruitlessly revisiting painful territory: "You made a formal commitment with me, then you broke it without even doing me the honour of telling me. So your monomania outweighs your conscience. I can do nothing, and neither can you. You created the situation. I can only accept it with a sadness I cannot describe."[8]

But Clemenceau could neither stay away from Giverny nor let the project die. At the end of February he wrote: "I'm in so much pain that I'm ready, if you agree, to make one last try. You have only to telegraph me your answer. But if you feel your decision is unchangeable, do not make me suffer the grief of an increasingly painful recommencement."[9]

These tense and crestfallen missives were not an encouraging prologue to the visit to Giverny. However, the two men agreed not to discuss the status of the donation during the visit and to keep their conversation to safer topics, such as gardens, the "horrid weather" that prevented Clemenceau's departure for the Vendée, and even the international political situation. The dismal failure of the Treaty of Versailles was evidently a happier subject for Clemenceau than the state of the Grande Décoration.[10]

Clemenceau also, no doubt, had little wish to hear about Monet's continuing problems with his eyesight. However, around the time of the visit, Monet finally received his Zeiss glasses, which had been seven or eight months in the making. At first there was little improvement. He wrote to Dr. Mawas regretting that the spectacles had not performed the miracles for which he had been hoping. He claimed that they caused blurred vision, while the subtler colors were "fragmented and distorted." Moreover, they had arrived "at a very bad time, when I was very discouraged and no longer able to believe in better results, so I did not persist with the use of these glasses." He promised to give them another try when he was in a "better frame of mind…although I am more convinced than ever that the lost sight of a painter cannot be found. When a singer loses his voice, he retires. The painter after cataract surgery should abandon painting."[11]

Monet was still in this state of discouragement when, in early May, he was struck by yet another severe blow. He had already outlived his son Jean and his stepdaughter Suzanne. Now he lost a second stepdaughter,

Marthe, who passed away suddenly in Giverny at the age of sixty-one. She had been the eldest of Alice's children and the wife of Theodore Earl Butler, who found himself a widower for the second time. Monet was badly shaken by her death. He canceled visits from friends such as Geffroy, Helleu, and Joseph Durand-Ruel, lapsing into "sadness and discouragement"[12] and maintaining a long silence that, by June, began to concern Clemenceau. The Tiger had sent his commiserations from Belébat: "I'm sorry about this sudden blow that has struck so cruelly. Our poor Blue Angel did not need this pain after so many others. There are no comforting words."[13]

Furthermore, Clemenceau was, almost for the first time, forced to confront his own failing health. He had suffered from a bad cough for much of the previous year. He summoned a doctor, Antoine Florand, from Paris, and then complained, quite ungraciously after the doctor endured the long train journey, that he was annoyed by his presence.[14] Clemenceau believed the problem was the bullet from the 1919 assassination attempt, still lodged in his chest. Then in the spring he began suffering from infections in one of his eyes followed by a heart condition that obliged him to undergo a "medical torture" in Paris.[15]

At least his relations with Monet gradually began to thaw and improve. Once again he began to look forward to lunches in Giverny. "In my case, my heart is weakening," he wrote to Monet in July. "I have only a faint pulse. I must learn to live with this, and my general way of life is not altered. However, I must take precautions. The first of them is that I must go to lunch on Sunday with Monet. This is better than digitalis and the antics of our doctors in their pointy caps."[16] Ominously, he was forced to cancel this visit to Giverny because, as he apologized, "I felt a great fatigue."[17] The Tiger's legendary energy was finally beginning to flag. Over the next few months his letters to Monet were uncharacteristically filled with references to his own poor health. In a kind of emotional blackmail, he even raised the specter of his death, halfheartedly joking that he would remain in the Vendée for a few more weeks "unless I stay there because of a final immobility." In August he informed Monet that he hoped to live long enough to see the opening of the "Salon Monet."[18]

*

THE DEATHS OF those closest to him often seemed to spring Monet into action at his easel, almost as if he believed the act of furiously painting might hold his own death at bay. The tragic passing in 1899 of his stepdaughter Suzanne Hoschedé-Butler had appeared to release something within him: a short time after her death, after having not painted for a year because of his disillusionment with the Dreyfus Affair, he produced a dozen views of his Japanese bridge and then scores of canvases of London. Likewise, the death in 1914 of his son Jean, harrowing as it was, shook him from the long depression into which he had fallen after his beloved Alice died. The Grande Décoration was conceived and started within months of Jean's funeral.

Monet's most startling reaction with his paintbrush had been at the deathbed of his first wife, Camille. She died in Vétheuil in September 1879, after horrendous sufferings. Monet was, quite naturally, devastated. But as he told Clemenceau many years later: "I found myself with my eyes fixed on her tragic brow, in the act of automatically studying the succession and duration of fading colours that death came to impose on her motionless face. Shades of blue, yellow, grey, what have you."[19] He began a rapid sketch of her postmortem features, and the result was *Camille Monet on Her Deathbed*. The act showed him painting, quite literally, in the face of death. If today his act seems callous, it must be put in the context of a time when families photographed themselves posing with their deceased loved ones, and when John James Audubon, early in his career, made money by painting deathbed portraits and, on one occasion, having his subject—a minister's son—exhumed for the purpose.[20]

The sudden death of Marthe yet again seemed to send Monet eagerly to his brushes and paints. "It's a true resurrection," he rejoiced of his improved eyesight and renewed activity.[21] André Barbier claimed that he turned up in Giverny one day in May 1925 (only a few days, presumably, after Marthe's funeral) with a collection of colorful specimens: exotic butterflies, seashells, minerals, and reproductions of Degas's drawings. "Monet examined all of them with joy—proving to me that he saw every nuance."[22] The new Zeiss lenses undoubtedly had much to do with this well-nigh miraculous recovery, although he was still occluding his left (unoperated-on) eye. In any case he was elated. "I've finally regained my true sight," he told Marc Elder, "which for me is like a second youth, and I have begun to work from life with a strange euphoria."[23]

Indeed, Monet claimed to one and all throughout the summer and autumn of 1925 that he was back to work "as never before" on the Grande Décoration, painting with "passion and joy" despite the uncooperative weather, which on one occasion left him completely drenched.[24] By October he had told Elder that he was putting the "finishing touches" on the paintings. "I don't want to lose a moment until I have delivered my panels."[25] To Barbier he claimed that this momentous date would finally arrive in the spring of 1926[26] — though his proposed deliveries had always been mirages that shimmered tantalizingly on the horizon before suddenly receding and evaporating like the fogs he had once painted on the Seine. Despite his claim about finishing touches, the lower right-hand corner of *The Setting Sun* still remained blank, as if Monet wished to emphasize the provisional and incomplete nature of his efforts — or perhaps because he simply could not bear to bring his labors to an end, and to let the sun finally set on his Grande Décoration.

Clemenceau was naturally delighted at this new and unexpected development, writing that he was reminded of the Monet of "the good old days."[27] "You will make a few more miracles," he wrote to him at the end of November. "I've come to believe you can do anything."[28] Yet doubts and anxieties lingered. His newfound faith in a resurrected Monet was not enough to make him resist, a month later, the pointed reminder that "I shall be happy if, as you have definitively stated, you can, in the spring, enjoy a triumph like no other."[29] A few weeks later, pressing the point home, he reiterated his concerns about his health: "I don't want to die without seeing your results."[30] He may have been exaggerating his physical plight, but he was still in poor health. He suffered from influenza throughout January 1926, for which he was treated with iodine and suction cups on his back. Around the same time he began a new treatment for his diabetes, arranging with the American ambassador to France, Myron T. Herrick, for shipments of American insulin (superior, he believed, to the French variety) to be smuggled into the country in diplomatic bags—an illegal task for which the ambassador would be rewarded, he assured him, "either in this world or the next."[31] He was given daily injections by his faithful valet, Albert Boulin.

It was, however, to be another friend that Monet lost that year. At the beginning of April, Gustave Geffroy died in his book-filled apartment at the Manufacture des Gobelins. His beloved sister Delphine had passed away a week earlier, the trauma of her death worsened by her frantic hallucinations and violent fits that exhausted Geffroy—her devoted caregiver of many years—both physically and emotionally. He died of a cerebral embolism a few days after her funeral. On April 7, at the cemetery in Montrouge, Clemenceau walked at the head of a large funeral cortège that included many writers and government officials, including the members of the Académie Goncourt and Paul Léon. "His life and his death are a great example," Clemenceau intoned at Geffroy's graveside, his voice shaking with emotion. "He struggled, he suffered, he was happy, and we must not be ashamed to say that he experienced life. His work is enough for us to judge him and to justify our admiration and our love."[32]

That morning Clemenceau had written to a friend: "I leave in a few minutes to bury a part of my past. I shall be seeing too many friends who are dead without being in the cemetery."[33] Although Monet no doubt qualified for this unflattering description, his poor health prevented him from joining the mourners in Montrouge. By the spring of 1926 it had become clear that he was in a worse state than Clemenceau. He was fatigued and suffering from pains successively diagnosed as intercostal neuralgia and gout. "I suppose that your doctor had to ban your little glass of Schnick, which will make you curse," joked Clemenceau.[34] Monet also suffered for several months from tracheitis, which made it difficult for him to eat, drink, and smoke.

Visiting Monet in April, shortly after Geffroy's funeral, Clemenceau found him in decline. "The human machine is cracking on all sides," he reported to a friend. "He is stoical and even cheerful at times. His panels are finished and will not be touched again, but he's unable to let them go. The best thing is to let him live day by day."[35]

Clemenceau knew by this point that the "Salon Monet" would open only with the death of the artist. At some point in 1925, Monet had assured him that he would make the donation after all, but that it would be a posthumous one. "When I am dead," he told Clemenceau, "I shall find their imperfections more bearable."[36] Clemenceau also knew by this point that Monet's death could not be far off. The painter no longer possessed the strength to walk around his garden, the expense of which was so great that he began contemplating giving it up. Such a measure would have been drastic and agonizing, since his garden, unlike painting, gave him nothing but pleasure. The company of Clemenceau, however, had temporarily raised his spirits during the visit that April. "I reminded him of the times of our youth, and this cheered him up. He was still laughing when I left."[37]

MONET CONTINUED TO receive visitors. On a May afternoon humming with bees, Evan Charteris arrived to interview him for a book on John Singer Sargent. Charteris, the future chairman of the Tate Gallery in London, found the painter "conversing in his garden with two devout visitors from Japan, who presently took their leave with reverential obeisances." Charteris was impressed with the painter's vitality. "The vigour of his voice and the alertness of his mind pointed to an astonishing discrepancy between constitution and age. He struck a visitor as at once gay and kindly, keen in his wit, and emphatic in his prejudices." Even Monet's occluded left eye and thick Zeiss lenses did not detract from his impression of alert and responsive acuity. His right eye, "magnified behind the lens of powerful spectacles, seemed to possess some of the properties of a searchlight and be ready to seize on the innermost secrets of a visible world."[38]

Around the same time, the painter Jacques-Émile Blanche, spying Monet in his garden from the chemin du Roy, was surprised by the painter's "robust appearance."[39] He was not the only one peeping over the fence at Monet. As he observed a short time later, Monet was regarded by many foreigners, especially Americans, as one of France's greatest celebrities: a figure on par with Louis Pasteur and Sarah Bernhardt.[40]

Monet in the
summer of 1926

Later that summer another visitor to Giverny, the poet Michel Sauvage, witnessed "a line of cars" filing slowly past Monet's "beflowered paradise." "Many admirers of the painter come here each day," he wrote, "among them many foreigners. They stop, look round, and would like to enter, but no visitors are received."[41]

To Louis Gillet, Monet was likewise still powerful and radiant. "Age only added to his majesty," he claimed, comparing him to the Manneporte, the massive rock formation at Étretat that he had painted so many times. He was "besieged by the waves and assaulted by storms" but still defiantly standing.[42]

Yet no matter how impressive the figure he cut, by the summer of 1926 Monet was rapidly losing weight as well as strength. In June he was too unwell to attend the wedding in Giverny of his granddaughter Lili Butler to Roger Toulgouat. For two weeks he was unable to leave the house. Visits from all friends except Clemenceau, who came at the end of the month, were canceled. "He's getting old, that's all," Clemenceau bleakly observed.[43] He managed to lure him into the garden and then to eat something. A few days later Monet was well enough to entertain other visitors, the painters Édouard Vuillard and Ker-Xavier Roussel, along with Vuillard's niece Annette and her husband, Jacques Salomon, who drove the party to Giverny in a red Ford convertible. Salomon found Monet surprisingly short but admired his "magnificent head." He noted that the painter "wears thick glasses, the left eye entirely masked by a dark lens, and the other is extraordinary, as if it were hugely enlarged by a magnifying glass." Monet served his guests duck seasoned with nutmeg and treated himself—despite concerned looks from Blanche—to great swigs of white wine.

Any impression of infirmity was cast aside when Monet took his guests into the grand atelier. "On twelve or fifteen canvases two meters high by four or six wide," Salomon wrote, "are the magnificent landscapes...We moved the heavy frames around to place them in the order in which they will be exposed in the rotunda." They were, he declared, "the work of a colossus."[44] Vuillard, himself the painter of large-scale decorations, was stunned. Later, trying to explain them to a fellow painter, he was struck dumb: "It's beyond words! It has to be seen to be believed!"[45]

Blanche was still hoping that Monet would go back to work, but Clemenceau knew that the painter's work was finished and the end fast approaching. During the summer, Monet began coughing up blood. After he was X-rayed at a surgery in Bonnières, doctors were summoned from Paris, including Clemenceau's physician, Dr. Florand ("all of whose patients," the Tiger once dryly observed, "die cured").[46] Monet was given a diagnosis of pulmonary sclerosis, but "he will never know his true illness," Clemenceau wrote. "This isn't necessary."[47] In fact, the radiological exam had revealed lung cancer. The only thing that remained,

Clemenceau knew, was to keep his friend's spirits high. "What more could one ask for?" he wrote to him in September. "You've had the best life that a man could dream of. There's an art to leaving as well as to entering."[48] Or, as he had commanded him a few weeks earlier: "Stand up straight, lift your head and send your slipper to the stars. There is nothing like doing it well."[49]

MONET DIED AT noon on a Sunday, December 5. The hour was an appropriate one for his quietus. Sunday lunches had always been precious to him: a time when a bell summoned him from the water lilies to his lunch, where a glass of homemade plum brandy would be waiting on the terrace or in the yellow dining room, along with any guests who had been lucky enough to receive an invitation.

"You shall die before the easel," Clemenceau once wrote to him, "and the devil take me if, arriving in heaven, I don't find you with a brush in your hand."[50] In the event, Monet died in his bedroom, in the "museum of his admired companions," surrounded by the works of Manet, Degas, Pissarro, Renoir, and Cézanne. He died surrounded by other companions, too: his son Michel, the devoted Blanche, and Clemenceau, who for the previous few days had been poised to come from Paris at short notice, and who arrived on the morning of the fifth—supposedly barking at his chauffeur "Faster! Faster! Faster!"—on time to take his friend's hand. "Are you in pain?" Clemenceau asked. "No," replied Monet in a barely audible voice, and a few moments later, with a soft groan, he passed away.[51] That afternoon telegrams were sent to the newspapers stating that the painter Claude Monet had died at noon at his property at Giverny at the age of eighty-six, with Georges Clemenceau at his side.

On the following day, Monet's death featured on the front page of all of the newspapers, which variously extolled him as the "Prince of Light" and the "true father of Impressionism." They recapped his glorious career, covering his trajectory from the withering early reviews and the legendary winter spent eating nothing but potatoes, to his acclaim, as Le Figaro put it, as "the most illustrious representative of the

Impressionists." In *Le Temps*, Thiébault-Sisson called him *le vieux lut-teur*—the old wrestler—and noted that much of his long life had been "nothing but a fight" as he pushed painting to its limits. In *Le Gaulois*, the faithful Louis Gillet waxed poetical: "Weep, O water lilies, the master is no more who came to find upon the waves, among reflections of sky and water, the figure of life's eternal dream."

The funeral was conducted on December 8, at 10:30 on a hushed and misty morning. It was such a day as Monet had once loved to paint. As the correspondent for *Le Figaro* observed: "Normandy was dressed as her painter would have wished. In the still waters of the river vibrated the thousands of glitters of gold, pink and purple from which he had made his palette. The waters reflected a mysterious sky of pink, purple and gold, dissolving poplars, and the misty outlines of low hills. Normandy was a Monet."[52] Flowers, however, were conspicuously lacking. Monet wanted no flowers or wreaths at his funeral, supposedly having claimed it would be "a sacrilege to plunder the flowers of my garden for an occasion such as this"[53]—although the pickings would have been slim, in any case, in the first week of December. Touchingly, the local schoolchildren wished to lay flowers on the coffin as a tribute to "the departed artist," but Monet's wishes were respected to the letter.[54]

Automobile after automobile loomed out of the Givernian mist that morning, conducting friends from Paris. The procession along the narrow road from the house to the church was led by the mayor of Giverny. The maplewood coffin was borne on a small handcart with a fringed canopy decorated with stars. Two of Monet's gardeners pulled the cart while a pair of others pushed from behind, "using the same gestures," as one correspondent observed, "with which they carried out their daily chores."[55] All of them were dressed, as Monet had commanded, in their work clothes. The coffin was draped with a violet cloth decorated in a floral pattern of forget-me-nots, periwinkles, and hydrangeas. The undertaker had been about to cover it with the traditional black cloth when Clemenceau intervened and protested, going to the window and tearing down the floral-patterned curtain. "No black for Monet," he said in a quiet voice, shrouding the coffin himself.[56]

Monet's funeral procession, December 8, 1926

Clemenceau had been angered by the crush of journalists, photographers, and curious onlookers outside Monet's house, a reaction
put down by one of the interlopers to the intensity of his grief.[57] Too
exhausted, grief stricken, or harassed to walk the half mile to Sainte-
Radegonde, he followed the creaking procession in his chauffeur-driven
automobile. Outside the church, leaning on a cane, tears in his eyes
and hands trembling, he joined the other mourners. Blanche and the
other women were veiled in crêpe. The men bowed their hatless heads
as they gathered around the rectangle of freshly turned earth. A few
handshakes and muted greetings were exchanged. Monet had asked for
a civil service, so no priest was present, and no prayers were said or

hymns sung. "How much more beautiful is silence," as Clemenceau had once observed.[58] He was buried next to his beloved Alice, his two step-daughters, and his son Jean.

As befit a man who detested crowds and ceremonies, it was all over very quickly. After the family departed, Clemenceau stayed to watch as the coffin was lowered by the gravediggers into the ground. "Soon the graveyard was deserted," reported a journalist. "Silence and mist wrapped for the first time the man whose brushes had so often told the poignant struggle of light and shadow."[59]

TWO WEEKS LATER, another solemn ceremony took place in Giverny. This one, carried out in the absence of journalists and onlookers, was presided over by Paul Léon, two curators from the Musées Nationaux, and the architect Camille Lefèvre. Twenty-two of Monet's enormous canvases were removed from the grand atelier. They were rolled up and transported to Paris to be photographed in the Louvre before being taken to the Orangerie. There, along the swoop of walls, they would be carefully unspooled: almost ninety meters, or almost three hundred feet, of painting. The work of a colossus.

EPILOGUE

THE PRINCE OF LIGHT

IN THE MIDDLE of May in 1927, a journalist named Gaëtan Sanvoisin arrived in the rue Franklin to interview Georges Clemenceau. He was greeted at the door by a maid in a traditional laced cap from the Vendée who conducted him into a small study. In the center of the room sat a horseshoe-shaped table almost every inch of whose surface was piled with bundles of papers and pyramids of books, among which Sanvoisin spied Winston Churchill's *The World Crisis*. Above the mantelpiece hung several sketches by Impressionist painters.

"Monsieur le Président," Sanvoisin greeted Clemenceau when his host finally appeared in the study wearing gray suede gloves and a curious policeman's hat, also gray, that reminded Sanvoisin of a Tartar's helmet. "Do you wish to talk to me about Monet?"[1]

The "Salon Monet" had finally been inaugurated one day earlier in the two rooms in the Orangerie. Clemenceau had been present for the occasion in the company of Blanche and Michel. "The Monets created the greatest effect," he had written to a friend. "It's a new kind of painting."[2] But to Sanvoisin he was more guarded, informing him that he did not want to speak about Monet, having little desire to put his thoughts and opinions on art before the public. He was easily enticed into revelation, however, and for the next few minutes he regaled his visitor with tales of how he had known Monet in the days when he was too poor to buy pigments, how buyers who spurned Monet's early works were later eager to part with huge sums for them, and how Monet had not wanted to relinquish his Grande Décoration until he was dead, because only at that point would he be able to bear their imperfections.

Mention of imperfections sparked a memory in the mind of Sanvoisin, who had also attended the opening at the Orangerie. "Did

Clemenceau at the opening of the Monet galleries at the Orangerie, May 1927

you notice, Monsieur le Président," he inquired, "that one of the canvases bears a long gash?" Indeed, several visitors to the first room had
noticed a distinctive scar on the rightmost section of *Morning*, one of
the canvases in the first of the two oval rooms.

"A slash from his knife," replied Clemenceau. "Monet attacked his
canvases when he was angry. And his anger was born of a dissatisfac-
tion with his work. He was his own greatest critic!" He explained that
Monet had destroyed more than five hundred canvases in his quest for
perfection.

"There are those, Monsieur le Président, who fear that these works
will not stand the test of time."

Clemenceau studied Sanvoisin, suddenly forlorn. "Perhaps," he
replied. He went on to explain that Monet had used the most expensive

THE PRINCE OF LIGHT

materials, but that he could not vouch for their quality, and anyway, no painting could withstand the depredations of time. "I went to the Louvre yesterday and saw the *Mona Lisa* again. She has changed a lot in fifty years."

Sanvoisin was voicing the fears of one of the curators at the Luxembourg Museum who a few months earlier had speculated that Monet's "hastily applied colours," blended in "dangerous mixtures," might be difficult to preserve.[3] In fact, there was little reason to fret about Monet's canvases. Despite their gossamer appearance, his paintings were not painted with "dew and the powder of butterfly wings," as the curator joked, but with tried-and-trusted pigments that Monet—a man obsessed with "the chemical evolution of colors"[4]—bought from specialist suppliers.

In fact, it was Monet's deteriorating reputation rather than his deteriorating canvases that brought the forlorn expression to Clemenceau's face. It had not escaped his notice that what was officially known as le Musée Claude-Monet à l'Orangerie des Tuileries had opened to little fanfare. By contrast, two days later, in New York, the *Panthéon de la Guerre* would be inaugurated in Madison Square Garden before a crowd of 25,000 people and a live radio broadcast. Monet received no such attention. Clemenceau observed bitterly that a sign announcing a dog show in another part of the building (for the growling canines had returned to the Orangerie) was much more prominent than the sign announcing the inauguration of the Musée Claude-Monet.

A number of respectful and flattering reviews appeared, to be sure, such as the one in *Le Populaire*. It praised the canvases as a summation of the master's aesthetics that revealed "the penetrating intensity of his vision and the tremendous flexibility of his brush technique."[5] But other reviews were less than complimentary. "The work of an old man," pronounced the *Comoedia*, France's most important daily arts newspaper. "One senses the fatigue," sniffed *Le Petit Journal*.[6] The painter Walter Sickert complained that they were too big, while even before they were marouflaged to the walls of the Orangerie an assistant curator at the Luxembourg Museum—Robert Rey, nominally in charge of looking

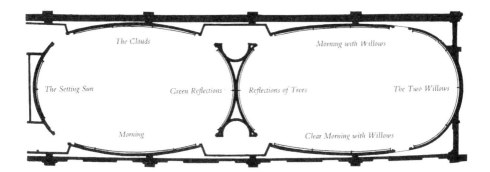

The Clouds — Morning with Willows — The Setting Sun — Green Reflections — Reflections of Trees — The Two Willows — Morning — Clear Morning with Willows

Original plan of the Monet galleries at the Orangerie

after these works — summarily dismissed them: "For me this period is no longer Impressionism, but its decline."[7]

The history of French art was filled with Ozymandias figures. As one of the prime examples, Jean-Louis-Ernest Meissonier, had observed: "Many people who had great reputations are nothing but burst balloons now."[8] Even before Monet was laid to rest, it appeared that his balloon might be about to burst and that, like Meissonier, he would pay for the fabulous success of his lifetime with scorn and obscurity in the hereafter. Some of the obituaries had been all too eager to point out his supposed shortcomings, along with those of Impressionism in general. One of them reported that Impressionism was "a doctrine against which a generation reacts with good reason," while the obituary in *L'Écho de Paris* took Monet to task for creating in his "long and peaceful old age" paintings that were nothing more than "scattered bits of fairy gossamer. We prefer the surprising feats of virtuosity of his youth and maturity." In 1927 a special issue of *L'Art Vivant* devoted six articles to Monet. One of them, by Jacques-Émile Blanche, was filled with damning invective: Monet's paintings were merely "postcard niceties of a certain American taste" purchased by the vulgar nouveaux riches.[9]

Several months after Monet's works had been inaugurated in the Orangerie, Jacques-Émile Blanche was at it again: "These spots, these splashes, these scratches inflicted on the surface of canvases of who knows how many square meters…a theatrical set designer with his bag of tricks could succeed in producing much the same effect."[10] Mixed in with his complaints about Monet's canvases were comments about the ugliness and sterility of the two oval rooms in which they were displayed: they had the "solemnity of the hall of an empty palace." He could not resist pointing out that few people were present in these rooms and that no one lingered for long. Viewing the paintings, he observed, was a disagreeable experience due to the lack of seats, the hard marble-like floor, and the meager light source.

Clemenceau would hardly have disputed the dearth of visitors and the poor light. More than a year after the inauguration, in June 1928, he was disappointed by his visit to the Orangerie. "There wasn't a soul there," he lamented. "During the day forty-six men and women came, of whom forty-four were lovers looking for a solitary spot."[11] In 1929 he complained that the paintings were exhibited in darkness: "On my last visit, the visitors asked for candles. When I complained to Paul Léon, I received nothing but a pale smile."[12] Another visitor compared the rooms to a dark and featureless crypt, claiming that he succumbed almost instantly to a migraine.[13]

The paintings were subjected to further indignities besides the poor light and lack of publicity. The oval rooms were used to stage other exhibitions. On one occasion, Flemish tapestries were hung in front of the paintings; at another point, water leaked through the vellum skylight and dripped down the front of the canvases. At other times, one of the two rooms was used as a storage area.[14] Such a combination of indifference, hostility, and neglect prompted Paul-Émile Pissarro, the youngest son of the painter and Monet's godson, to claim that Monet had been buried twice: once in 1926, after his death, and a second time in 1927, with the opening of the Orangerie.[15]

MONET'S REPUTATION WAS kept alive in the years following his death by his dwindling band of surviving friends. Clemenceau was to perform one final service: the publication in 1928 of a book entitled *Claude Monet:*

Les Nymphéas. It was part of the Paris-based publisher Plon's "Noble Lives, Great Works" series, whose earlier volumes included studies of such luminaries as Racine, Victor Hugo, and Saint Louis of Toulouse. A year later another faithful friend, Sacha Guitry, paid tribute to Monet by likewise placing him among the pantheon of French heroes. In October 1929 his four-act play *Histoires de France* opened at the Théâtre Pigalle in Paris. It featured inspiring episodes from French history, with actors taking the parts of Joan of Arc, Henri IV, Louis XIV, Napoleon, and Talleyrand. Guitry did not fail to include the events of Monday, November 18, 1918, when Clemenceau came to Giverny and Monet pledged to donate canvases to the state. The role of Monet was played by Guitry himself, who gave, in the words of one reviewer, a "remarkable impersonation."[16]

Clemenceau died the following month, in November 1929. In the years that followed, the critical curses fell steadily on Monet and Impressionism, and in particular on Monet's final works. In 1931 a guidebook to Paris's museums could still extoll Monet's paintings in the Orangerie as a "colorful poem of a refined sensibility" that transcended the limits of painting.[17] Yet even an old ally, Arsène Alexandre, lamented that in these last works Monet had abandoned the "direct communication with nature" found in his early paintings in favor of conveying "internal impressions." He had been the leader, wrote Alexandre, of a "frantic cult of color" whose time had come and gone.[18]

Such were the critical suspicions of Monet that a retrospective exhibition of 128 of his paintings staged at the Orangerie in 1931 began with a series of pleas and apologies. The curator, Paul Jamot, admitted that Impressionism had fallen out of critical favor among young painters and critics, "many of whom have moved beyond indifference and reached a stage of disdainful disapproval."[19] He allowed that Impressionism was excessive in exalting the sensuous over the intellectual, the eye over the brain. This emphasis had led to a reaction that sought to restore "the principles of solidity, order and composition." Jamot called this movement a *"retour classique"* (return to the classics). It had become fashionable to argue that, later in their careers, many of the Impressionists and

Post-Impressionists had actually turned for their inspiration to the firm contours of classical art. But of course Monet with his shifting fogs and shimmering prisms of light could never be counted among those who embraced the solidity and reassurance of bold, clear lines and hard-edged, simplified forms.[20]

The 1931 retrospective at the Orangerie included a small section called *Les Nymphéas*. However, the works on show consisted merely of five small canvases of the lily pond sent by Michel Monet from among the unsold works in the grand atelier. The curators evidently had no appetite to put on display any of the large-scale canvases that Monet had painted in the last dozen years of his life. Some twenty of these paintings could still be found in the studio, languishing unseen and unsold. The catalogue was dismissive of such late works, noting that Monet's problems with his eyes meant that many of the canvases consisted of "scatterings of color increasingly detached from the constraints of visual reality."[21] Reviews of the exhibition were as vicious as they were sparse, as critics took the opportunity for further swipes at the donation to the Orangerie. The two oval rooms of painted canvas resembled, according to one critic, Alexandre Benoît, "the first-class cabin of an ocean liner." The paintings of *Les Nymphéas* were, he said, a catastrophe, the "truly pitiful crowning of Monet's career."[22]

That same year Florent Fels, who six years earlier had seen (and been impressed by) these large canvases, asked a bit plaintively: "What will become of his last panels?" He praised them as "a sensual delirium of pure color"—although this sort of work, he bleakly acknowledged, did not match the "virility of design and form" demanded by young painters.[23] Indeed they did not. A year later, in 1932, the Cubist painter André Lhote, another aggressive and persistent anti-Monet crusader, claimed the Impressionist master had committed "artistic suicide" at the Orangerie, where the "soul of the Ophelia of painting is dragged down ingloriously by a shroud of waterlilies."[24]

Such criticism revealed how Monet had become a victim of the "return to order" that followed the trauma of the Great War, when there was a call in many quarters for a nostalgia-tinged, pastoral subject matter conjuring the antebellum world.²⁵ This world had been captured evocatively in Monet's wheat stacks, poplars, and riverscapes—all of which retained their commercial and critical appeal—but the Grande Décoration responded to this call neither in its hazy, high-keyed style nor in its exotic subject matter, which appeared to have little to do with rural France. For Lhote, Monet in his last decades had perversely disdained "landscapes that only begged to be copied"—the supposedly timeless views of rural Normandy—in favor of concentrating on his garden pond.²⁶

Monet may have submerged himself, in Lhote's opinion, in stagnant, florid waters. Unlike Ophelia, however, he was destined to rise from his watery grave.

IN 1949 A newspaper reported that each year Félix Breuil, Monet's old gardener, made the journey to Paris to visit the Orangerie.²⁷ Breuil had been one of the few regular visitors over the previous two decades to what, in 1952, a painter called a "deserted place in the heart of the city."²⁸

However, things were beginning to change. In the years after World War II, the Orangerie became a place of pilgrimage for many enthusiastic young Americans who wanted something different from the carefully controlled, Cubist-inspired geometrical constructions—the "virility of design and form"—that had dominated much of the previous generation of avant-garde painters. A Parisian gallerist later claimed that the American art students who came to France on the GI Bill in the late 1940s and early 1950s "all rushed like flies to one place: the Orangerie, to look at the Nymphéas by Monet, those colored rhythms with no beginning or end."²⁹ Here they found what appeared to be exuberant and spontaneous expressions, luxuriant nature abstracted into pullulating colors and visual grace.

One of these ex-soldiers studying in Paris, Ellsworth Kelly, wrote to Jean-Pierre Hoschedé asking if he might visit Giverny. The house and garden had retained much of their magical allure in the years following Monet's death, when the rue de Haut, the road running past his house, was christened rue Claude-Monet. In May 1939 the garden received the ultimate in fashion accolades when it was featured in the pages of the French edition of *Vogue*, which described it as a "paradise of flowers." The photographs were taken by none other than Willy Maywald, soon to become famous for his work with Christian Dior. But during and after the war, the property fell into disrepair. A year following the *Vogue* spread, Blanche left Giverny for Aix-en-Provence, dying in Nice in 1947 at the age of eighty-two. Following her departure, the upkeep of the house was paid for by Michel Monet and Jean-Pierre Hoschedé. The latter remained in Giverny, in the Maison Bleue, while Michel—"the solitary Michel Monet," as a newspaper called him[30]—moved twenty-five miles south to the village of Sorel-Moussel. There he lived among a clutter of Monet's unsold paintings and his own trophies from African safaris, including a pet monkey.

Kelly was deeply moved by his visit to Giverny. "There must have been at least a dozen huge canvases," he later remembered of his tour of the studio, "each on two easels. There were birds flying around. The paintings were more or less abandoned."[31] He was so impressed by the works—their vast scale, their gestural brushwork, their subtle manipulation of colors—that on the following day he produced *Tableau Vert* as an homage. Many decades later he would donate this painting to the Art Institute of Chicago, a museum in a city that had always been particularly receptive to Monet's art.

Another American studying on the GI Bill, Sam Francis—destined to become "the hottest American painter in Paris" by the mid-1950s[32]—was equally impressed by Monet's late works. "I make the late Monet pure," he proudly proclaimed at a dinner party hosted by Kandinsky's wife.[33] He became friends in Paris with the expatriate Canadian painter Jean-Paul Riopelle, one of whose paintings, *Man with Monet's White Waterlilies*, revealed the importance for him of Monet's work in the Orangerie, which he saw for the first time in 1951. In 1957 *Life* magazine called Francis and Riopelle "Monet's heirs."[34] Riopelle lived for many years in Monet country, in a house at Vétheuil, purchased in 1967 by his long-term partner and fellow painter, Joan Mitchell; almost a century earlier, the gardener's cottage on the property had been Monet's home.

Mitchell would remain there until her death in 1992 as Monet (according to one art critic) "hovered over her private landscape."³⁵

The painter Barnett Newman, an exponent of Abstract
Expressionism, was therefore not exaggerating when he claimed in 1953
that Monet's late work was of great interest to "the younger artists today."³⁶
A 1954 Impressionist exhibition at the Brooklyn Museum proved a revelation. Robert Rosenblum, a future Guggenheim curator and professor
of fine arts at New York University, noted that Monet's paintings bore
"unexpected analogies" to recent developments in modern American
painting—namely, to compelling new movements such as Abstract
Expressionism, Action Painting, and Color Field Painting. "Above all,
there are three late Monets, surely the finest group in the show," wrote
Rosenblum. "Before these iridescent canvases one thinks inevitably of
the pictorial explorations of a Rothko, a Pollock, a Guston." He observed
that these young painters, like Monet, challenged Cubist notions of
formal structure in favor of making "a cohesive work of art from
unbounded color areas, from the immediate excitement of the paint surface itself."³⁷ These connections with the Abstract Expressionists were
pointed out a few years later by an even more influential critic, Clement
Greenberg. "Monet is beginning to receive his due," he wrote in an essay
published in 1957. The influence of Monet's late paintings, he pointed out,
"is felt—whether directly or indirectly—in some of the most advanced
painting now being done in this country."³⁸ For this reason, he argued in
1959, Monet's paintings seemed "to belong to our age."³⁹

THAT MONET'S RENEWED popularity should have come about
because of the example he provided for a group of thrusting young
American artists was deeply ironic. Monet had disliked both Americans
and the work of many of his *avant-gardiste* younger contemporaries. He
was occasionally almost as dismissive of the work of the younger generation as, decades earlier, the older generation had been of him and his
friends. "I don't want to see it," he stubbornly declared of Cubism, "it
would make me angry."⁴⁰ Abstract Expressionism might have made him
even more furious.

Equally ironic was Greenberg's claim that Monet seemed to belong to the modern world of the 1950s, described by Jackson Pollock as the age of "the airplane, the atom bomb, the radio."[41] As Jean-Pierre Hoschedé wrote, Monet did not like technological progress: he was outraged by the appearance in Giverny of telegraph poles, he never made a telephone call in his life, and he "ignored the radio, even the phonograph. He never took a photograph...The cinema barely interested him...He had neither the idea nor the inclination to learn how to ride a bicycle."[42] Monet was not comfortably at home in the world of the 1920s, let alone that of the 1950s or 1960s.

It was, moreover, something of an injustice to Monet's work that he should suddenly have been celebrated because he could be ushered into the company of the Abstract Expressionists. Writing in 1971, Robert Hughes acknowledged Monet's importance to these artists of the 1950s, but called him "a prophetic figure who was much greater than what he foretold" and pointed out that "Monet did not labor for the sake of Philip Guston or Sam Francis." Or, as Hughes stressed two decades later: "You can hardly imagine Jackson Pollock's all-over drip paintings...without the example of late Monet. But the real value of Monet's work lies not in what it predicted or how it was used by later artists but in itself: its intensity and breadth of vision, its lyrical beauty and the disciplined subtlety of its address to the world."[43]

The Abstract Expressionists nonetheless taught others to see Monet with new eyes. Admiration for his intense vision and lyrical beauty was soon shared by museum directors and curators as well as by important, well-heeled collectors. In 1949, Michel Monet loaned five of the large-scale *Water Lilies* for an Impressionist exhibition at the Öffentliche Kunstsammlung in Basel—the first time they had ever left the studio or been seen by anyone but a handful of visitors to Giverny. There the enormous canvases were spotted by the arms dealer and art collector Emil Georg Bürhle, who made haste to Giverny and purchased three works, two of which he promptly offered to the Kunsthaus in Zurich. Next came American collectors like Walter P. Chrysler, the automotive heir and one of the driving forces behind the Museum of

Modern Art in New York. In 1950 he purchased the nineteen-and-a-half-foot-wide canvas simply called *Water Lilies*. Chrysler convinced the Museum of Modern Art to acquire a large-scale composition from the studio in Giverny despite the museum's director of collections, Alfred H. Barr, having scorned Monet as a "bad example."[44] When the eighteen-foot-wide painting arrived in New York in the summer of 1955, it quickly became one of the museum's most popular and beloved works. Barr performed an abrupt U-turn, suddenly hailing Monet as the grandfather of Abstract Expressionism. The painting's object label identified it as an example of a hastily coined movement: "Abstract Impressionism." After the work was destroyed in a fire in 1958, MoMA urgently purchased a replacement from a dealer in Paris, Katia Granoff, who had bought the contents of the studio in Giverny from Michel Monet a few years earlier and then began exhibiting the large canvases in her gallery. The replacement was the stunning *Water Lilies*, an immense triptych that, once installed, stretched almost forty-two feet along the wall. The rise in Monet's reputation was signaled by the fact that while MoMA had paid $11,500 in 1955, four years later *Water Lilies* could only be acquired at a cost of $150,000.

There then followed what one American collector called "a regular gold rush" in which prices for Monet's paintings of his pond seemed to increase by tens of thousands of pounds per week.[45] Monet even got the seal of approval from Joseph Pulitzer III, one of America's most passionate and discriminating collectors of modern art. He displayed his six-and-a-half-foot-wide *Water Lilies*, in keeping with its aquatic theme, in the pool house of his St. Louis mansion—thus fulfilling René Gimpel's prophecy, made decades earlier, that the paintings would make good decorations for a swimming pool.

IN 1952, AS the enthusiastic American artists were gathering in its two oval rooms, the painter André Masson, an important influence on Pollock, called the Orangerie the "Sistine Chapel of Impressionism." In words that must have cheered Sacha Guitry, who in that same year rereleased *Ceux de chez nous*, Masson called these huge canvases "one of the summits of French genius."⁴⁶ However, the official ambivalence and neglect of Monet's paintings persisted. In August 1944, during the liberation of Paris, the Orangerie narrowly escaped destruction when five artillery shells fell on the building, damaging *Reflections of Trees*, on the entrance wall of the second room. Such was the official indifference that the shrapnel would not be removed for another twenty years.

By that point the paintings had been subjected to further indignities. In 1966, 144 paintings from the Jean Walter–Paul Guillaume collection—a treasure trove that included ten Matisses, a dozen Picassos, sixteen Cézannes, and twenty-three Renoirs—were unveiled in a newly built extension to the Orangerie, one constructed directly above Monet's elliptical rooms, which found themselves encased beneath slabs of concrete. The natural light, such as there had been, was abruptly extinguished. Works intended to show the delicious vibrations of color, weather, and the subtle alterations of sunlight were relegated to a basement, under artificial illumination. For the next thirty years the *Water Lilies* canvases were effectively entombed in this gloomy cellar.

Finally, in 1996, France's Ministry of Culture and Communication decided to redevelop the site in order "to rethink the museographical articulation" between the Walter-Guillaume collection and Monet's *Water Lilies*.⁴⁷ The Orangerie closed its doors in January 2000, supposedly for eighteen months, although in the end the construction, which cost $36 million, exhausted six years of work. Too fragile to be removed from the walls, Monet's paintings were hermetically sealed inside reinforced boxes with security alarms, protected by polyester film, and maintained at a constant temperature and humidity. After demolition began in February 2003, they occasionally beeped in distress, like agitated ICU patients, when vibrations from the jackhammers exceeded safe levels. When the doors reopened to the public in 2006, the "museographical articulation" between the two donations had indeed been rethought: Monet's *Water Lilies* paintings were now in pride of place, bathed in natural light, while the Walter-Guillaume collection went to an annex.

Today, Claude Monet's house, gardens, and paintings are some of France's greatest tourist attractions. Each year, some 600,000 people

visit his house and garden in Giverny, many now departing from the
Gare Saint-Lazare on the special "Train de l'Impressionnisme" launched
in 2015 by the SNCF, France's national railway company. Its route
through the Pays des Impressionnistes passes many of Monet's old
painting grounds and retraces the dozens of journeys he took back and
forth from Paris to Giverny and Rouen. Meanwhile, almost a million
people visit the Orangerie, making it not the deserted place deplored by
Clemenceau and Masson but an attraction for which one often has to
join a lengthy queue.

The experience of the two elliptical rooms—at once immersive,
interactive, and contemplative—is certainly worth the wait. The first
thing we see as we pass through an antechamber and enter the first room
is, on the far wall, *Green Reflections*. It is arguably the most beautiful of
all the paintings in the Orangerie. From a background of brilliant blues
and deep greens leap bright blossoms of water lilies: flames of burgundy
and yellow, amaranthine tongues, flashes of salmon pink—what seem to
be dozens of distinctive colors all delicately harmonized. So brilliant is
the performance here that one suspects Monet must indeed have been
going blind if, in the terrible years of 1923 and 1924, he doubted the
worth of what he was doing on canvases such as these.

The paintings along the room's lateral walls are *Morning*—the victim
of the knife attack—and *The Clouds*, the panel that amazed Clemenceau,
filled with reflections of rococo-style cotton-candy cumulus billows.
The compositions are spectacular in size: wraparound art so enormous
they could astonish even a veteran painter of large-scale canvases such as
Édouard Vuillard. Mirbeau wrote in 1889 that Monet's works sometimes
took sixty sessions, but here the quantity of paint, variety of brushstrokes, and sheer square footage make it possible to imagine the panels
consuming hundreds, even thousands of hours. We can imagine the old
man in his vast studio, prodding, slashing, scribbling. Layer upon layer
of paint is added as cigarettes burn to ash and rays filtered through the
skylight sneak across the floor. He stands back at the end of the day, in
eye patch and thick spectacles, to appraise the work with dimming eyes
as Blanche trundles it across the floor, the two of them perhaps slowly

promenading (as all visitors do) along the reams of canvas, staring into their florid depths.

From this close range we can see how the paintings were not fashioned from dewdrops and the powder of butterfly wings. The paint is thick, textured, even encrusted in places, with the brushstrokes broad and bold, at times added in the controlled *automatiste* frenzy that so impressed Masson and influenced other painters such as Pollock and Riopelle. And yet from these dense layers of impasto come, incredibly, the most delicate effects of light and form, such as the calligraphy of crisscrossing lavender and violet that creates the ruffled waters in the center of *Morning*, or the undulant swipes of the paintbrush, charged with a mix of green and yellow, with which he created the water lilies floating on top of the reflections of willow branches in *The Setting Sun*—the sulfurous vision on the entrance wall.

Intriguingly, the lower right-hand corner of *The Setting Sun* remains blank but for a few swipes and squiggles, as if to emphasize that this giant canvas is unfinished and, like the other compositions, still awaits the master's further ruminations. Yet the rest of the canvas's 125 square feet have been painstakingly and emphatically painted. The reflection of sunset on water is created with thick slatherings of cadmium yellow in which we see the imprint of Monet's brush and thick gobs of paint that seem to have been squeezed straight from the tube. The result, as we stand back, is the hot glare of sundown spreading its molten light across a peaceful pond. "To create impalpable matter from canvas and paste," an art critic wrote of Monet's works in 1922, "to trap the sun, to focus and diffuse its light. *Quel miracle!*"[48]

With our backs to the fiery glory of *The Setting Sun*, we are entranced by keynotes of tender blues, woolly pinks, spongy greens. The first room appears, from this perspective, as a place of calm and quiet meditation, the haven for neurasthenics of which Marcel Proust had dreamed more than a century earlier. But a new note strikes as we pass through the gracefully arching doorway and enter the second room. Here, three of the compositions are flanked by the graceful curves of truncated willow trees showering their branches in fragile, flickering cascades as they gather us in a sweeping embrace. They are, as Monet intended, symbols of mourning. Not merely honoring—as he had first envisaged on that long-ago November day—the glorious dead of the Grand Guerre, they mark an apotheosis of mourning. It is not difficult to see in them the commemoration of all those whom Monet had lost, from Alice and Jean to Mirbeau and Geffroy, in those years of anguished struggle.

The panels become even more acutely personal as we turn around and see on the entrance wall of this second room the darkest and most unsettling of the compositions: *Reflections of Trees*, the wounded, bomb-scarred canvas. As Paul Hayes Tucker has pointed out, this composi-tion—"dark and haunting...if not slightly disturbing"—is very rarely reproduced because of its gloomily unnerving qualities.[49] It offers what is undoubtedly Monet's most disquieting vision, a sharp rejoinder to those who might still think of him only as "the great anti-depressant" churning out dappled riverbanks and sun-kissed meadows. The lily pads glow an eerie radium blue, their blooms like candles—like the lanterns of Rollinat's hobgoblins—against the creep of shadows and the last fall of light. The colors shimmer and seem to float from the wall.

In the midst of this gently fluorescing twilight, at the joining of the two canvases, we see an indistinct silhouette: the sinuous apparition of a willow glimpsed upside-down in reflection, a liquid shadow wreathed in clouds of blue lily pads. Its bifurcated trunk forms an anguished human body, even perhaps a drowned shape passing through the shadowy fath-oms. If the other walls of this room speak to us of sorrow and loss, in this wraithlike afterimage we feel the painter's rage and suffering but also his defiance and resilience. Monet did not believe in God, but he believed in the sanctity of nature, and the forked creature formed by the willow sug-gests a calvary. It brings with it the promise of resurrection and renewal, of a "sea-change / Into something rich and strange."

Reflections of Trees is the most emblematic of all the paintings of those long years of toil and trouble: the self-portrait of a man who, like golden-haired Hylas, was irresistibly drawn into the luminous abyss of the lily pond.

ACKNOWLEDGMENTS

I AM GRATEFUL to everyone who assisted me over the course of my research and writing. I'm extremely thankful, as always, to have George Gibson as my editor and publisher. His editorial acumen and patient advice are much appreciated, as is the friendship that now stretches back over five books and more than fifteen years. George was part of this book from conception through publication, and he was never too busy—despite being the busiest person I've ever known—to discuss the most abstruse details or to ponder how they fit into the larger picture. His many strokes of the pen and thoughtful injunctions improved the manuscript immeasurably.

My other huge debt is to Paul Hayes Tucker. Despite a hectic schedule and numerous other commitments, he responded to my queries and then generously read the manuscript in full. Over the course of his career, Dr. Tucker has enlarged and deepened our understanding of Monet's life and work through both his books and the major exhibitions he has curated. Particularly important for me was *Monet in the 20th Century*, which I saw at the Royal Academy in London in 1999. My well-thumbed and much-pored-over copy of his catalogue for this exhibition was—like his 1995 biography of Monet—never far from my reach as I worked. I was truly privileged to have him offer his expertise, and to suggest refinements, nuances, and outright corrections.

Many other people responded to my pleas for help. Mark Asquith was once again among my first readers, giving the manuscript the benefit of his perceptive and quizzical attention. A good friend for the past twenty years, Mark is in many respects my "ideal reader" whose impeccable literary instincts I have come to rely on. Two other friends,

Anne-Marie Rigard-Asquith and Frederike Mulot, offered valuable advice on some of the knottier translations.

For help with other points and problems, or for supplying information, I thank Camille Bidaud (Université Paris-Est); Corinne Charlery (Archives Municipales, Chatou); Danielle Chapelin (Secrétariat de Histoire et Patrimoine de Saint-Étienne); Yann Harlaut; Mark Levitch; Claire Maingon (Université de Rouen); Bernard Rivatton (Musée du Vieux Saint-Étienne); Jean-Michel Peers; Cyrille Sciama (Musée des Beaux-Arts de Nantes); and Dieter Schwarz (Kunstmuseum, Winterthur). I also thank my friend Jean Glasel—like Monet, a Norman by inclination if not quite by birth—for giving me the opportunity to conduct a group tour to Giverny in 2010, and so to begin thinking in earnest about the stories and paintings I would begin exploring in this book.

My research would not have been possible without the prodigious collections and generous staff of two great libraries where it is always a pleasure to work: the London Library and, in Oxford, the Sackler Library. I was also the beneficiary of the technological wonder that is Gallica, the online digital library of the Bibliothèque nationale de France, which permitted me the pleasure of reading one-hundred-year-old newspapers from the comfort of the studio at the bottom of my garden in Oxfordshire.

For turning my manuscript into a book I thank the wonderful teams at Bloomsbury in New York and London. Linda Johns did a superb job of identifying and tracking down the images for the book, and Jeff Ward created all the maps. I am grateful to the painstaking attention to detail shown by Gleni Bartels; my copyeditor, David Chesanow; my proofreader, Megha Jain; and to Lee Gable for the index. For the cover of the North American edition, I was fortunate to have Patti Ratchford as my designer, and for the UK cover, David Mann. The interior was designed by Sara Stemen. I also thank, among others in the London office, Michael Fishwick, Vicky Beddow, Rachel Nicholson, Marigold Atkey, Rebecca Thorne, and Laura Brooke, and among those on the American team, Laura Keefe, Sara Mercurio, and Callie Garnett. For their efforts on my behalf in Canada, I thank the marvellous people at Doubleday with whom I've been fortunate to work for much of the past ten years: Kristin Cochrane, Amy Black, Sheila Kay, Martha Leonard, and Brad Martin.

I am indebted, as always, to my agent, Christopher Sinclair-Stevenson, who not only read the manuscript carefully—as he always does—but who also, along with his wife, Deb, is a constant source of good conversation and entertaining companionship.

The last stages of work on the manuscript were completed while I was the 2015 writer-in-residence at L'Ancienne-Auberge in the beautiful hilltop village of Puycelsi. I thank Dorothy and David Alexander for their generous hospitality, and also Danny Lewis for kindly providing me with Internet access during my stay. I would never have known of this splendid opportunity for writing and relaxation had it not been for my friend Prajwal Parajuly, a previous writer-in-residence, and I heartily thank him for recommending me. My wife, Melanie, was my fellow writer-in-residence in Puycelsi, which made the experience even more rewarding. Melanie was, as ever, a constant source of enthusiasm and encouragement for my research and writing—and equally important, a welcome and healthy distraction from it.

Finally, I thank my brothers and sisters and their families. All of us have come a long way over the past few years. Our mother, Claire King, passed away during the course of my work on this book, and she is very much in my thoughts as I finish it. I dedicate it to her in gratitude for her lifetime of humor, inspiration, encouragement, and love.

IMAGE CREDITS

INTERIOR IMAGES

Pages ix, x: maps © Jeff Ward

Pages 7, 51, 52: © Bridgeman Images

Pages 22, 28, 62, 90, 123, 134, 162, 181, 232, 244, 253, 275, 282, 288: © Getty Images

Page 221: © Archives Durand-Ruel © Durand-Ruel & Cie

PLATE SECTION

Pages 1 (top and bottom), 2, 3, 4 (top): Photograph by DeAgostini/Getty Images

Page 4 (bottom): Image courtesy Saint Louis Art Museum, funds given by Mrs. Mark C. Steinberg

Page 5: © Foundation Claude Monet, Giverny

Pages 6: Photograph by National Museum Galleries of Wales Enterprises Limited/Heritage Images/Getty Images

Page 7: Photograph by Fine Art Images/Heritage Images/Getty Images

Page 8 (top): © 2016 Succession H. Matisse/Artists Rights Society (ARS) New York

Page 8 (bottom), 9 (top), 11 (bottom): © Bridgeman Images

Page 9 (bottom): Photograph © Museum of Fine Arts, Boston. All Rights Reserved

Page 10: © Kimbell Art Museum, Fort Worth

Page 11 (top): © Musée d'Art Moderne de Saint-Etienne Métropole

Page 12: Photograph by Photo IZ/UIG/Getty Images

Page 13: © Getty Images

Page 14: Photograph by Hubert Fanthomme/Paris Match via Getty Images

Page 15: Photograph by View Pictures/UIG via Getty Images

Page 16: Photograph by Chesnot/Getty Images

SELECTED BIBLIOGRAPHY

Alphant, Marianne. *Claude Monet: une vie dans le paysage*. Paris: Hazan, 1993.

Apter, Emily. "The Garden of Scopic Perversion from Monet to Mirbeau." *October* 47 (Winter 1988): 91–115.

Archives Claude Monet, *Correspondance d'artiste: Collection Monsieur et Madame Cornebois. Artcurial auction catalogue*. Paris: Hôtel Dassault, 2006.

Avtonomova, Natalya. "Vasilii Kandinsky and Claude Monet." *Experiment: A Journal of Russian Culture* 9 (2003): 57–68.

Becker, Jean-Jacques. *The Great War and the French People*. Trans. Arnold Pomerans. Leamington Spa: Berg, 1985.

Bernier, Ronald R. *Monument, Moment, and Memory: Monet's Cathedral in Fin de Siècle France*. Cranbury, NJ: Associated University Press, 2007.

Bourguignon, Katherine M., ed. *Impressionist Giverny: A Colony of Artists, 1885–1915*. Giverny: Musée d'art Américain, 2007.

Buffet, Eugénie. *Ma vie, mes amours, mes aventures: confidences recueillies par Maurice Hamel*. Paris: Eugène Figuière, 1930.

Burke, Janine. "Monet's 'Angel': The Artistic Partnership of Claude Monet and Blanche Hoschedé-Monet." *Colloquy: text theory critique* 22 (2011): 68–80.

Butler, Ruth. *Hidden in the Shadow of the Master: The Model-Wives of Cézanne, Monet, and Rodin*. New Haven, CT: Yale University Press, 2008.

Butler, Ruth. *Rodin: The Shapes of Genius*. New Haven, CT: Yale University Press, 1993.

Carr, Reg. *Anarchism in France: The Case of Octave Mirbeau*. Manchester, UK: Manchester University Press, 1977.

Charteris, Evan. *John Sargent*. New York: Charles Scribner's Sons, 1927.

Churchill, Winston. *Great Contemporaries*. London: Thornton Butterworth, 1937.

Clemenceau, Georges. *Claude Monet: Les Nymphéas*. Paris: Plon, 1928.

Clemenceau, Georges. *Discours de Guerre: Recueillis et publiés par la Société des Amis de Georges Clemenceau*. Paris: Presses Universitaires de France, 1968.

Clemenceau, Georges. *Georges Clemenceau à son ami Claude Monet: Correspondance*. Annotated by Jean-Claude Montant. Paris: Éditions de la Réunion des musées nationaux, 1993.

Clemenceau, Georges. *Lettres à une Amie, 1923–1929*. Ed. Pierre Brive. Paris: Gallimard, 1970.

Dallas, Gregor. *At the Heart of a Tiger: Clemenceau and His World, 1841–1929*. London: Macmillan, 1993.

Dallas, Gregor. *1918: War and Peace*. London: Pimlico, 2002.

Delouche, Danielle. "Cubisme et camouflage." *Guerres mondiales et conflits contemporains* 171: *Représenter la Guerre de 1914–1918* (July 1993): 123–37.

Duroselle, Jean-Baptiste. *Clemenceau*. Paris: Fayard, 1988.

Edwards, Hugh. "The Caricatures of Claude Monet." *Bulletin of the Art Institute of Chicago* (1907–51) (September–October 1943): 71–2.

Elder, Marc. *À Giverny, chez Claude Monet*. Paris: Bernheim-Jeune, 1924. Reprint, Paris: Mille et une nuits, 2010.

Fels, Marthe de. *La Vie de Claude Monet*. Paris: Gallimard, 1929.

Flam, Jack. *Matisse and Picasso: The Story of Their Rivalry and Friendship*. Cambridge, MA: Westview Press, 2004.

Fussell, Paul. *The Great War and Modern Memory*. Oxford: Oxford University Press, 1975. Reprint, Oxford: Oxford University Press, 2013.

Gasquet, Joachim. *Cézanne*. Paris: Les Éditions Bernheim-Jeune, 1921.

Geffroy, Gustave. *Claude Monet: sa vie, son temps, son oeuvre*. Paris: G. Crès, 1922.

Gibbons, Helen Davenport. *Paris Vistas*. New York: The Century Co., 1919.

Gillet, Louis. *Trois variations sur Claude Monet*. Paris: Librairie Plon, 1927.

Gimpel, René. *Diary of an Art Dealer*. Trans. John Rosenberg. London: Hodder & Stoughton, 1966.

Golan, Romy. *Modernity and Nostalgia: Art and Politics in France Between the Wars*. New Haven, CT: Yale University Press, 1995.

Golan, Romy. "Oceanic Sensations: Monet's Grandes Décorations and Mural Painting in France from 1927 to 1952." In Paul Hayes Tucker, George T. M. Shackleford, and MaryAnne Stevens, *Monet in the 20th Century*. New Haven and London: Yale University Press, 1998, 86–97.

Golding, John. *Matisse and Cubism*. Glasgow: University of Glasgow Press, 1978.

Goncourt, Edmond, and Jules de. *Journal: Mémoires de la vie littéraire*. 3 vols. Annotated by Robert Ricatte. Preface and chronology by Robert Kopp. Paris: Robert Laffont, 1989.

Gréard, Valéry C. O. *Meissonier: His Life and Art*. Trans. Lady Mary Loyd and Miss Florence Simmonds. London: William Heinemann, 1897.

Griel, Jacques Le. "Voyage fait à Giverny (Eure) par les conseillers municipaux de Saint-Étienne qui y allèrent pour acquérir pour le musée un tableau de M. Claude Monet." *Les Amitiés Foréziennes et Vellaves* (April 1925). Reprinted, *Bulletin du Vieux Saint-Étienne* 218 (June 2005): 36–41.

Groom, Gloria, and Jill Shaw, eds. *Monet: Paintings and Drawings at the Art Institute of Chicago*. Chicago: Art Institute of Chicago, 2014.

Guitry, Sacha. *If I Remember Right*. Trans. Lewis Galantière. London: Methuen, 1935.

Harding, James. *Sacha Guitry: The Last Boulevardier*. London: Methuen, 1968.

Herbert, Robert L. *Impressionism: Art, Leisure, and Parisian Society*. New Haven, CT: Yale University Press, 1988.

Herbert, Robert L. "Method and Meaning in Monet." *Art in America* 67 (September 1979): 91–108.

Holt, Edgar. *The Tiger: The Life of Georges Clemenceau, 1841–1929*. London: Hamish Hamilton, 1976.

Hoog, Michel. "La Cathédrale de Reims de Claude Monet, ou le tableau impossible." *Revue du Louvre* (1981): 22–4.

Horne, Alistair. *The Price of Glory: Verdun 1916*. London: Macmillan, 1962.

Hoschedé, Jean-Pierre. *Claude Monet, ce mal connu: intimité familiale d'un demi-siècle à Giverny de 1883 à 1926*. 2 vols. Geneva: Pierre Cailler, 1960.

House, John. *Monet: Nature into Art*. New Haven, CT: Yale University Press, 1986.

Joyes, Claire. *Monet's Table: The Cooking Journal of Claude Monet.* New York: Simon & Schuster, 1989.

Keiger, J. F.V. *Raymond Poincaré.* Cambridge, UK: Cambridge University Press, 1997.

Kelly, Simon. *Monet's Water Lilies: The Agapanthus Triptych.* St. Louis: St. Louis Art Museum, 2011.

Kipling, Rudyard. *The Letters of Rudyard Kipling.* Vol. 5. Ed. Thomas Pinney. Iowa City: University of Iowa Press, 2004.

Levine, Steven Z. *Monet, Narcissus, and Self-Reflection: The Modernist Myth of the Self.* Chicago: University of Chicago Press, 1994.

Levitch, Mark. "The Great War Re-remembered: The Fragmentation of the World's Largest Painting." In Nicholas J. Saunders, ed., *Matters of Conflict: Material Culture, Memory and the First World War.* London: Routledge, 2004, 90–108.

Limousin, Christian. "Monet au Jardin des supplices." *Cahiers Octave Mirbeau* 8 (April 2001): 256–78.

Lyon, Christopher. "Unveiling Monet." *MoMA* 7 (Spring 1991): 14–23.

MacMillan, Margaret. *Paris 1919: Six Months that Changed the World.* New York: Random House, 2001.

Maingon, Claire, and David Campserveux. "A Museum at War: The Louvre 1914–1921." *L'Esprit Créateur* 54 (Summer 2014): 127–40.

Maloon, Terence. "Monet's Posterity." In George T. M. Shackleford, ed., *Monet and the Impressionists.* Sydney: Art Gallery of New South Wales, 2008, 177–89.

Martet, Jean. *Clemenceau: The Events of His Life as Told by Himself to His Former Secretary.* Trans. Milton Waldman. London: Longmans, Green & Co., 1930.

Masson, André. "Monet the Founder." Trans. Terence Maloon. In George T.M. Shackleford, ed., *Monet and the Impressionists.* Sydney: Art Gallery of New South Wales, 2008. 190–91.

Matisse, Henri. *Matisse on Art.* Ed. Jack Flam. Los Angeles and Berkeley: University of California Press, 1995.

Mauclair, Camille. *L'Impressionnisme: son histoire, son esthétique, ses maîtres.* Paris: Librairie de l'Art Ancien et Moderne, 1904.

Michel, Pierre, and Jean-François Nivet. *Combats politiques de Mirbeau.* Paris: Librairie Séguier, 1990.

Michel, Pierre, and Jean-Francois Nivet. *Octave Mirbeau: l'imprécateur au cœur fidèle.* Paris: Librairie Séguier, 1990.

Mirbeau, Octave. *Correspondance avec Claude Monet.* Ed. Pierre Michel and Jean-François Nivet. Tusson: Du Lérot, 1990.

Mirbeau, Octave. *Correspondance Générale.* Ed. Pierre Michel with the assistance of Jean-François Nivet. 3 vols. Lausanne: L'Age d'Homme, 2003–09.

Mirbeau, Octave. *Le Jardin des Supplices.* Paris: Eugène Fasquelle, 1899.

Patry, Sylvie. "Monet and Decoration." In *Claude Monet, 1840–1926.* Paris: Réunion des musées nationaux, 2010, 318–25.

Piguet, Philippe. *Claude Monet au temps de Giverny.* Paris: Centre culturel du Marais, 1983.

Pilon, Edmond. *Octave Mirbeau.* Paris: Bibliothèque Internationale, 1903.

Rewald, John. *The History of Impressionism.* New York: Museum of Modern Art, 1961.

Roy, Ashok. "Monet's Palette in the Twentieth Century: *Water-Lilies* and *Irises.*" *National Gallery Technical Bulletin* 28 (London: National Gallery, 2007): 61–7.

Royer, J., J. Haut, and P. Almaric, eds. "L'Opération de la cataracte de Claude Monet:

Correspondance inédite du peintre et de G. Clemenceau au docteur Coutela." *Histoire des Sciences Médicales* 18 (1984): 109–27.

Saint-Marceaux, Marguerite de. *Journal 1894–1927.* Ed. Myriam Chimènes. Paris: Fayard, 2007.

Séguéla, Matthieu. "Le Japonisme de Georges Clemenceau." *Ebisu* 27 (Autumn–Winter 2001): 7–44.

Shackleford, George T. M. "Monet and Japanese Art." In George T. M. Shackleford, *Monet and the Impressionists.* Sydney: Art Gallery of New South Wales, 2008, 91–4.

Shackleford, George T. M., with contributions by Jonathan Mane-Wheoki, Clare Durand-Ruel Snollaerts, and Terence Maloon. *Monet and the Impressionists.* Sydney: Art Gallery of New South Wales, 2008.

Silver, Kenneth E. *Chaos and Classicism: Art in France, Italy, and Germany, 1918–19.* New York: Guggenheim Museum Publications, 2010.

Silver, Kenneth E. *Esprit de Corps: The Art of the Parisian Avant-Garde and the First World War, 1914–1925.* Princeton, NJ: Princeton University Press, 1989.

Silvestre, Armand. *Au Pays des souvenirs: mes maîtres et mes maîtresses.* Paris: La Librairie Illustrée, 1892.

Spate, Virginia. *Claude Monet: The Colour of Time.* London: Thames & Hudson, 1992.

Spurling, Hilary. *The Unknown Matisse: A Life of Henri Matisse: The Early Years, 1869–1908.* Berkeley and Los Angeles: University of California Press, 1998.

Stanley, Edward, Earl of Derby. *Paris 1918: The War Diary of the 17th Earl of Derby.* Ed. David Dutton. Liverpool: Liverpool University Press, 2001.

Stuckey, Charles F. "Blossoms and Blunders: Monet and the State." Part I: *Art in America* (January–February 1979): 102–17. Part II: (September 1979): 109–25.

Stuckey, Charles F. *Claude Monet, 1840–1926.* London: Thames & Hudson, 1995.

Suarez, Georges. *La vie orgueilleuse de Clemenceau.* Paris: Éditions P. Saurat, 1987.

Temkin, Anne, and Nora Lawrence. *Claude Monet: Water Lilies.* New York: Museum of Modern Art, 2009.

Tucker, Paul Hayes. *Claude Monet: Life and Art.* New Haven and London: Yale University Press, 1995.

Tucker, Paul Hayes. *Monet in the '90s: The Series Paintings.* Boston: Museum of Fine Arts, 1989.

Tucker, Paul Hayes. "Revolution in the Garden: Monet in the Twentieth Century." In Paul Hayes Tucker, *Monet in the 20th Century.* New Haven, CT, and London: Yale University Press, 1998.

Vollard, Ambrose. *Paul Cézanne.* Trans. H. L. van Doren. London: Brentano, 1924.

Vollard, Ambrose. *Recollections of a Picture Dealer.* Trans. Violet M. MacDonald. Mineola, NY: Dover, 2002.

Vollard, Ambrose. *Renoir: An Intimate Record.* Trans. Harold L. Van Doren and Randolph T. Weaver. New York: Alfred A. Knopf, 1925.

Watson, D. R. *Clemenceau: A Political Biography.* London: Eyre Methuen, 1974.

Wildenstein, Daniel. *Claude Monet: Biographie et catalogue raisonné.* 5 vols. Lausanne-Paris: La Bibliothèque des Arts, 1974–91.

Wildenstein, Daniel. *Monet, or the Triumph of Impressionism.* Cologne and Paris: Taschen, 1996.

Williams, Wythe. *The Tiger of France: Conversations with Clemenceau.* New York: Duell, Sloan & Pearce, 1949.

Zeldin, Theodore. *France 1848–1945: Politics and Anger.* Oxford: Oxford University Press, 1979.

NOTES

CHAPTER ONE: THE TIGER AND THE HEDGEHOG

1   *Gil Blas*, April 26, 1914. All translations, unless otherwise noted, are my own.

2   *Gil Blas*, February 23 and May 6, 1912.

3   *Gil Blas*, September 7, 1909. For Clemenceau's house and garden in Bernouville, see Gregor Dallas, *At the Heart of a Tiger: Clemenceau and His World, 1841–1929* (London: Macmillan, 1993), p. 442.

4   Marc Elder, *À Giverny, chez Claude Monet* (Paris: Bernheim-Jeune, 1924; reprinted, Paris: Mille et une nuits, 2010), Kindle edition, loc. 658.

5   Georges Clemenceau, *Lettres à une Amie, 1923–1929*, ed. Pierre Brive (Paris: Gallimard, 1970), p. 17.

6   *Gil Blas*, August 31, 1911.

7   The population is given as 250 in M. G. Quilbeuf, *La Loi sur l'assistance: ses conséquences financières pour les communes* (Rouen, 1906), p. 9.

8   Quoted in Katherine M. Bourguignon, ed., *Impressionist Giverny: A Colony of Artists, 1885–1915* (Giverny: Musée d'art Américain 2007), pp. 19 and 29.

9   Marguerite de Saint-Marceaux, *Journal 1894–1927*, ed. Myriam Chimènes (Paris: Fayard, 2007), p. 308.

10   Jean-Pierre Hoschedé tells the story of the wedding party on the train in *Claude Monet, ce mal connu: intimité familiale d'un demi-siècle à Giverny de 1883 à 1926* (Geneva: Pierre Cailler, 1960), vol. 1, p. 24.

11   Hoschedé, *Claude Monet*, vol. 1, p. 52.

12   *Je sais tout*, January 15, 1914.

13   Daniel Wildenstein, *Claude Monet: Biographie et catalogue raisonné*, 5 vols. (Lausanne-Paris: La Bibliothèque des Arts, 1974–91), vol. 1, 1840–1881, letter 50. All subsequent letters of Monet quoted in the text will be designated by the numbers given to them by Wildenstein, following the abbreviation WL. All translations, unless otherwise noted, are my own.

14   WL 108. See also WL 117 (January 1878) for a similar threat.

15   The legend of the potatoes is found in *L'Écho de Paris*, December 6, 1926. For the lack of food and paints, see WL 46, 51 and 52. For the story of the butcher, see René Gimpel, *Diary of an Art Dealer*, trans. John Rosenberg (London: Hodder & Stoughton, 1966), pp. 72–3. For the baker and the laundress: Daniel Wildenstein, *Monet, or the Triumph of Impressionism* (Cologne and Paris: Taschen, 1996), pp. 130 and 150. For the draper: Ruth Butler, *Hidden in the Shadow of the Master: The Model-Wives of Cézanne, Monet, and Rodin* (New Haven: Yale University Press, 2008), p. 199. The figure of 20 francs is given by Monet's dealer, Paul Durand-Ruel, in *Le Bulletin de la Vie Artistique*, April 15, 1920.

16   WL 148, 155.

17   Paul Mantz, *Gazette des Beaux-Arts*, July 1865, and Gonzague Privat, *Place aux jeunes! Causeries critiques sur le Salon de 1865* (F. Cournol: Paris, 1865), p. 190.

18   *Le Charivari*, April 25, 1874.

19   Quoted in Wildenstein, *Monet, or the Triumph of Impressionism*, p. 216; and Georges Clemenceau, *Claude Monet: Les Nymphéas* (Paris: Plon, 1928), p. 70.

20   Gustave Geffroy, *Claude Monet: sa vie, son temps, son oeuvre* (Paris: G. Crès, 1922), p. 312.

21   *La Vie Moderne*, June 12, 1880.

22   Lilla Cabot Perry, "Reminiscences of Claude Monet," *American Magazine of Art*, March 1927.

23   *Gazette des Beaux-arts*, April 1, 1883.

24   Paul Hayes Tucker has pointed out that *Impression, Sunrise* was "not the actual source for the term 'Impressionists' that was first applied to the group" by Louis Leroy in his much-quoted review in *Le Charivari*, April 25, 1874. Leroy instead used the term, Tucker argues, in the context of his discussion of Monet's *Boulevard des Capucines*, two paintings by Cézanne, and one by Eugène Boudin. See Tucker, *Claude Monet: Life and Art* (New Haven, CT, and London: Yale University Press, 1995), pp. 77–8.

25   On these transactions, see Daniel Wildenstein, *Claude Monet: Biographie et catalogue raisonné*, vol. 1: 1840–1881 (1974), p. 226.

26   Hoschedé, *Claude Monet*, vol. 1, p. 45.

27   Quoted in Paul Hayes Tucker, *Monet in the '90s: The Series Paintings*, exhibition catalogue (Boston: Museum of Fine Arts, 1989), p. 3. For the success of Monet in 1889, see Tucker, ibid., p. 59.

28   *L'Art moderne*, July 7, 1889; *L'Art et les Artistes*, July 1909; and Gourmont, "L'Oeil de Claude Monet," in *Promenades philosophiques* (Paris, 1905), quoted in Wildenstein, *Monet, or the Triumph of Impressionism*, p. 376.

29   Joachim Gasquet, *Cézanne* (Paris: Les Éditions Bernheim-Jeune, 1921), p. 90.

30   *Le Carnet de la semaine*, July 1, 1917.

31   *Modern Art*, January 1897. For the "Giverny trick," see Bourguignon, ed., *Impressionist Giverny*, p. 23.

32   *Le Temps*, June 7, 1904.

33   WL 1151.

34   Sacha Guitry, *If I Remember Right*, trans. Lewis Galantière (London: Methuen, 1935), p. 232.

35   For Monet's earnings: Wildenstein, *Monet, or the Triumph of Impressionism*, p. 399. For the salary of Paris workmen: Paul Hayes Tucker, "Revolution in the Garden: Monet in the Twentieth Century," in Tucker et al., *Monet in the 20th Century* (New Haven, CT, and London: Yale University Press, 1998), p. 17 and note 7 on p. 286.

36   *Brush and Pencil*, March 1905.

37   *Revue Mensuelle du Touring-Club de France*, May and September 1906. Automobiles owned by Monet and his family included several Panhards, a Mendelssohn, a Mors, a Peugeot, a Lion-Peugeot, a Peugeot Torpedo, a Zédel, a De Dion–Bouton, and a Clément-Bayard.

38   *Le Temps*, July 19, 1901.

39   WL 1736.

40   *L'Art et les Artistes*, November 1905.

41 Hoschedé, vol. 1, p. 37.

42 Gustave Geffroy, *L'Art et les artistes*, November 1920.

43 WL 2024a.

44 WL 1962, 1968, and 1977.

45 Quoted in Wildenstein, *Monet, or the Triumph of Impressionism*, p. 217.

46 WL 1972.

47 Quoted in Marianne Alphant, *Claude Monet: une vie dans le paysage* (Paris: Hazan, 1993), p. 644; and WL 1989.

48 WL 2023.

49 Quoted in Wildenstein, *Monet, or the Triumph of Impressionism*, p. 331.

50 *Gazette des Beaux-Arts*, April 1, 1883.

51 Ambrose Vollard, *Paul Cézanne*, trans. H. L. van Doren (London: Brentano, 1924), p. 117; and Gasquet, *Cézanne*, p. 90

52 *Le Petit Parisien*, August 3, 1912.

53 *Gil Blas*, September 3, 1913.

54 WL 2097.

55 *Brush and Pencil*, March 1905.

56 Where and when the two men first met is not recorded. Clemenceau's biographer speculates that they may have met in the studio of the painter Jean-Baptiste Delestre. See Jean-Baptiste Duroselle, *Clemenceau* (Paris: Fayard, 1988), p. 43. Dallas reports that Clemenceau came to Giverny for the first time in 1890 (*At the Heart of a Tiger*, p. 267).

57 Hoschedé, vol. 1, p. 40, and vol. 2, p. 111. Hoschedé claims that Monet voted for the first time after World War I.

58 Geffroy, *L'Art et les artistes*, November 1920. Marianne Alphant has pointed out their similarities: "The audacity, the pride, the stubbornness, the spontaneous enthusiasm, the passion and lyricism, the violent nature, the incredible youthfulness of the two men—all very similar" (*Claude Monet*, p. 677).

59 *Georges Clemenceau à son ami Claude Monet: Correspondance*, annotated by Jean-Claude Montant (Paris: Éditions de la Réunion des musées nationaux, 1993), pp. 161, 168, and 182.

60 *Gil Blas*, January 31, 1914.

61 *La Croix*, February 8–9, 1914.

62 Quoted in Duroselle, *Clemenceau*, p. 35.

63 Quoted Duroselle, p. 34.

64 *Lettres à une Amie*, p. 184.

65 *Gil Blas*, January 31, 1914.

66 Quoted in Dallas, *At the Heart of a Tiger*, p. 439.

67 Quoted in Wythe Williams, *The Tiger of France: Conversations with Clemenceau* (New York: Duell, Sloan & Pearce, 1949), p. 282.

68 Quoted in Dallas, *At the Heart of a Tiger*, p. 102.

69 Quoted in Dallas, *At the Heart of a Tiger*, p. 192.

70 *The Letters of Rudyard Kipling*, ed. Thomas Pinney, vol. 5 (Iowa City: University of Iowa Press, 2004), p. 325.

71 *La Justice*, January 16, 1880.

72 Quoted in Duroselle, *Clemenceau*, p. 310.

73   Guitry, *If I Remember Right*, p. 234.

74   Violet Milner, *My Picture Gallery, 1886–1901* (London: John Murray, 1951), pp. 62–3.

75   Adolphe Tabarant, *Manet et ses oeuvres* (Paris: Gallimard, 1947), p. 358. The paintings are now in the Kimbell Art Museum in Fort Worth and the Musée d'Orsay.

76   *La Justice*, May 20, 1895.

77   WL 2287.

CHAPTER TWO: DU CÔTÉ DE CHEZ MONET

1   *Claude Monet*, p. 327.

2   *Je sais tout*, January 15, 1914.

3   WL 2642.

4   *Gil Blas*, March 20, 1906.

5   Hoschedé, *Claude Monet*, vol. 1, p. 92. For a good assessment of Blanche Hoschedé-Monet's career as well as her relationship to Monet, see Janine Burke, "Monet's 'Angel': The Artistic Partnership of Claude Monet and Blanche Hoschedé-Monet," *Colloquy: text theory critique* 22 (2011), pp. 68–80.

6   For Michel's wheeling and dealing, see *Revue Mensuelle du Touring-Club de France*, September and December 1906, April 1907, January and December 1913, and April 1914. The "Offres et Demandes" columns of this publication reveal Jean-Pierre Hoschedé to have been equally active.

7   Jean Martet, *Clemenceau: The Events of His Life as Told by Himself to His Former Secretary*, trans. Milton Waldman (London: Longmans, Green & Co., 1930), p. 220. Michel Monet was indeed destined to die at the wheel of a fast car, although not until 1966, when, a few weeks shy of his eighty-eighth birthday, he would crash on the bridge in Vernon that bore Clemenceau's name.

8   *La Presse*, August 1, 1910. For the garage and cycle shop in Vernon (Moché & Hoschedé): *La Croix*, July 19, 1906; and *Guide Michelin* (1912), p. 35. This garage, at 105 route de Paris, later became Hoschedé & Veilleux (*L'Ouest-Éclair*, October 22, 1922).

9   Hoschedé, *Claude Monet*, vol. 1, p. 123. Hoschedé's work appears as early as his 1898 publication, "Flore de Vernon et de la Roche-Guyon," in the *Bulletin de la Société des amis des sciences naturelles de Rouen*. For his membership of the Linnean Society, see *Bulletin de la Société Linnéenne de Normandie* (Caen: Lanier, 1901), p. x. For his Irish water spaniel: *L'Ouest-Éclair*, July 24, 1913.

10   *L'Art dans les Deux Mondes*, March 7, 1891.

11   *Je sais tout*, January 15, 1914.

12   See Muriel Giolkowska, "Memories of Monet," *Canadian Forum* (March 1927), reprinted in George T. M. Shackleford et al., *Monet and the Impressionists* (Sydney: Art Gallery of New South Wales, 2008), p. 203; and Geffroy, *Claude Monet*, p. 1.

13   Geffroy, *Claude Monet*, p. 122.

14   Quoted in John M. Merriman, *The Margins of City Life: Explorations on the French Urban Frontier, 1815–1851* (Oxford: Oxford University Press, 1991), p. 216. For Ingouville's unsavory reputation (which Merriman points out was not entirely deserved), see pp. 210–17.

15   Geffroy, *Claude Monet*, p. 5.

16   Ibid. For Monet's earliest sketches, see Charles F. Stuckey, *Claude Monet, 1840–1926* (London: Thames & Hudson, 1995), p. 186.

17 Armand Silvestre, *Au Pays des souvenirs: mes maîtres et mes maîtresses* (Paris: La Librairie Illustrée, 1892), p. 161.

18 Evan Charteris, *John Sargent* (New York: Charles Scribner's Sons, 1927), p. 129

19 Hoschedé, vol. 1, p. 36.

20 Clemenceau, *Claude Monet*, p. 15.

21 Hoschedé, vol. 1, p. 37.

22 *La Revue de l'art ancien et moderne*, June 1927.

23 See Maloon, "Meeting Monsieur Monet," in *Monet and the Impressionists*, p. 194; and Alphant, *Claude Monet,* p. 649.

24 *La Revue de l'art ancien et moderne*, June 1927.

25 Gimpel, *Diary of an Art Dealer*, p. 8.

26 Gimpel, p. 60; Hoschedé, vol. 1, p. 53.

27 *Gil Blas*, August 31, 1911. André Arnyvelde describes the progress up the stairs of the Japanese prints (*Je sais tout*, January 15, 1914).

28 Sacha Guitry tells this story about Renoir in his commentary for the 1952 version of his film *Ceux de chez nous*.

29 Hoschedé, vol. 1, p. 80.

30 Gimpel, p. 8.

31 Hoschedé, vol. 1, p. 82. For Monet's food and recipes, see Claire Joyes, *Monet's Table: The Cooking Journal of Claude Monet* (New York: Simon & Schuster, 1989).

32 Hoschedé, vol. 1, p. 61.

33 *La Revue de l'art ancien et moderne*, June 1927.

34 Quoted in Tucker, *Claude Monet: Life and Art*, p. 177.

35 On these matters, see Hoschedé, vol. 1, pp. 45–8.

36 Albert Cim, "Un homme de lettres messin: Albert Collignon," *Le Pays Lorrain et Le Pays Messin: Revue mensuelle illustré* (1922), p. 476.

37 WL 2319.

38 Monet's complete order can be found in the website for Latour-Marliac: http://www.latour-marliac.com.

39 *La Revue illustrée*, March 15, 1898.

40 For the cost of the garden: Philippe Jullian, *Jean Lorrain ou le satiricon de 1900* (Paris: Fayard, 1974), p. 244. For Monet's interest payments: Virginia Spate, *Claude Monet: The Colour of Time* (London: Thames & Hudson, 1992), p. 331, n. 3.

41 Paul Hayes Tucker, *Monet in the '90s: The Series Paintings* (Boston: Museum of Fine Arts, in association with Yale University Press, 1989), p. 37.

42 Ibid., p. 148.

43 Quoted in Tucker, "Revolution in the Garden," p. 17.

44 Geffroy, *Claude Monet*, p. 314.

45 For the Dreyfus Affair and Monet's responses to it, see Tucker, *Monet in the '90s*, pp. 253–6; and idem, "Revolution in the Garden", pp. 20–3.

46 WL 1397. Monet's letter, which predates the appearance of "J'Accuse," was in support of Zola's journalistic efforts on Captain Dreyfus's behalf in *Le Figaro* in November and December 1897.

47 *L'Aurore*, January 13, 1898.

48 *Claude Monet*, p. 314.

49 *Gazette des Beaux-Arts*, June 1909; *L'Art et les Artistes*, July 1909.

50 Tucker, *Claude Monet: Life and Art*, p. 197.

51 *L'Art et les Artistes,* November 1905.

52 Valéry C. O. Gréard, *Meissonier: His Life and Art*, trans. Lady Mary Loyd and Miss Florence Simmonds (London: William Heinemann, 1897), p. 345. I discuss the rise and fall of Meissonier in *The Judgment of Paris: The Revolutionary Decade that Gave the World Impressionism* (New York: Walker, 2006).

53 *Gil Blas*, January 31, 1912.

54 Gimpel, *Diary of an Art Dealer*, pp. 12 and 15.

55 Paul Valéry, *Degas Manet Morisot*, trans. David Paul, ed. Jackson Mathews (New York: Bollingen, 1960), p. 99.

56 Quoted in Judith A. Barter, ed., *Mary Cassatt: Modern Woman*, exhibition catalogue (Chicago: Art Institute of Chicago, 1998), p. 350.

57 *La Chronique des Arts et de la Curiosité*, June 25, 1898.

58 Maurice Denis (in 1907) and Émile Bernard (in 1904), quoted in Robert Herbert, "Method and Meaning in Monet," *Art in America* 67 (September 1979), pp. 90 and 92.

59 Quoted in Harry E. Buckley, *Guillaume Apollinaire as an Art Critic* (Ann Arbor: UMI Research Press, 1969), p. 55.

60 *André Salmon on Modern French Art*, ed. and trans. Beth S. Gersh-Nesic (Cambridge, UK: Cambridge University Press, 2005), p. 83.

61 *Archives Claude Monet*, p. 74.

62 *Gil Blas*, January 25, 1914.

63 WL 2076.

64 Paul Reboux, *Mes mémoires* (Paris: Éditions Haussmann, 1956), p. 195.

65 *Gil Blas*, September 3, 1913.

66 *Archives Claude Monet*, p. 83. For Monet's work at Les Zoaques, see WL 2112 and 2115.

67 *Gil Blas*, September 3, 1913.

68 *Je sais tout*, January 15, 1914.

69 WL 2050.

70 Martet, *Clemenceau*, p. 237.

71 Ibid. In 1927 Clemenceau would tell Gaëtan Sanvoisin: "I gave him the idea for the *Water Lilies*. 'What if you paint for some wealthy patron,' I told him, 'a circular ensemble of large canvases?'" (*Le Gaulois*, May 18, 1927).

72 WL 2116.

73 Clemenceau, *Claude Monet: Les Nymphéas* (Paris: Plon, 1928), pp. 19 and 18.

CHAPTER THREE: LANDSCAPES OF WATER

1 Charteris, *John Sargent*, p. 131.

2 Quoted in Wildenstein, *Monet, or the Triumph of Impressionism*, p. 259.

3 Quoted in Ronald R. Bernier, *Monument, Moment, and Memory: Monet's Cathedral in Fin de Siècle France* (Cranbury, NJ: Associated University Press, 2007), p. 73.

4 Hoschedé, vol. 2, p. 112. For Monet on the *enveloppe*, see *Gil Blas*, March 3, 1889.

5 *Gil Blas*, March 3, 1889.

6 *American Magazine of Art*, March 1927.

7 Martet, *Clemenceau,* p. 216.

8   *Gil Blas*, September 28, 1886.

9   *Le Temps*, June 7, 1904.

10 Charteris, *John Sargent*, p. 126.

11 *Modern Art*, Winter 1897.

12 For an excellent study of how Monet's works were not merely spontaneously improvised compositions created before the motif, see Herbert, "Method and Meaning in Monet," pp. 90–108.

13 *Gil Blas*, June 22, 1889.

14 Christopher Lyon, "Unveiling Monet," *MoMA*, No. 7 (Spring, 1991), p. 22.

15 Quoted in Geffroy, *Claude Monet*, p. 121

16 *Gazette des Beaux-Arts*, June 1909.

17 Marcel Proust, "Journées de lecture," in *Contre Sainte-Beuve*, ed. Pierre Clarac and Yves Sandre (Paris: Gallimard, 1971), p. 178, quoted in Levine, p. 314, n. 34.

18 Philip Hook, quoted in the *Times*, December 31, 2014.

19 Geffroy, *Claude Monet*, p. 335; Hoschedé, vol. 1, p. 96.

20 *Georges Clemenceau à son ami Claude Monet*, p. 179.

21 *Archives Claude Monet*, p. 96.

22 Théodore Licquet, *Rouen: précis de son histoire, son commerce, son industrie, ses manufactures, ses monumens* (Rouen: Édouard Frère, 1831), p. 17.

23 WL 1343.

24 *The American Magazine of Art*, March 1927.

25 WL 40.

26 Hoschedé, vol. 1, p. 73.

27 *The American Magazine of Art*, March 1927.

28 Mirbeau, *Correspondance avec Claude Monet*, ed. Pierre Michel and Jean-François Nivet (Tusson: Du Lérot, 1990), p. 210.

29 WL 1064.

30 *Modern Art*, Winter 1897.

31 The story is told in Léon Daudet, "Un Prince de la Lumière," *L'Action française*, December 8, 1926.

32 *Claude Monet*, p. 335.

33 *Georges Clemenceau à son ami Claude Monet*, p. 101.

34 Martet, *Clemenceau*, p. 238.

35 WL 1066.

36 *Le Temps*, June 7, 1904.

37 WL 1831 and 1832.

38 WL 1850.

39 Quoted in Philippe Piguet, *Claude Monet au temps de Giverny* (Paris: Centre culturel du Marais, 1983), p. 270.

40 *Chicago Tribune*, May 16, 1908. Tucker suggests that the much-publicized accounts of Monet's destruction of his canvases "might even have been a sly public relations campaign to encourage already enthusiastic American collectors to acquire more of his pictures, since they seemed to be becoming rarer" (*Claude Monet: Art and Life*, p. 190).

41 *Correspondence avec Claude Monet*, p. 215.

42 WL 1854.

43   *Le Gaulois*, May 5, 1909; *Comoedia*, May 8, 1909.

44   Christopher E. Forth, "Neurasthenia and Manhood in fin de siècle France," in *Cultures of Neurasthenia from Beard to the First World War*, ed. Marijke Gijswijt-Hofstra and Roy Porter (Amsterdam: Éditions Rodopi, 2001), pp. 329–62.

45   *La Revue de l'art ancien et moderne*, June 1927.

46   Antonin Proust, *Édouard Manet: Souvenirs* (Paris: Librairie Renouard, 1913), p. 84.

47   WL 1060.

48   *Cahiers Octave Mirbeau*, ed. Pierre Michel, no. 8 (2001), p. 261.

49   For the following information I am indebted to Herbert, "Method and Meaning in Monet," pp. 90–108.

50   André Masson, "Monet the Founder," trans. Terence Maloon, in Shackleford et al., *Monet and the Impressionists*, p. 190.

51   Herbert, "Method and Meaning in Monet," p. 98.

52   Lyon, "Unveiling Monet," p. 22.

53   *Revue Hebdomadaire*, August 21, 1909, quoted in Levine, *Monet, Narcissus, and Self-Reflection*, p. 246.

54   For good discussions of Monet's revolutionary technique at this point, see Tucker, *Claude Monet: Life and Art*, pp. 190–8; and Spate, *Claude Monet: The Colour of Time*, pp. 254–62. Tucker points out that Monet reversed "one of the most fundamental tenets of landscape painting—that sky is up and land is down" (p. 191), while Spate writes that he "destroyed the notion of the "view" (p. 254).

55   *Revue Hebdomadaire*, August 21, 1909, quoted in Levine, *Monet, Narcissus, and Self-Reflection*, p. 247.

56   Hoschedé, vol. 1, p. 135.

57   Quoted in Geffroy, *Claude Monet*, p. 240.

58   *Comoedia*, May 8, 1909, quoted in Levine, *Monet, Narcissus, and Self-Reflection*, p. 214.

59   Quoted in Roger Benjamin, "The Decorative Landscape, Fauvism and the Arabesque of Observation," *Art Bulletin* (June 1993), p. 299. For the fin de siècle interest in decorative painting, see Tucker, *Monet in the '90s*, pp. 133–4.

60   *Revue des Deux Mondes,* June 1906.

61   *Le Gaulois*, May 22, 1909.

62   *Gazette des Beaux-Arts*, June 1909.

63   *L'Art moderne*, July 7, 1889.

64   Quoted in Anne Y. Smith, "The Whittemores of Connecticut: Pioneer Collectors of French Impressionism," *Antiques & Fine Art* (Spring 2010), p. 158.

CHAPTER FOUR: A GREAT PROJECT

1   *Claude Monet*, p. 331.

2   *L'Art et les Artistes*, December 1905, trans. Terence Maloon in Shackleford et al., *Monet and the Impressionists*, p. 198.

3   Michel Georges-Michel, *Peintres et sculpteurs que j'ai connu, 1900–1942* (New York: Brentano's, 1942), p. 35.

4   *Gil Blas*, June 5, 1914. Monet claimed in 1920 to have fourteen Cézannes in his bedroom (*La Revue de l'art ancien et moderne*, January—May 1927), but other reports place at least some of them in his studio.

5   *If I Remember Right*, p. 223. On alcohol at breakfast, see W. Scott Haine, *The World of the Paris Café: Sociability Among the French Working Class, 1789—1914* (Baltimore: Johns Hopkins University Press, 1998), p. 94.

6   Louis Gillet, *Trois variations sur Claude Monet* (Paris: Librairie Plon, 1927), p. 45.

7   WL 2123.

8   WL 2119.

9   WL 2113.

10 Quoted in Ray Rushton, "Ingres: Drawings from the Musée Ingres at Montauban and Other Collections," *Journal of the Royal Society of Arts* (February 1980), p. 159.

11 On the Le Havre caricatures, see Tucker, *Claude Monet: Life and Art*, p. 9; and Hugh Edwards, "The Caricatures of Claude Monet," *Bulletin of the Art Institute of Chicago (1907–1951)*, vol. 37 (September–October, 1943), pp. 71–2. For his sketching portraits in the Brasserie des Martyrs, see Firmin Maillard, *Les Derniers Bohèmes: Henri Murger et son temps* (Paris: Librairie Satorius, 1874), p. 42.

12 Marmottan inventory no. 5128 (Sketchbook 1); and Marmottan inventory no. 5129 (Sketchbook 6).

13 *Georges Clemenceau à son ami Claude Monet*, pp. 78–9.

14 *La Revue de l'art ancien et moderne*, June 1927. For his improved eyesight in 1914, see WL 2123.

15 *La Renaissance: Politique, Littéraire et Artistique*, June 13, 1914.

16 WL 642.

17 Quoted in Spate, *Claude Monet: The Colour of Time*, p. 280.

18 WL 2103.

19 Geffroy, *Claude Monet*, p. 332. For Blanche's support and encouragement at this time, see also Burke, "Monet's 'Angel,'" pp. 74–5.

20 *Manette Salomon* (Paris: Charpentier, 1902), pp. 162 and 267–8.

21 *L'Artiste*, June 1, 1873.

22 Pissarro, quoted in Christoph Becker et al., *Camille Pissarro, Impressionist Artist* (Staatsgalerie, Stuttgart, 1999), p. 103. For Pissarro's view on the ideal distance from the canvas, see John Gage, "The Technique of Seurat: A Reappraisal," *Art Bulletin*, vol. 69 (September 1987), pp. 451–2.

23 Gimpel, *Diary of an Art Dealer*, p. 75.

24 Quoted in Philip Ball, *Bright Earth: The Invention of Colour* (London: Viking, 2001), p. 153.

25 Quoted in Ball, *Bright Earth*, p. 13.

26 Gimpel, *Diary of an Art Dealer*, p. 59. On Monet's pigments and techniques in his later career, see Ashok Roy, "Monet's Palette in the Twentieth Century: *Water-Lilies* and *Irises*," *National Gallery Technical Bulletin*, vol. 28 (London: National Gallery, 2007), pp. 61–7.

27 Léonce Bénédite, quoted in Sarah J. Moore, *John White Alexander and the Construction of National Identity: Cosmopolitan American Art, 1880–1915* (Cranbury, NJ: Associated University Presses, 2003), p. 49.

28 WL 2617.

29 WL 1132.

30 *L'Art et les Artistes*, December 1905, trans. Terence Maloon in Shackleford et al., *Monet*

and the Impressionists, p. 197.

31 Hoschedé, vol. 1, p. 86

32 *La Renaissance de l'art français et des industries de luxe*, January 1920. The friend was Georges Lecomte and the date of this visit the early 1890s.

33 *Gil Blas*, June 3, 1914.

34 Monet's trip to Paris to view the Camondo rooms is confirmed in the *Journal des débats politiques et littéraires,* June 9, 1914.

35 *La Revue de Paris*, February 1927.

36 Quoted in Tucker, *Monet in the '90s*, p. 246.

37 WL 243.

38 Quoted in Howard Isham, *Image of the Sea: Oceanic Consciousness in the Romantic Century* (New York: Peter Lang, 2004) p. 335.

39 Juliet Wilson-Bareau, ed., *Manet by Himself: Correspondence and Conversation* (London: MacDonald & Co., 1991), p. 31.

40 Quoted in Tucker, *Claude Monet: Life and Art*, p. 96.

41 *Burlington Magazine for Connoisseurs*, May 1911.

42 Ambrose Vollard, *Recollections of a Picture Dealer*, trans. Violet M. MacDonald (Mineola, NY: Dover, 2002), p. 103.

43 *Le Carnet de la semaine*, June 24, 1917.

44 *Journal des débats politiques et littéraires*, June 9, 1914.

45 *La Lanterne*, June 17, 1914.

46 *Gil Blas*, June 16, 1914. Reports of the destruction are taken from *La Lanterne*, June 16, 1914.

47 *Le Figaro*, June 20, 1913.

48 *Archives Claude Monet*, p. 152. The novelist was Léon Werth.

49 WL 2120 and 2121.

50 WL 2122 and 2123.

51 Quoted in Edgar Holt, *The Tiger: The Life of Georges Clemenceau, 1841–1929* (London: Hamish Hamilton, 1976), p. 165.

52 *L'Homme Libre*, June 25, 1914.

53 Quoted in Holt, *The Tiger*, p. 164.

54 See Theodore Zeldin, *France 1848–1945: Politics and Anger* (Oxford: Oxford University Press, 1979), p. 397.

55 Quoted in Harvey Goldberg, *The Life of Jean Jaurès* (Madison: University of Wisconsin Press, 1962), pp. 460 and 463.

56 *Le Figaro*, March 13, 1914. For a full account of the affair, see Edward Berenson, *The Trial of Madame Caillaux* (Berkeley: University of California Press, 1992).

57 *L'Homme Libre*, 21 July 1914.

58 For the weather on August 3: *Le Matin*, 4 August 1914.

CHAPTER FIVE: INTO THE UNKNOWN

1 WL 2128.

2 WL 3102.

3 *Le Matin*, August 4, 1914.

4 *Le Temps*, September 4, 1914.

5   *The Times*, September 3, 1914.
6   I am grateful to Claire Maingon for this information (personal email correspondence, December 17, 2014). See Claire Maingon and David Campserveux, "A Museum at War: The Louvre 1914–1921," *L'Esprit Créateur*, vol. 54 (Summer 2014), pp. 127–40.
7   WL 2642.
8   Eugénie Buffet, *Ma vie, mes amours, mes aventures: confidences recueillies par Maurice Hamel* (Paris: Eugène Figuière, 1930), p. 129.
9   *Le Radical*, November 19, 1914.
10 Buffet, *Ma vie, mes amours, mes aventures*, pp. 129–30.
11 WL 2132.
12 WL 2124.
13 WL 2126.
14 On this accident, see WL 1673. Monet describes him as being exempted from service in WL 2128.
15 WL 2125.
16 WL 2127.
17 Octave Mirbeau, *Correspondance Générale*, ed. Pierre Michel with the assistance of Jean-François Nivet (Lausanne: L'Age d'Homme, 2005), vol. 2, p. 260.
18 *If I Remember Right*, p. 222.
19 Ibid., p. 227.
20 Elder, *À Giverny, chez Claude Monet*, loc. 835.
21 *L'Homme Libre*, August 2, 1913.
22 Ibid., September 14, 1913.
23 James Harding, *Sacha Guitry: The Last Boulevardier* (London: Methuen, 1968), p. 51.
24 *Le Figaro*, October 22, 1932.
25 *Le Journal*, September 16, 1894.
26 Mirbeau, *Correspondance Générale*, vol. 2, p. 284.
27 Ibid., vol. 2, p. 261.
28 *Le Figaro*, February 17, 1917.
29 Pierre Michel discusses the faithful dingo as Mirbeau's "fraternal twin" in his Preface to the Éditions du Boucher version of Mirbeau's *Dingo* (Société Octave Mirbeau, 2003), p. 6. The edition is available online at: http://www.leboucher.com/pdf/mirbeau/dingo.pdf.
30 Reg Carr, *Anarchism in France: The Case of Octave Mirbeau* (Manchester, UK: Manchester University Press, 1977), p. 147.
31 *L'Écho de Paris*, March 31, 1891.
32 Quoted in Pierre Michel and Jean-Francois Nivet, *Octave Mirbeau: l'imprécateur au cœur fidèle* (Paris: Librairie Séguier, 1990), pp. 905–6.
33 *Sébastien Roch*, preface by Pierre Michel (Angers: Éditions du Boucher, 2003), pp. 268, 269.
34 *Le Petit Parisien*, August 13, 1915.
35 Marc Elder, *Deux essais: Octave Mirbeau, Romain Rolland* (Paris: Georges Cres, 1914), p. 22.
36 Mirbeau, *Correspondance avec Claude Monet*, p. 215.
37 *Gil Blas*, September 3, 1913.
38 WL 2124.

39   Ibid.

40   See "Le Temps Qu'il Fait" on page 3 of *Le Matin* throughout the month of July 1914.

41   *Le Matin*, September 14, 1914.

42   The term "La Grande Guerre" was in use by the early autumn of 1914. See René Mercier, ed., *La Grande Guerre: La Vie en Lorraine* (Nancy: L'Est Républicain, 1914), dated September 1914; and Gustave Geffroy, ed., *La Grande Guerre par les artistes* (Paris: Georges Crès, 1914), the first edition of which was issued in November 1914. Also published in the autumn of 1914 was Charles de Preissac's collection, *Photographies de la Grande Guerre*. The term "La Guerre Mondiale" appears in *Revue Générale Militaire* 16, July–December 1914 (Paris: Berger-Levrault, 1914), p. 104.

43   WL 2642.

44   WL 2129.

45   WL 2130.

46   *L'Écho de Paris*, November 8, 1914, lists only four hotels in Paris "open during the war."

47   *Le Petit Parisien*, November 10, 1914.

48   Ibid.

49   Geffroy, *Claude Monet*, p. 1.

50   Jules-Amédée Barbey d'Aurevilly, cited in Hoschedé, vol. 1, p. 103.

51   *L'Art et les Artistes*, December 1905, trans. Terence Maloon in Shackleford et al., *Monet and the Impressionists*, p. 197.

52   Geffroy, *Claude Monet*, p. 313.

53   See Dallas, *At the Heart of a Tiger*, p. 440.

54   *Georges Clemenceau à son ami Claude Monet*, p. 79.

55   *L'Homme Libre*, August 2, 1914.

56   Clemenceau, *Discours de Guerre: Recueillis et publiés par la Société des Amis de Georges Clemenceau* (Paris: Presses Universitaires de France, 1968), p. 43.

57   Quoted in D. R. Watson, *Clemenceau: A Political Biography* (London: Eyre Methuen, 1974), p. 252.

58   Quoted in Georges Suarez, *La vie orgueilleuse de Clemenceau* (Paris: Éditions P. Saurat, 1987), p. 128.

59   Quoted in Jean-Jacques Becker, *The Great War and the French People*, trans. Arnold Pomerans (Leamington Spa: Berg, 1985), p. 45.

60   WL 2135.

61   *The International Journal of Ethics*, November 1915.

62   *Le Figaro*, February 20, 1915.

63   Quoted in Danielle Delouche, "Cubisme et camouflage," in *Guerres mondiales et conflits contemporains*, No. 171: *Représenter la Guerre de 1914–1918* (July 1993), p. 125.

64   Quoted in Delouche, pp. 131–2. On Cubism as unpatriotic, see ibid., p. 129.

65   *Le Figaro*, June 2, 1915.

66   *L'Homme Libre*, August 9, 1914.

67   *Le Matin*, August 30, 1914.

68   *Revue de Paris*, December 15, 1914, translated in Joseph F. Byrnes, "Reconciliation of Cultures in the Third Republic: Émile Mâle (1862–1954)," *Catholic Historical Review*, vol. 83, no. 3 (July 1997), pp. 417–18. For Rodin on Reims, see Judith Cadel, *Rodin: Sa vie glorieuse, sa vie inconnue* (Paris: Grasset, 1937), p. 110.

69 Quoted in Barbara L. Kelly, "Debussy and the Making of a *musicien français*: *Pelléas*, the Press, and World War I," in Barbara L. Kelly, ed., *French Music, Culture, and National Identity, 1870–1939* (Rochester NY: University of Rochester Press, 2008), p. 69.

70 Becker, *The Great War and the French People*, p. 91.

71 *L'Écho de Paris*, September 19, 1914.

72 WL 2143.

73 *Les Allemands: destructeurs des cathédrales et de trésors du passé* (Paris: Hachette, 1915), p. 76.

CHAPTER SIX: A GRANDE DÉCORATION

1 Quoted in Gregor Dallas, *1918: War and Peace* (London: Pimlico, 2002), p. 170.

2 *Le Matin*, December 5, 1914.

3 *L'Écho de Paris*, January 2. 1915.

4 *Georges Clemenceau à son ami Claude Monet*, p. 80.

5 *Le Figaro*, December 10, 1914.

6 *Le Matin*, February 25, 1915, and *Le Petit Parisien*, February 29, 1915.

7 *L'Homme Libre*, December 15, 1914.

8 *Le Petit Parisien*, February 12, 1922.

9 Guitry, *If I Remember Right*, p. 23.

10 Marthe de Fels, *La Vie de Claude Monet* (Paris: Gallimard, 1929), p. 173.

11 *If I Remember Right*, p. 236.

12 See Geffroy, *Claude Monet*, pp. 14–15.

13 *Gil Blas*, December 9, 1909.

14 Elder, *À Giverny, chez Claude Monet*, loc. 662.

15 Quoted in Rosemary Lloyd, *Mallarmé: The Poet and His Circle* (Ithaca: Cornell University Press, 1999), p. 138. Monet provides the text of Mallarmé's poem in a 1920 letter to Geffroy: WL 2390. The translation is mine. André Arneveldt reports that it was on display on a small stand on a glazed bureau in the second studio (*Je sais tout*, January 15, 1914).

16 See *Le Figaro*, June 15, 1907. Proust's book was to be called *Six Gardens of Paradise* — the gardens in question being that of the Countess of Noailles, that of Ruskin on Coniston Water, that of Maurice Maeterlinck (whom he calls the "Virgil of Flanders"), those of the poets Henri de Régnier and Francis Jammes, and Monet's garden at Giverny.

17 *Marcel Proust on Art and Literature, 1896–1919*, trans. Sylvia Townsend Warner (New York: Meridian Books, 1958), p. 357.

18 *Nouvelle Revue Française*, July 1, 1909.

19 WL 2640.

20 *Le Figaro*, November 20, 1914.

21 Ibid., December 23, 1914.

22 Arthur Banks and Alan Palmer, *A Military Atlas of the First World War* (London: Leo Cooper, 1989), p. 13 (Kaiser Wilhelm); Matthew Stibbe, *Germany, 1914–1933: Politics, Society and Culture* (Abingdon: Routledge, 2013), p. 16 (Moltke); and Malcolm Chandler, *Home Front 1914–18* (Oxford: Heinemann, 2001), p. 7 (Asquith).

23 *Le Temps*, December 27, 1914.

24 WL 3103.

25 Raymond Koechlin, *Souvenirs d'un vieil amateur d'art de l'Extrême-Orient*

(Chalon-sur-Saone: Imprimerie Française et Orientale E. Bertrand), pp 3 and 38. For his father, Alfred Kocchlin, see *Tableaux Généalogiques de la Famille Koechlin, 1460–1914* (Mulhouse: Ernest Meinenger, 1914), p. 19.

26 *Archives Claude Monet*, p. 82.

27 WL 2142.

28 *Les Musées de France: Bulletin publié sous le patronage de la Direction des Musées Nationaux avec le concours de la Société des Amis du Louvre et de l'Union Centrale des Arts Décoratifs*, ed. Paul Vitry (Paris: D.-A. Longuet, 1913), pp. 55–6.

29 On the latter occasion, in 1892, the commissioners for the decoration of the Hôtel de Ville voted for Pierre Lagarde (10 votes) over Monet (4 votes). See Sylvie Patry, "Monet and Decoration," in *Claude Monet, 1840–1926* (Paris: Réunion des musées nationaux, 2010), p. 323. Wildenstein points out the absence of references to the campaign in Monet's letters, suggesting that "it seems not to have concerned him greatly. Indeed, it is by no means certain that he ever requested the commission" (*Monet, or the Triumph of Impressionism*, p. 288).

30 Quoted in Marc J. Gotlieb, *The Plight of Emulation: Ernest Meissonier and French Salon Painting* (Princeton, NJ: Princeton University Press, 1996) p. 24.

31 Quoted in Gotlieb, *The Plight of Emulation*, p. 21.

32 *Lettres de Eugène Delacroix*, ed. Philippe Burty (Paris: A. Quantin, 1878), p. 147.

33 *Revue des Deux Mondes*, June 1906.

34 *Mercure de France*, September 16, 1912.

35 Quoted in Patry, "Monet and Decorations," p. 318.

36 WL 2145.

37 WL 2145.

38 *Discours de Guerre*, p. 46.

39 WL 2145.

40 *Le Figaro*, May 31, 1912.

41 Ibid., February 18, 1913.

42 Ibid., February 20, 1913.

43 *Gil Blas*, April 3, 1913.

44 WL 2148.

45 *Georges Clemenceau à son ami Claude Monet*, p. 155.

46 Clemenceau, *Claude Monet: Les Nymphéas* (Paris: Plon, 1928), p. 16.

47 *Je sais tout*, January 15, 1914.

48 *L'Art et les Artistes*, December 1905, trans. Terence Maloon in Shackleford et al., *Monet and the Impressionists*, p. 197.

49 WL 2127, 2134, 2136 and 2149.

CHAPTER SEVEN: A GRAND ATELIER

1 WL 2153.

2 Quoted in "The Prix Goncourt", *Encyclopedia of Library and Information Science*, ed. Allen Kent, Harold Lancourt and Jay E. Daley (New York: Marcel Dekker, 1978), vol. 24, p. 206.

3 Edmond and Jules de Goncourt, *Journal: Mémoires de la vie littéraire*, vol. 3, ed. Robert Ricatte (Paris: Robert Laffont, 1989), p. 348.

4   Elder, *À Giverny, chez Claude Monet*, loc. 674. *La Guerre du Feu* was filmed by Jean-Jacques
    Annaud in 1981 as *Quest for Fire*.

5   Geffroy, *Claude Monet*, p. 329.

6   *Paris-Magazine*, August 25, 1920, quoted in Wildenstein, *Monet, or the Triumph of
    Impressionism*, p. 406.

7   Lucien Descaves, in *L'Oeuvre*, December 11, 1926.

8   Quoted in Georges Ravon, *L'Académie Goncourt en dix couverts* (Avignon: E. Aubanel,
    1943), p. 59.

9   Quoted in Wildenstein, *Monet, or the Triumph of Impressionism*, p. 46.

10 Stuckey, *Claude Monet, 1840–1926*, p. 247.

11 *La Guerre Mondiale*, July 22, 1915.

12 WL 2155.

13 Hoschedé, vol. 1, p. 83. Monet's campaign against the starch factory is amply reported
    in the newspapers of the day: See, for example, *La Chronique des arts et de la curiosité*,
    September 21, 1895.

14 Geffroy, *Claude Monet*, p. 324.

15 *La Vie Moderne*, July 12, 1880.

16 *Revue illustrée*, March 15, 1898, quoted in Wildenstein, *Monet, or the Triumph of
    Impressionism*, p. 321.

17 Hoschedé, vol. 1, p. 130.

18 Jean Martet, *M. Clemenceau peint par lui-même* (Paris: Albin Michel, 1929), pp. 52–53. For
    a good discussion of this passage, as well as its variation from both the 1930 English
    translation (Martet, *Clemenceau*, p. 217) and the claims of Blanche Hoschedé-Monet
    (Hoschedé, vol. 1, p. 163), see Burke, "Monet's 'Angel,'" pp. 75–6. Burke speculates that
    Blanche may have performed an even more active role in the painting of the Grande
    Décoration because of her ability "to beautifully interpret and emulate the master's
    style." She argues that Blanche may have added some of the layers of color, leaving
    Monet to add the gestural brushwork and other more sophisticated touches (p. 76).
    Blanche's denials and a lack of evidence leave this intriguing thesis unproven.

19 Hoschedé, *Claude Monet*, vol. 1, p. 163.

20 Hoschedé, *Claude Monet*, vol. 1, p. 81.

21 *Le Temps*, July 8 and 9, 1915.

22 *Le Figaro*, July 8, 1915.

23 See E. L. Hawke's review of Alfred Angot's article "Le Canon et La Pluie," *Monthly
    Weather Review*, vol. 45 (September 1917), pp. 450–1 (reprinted from Hawke's review in
    Nature, August 9, 1917); and W. W. Campbell, "The War and the Weather," *Publications
    of the Astronomical Society of the Pacific*, vol. 29 (October 1917), pp. 200–202.

24 For the dinners in Paris: *Gil Blas*, May 15, 1913. For the eye doctors: Alphant, *Claude
    Monet*, p. 658. For the stay at Bois-Lurette: WL 2079.

25 Harding, *Sacha Guitry*, p. 77.

26 Such is Guitry's description in the expanded-minute 1952 version of *Ceux de chez nous*.
    In this later version, done for television in collaboration with Frédéric Rossif, Guitry
    mistakenly identifies Claude Renoir as his older brother Jean.

27 Harding, *Sacha Guitry*, p. 77.

28 For Monet's aversion to dogs and cats in the garden, see Hoschedé, vol. 1, p. 123. For the

Japanese chickens, see Elder, *À Giverny, chez Claude Monet*, loc. 677. For Lassis: *L'Ouest-Éclair*, July 24, 1913.

29 WL 2158.

30 WL 2161a.

31 WL 2160.

32 WL 2157 and 2158.

33 *Le Petit Parisien*, November 4, 1915; *L'Homme Libre*, November 5, 1915.

34 *Le Petit Journal*, March 22, 1915. Photographs and locations of the damage are found in *Le Petit Parisien*, March 22, 1915.

35 *Le Petit Parisien*, May 2, 1915.

36 *La Croix*, August 25, 1915.

37 Ibid., October 2, 1915.

38 See Watson, *Clemenceau*, p. 256.

39 WL 2162.

40 Hoschedé, vol. 1, p. 83.

41 *Le Figaro*, November 24, 1915.

42 *Le Gaulois*, November 23, 1915.

43 *Le Figaro*, December 6, 1915.

44 *Le Petit Parisien*, November 25, 1915.

45 *Le Figaro*, December 6, 1915.

46 *Le Figaro*, November 24, 1915.

47 Quoted in Harding, *Sacha Guitry*, p. 79.

48 *Le Figaro*, December 10, 1915.

49 Ibid., June 2, 1915.

50 *Le Gaulois*, July 23, 1921.

51 WL 2164 and 2165.

CHAPTER EIGHT: UNDER FIRE

1   *Le Matin*, January 1, 1916.

2   Quoted in Alistair Horne, *The Price of Glory: Verdun 1916* (London: Macmillan, 1962), p. 34.

3   Quoted in Robert T. Foley, *German Strategy and the Path to Verdun: Erich Von Falkenhayn and the Development of Attrition, 1870–1916* (Cambridge, UK: Cambridge University Press, 2005), p. 189.

4   *L'Echo de Paris*, January 5, 1915.

5   *Le Petit Parisien*, March 22, 1915.

6   Ibid., January 30, 1916.

7   Quoted in Horne, *The Price of Glory*, p. 76.

8   Ibid.

9   *Le Petit Parisien*, March 1, 1916.

10 Ibid., October 11, 1914, and October 3, 1915.

11 Helen Davenport Gibbons, *Paris Vistas* (New York: The Century Co., 1919), p. 224.

12 *Le Petit Journal*, December 23 and 24, 1874.

13 WL 2172.

14 WL 2172 and 2173.

15 WL 2170.

16 WL 2163.

17 WL 2177.

18 *Journal des débats politiques et littéraires,* April 14 and July 24, 1915; WL 2151.

19 WL 2176.

20 The *Times,* November 11, 1914.

21 *Gil Blas,* June 2, 1912.

22 Quoted in Wildenstein, *Monet, or the Triumph of Impressionism,* p. 253.

23 *Archives Claude Monet,* p. 137.

24 *Le Figaro,* November 10, 1916.

25 WL 2188.

26 WL 2183.

27 WL 2180.

28 Alexander McAdie, "Has the War Affected the Weather?" *Atlantic Monthly* (September 1916), pp. 392–95. McAdie writes that it is a "commonplace of conversation that for some months past the weather conditions have been abnormal" (p. 392). For Monet's complaints about the weather, see WL 2188.

29 *Rapports de M. Paul Peytral, Préfet de L'Allier et des Chefs de Service,* part 3: *Rapports des Chefs de Service et Renseignments Divers: Finances* (Moulins: Fudez Frères, 1915), p. 11.

30 WL 2178.

31 Hoschedé, vol. 1, p. 37.

32 *Bulletin de la Statistique générale de la France,* vol. 6 (October 1916), pp. 18, 25, and 25.

33 *Le Matin,* September 19, 1916.

34 WL 2187.

35 WL 2178.

36 WL 2190.

37 Carr, *Anarchism in France,* p. 164, n. 17.

38 Quoted in Ruth Butler, *Rodin: The Shapes of Genius* (New Haven, CT: Yale University Press, 1993), p. 88.

39 *Le Figaro,* February 23, 1916.

40 Quoted in Holt, *The Tiger,* p. 174.

41 *Le Figaro,* February 23, 1916.

42 WL 2192.

43 *Le Matin,* August 22, 1916.

44 Quoted in Horne, *The Price of Glory,* p. 304.

45 Quoted in Alexander John Watson, *Marginal Man: The Dark Vision of Harold Innis* (Toronto: University of Toronto Press, 2006), p. 77.

46 Henri Barbusse, *Under Fire,* trans. W. Fitzwater Wray (London: Dent, 1988), p. 325. The novel was first published in Wray's English translation in 1917.

47 WL 2182 and 2184.

48 *Le Figaro,* November 10, 1916.

49 *Législation de la guerre de 1914–1916: Lois, décrets, arrêtés ministériels et circulaires ministéri-elles,* vol. 5 (Paris: Librairie Générale de Droit et de Jurisprudence, 1917), p. 267.

50 Martet, *Clemenceau,* p. 223.

51 Quoted in *Georges Clemenceau à son ami Claude Monet,* p. 19.

52 Quoted in Albert E. Elsen and Rosalyn Frankel Jamison, *Rodin's Art. The Rodin Collection of Iris & B. Gerald Cantor Center of Visual Arts at Stanford University*, ed. Bernard Barryte (New York: Oxford University Press, 2003), p. 480.

53 *Le Gaulois*, March 11, 1917.

54 Quoted in Mark Levitch, "The Great War Re-remembered: The Fragmentation of the World's Largest Painting," in Nicholas J. Saunders, ed., *Matters of Conflict: Material Culture, Memory and the First World War* (London: Routledge, 2004), p. 96.

55 WL 2200.

56 WL 2191.

57 WL 2192.

58 WL 2201.

CHAPTER NINE: A STATE OF IMPOSSIBLE ANXIETY

1 WL 2205.

2 *Gil Blas*, October 17, 1905. It is in this review that Vauxcelles christens Matisse, Derain et al. as the *fauves*.

3 M. J. Péladan, quoted in Russell T. Clement, ed., *Les Fauves: A Sourcebook* (Westport, CT: Greenwood Press, 1994), p. xxix.

4 *Archives Claude Monet*, p. 105.

5 Quoted in John O'Brian, *Ruthless Hedonism: The American Reception of Matisse* (Chicago: University of Chicago Press, 1999), p. 6.

6 *L'Art et les Artistes*, December 1905, trans. Terence Maloon in Shackleford et al., *Monet and the Impressionists*, p. 198.

7 Quoted in Hilary Spurling, *The Unknown Matisse: A Life of Henri Matisse: The Early Years, 1869–1908* (Berkeley and Los Angeles: University of California Press, 1998), p. 126.

8 Quoted in Spurling, *The Unknown Matisse*, p. 133.

9 Quoted in Benjamin, "The Decorative Landscape," p. 304.

10 *Matisse on Art*, ed. Jack Flam (Los Angeles and Berkeley: University of California Press, 1995), p. 39.

11 *Archives Claude Monet*, p. 105.

12 *Matisse on Art*, p. 5.

13 The story of this artistic competition is wonderfully told in Jack Flam, *Matisse and Picasso: The Story of Their Rivalry and Friendship* (Cambridge, MA: Westview Press, 2004). For their competition in the early years of the war—including a discussion of *Bathers by a River*—see pp. 102–12. For Matisse's experiments with Cubism: John Golding, *Matisse and Cubism* (Glasgow: University of Glasgow Press, 1978), pp. 14–19.

14 Quoted in Flam, *Matisse and Picasso*, p. 109.

15 *L'Anti-Boche*, July 8, 1916.

16 On this transition, see Jack Flam, "Introduction", *Matisse on Art*, p. 5.

17 WL 2207.

18 WL 2205a.

19 WL 2208.

20 *New York Herald*, March 11, 1917.

21 WL 2014.

22 WL 2212.

23   WL 2210.

24   WL 2211.

25   *Le Figaro*, February 1, 1917.

26   *Le Matin*, February 3, 1917.

27   *Le Figaro*, January 30, 1917.

28   WL 2217.

29   Quoted in Stuckey, *Claude Monet*, p. 248.

30   WL 2216.

31   Quoted in Wildenstein, *Monet, or the Triumph of Impressionism*, p. 408.

32   WL 2219.

33   *Le Petit Parisien*, February 19, 1917.

34   Ibid., July 28, 1915.

35   Ibid., August 13, 1915.

36   Paul Léautaud, quoted in Carr, *Anarchism in France*, p. 161.

37   Quoted in Carr, *Anarchism in France*, p. 161

38   For a discussion of the affair, see Carr, *Anarchism in France*, pp. 161ff; Léon Werth, "Le 'Testament politique d'Octave Mirbeau' est un faux," in *Combats politiques de Mirbeau*, ed. Pierre Michel et Jean-François Nivet (Paris: Librairie Séguier, 1990), pp. 268–73; and Michel et Nivet, *Octave Mirbeau: l'imprécateur au cœur fidèle*, pp. 920–24.

39   WL 2232.

40   Clemenceau, *Claude Monet: Les Nymphéas*, p. 25.

41   WL 2242.

42   Gimpel, *Diary of an Art Dealer*, p. 58.

43   Clemenceau, *Claude Monet*, pp. 28 and 31.

44   Quoted in Watson, *Clemenceau*, p. 258.

45   See Vollard, *Recollections of a Picture Dealer*, pp. 238–40.

46   Vollard, *Recollections of a Picture Dealer*, p. 240. For Clémentel sketching his colleagues, see "Exposition de Peintures et Dessins d'Étienne Clémentel," *La Renaissance de l'art français et des industries de luxe* (July 1926), p. 637.

47   WL 2230.

48   Quoted in House, *Nature into Art*, p. 246, n. 56.

49   Charles Morice, "Introduction" to Auguste Rodin, *Les Cathédrales de France* (Paris. Librairie Armand Colin, 1914), p. 22.

50   Quoted in Stefan Goebel, *The Great War and Medieval Memory: War, Remembrance and Medievalism in Britain and Germany* (Cambridge, UK: Cambridge University Press, 2007), p. 181. For the use of Reims in French propaganda, see Yann Harlault, "La Cathédrale de Reims, du 4 septembre 1914 au 10 juillet 1938: Idéologies, controverses et pragmatisme," thesis directed by Marie-Claude Genet-Delacroix, Université de Reims Champagne-Ardenne, 2006; idem, *Naissance d'un mythe: l'Ange au Sourire de Reims* (Reims: Éditions Guéniot, 2008); and Patrick Demouy, "Le Sourire de Reims," *Comptes rendus des séances de l'Académie des Inscriptions et Belles-Lettres* 153, no. 4 (2009), pp. 1609–27.

51   Quoted in Demouy, "Le Sourire de Reims," pp. 1613 and 1615.

52   *Le Matin*, October 9, 1914.

53   Ibid., February 24, 1917.

54   *Le Matin*, April 9, 10 and 21, 1917; *Le Croix*, April 14, 1917.

55   *Le Matin*, April 21, 1917.

56   Ibid., April 30, 1917.

57   WL 2230.

58   *L'Homme Libre*, December 16, 1914.

59   WL 2231.

60   "La Réglementation de la Consommation de l'Essence," *Bulletin des Usines de Guerre* (May 21, 1917), p. 27.

61   WL 2232a.

62   *Le Matin*, April 15, 1917.

63   Ibid., May 10, 1917.

64   See Becker, *The Great War and the French People*, pp. 210ff.

65   WL 2232.

66   WL 2229.

67   Ibid.

68   Marianne Alphant dates the visit to May 10: See *Claude Monet: une vie dans le paysage*, p. 654. For the violent thunderstorms: *Le Matin*, May 11, 1917.

69   Tucker discusses how Matisse "might have been thinking of the elder Impressionist" when he painted *The Music Lesson*: see "Revolution in the Garden," pp. 70–71.

CHAPTER TEN: THE SMILE OF REIMS

1   For reports of the bombardment in the month before Monet's July 23 letter to Clémentel, see *Le Matin*, June 22, 27, and 30 and July 7, 8, 11, 13 and 16, 1917.

2   *Le Matin*, July 4, 1917.

3   *Le Carnet de la semaine*, September 16, 1917.

4   Quoted in John Rewald, *The History of Impressionism*, vol. 1 (New York: Museum of Modern Art, 1961), p. 220.

5   On some of these changes, see Herbert, "Method and Meaning in Monet," p. 102. For a good account of how the Reims painting would have been at odds with Monet's usual approach, see Michel Hoog, "La Cathédrale de Reims de Claude Monet, ou le tableau impossible," *Revue du Louvre*, no. 1 (1981), pp. 22–24. Hoog writes that "pictorial intention trumps concern for representation" in Monet's paintings, and that "representing the cathedral, let alone describing the damages it sustained, would have meant renouncing all his work, both past and present" (p. 24). Similarly, John House writes that even in Monet's series paintings of poplars and wheat stacks the "conventional rhetoric of thematic significance" is suppressed "in favor of a parading of the artist's powers of vision and creativity." See his review article in the *Art Bulletin* (June 1996), p. 366.

6   *American Magazine of Art* (March 1927).

7   Louis Gillet, *Trois variations sur Claude Monet* (Paris: Librairie Plon, 1927), p. 53.

8   *Kandinsky: Complete Writings on Art*, vol. 1, ed. Kenneth C. Lindsay and Peter Vergo (Boston: G. K. Hall, 1982), p. 363. For a discussion of Kandinsky's encounter with Monet's work, see Natalya Avtonomova, "Vasilii Kandinsky and Claude Monet," *Experiment: A Journal of Russian Culture* 9 (2003), pp. 57–68.

9   *French Cathedrals, by B. Winkles, from Drawings Taken on the Spot by R. Garland, Architect, with an Historical and Descriptive Account* (London: Charles Tilt, 1837), p. 149.

10   Kenneth Clark, *Landscape into Art* (London: John Murray, 1976), p. 94.

11   *Le Carnet de la Semaine*, November 4, 1917.

12   WL 2235a.

13   *Le Matin*, July 24, 1917.

14   *Le Carnet de la Semaine*, September 16, 1917. Vauxcelles wrote the article under his pseudonym, "Pinturicchio."

15   Winston Churchill, *Thoughts and Adventures* (London: Thornton Butterworth, 1932), pp. 169, 175, and 177.

16   WL 2238a.

17   *Le Matin*, September 30, 1917.

18   WL 2233.

19   WL 2235.

20   WL 2238.

21   Gimpel, *Diary of an Art Dealer*, p. 16.

22   Ibid., p. 154.

23   Geffroy, *Claude Monet*, p. 332.

24   WL 2245.

25   WL 2240.

26   WL 2242.

27   Geffroy, *Claude Monet*, p. 5.

28   *Gil Blas*, March 3, 1889.

29   Geffroy, *Claude Monet*, p. 8.

30   WL 2247.

31   Ibid.

32   Quoted in Alphant, *Claude Monet: une vie dans le paysage*, p. 682.

33   WL 2248.

34   WL 2249.

35   Hoog, "La Cathédrale de Reims de Claude Monet," p. 24, n. 13.

36   WL 2251.

37   WL 2248.

38   WL 2254.

39   Quoted in J. F. V. Keiger, *Raymond Poincaré* (Cambridge, UK: Cambridge University Press), p. 3.

40   Quoted in Keiger, *Raymond Poincaré*, p. 11.

41   Marcel Berger and Paul Allard, *Les Secrets de la censure pendant la guerre* (Paris: Éditions des portiques, 1932), p. 63.

42   Quoted in Zeldin, *Politics and Anger*, p. 233.

43   Quoted in Keiger, *Raymond Poincaré*, p. 236.

44   Quoted in Margaret MacMillan, *Paris 1919: Six Months that Changed the World* (New York: Random House, 2001), pp. 33–4.

45   Quoted in Watson, *Clemenceau*, p. 269.

46   Quoted in Keiger, *Raymond Poincaré*, p. 372.

47   *La Croix*, November 17, 1917.

48   *L'Opinion*, November 24, 1917.

49   Clemenceau, *Discours de Guerre*, p. 133.

50 Winston Churchill, *Great Contemporaries* (London: Thornton Butterworth, 1937), p. 312.

51 WL 2259.

52 *La Revue de l'art ancien et moderne*, June 1927.

53 WL 2285.

54 Delouche, "Cubisme et camouflage," p. 127; and the *Illustrated London News*, November 6, 1920.

55 Étienne Clémentel, *La France et la Politique économique interalliée* (Paris: Les Presses Universitaires de France, 1931), p. 217.

56 *Archives Claude Monet*, p. 29.

57 *Le Figaro*, January 29, 1918.

58 Tyler Stovall, *Paris and the Spirit of 1919: Consumer Struggles, Transnationalism, and Revolution* (Cambridge, UK: Cambridge University Press, 2012), p. 219.

59 *Milwaukee Journal*, November 25, 1929.

60 WL 2260.

61 Gibbons, *Paris Vistas*, p. 282.

62 Clémentel, *La France et la Politique économique interalliée,* p. 233.

63 *Le Gaulois*, November 25, 1917.

64 WL 2255a.

CHAPTER ELEVEN: THE WEEPING WILLOW

1   Quoted in Ronald Hayman, *Proust* (London: William Heinemann, 1990), p. 433.

2   Quoted in Watson, *Clemenceau*, p. 294.

3   Quoted in Paul Fussell, *The Great War and Modern Memory* (Oxford: Oxford University Press, 2013), p. 78.

4   *Le Matin*, March 30, 1918.

5   Ibid., March 23, 1918.

6   Clemenceau, *Discours de Guerre*, p. 177.

7   Quoted in Holt, *The Tiger*, pp. 189 and 206.

8   Quoted in Martin Gilbert, *Winston S. Churchill, 1874–1965*, vol. 4: *1916–1922* (London: Heinemann, 1975), p. 99.

9   Churchill, *Great Contemporaries*, p. 312.

10 WL 2275.

11 *Le Matin*, April 21, 1918, citing the *Cologne Gazette*, April 16, 1918.

12 WL 2277.

13 WL 2266 and 2274.

14 *Le Carnet de la semaine*, January 27, 1918.

15 WL 2275.

16 WL 2261, 2271, and 2272.

17 WL 2278.

18 J. J. Grandville, "Élégie: Le Saule Pleureur," in *Les Fleurs animées* (Paris: Garnier-Frères, 1847), pp. 211–12.

19 Maurice Rollinat, "La Lune," in *Choix de poésies* (Paris: Charpentier, 1926).

20 *Revue des Deux Mondes*, April 1, 1835 (my translation). The text from *Otello* is from *Edizione critica delle opere di Gioachino Rossini*, vol. 19, ed. Michael Collins (Fondazione Rossini: Pesaro, 1994), p. 786 (my translation).

21 Charles Virmaître and Henry Buguet, *Paris Croque-Mort* (Paris: Camille Dalou, 1889), p. 56.

22 Wildenstein Letter 2275.

23 Tucker, "Revolution in the Garden," pp. 76–77.

24 *Claude Monet: Life and Art*, p. 210. See also Tucker's discussion of these paintings as "bearers of deep meaning" in "Revolution in the Garden," p. 76–77.

25 *American Art News*, February 23, 1907.

26 For details of this encounter, see Gimpel, *Diary of an Art Dealer*, pp. 57–60.

27 *Le Matin*, August 3, 1918.

28 Quoted in Michael Carver, ed., *The War Lords* (London: Weidenfeld & Nicolson, 1976), p. 41.

29 Quoted in Holt, *The Tiger*, p. 212, n. 1.

30 Watson, *Clemenceau*, p. 314.

31 Quoted in Holt, *The Tiger*, p. 219.

32 *Paris 1918: The War Diary of the 17th Earl of Derby*, ed. David Dutton (Liverpool: Liverpool University Press, 2001), p. 217.

33 Quoted in Holt, *The Tiger*, p. 218.

34 Holt, *The Tiger*, p. 241.

35 Quoted in Holt, *The Tiger*, p. 251.

36 *Art & Life*, November 1919. On Clemenceau's Japanese collection, see Matthieu Séguéla, "Le Japonisme de Georges Clemenceau," *Ebisu* 27 (Autumn–Winter 2001), pp. 7–44.

37 Clemenceau, *Discours de Guerre*, p. 43.

38 *Discours de Guerre*, p. 211.

CHAPTER TWELVE: THIS TERRIBLE, GRAND, AND BEAUTIFUL HOUR

1 *Le Temps*, October 20, 1918.

2 Dallas, *1918*, p. 172. Dallas reports the poignant story that Apollinaire's last minutes coincided with news in Paris of the abdication of Kaiser Wilhelm, with the result that the poet, hearing crowds outside his window chanting "*À bas Guillaume!*," thought they were calling for his death.

3 Quoted in Pierre Darmon, "La grippe espagnole submerge la France," *L'Histoire*, no. 281 (Novembre 2003), p. 84. For information on the epidemic in Paris, I am indebted to this work and also to Olivier Lahaie, "L'épidémie de grippe dite 'espagnole' et sa perception par l'armée française (1918–1919)," *Revue historique des armées*, vol. 262 (2011), pp. 102–9.

4 Becker, *The Great War and the French People*, p. 318.

5 Quoted in Michael S. Neiberg, *Foch: Supreme Allied Commander in the Great War* (Dulles, VA: Potomac Books, 2003), p. 86.

6 Quoted in Neiberg, *Foch*, p. 86.

7 Quoted in Dallas, *1918*, p. 173.

8 These descriptions (and those in the following paragraphs) are taken from reports published on November 12 in *Le Figaro*, *L'Homme Libre*, *L'Humanité*, *Le Matin*, *Le Petit Parisien*, and *Le Temps*.

9 *L'Homme Libre*, November 12, 1918.

10 Quoted in Holt, *The Tiger*, p. 218.

11   *Great Contemporaries*, p. 302.

12   *Discours de Guerre*, p. 203.

13   Quoted in Watson, *Clemenceau*, p. 327.

14   WL 2290.

15   WL 2287.

16   *Le Matin*, November 14 and 18, 1918.

17   *La Renaissance: Politique, Economique, Littéraire et Artistique*, December 7, 1918. This report, "Le Tigre dans la Jungle," incorrectly places this visit on the day of the armistice.

18   Gimpel, *Diary of an Art Dealer*, p. 75.

19   Ibid., pp. 75–6.

20   Guitry, *If I Remember Right*, p. 238.

21   Marc Elder in *Le Bulletin de la Vie Artistique*, May 1, 1920.

22   Guitry, *If I Remember Right*, p. 238.

23   *La Renaissance: Politique, Economique, Littéraire et Artistique*, December 7, 1918.

24   Geffroy, *Claude Monet*, p. 333.

25   *L'Homme Libre*, December 1, 1918.

26   Geffroy, *Claude Monet*, p. 333. Wildenstein writes that Geffroy's account makes it "tempting to conclude that the idea of a more substantial donation had been adopted by 18 November" (Wildenstein, *Monet, or the Triumph of Impressionism*, p. 410).

27   *L'Art et les artistes*, November 1920.

28   *Excelsior*, January 26, 1921.

29   Mark Levitch, personal e-mail communication, February 26, 2015.

30   *Le Gaulois*, December 29, 1918. For a description of the immersive experience, see Levitch, "The Great War Re-remembered: The Fragmentation of the World's Largest Painting," pp. 94–5.

31   *France-États-Unis: revue mensuelle du Comité France-Amérique* (January 1919), p. 379.

32   *Le Figaro*, November 25, 1917. I have also used details from the description of the funeral in *Le Matin*, November 25, 1917.

33   *Archives Claude Monet*, p. 137.

34   WL 2288, 2289, 2290.

35   Gimpel, *Diary of an Art Dealer*, p. 74.

36   WL 2292.

37   *Le Matin*, December 5, 1918.

38   WL 2294.

39   *Le Matin*, August 2, 1918.

40   Ibid., September 6, 1918.

41   WL 2296 and 2299.

42   *Art et Décoration: Revue mensuelle d'Art moderne* (July–December 1910).

43   *New York Times*, January 11, 1914.

44   *New York Sun*, October 7, 1917.

45   Ibid., April 14, 1918.

46   WL 2280.

47   WL 2294.

CHAPTER THIRTEEN: AN OLD MAN MAD ABOUT PAINTING

1 See *Le Petit Parisien*, January 9, 1919, and numerous reports in other newspapers.
2 WL 2296.
3 WL 2297.
4 WL 2296.
5 WL 2308.
6 WL 2306.
7 *Archives Claude Monet*, p. 12.
8 WL 2306.
9 The *Times*, December 2 and 4, 1918.
10 *Paris 1918: The War Diary of the British Ambassador*, p. 83.
11 *Paris 1918*, p. 287.
12 On this controversy, and the distinction between *candeur* and *candour*, see Dallas, *1918*, p. 216.
13 Quoted in MacMillan, *Paris 1919*, p. 27.
14 Quoted in Dallas, *1918*, p. 212.
15 The *Times*, December 31, 1918.
16 Ibid., January 23, 1919.
17 Details of the assassination attempt come from reports in *L'Homme Libre*, *Le Petit Parisien*, the *Times*, and the *New York Times*, February 20, 1919.
18 *La Croix*, May 7, 1912.
19 *L'Homme Enchâiné*, October 20, 1916. Her presence in the rue Franklin in February 1919 is reported in *Le Figaro*, February 23 and 24.
20 L. Delamarre, *Lettre à mes soldats* (Paris: A. Rasquin, 1919), p. 4.
21 *Archives Claude Monet*, p. 31.
22 Quoted in Holt, *The Tiger*, p. 228. Cottin was released from prison, due to poor health, in August 1924.
23 Quoted in Dallas, *1918*, p. 177.
24 The *Times*, December 5, 1918.
25 For these statistics, see William McDonald, *Reconstruction in France* (London: Macmillan, 1922), pp. 24–30.
26 Dallas, *1918*, p. 84.
27 *Collected Writings of John Maynard Keynes*, vol. 2, ed. Donald Moggridge and Elizabeth Johnson (London: Macmillan, 1971), p. 94.
28 *Le Figaro*, April 9, 1919.
29 WL 2319.
30 WL 2316.
31 WL 2313.
32 WL 2319.
33 *Le Figaro*, August 16, 1919, and reports in the *Times*, August 14 and 18, 1919.
34 WL 2319.
35 *The Literary Digest*, February 3, 1917.
36 *Le Looping*, August 10, 1918.
37 Cocteau, *A Call to Order*, trans. Rollo H. Myers (London: Faber & Gwyer, 1926). On this subject, see the ground-breaking work by Kenneth Silver, *Esprit de Corps: The Art of the*

Parisian Avant-Garde and the First World War, 1914–1925 (Princeton: Princeton University Press, 1989). Silver shows how foreign, noncombatant artists working in France during the war fell under suspicion and how modernism in general and Cubism in particular came to be associated with the German enemy. Silver has subsequently expanded the scope of his argument in *Chaos and Classicism: Art in France, Italy, and Germany, 1918–19*, exhibition catalogue (New York: Guggenheim Museum Publications, 2010).

38   Pierre Lampué, *Rapport: Au nom de la 4e Commission (1), relatif aux diverses propositions de la glorification de la Victoire* (Paris: Conseil Municipal de Paris, 1919), p. 2.

39   Marius Vachon, *La Guerre artistique avec l'Allemagne: L'Organization de la Victoire* (Paris: Librairie Payot et Cie, 1916), pp. 138, 140.

40   For a good discussion of how Monet's late paintings went against the artistic grain of the postwar period, see Tucker, "Revolution in the Garden," pp. 78–9.

41   WL 2324.

42   Clemenceau, *Claude Monet: Les Nymphéas*, p. 31.

43   See *Archives Claude Monet*, p. 140.

44   WL 2326.

45   "L'Épitaphe," in *Les Névroses: les âmes, les luxures, les refuges, les spectres, les ténèbres* (Paris: G. Charpentier, 1885), my translation. For Rollinat's study of psychiatric patients, see Rae Beth Gordon, "From Charcot to Charlot," in Mark S. Micale, ed., *The Mind of Modernism: Medicine, Psychology, and the Cultural Arts in Europe and America, 1880–1940* (Stanford, CA: Stanford University Press, 2004), p. 105.

46   Quoted in Levine, *Monet, Narcissus, and Self-Reflection*, p. 148.

47   WL 923.

48   Levine, *Monet, Narcissus, and Self-Reflection*, p. 105.

49   Quoted in Émile Vinchon, "Maurice Rollinat dans la Creuse," in *Mémoires de la société des sciences naturelles et archéologiques de la Creuse*, vol. 27 (1938–40), p. 318. I am indebted to this work for details of Rollinat's life in Fresselines.

50   WL 2326.

51   Quoted in Lawrence Hanson, *Renoir: The Man, the Painter, and His World* (London: Leslie Frewin, 1972), p. 248. Hanson writes that there is more than one version of this remark, "but the sense of all is identical" (p. 270, n. 64). *Le Monde illustré* reports what it calls "la Légende" as early as December 20, 1919, with Renoir uttering as he expired: "*Je faisais encore des progrès!*" ("I'm still making progress!").

52   Quoted in Ray Rushton, "Ingres: Drawings from the Musée Ingres at Montauban and Other Collections," *Journal of the Royal Society of Arts* (February 1980), p. 159.

53   Quoted in A. Hyatt Mayor and Yasuko Betchaku, "Hokusai," *Metropolitan Museum of Art Bulletin*, New Series, vol. 43 (Summer 1985), p. 5.

54   Ambrose Vollard, *Renoir: An Intimate Record*, trans. Harold L. Van Doren and Randolph T. Weaver (New York: Alfred A. Knopf, 1925), pp. 225–6.

55   *Archives Claude Monet*, p. 135.

56   WL 2328 and 2329.

57   *Le Radical*, December 4, 1919.

CHAPTER FOURTEEN: MEN OF IMPECCABLE TASTE

1   *Le Gaulois*, January 19, 1920.

2   Gimpel, p. 127.

3   Quoted in Robert C. Byrd, *The Senate, 1789–1989*, vol. 1: *Addresses on the History of the United States Senate* (Washington, DC: Senate Historical Office, 1988), p. 424.

4   Quoted in the *Times*, December 11, 1919.

5   For Lloyd George's involvement, see Dallas, *1918*, p. 501.

6   *Le Monde illustré*, January 24, 1920.

7   Quoted in Holt, *The Tiger*, p. 247.

8   WL 2319b.

9   *La Revue hebdomadaire*, February 6, 1909.

10 *Le Bulletin de la vie artistique*, February 1, 1920.

11 *Archives Claude Monet*, p. 78.

12 WL 2333.

13 Wildenstein writes: "It has been alleged—though no evidence is forthcoming—that Clemenceau took a foreign collector to Giverny by way of revenge against his ungrateful countrymen" (*Monet, or the Triumph of Impressionism*, p. 412). If this collector was Zoubaloff, he was hardly foreign in the sense that he would have spirited the Grande Décoration out of the country. Nor, if he did bring Zoubaloff to Giverny, would Clemenceau necessarily have been acting out of spite: Zoubaloff almost certainly would have purchased the panels (as he did so many other works of art) for the nation.

14 WL 2335.

15 *Le Petit Parisien*, February 12, 1922.

16 WL 2341.

17 WL 2336. For the high prices fetched by Monet's paintings in America at this time, see *La Renaissance de l'art français et des industries de luxe* (January 1920), which reports (p. 193) that his works were being sold for as much as 130,000 francs.

18 *La Renaissance de l'art français et des industries de luxe*, May 1927.

19 *Le Bulletin de la Vie Artistique*, August 15, 1921.

20 Ibid., May 1, 1920.

21 "Bertha Palmer: Curatorial Entry," in Gloria Groom and Jill Shaw, eds., *Monet: Paintings and Drawings at the Art Institute of Chicago* (Chicago: Art Institute of Chicago, 2014), para. 6.

22 *Bulletin de la vie artistique*, April 15, 1921. For the Impressionist paintings in the Luxembourg, see Léonce Bénédite, *Le Musée du Luxembourg: Les Peintures, École Française* (Paris: H. Laurens, 1923), *passim*.

23 For the presence of the curator and architect, see *Le Temps*, October 14, 1920.

24 *Chicago Daily Tribune*, December 6, 1926. In 1920 the US dollar was worth 15 francs.

25 *Alumni Directory: University of Chicago* (Chicago: University of Chicago Press, 1920), pp. xiv–xv.

26 WL 2335a.

27 Alphant, *Claude Monet: une vie dans le paysage*, p. 675.

28 *La Revue de l'art ancien et moderne*, January–May 1927.

29 *Chicago Daily Tribune*, December 6, 1926.

30 WL 578.

31 *La Revue de l'art ancien et moderne*, January- May 1927.
32 WL 2358.
33 WL 2359.
34 WL 2355 and 2358.
35 WL 2362.
36 WL 2326 and 2355.
37 *Georges Clemenceau à son ami Claude Monet*, p. 80.
38 Ibid.
39 Duroselle, *Clemenceau*, p. 898.
40 Quoted in Duroselle, *Clemenceau*, p. 899.
41 *Georges Clemenceau à son ami Claude Monet*, p. 84.
42 WL 2366.

CHAPTER FIFTEEN: A GRAND DONATION

1 Paul Léon, *Du Palais-Royal au Palais-Bourbon: souvenirs* (Paris: Albin-Michel, 1947), p. 207.
2 For Léon's activities in Reims, see Camille Bidaud, "Paul Léon et la restauration monumentale: l'exemple de Saint-Remi de Reims," Diplôme Propre aux Écoles d'Architecture, directed by Jean-Philippe Garric, École Nationale Supérieure d'Architecture de Paris-Belleville (2012); and idem, "Des expérimentations légitimées par le traumatisme: Paul Léon à Saint-Remi de Reims," *In Situ: Revue des patrimoines*, no. 23 (2014), available online at http://insitu.revues.org/10974.
3 I am grateful to Camille Bidaud (personal e-mail correspondence, July 29, 2015) and Yann Harlaut (August 6, 2015) for having confirmed the lack of evidence for Paul Léon having been involved in Monet's Reims commission.
4 *Diary of an Art Dealer*, p. 150.
5 Quoted in Charles Lortsch, *La Beauté de Paris et la Loi* (Paris: Librairie de la Société du Recueil Sirey, 1913), p. 205. For the architectural changes wrought by Bonnier's 1902 regulations, see Andrew Ayers, *The Architecture of Paris* (Stuttgart and London: Axel Menges, 2004), p. 400.
6 *Le Cri de Paris*, June 8, 1913.
7 Alan Sheridan, *André Gide: A Life in the Present* (Cambridge, MA: Harvard University Press, 1998), p. 217.
8 Quoted in Wildenstein, *Monet, or the Triumph of Impressionism*, p. 414.
9 Quoted in Sheridan, *André Gide*, p. 223.
10 Wildenstein, *Claude Monet: Biographie et catalogue raisonné*, vol. 4, p. 97, n. 887.
11 Ibid., vol. 4, p. 98, n. 902; and p. 99, n. 912.
12 Ibid., vol. 4, p. 97, note 887.
13 *Le Petit Parisien*, October 14, 1920.
14 *L'Opinion*, October 16, 1920.
15 WL 2380.
16 WL 2391.
17 *Le Temps*, October 14, 1920.
18 *La Revue de l'art ancien et moderne*, February 1927.
19 *Le Temps*, October 14, 1920.

20 *Le Populaire*, October 20, 1920.

21 *L'Humanité*, October 29, 1920.

22 *Le Figaro*, October 21, 1920.

23 *La Renaissance de l'Art Français et des Industries de Luxe*, January 1921. This article, like Alexandre's in *Le Figaro* and all other contemporary documentation, including references by Monet himself, calls the work *Dames cueillant des fleurs* (*Women Picking Flowers*).

24 *Diary of an Art Dealer*, p. 153.

25 "Normand," in Centre National de Ressources Textuelles et Lexicales, available online at www.cnrtl.fr.

26 WL 2384.

27 *Le Figaro*, November 14, 1920.

28 Ibid., October 21, 1920.

29 *La Renaissance de l'art français et des industries de luxe,* January 1920.

30 *La Revue de l'art ancien et moderne*, January–May 1927.

31 *Le Populaire*, November 23, 1920.

32 *Le Journal*, September 26, 1911.

33 Elder, *À Giverny, chez Claude Monet*, loc. 641.

34 Camille Mauclair, *L'Impressionnisme: son histoire, son esthétique, ses maîtres* (Paris: Librairie de l'Art Ancien et Moderne, 1904), p. 220. Monet's paintings are listed in *Exposition universelle de 1900: Catalogue officiel illustré de l'exposition centennale de l'art français de 1800 à 1889* (Paris: Lemercier, 1900), p. 211.

35 Adolphe Tabarant, *Manet et ses oeuvres* (Paris: Gallimard, 1947), p. 316.

36 *Claude Monet, ce mal connu*, vol. 1, p. 40.

37 Quoted in Roger Peyrefitte, *L'Illustre écrivain* (Paris: Albin Michel, 1982), p. 197.

38 *Le Bulletin de la vie artistique*, December 1, 1920.

39 *Le Figaro*, January 30, 1921.

40 Ibid., December 31, 1920.

41 *Illustrated London News*, February 26, 1921.

42 Quoted in Wildenstein, *Monet, or the Triumph of Impressionism*, p. 415.

43 Quoted in Simon Kelly, *Monet's Water Lilies: The Agapanthus Triptych* (St. Louis: St. Louis Art Museum, 2011), pp. 30–31.

44 Quoted in Kelly, *Monet's Water Lilies*, p. 30.

45 Quoted in Paul Léon, *La Renaissance des ruines: maisons, monuments* (Paris: H. Laurens, 1918), p. 44.

46 WL 2406.

47 WL 2398.

48 WL 2402.

49 WL 2400 and 2402.

50 Quoted in Duroselle, *Clemenceau*, p. 914.

51 The *Times*, November 28, 1929.

52 *Georges Clemenceau à son ami Claude Monet*, p. 85.

53 Ibid., p. 101.

54 *Le Matin*, April 8, 1921.

55 *Georges Clemenceau à son ami Claude Monet*, p. 87.

56 WL 2418.

57 *Le Matin*, April 8, 1921.

58 WL 2419 and 2421.

59 WL 2422.

60 WL 2424.

61 WL 2426.

62 Monet complained to Arsène Alexandre that the Orangerie did not provide "the necessary distance" for viewing the paintings (WL 2437).

63 WL 2426.

CHAPTER SIXTEEN: A MOST ARDENT ADMIRER

1 On Clemenceau's friendship with Prince Saionji, see Séguéla, "Le Japonisme de Georges Clemenceau," p. 12; and on Clemenceau's bonsai tree and gardener, see ibid., p. 35.

2 *Archives Claude Monet*, p. 78.

3 *Le Bulletin de la vie artistique*, November 15, 1921. This article mentions visits recently made by the artists Yamagata and Hashimoto.

4 *Le Bulletin de la vie artistique*, December 15, 1922.

5 *L'Homme Libre*, March 16, 1924. I date the visit of Matsukata to Giverny to June on the basis of Monet's letter of June 19 to Arsène Alexandre (WL 2442).

6 *Le Bulletin de la vie artistique*, December 15, 1922.

7 Ibid.

8 See Libby Horner, "Brangwyn and the Japanese Connection," *Journal of the Decorative Arts Society 1850–the Present*, No. 26, *Omnium Gatherum: A Collection of Papers* (2002), pp. 72–83.

9 WL 2341a.

10 Octave Mirbeau, *La 628-E8* (Paris: Charpentier, 1910), pp. 207–9. Hoschedé also tells the story of the *épicier* in Holland (vol. 1, p. 54).

11 Hoschedé, vol. 1, p. 54.

12 *Gazette des Beaux-Arts*, June 1909, trans. Maloon, p. 201.

13 *Excelsior*, January 26, 1921, quoted in Shackleford et al., *Monet and the Impressionists*, cat. 37, p. 162.

14 Quoted in George T. M. Shackleford, "Monet and Japanese Art," in Shackleford et al., *Monet and the Impressionists*, p. 91.

15 See Hidemichi Tanaka, "Cézanne and *Japonisme*," *Artibus et Historiae* 22, no. 44 (2001), pp. 201–20. Tanaka cites the work of earlier Japanese scholars such as Kazuo Fukumoto, who in the 1950s pointed out the resemblances between Cézanne and Japanese artists. Tanaka and other Japanese critics have pointed out that Cézanne's Mont Sainte-Victoire paintings were inspired likewise by Monet's wheat stack paintings, "themselves influenced by Hokusai's landscape series" (p. 203).

16 *Le Temps*, June 7, 1904.

17 *Archives Claude Monet*, p. 142.

18 *Le Temps*, June 7, 1904.

19 For this coincidence, see Wildenstein, *Monet, or the Triumph of Impressionism*, p. 290.

20 *American Art News*, January 21, 1922.

21 *L'Homme Libre*, March 16, 1924.

22 Ibid. This report says the episode took place "two years ago," but Matsukata first met Monet and made his purchases in 1921.

23 *Le Bulletin de la vie artistique*, November 15, 1921.

24 *Le Bulletin de la vie artistique* reported that Matsukata "chose for himself...fifteen can-vases from Monet at Giverny...He must have twenty-five Monets today" (December 15, 1922). The article recorded his purchases as "wheatstacks, poplars, London bridges, water lilies, snowscapes, Belle-Île landscapes."

25 Quoted in Horner, "Brangwyn and the Japanese Connection," p. 75.

26 Ibid.

27 WL 2442.

28 *American Art News*, January 21, 1922. Matsukata is said in this article to own twenty-five Monet paintings.

29 WL 2437.

30 WL 2442.

31 WL 2435.

32 WL 2444.

33 *Georges Clemenceau à son ami Claude Monet*, p. 89.

34 The *Times*, June 23, 1921.

35 *Georges Clemenceau à son ami Claude Monet*, p. 89.

36 *Le Petit Parisien*, October 3, 1921.

37 Ibid., October 3, 1921.

38 *Georges Clemenceau à son ami Claude Monet*, p. 89.

39 Ibid., p. 119.

40 *Le Petit Parisien*, October 1, 1921.

41 *Georges Clemenceau à son ami Claude Monet*, p. 90.

42 I have taken the following details from the article in *Le Petit Parisien*, October 1, 1921.

43 *Georges Clemenceau à son ami Claude Monet*, pp. 107–8.

44 Ibid., pp. 149 and 151.

45 Ibid., p. 89.

46 Duroselle, *Clemenceau*, p. 900.

47 *Le Petit Parisien*, October 1, 1921.

48 *Lettres à une amie*, p. 323n.

49 *Le Petit Parisien*, October 1, 1921.

50 *Lettres à une Amie*, p. 81; and *Le Temps*, August 31, 1924.

51 *Georges Clemenceau à son ami Claude Monet*, p. 90.

52 Ibid., p. 91.

53 WL 2458.

54 *Georges Clemenceau à son ami Claude Monet*, p. 91.

55 WL 2463.

56 WL 2470.

57 *Georges Clemenceau à son ami Claude Monet*, p. 94.

58 WL 2474.

59 *Georges Clemenceau à son ami Claude Monet*, p. 94.

60 Ibid., p. 98.

61 WL 2489. The phrase he uses is *que sale type je suis.*

62 WL 2490.

63 WL 2491.

64 For a good discussion of the contract, see Charles F. Stuckey, "Blossoms and Blunders: Monet and the State," Part I: *Art in America* (January–February 1979), pp. 114–15.

65 *Georges Clemenceau à son ami Claude Monet*, p. 101.

CHAPTER SEVENTEEN: THE LUMINOUS ABYSS

1 WL 2500.

2 *Le Figaro*, November 19, 1922.

3 *Claude Monet*, pp. 324 and 335.

4 *L'Art dans les deux mondes*, March 7, 1891.

5 *La Revue Indépendante de Littérature et d'Art*, March 1892.

6 *Claude Monet*, pp. 335–6.

7 *Fermes et Château*, September 1, 1908.

8 *Claude Monet*, pp. 334 and 336.

9 *Metamorphoses*, trans. Frank Justus Miller (Cambridge MA: Loeb Classical Library, 1916), Book 9, line 347.

10 William E. Ward, "The Lotus Symbol: Its Meaning in Buddhist Art and Philosophy," *Journal of Aesthetics and Art Criticism* 11 (December 1952), p. 136, n. 9. Ward discusses Egyptian meanings on p. 135.

11 Marlene Dobkin de Rios, "The Influence of Psychotropic Flora and Fauna on Maya Religion", *Current Anthropology* 15 (June 1974), pp. 150–51; and Esther Pasztory, "The Iconography of the Teotihuacan Tlaloc," *Studies in Pre-Columbian Art and Archaeology*, no. 15 (1974), pp. 7 and 10.

12 *Claude Monet, ce mal connu*, vol. 1, pp. 68–9.

13 Maeterlinck, *The Intelligence of Flowers*, trans. Alexander Teixeira de Mattos (New York: Dodd Mead & Co., 1907), p. 34.

14 George Sand, *François le Champi* (Paris: Hachette, 1855), p. ii. Sand writes that *nape* was a colloquial name for "the beautiful plant called *nénuphar* or *nymphéa*," which she speculates referred to the *napées*, mythological goddesses who presided over the meadows and forests (p. 1).

15 L'Abbé Thiébaud, *Marie dans les Fleurs: ou, reflet symbolique des privilèges de la Sainte Vierge dans les beautés de la Nature* (Paris: Lecoffre Fils et Cie., 1867), pp. 284–5.

16 Maurice Rollinat, "L'Étang," in *Les névroses* (my translation).

17 Maurice Rollinat, "L'Étang Rouge," *En errant, proses d'un solitaire* (Paris: Charpentier, 1903) p. 132. Rollinat's poems mentioning water lilies include "Les Yeux des Vierges" and "La Lune."

18 Octave Mirbeau, *Le Jardin des Supplices* (Paris: Eugène Fasquelle, 1899), p. 191.

19 Ibid., p. 287.

20 *L'Art dans les deux Mondes*, March 7, 1891.

21 *Mercure de France*, February 1901, quoted in Levine, *Monet, Narcissus, and Self-Reflection*, p. 196.

22 Edmond Pilon, *Octave Mirbeau* (Paris: Bibliothèque Internationale), 1903, p. 8.

23 Emily Apter, "The Garden of Scopic Perversion from Monet to Mirbeau," *October* 47 (Winter, 1988), p. 106. See also Christian Limousin, "Monet au Jardin des supplices," *Cahiers Octave Mirbeau*, Angers, no. 8 (April 2001), pp. 256–78, available online at http://mirbeau.asso.fr/darticlesfrancais/Limousin-JDSmonet.pdf

24 Gimpel, *Diary of an Art Dealer*, p. 58.

25 "Le Nénuphar Blanc," trans. Bradford Cook, in Mary Ann Caws, ed., Stéphane Mallarmé, *Selected Poetry and Prose* (New York: New Directions, 1982), p. 67.

26 Apter, "The Garden of Scopic Perversion," pp. 110–11.

27 Gimpel, *Diary of an Art Dealer*, p. 339.

28 Limousin, "Monet au Jardin des supplices," available at http://mirbeau.asso.fr/darticles francais/Limousin-JDSmonet.pdf

29 Levine, *Monet, Narcissus, and Self-Reflection*, p. 252.

30 Quoted in Geffroy, *Claude Monet*, p. 244.

31 Quoted in Levine, *Monet, Narcissus, and Self-Reflection*, p. 223.

32 Robert Rey, *La Renaissance du sentiment classique dans la peinture française à la fin du 19e siècle: Degas, Renoir, Gauguin, Cézanne, Seurat* (Paris: Les Beaux-Arts, Édition d'Études et de Documents, 1931), pp. 136–7. Writing following Monet's death, Rey predicted that, had the master lived another decade, these human forms would have emerged in his landscapes.

33 *Claude Monet, ce mal connu*, vol. 1, p. 129, n. 2.

34 Georges Cuvier, *Leçons d'anatomie comparée*, vol. 5 (Paris: Crochard, 1805), p. 122.

35 Huysmans, *Against Nature*, trans. Robert Baldick (Baltimore: Penguin, 1966), p. 67.

36 *Le Gaulois*, December 6, 1926.

37 *Variations*, May 27, 1927.

38 *Dictionnaire encyclopédique usuel*, 4th edition (Paris: Librairie Scientifique, Industrielle et Agricole de Lacroix-Comon, 1858), vol. 2, p. 969.

39 *Apollonius Rhodius: Argonautica*, ed. and trans. William H. Race (Cambridge, MA: Harvard University Press, 2009), lines 1236–9.

40 See, for example, Félix Jahrer's *Étude des Beaux-arts: Salon de 1865* (Paris, 1865), p. 55; and *Revue française*, May–August 1865. I discuss the scandal of Manet's *Olympia* in *The Judgment of Paris*, pp. 151–5.

CHAPTER EIGHTEEN: THE FATAL PROTUBERANCE

1   Clemenceau, *Claude Monet: Les Nymphéas*, p. 19.

2   *Selected Writings of Jules Laforgue*, ed. and trans. William Jay Smith (New York: Grove Press, 1956), p. 192.

3   Nordau, *Degeneration* (New York: D. Appleton & Co., 1895), p. 43.

4   Ibid., p. 37.

5   Quoted in Apter, "The Garden of Scopic Perversion," pp. 104 and 105.

6   Quoted in Philippe Lanthony, *Art and Ophthalmology: The Impact of Eye Diseases on Painters*, trans. Colin Mailer (Amsterdam: Kugler, 2009), p. 134.

7   WL 2494.

8   *À Giverny, chez Claude Monet*, loc. 930.

9   WL 2503.

10 Quoted in Tucker, "Revolution in the Garden," p. 82.

11 Dating these late works is difficult, given the persistent failure of Monet to sign and date his works after 1919. However, Tucker dates the completion of the Japanese bridge canvases (of which three had been begun in 1918) and the alley of roses (a motif resumed in 1920) to the summer of 1922: *Claude Monet: Life and Art*, pp. 218–19.

12 WL 2504a.

13 Quoted in Wildenstein, *Monet, or the Triumph of Impressionism*, p. 423.

14 *Le Journal*, May 22, 1922.

15 Paul Hayes Tucker, personal e-mail correspondence, August 2, 2015. I am grateful to Dr. Tucker for information on this transaction and for confirming my suspicions about the identity of the painting purchased by Matsukata.

16 WL 2505.

17 J. Royer, J. Haut, and P. Almaric, "L'Opération de la cataracte de Claude Monet: Correspondance inédite du peintre et de G. Clemenceau au docteur Coutela," *Histoire des Sciences Médicales* 18 (1984), p. 110.

18 Royer et al., "L'Opération de la cataracte de Claude Monet," p. 110.

19 WL 2507.

20 "L'Opération de la cataracte de Claude Monet," p. 111.

21 *New York Times*, September 10, 1922.

22 Quoted in Holt, *The Tiger*, p. 251.

23 For Kipling's denial, see *The Letters of Rudyard Kipling*, vol. 5, pp. 127–8. Pinney observes that there is "no doubt he had in fact said them" (p. 128).

24 The *Times*, September 11, 1922.

25 *New York Times*, September 10, 1922.

26 *Le Petit Journal*, September 12, 1922.

27 *New York Tribune*, October 22, 1922.

28 The *Times*, November 11, 1922.

29 *New York Tribune*, October 22, 1922.

30 Ibid., November 20, 1922.

31 Ibid., November 19, 1922.

32 *New York Evening World*, November 20, 1922.

33 *New York Tribune*, November 24, 1922.

34 Ibid., November 24, 1922.

35 *New York Evening World*, December 5 and 13, 1922.

36 *Le Figaro*, November 19, 1922.

37 WL 2517.

38 Hoschedé, *Claude Monet, ce mal connu*, vol. 1, p. 142.

39 Quoted in Wildenstein, *Monet, or the Triumph of Impressionism*, pp. 423–4.

40 Hoschedé, vol. 1, p. 142.

41 Ibid., vol. 1, pp. 142–3.

42 Léon Heuraux, *Cocaïne et stovaïne en ophtalmologie: leurs indications particulières* (Lyon: Delaroche et Schneider, 1906), p. 51.

43 E. Fuchs, *Manuel d'ophtalmologie*, 2nd French edition, trans. C. Lacompte and L. Leplat (Paris: Georges Carré and C. Naud, 1897), p. 787.

44 Hoschedé, vol. 1, p. 143.

45 Quoted in Wildenstein, *Monet, or the Triumph of Impressionism*, pp. 424–5.

46 WL 2505.

47 *La Lanterne*, May 24, 1922.

48 *Le Bulletin de la vie artistique*, October 15, 1923.

49 WL 2522.

50 This point is made in Romy Golan, "Oceanic Sensations: Monet's *Grandes Décorations* and Mural Painting in France from 1927 to 1952," in Tucker et al., *Monet in the 20th Century*, p. 92.

51 Royer et al., "L'Opération de la cataracte de Claude Monet," p. 111.

52 *Georges Clemenceau à son ami Claude Monet*, p. 116.

53 Royer et al., "L'Opération de la cataracte de Claude Monet," p. 112.

54 Hoschedé, *Claude Monet, ce mal connu*, vol. 1, p. 144.

55 *Georges Clemenceau à son ami Claude Monet*, p. 116.

56 Ibid., p. 118.

57 Ibid., p. 119.

58 Royer et al., "L'Opération de la cataracte de Claude Monet," pp. 113–14.

59 *Georges Clemenceau à son ami Claude Monet*, p. 119.

60 Ibid., p. 122.

61 WL 2526.

62 *Georges Clemenceau à son ami Claude Monet*, p. 124.

63 WL 2528; and Royer et al., "L'Opération de la cataracte de Claude Monet," p. 114.

64 Royer et al., "L'Opération de la cataracte de Claude Monet," p. 115.

65 *Georges Clemenceau à son ami Claude Monet*, p. 125.

66 Ibid., p. 126; and WL 2538.

67 WL 2529.

68 Dr. Coutela's report of this consultation can be found in *Georges Clemenceau à son ami Claude Monet*, pp. 128–30.

69 WL 2530.

70 WL 2531.

71 Philippe Lanthony, "La xanthopsie de Van Gogh," *Bulletin des Sociétés d'ophtalmologie de France* (October 1989), pp. 133–4; and W. N. Arnold and L. S. Loftis, "Xanthopsia and van Gogh's Yellow Palette," *Eye* 5 (1991), pp. 503–10.

72 Royer et al., "L'Opération de la cataracte de Claude Monet," p. 116.

73 *If I Remember Right*, p. 233.

74 *Georges Clemenceau à son ami Claude Monet*, pp. 126 and 127.

75 Royer et al., "L'Opération de la cataracte de Claude Monet," p. 116.

76 *Georges Clemenceau à son ami Claude Monet*, p. 132–4.

77 Ibid., p. 137.

78 WL 2535.

79 WL 2539.

80 WL 2534.

81 Gimpel, *Diary of an Art Dealer*, pp. 9 and 58.

82 *Georges Clemenceau à son ami Claude Monet*, p. 139.

83 WL 2664.

84 *Georges Clemenceau à son ami Claude Monet*, pp. 140–41.

85 Ibid., pp. 142 and 143. The accident was widely reported in the press: See, for example, *Le Petit Parisien* and *Le Figaro*, December 17, 1923.

CHAPTER NINETEEN: THE SOUL'S DARK COTTAGE

1   Quoted in Gennifer Weisenfeld, *Imaging Disaster: Tokyo and the Visual Culture of Japan's Great Earthquake of 1923* (Berkeley and Los Angeles: University of California Press, 2012), p. 2.

2   See, for example, *L'Humanité*, September 5, 1923.

3   *Le Petit Parisien*, December 1, 1923.

4   *Le Rappel*, January 15, 1924.

5   WL 2554.

6   WL 2545.

7   Wildenstein, *Monet, or the Triumph of Impressionism*, p. 137.

8   Louis Gillet, *Trois variations sur Claude Monet* (Paris: Librairie Plon, 1927), p. 45. All quotations are taken from this text.

9   *Georges Clemenceau à son ami Claude Monet*, p. 143.

10   Royer et al., "L'Opération de la cataracte de Claude Monet," p. 119.

11   *Georges Clemenceau à son ami Claude Monet,* p. 147.

12   WL 2489.

13   *Lettres à une Amie*, p. 89.

14   *Georges Clemenceau à son ami Claude Monet*, pp. 148, 149, 150, and 157.

15   Ibid., p. 113.

16   Martet, *Clemenceau*, p. 219.

17   *Georges Clemenceau à son ami Claude Monet*, p. 149.

18   Ibid., p. 150.

19   Royer et al., "L'Opération de la cataracte de Claude Monet," p. 120.

20   WL 2567.

21   Hoschedé, *Claude Monet, ce mal connu*, vol. 1, p. 102.

22   This account is provided in Hoschedé, *Claude Monet, ce mal connu*, vol. 1, p. 146.

23   Quoted in Wildenstein, *Monet, or the Triumph of Impressionism*, p. 434.

24   Quoted in Hoschedé, vol. 1, p. 146.

25   The required measurements for Katral lenses are described in M. Dufour, "Sur le centrage des verres de lunettes," *Comptes rendus des séances de la Société de biologie et de ses filiales* (Paris: Masson et Cie., 1914), pp. 220–22.

26   Georges-Paul Collet, ed., *Correspondance: Jacques-Émile Blanche–Maurice Denis (1901–1939)* (Geneva: Droz, 1989), p. 61.

27   *La Renaissance de l'art français et des industries de luxe* (May 1923), p. 310. The tenants of the rue de Castiglione in 1923 are given on pp. 374–5.

28   *Georges Clemenceau à Son Ami Claude Monet*, p. 154.

29   Ibid., p. 157.

30   WL 2575.

31   Quoted in Levine, *Monet, Narcissus, and Self-Reflection*, p. 266.

32   See Stuckey, "Blossoms and Blunders," p. 120.

33   *Georges Clemenceau à Son Ami*, p. 158.

34   The letter to Léon has since disappeared. In its absence, the question remains of how definitive Monet was in his termination of the contract.

35   Quoted in Wildenstein, *Monet, or the Triumph of Impressionism*, p. 432.

36   Quoted in Spate, *Claude Monet: The Colour of Time*, p. 285.

37 *Claude Monet: The Colour of Time*, p. 285.

38 See Simon Kelly, *Monet's Water Lilies: The Agapanthus Triptych*, pp. 40–41.

39 Christopher Lyon, "Unveiling Monet," *MoMA*, No. 7 (Spring, 1991), p. 16.

40 Walter Friedländer, "Poussin's Old Age," *Gazette des beaux-arts*, vol. 60 (July–August 1962), p. 249.

41 Kenneth Clark, "The Artist Grows Old," *Daedalus* 135 (Winter 2006), p. 85.

42 Quoted in Glen A. Mazis, "'Modern Depths,' Painting, and the Novel: Turner, Melville, and the Interstices," *Soundings: An Interdisciplinary Journal*, vol. 70 (Spring/Summer 1987), p. 125.

43 *Georges Clemenceau à Son Ami Claude Monet*, p. 158.

44 Ibid., p. 161.

45 WL 2583, 2584 and 2585.

46 *Georges Clemenceau à Son Ami Claude Monet*, p. 163.

47 Quoted in Hoschedé, vol. 2, p. 15.

48 *Georges Clemenceau à Son Ami Claude Monet*, pp. 162–3.

CHAPTER TWENTY: "SEND YOUR SLIPPER TO THE STARS"

1   For details of this visit, see Jacques Le Griel, "Voyage fait à Giverny (Eure) par les conseillers municipaux de Saint-Étienne qui y allèrent pour acquérir pour le musée un tableau de M. Claude Monet," *Les Amitiés Foréziennes et Vellaves* (April 1925), reprinted in *Bulletin du Vieux Saint-Étienne*, no. 218 (June 2005), pp. 36–41.

2   Quoted in Maloon, "Monet's Posterity," p. 179.

3   Quoted in Wildenstein, *Monet, or the Triumph of Impressionism*, p. 438.

4   WL 2589.

5   WL 2589 and 2590.

6   *Georges Clemenceau à Son Ami Claude Monet*, pp. 163–4.

7   Ibid., p. 164.

8   Ibid.

9   Ibid., p. 165.

10 For gardens and the weather, see Clemenceau's letter from later that same month, in *Georges Clemenceau à Son Ami Claude Monet*, p. 165. For their discussion of the political situation, see *Lettres à une Amie*, p. 136.

11 Royer et al., "L'Opération de la cataracte de Claude Monet," p. 123.

12 WL 2606.

13 *Georges Clemenceau à Son Ami Claude Monet*, p. 166.

14 *Lettres à une Amie*, p. 103.

15 Ibid., pp. 166.

16 *Georges Clemenceau à Son Ami Claude Monet*, p. 167.

17 Ibid., p. 168.

18 Ibid., p. 167.

19 Clemenceau, *Claude Monet*, p. 19.

20 Jay Ruby, *Secure the Shadow: Death and Photography in America* (Cambridge, MA: MIT Press, 1995); and John Moring, *Early American Naturalists: Exploring the American West, 1804–1900* (Lanham, MD: Taylor Trade Publishing, 2005), pp. 124–25.

21 WL 2612.

22 Hoschedé, vol. 1, pp. 146–47.
23 WL 2683.
24 WL 2609 and 2611.
25 WL 2683.
26 WL 2615.
27 *Georges Clemenceau à Son Ami Claude Monet*, p. 171.
28 Ibid., p. 173.
29 Ibid., p. 174.
30 Ibid., p. 176.
31 *Milwaukee Journal*, May 6, 1943.
32 Quoted in Denommé, *The Naturalism of Gustave Geffroy*, p. 29. Clemenceau's shaking voice is reported in *Le Petit Parisien*, April 8, 1926.
33 *Lettres à une Amie*, p. 268.
34 *Georges Clemenceau à Son Ami Claude Monet*, p. 173.
35 *Lettres à une Amie*, p. 266.
36 *Le Gaulois*, May 18, 1927.
37 *Lettres à une Amie*, p. 266.
38 Charteris, *John Sargent*, pp. 128–9.
39 Quoted in Wildenstein, *Monet, or the Triumph of Impressionism*, p. 444.
40 *La Revue de Paris*, February 1927.
41 Quoted in Wildenstein, *Monet, or the Triumph of Impressionism*, p. 453.
42 *Le Gaulois*, December 6, 1926.
43 *Lettres à une Amie*, p. 294.
44 Quoted in Hoschedé, vol. 1, p. 151. For a description of this visit, see also Wildenstein, *Monet, or the Triumph of Impressionism*, p. 446.
45 Quoted in Alphant, *Claude Monet*, p. 674.
46 *Lettres à une Amie*, p. 35.
47 Ibid., pp. 348–9.
48 *Georges Clemenceau à son Ami Claude Monet*, p. 186.
49 Ibid., p. 181.
50 Ibid., p. 111.
51 Thiébault-Sisson, *Le Temps*, January 8, 1927. Clemenceau's supposed commands to his chauffeur are given in Guitry, *If I Remember Right*, p. 233. However, Guitry incorrectly reports that Clemenceau came from Belébat rather than Paris, which was actually the case.
52 *Le Figaro*, December 9, 1926.
53 Quoted in Wildenstein, *Monet, or the Triumph of Impressionism*, p. 458.
54 R. Hubert, L'Inspecteur de l'Enseignement Primaire des Andelys, to Achille Delaplace, L'Instituteur de Giverny, December 7, 1926. My thanks to Jean-Michel Peers for granting permission to cite this letter.
55 *L'Écho de Paris*, December 9, 1926.
56 Guitry, *If I Remember Right*, pp. 233–4.
57 *L'Écho de Paris*, December 9, 1926.
58 *Lettres à une Amie*, p. 268.
59 *Le Petit Parisien*, December 9, 1926.

EPILOGUE: THE PRINCE OF LIGHT

1   For this interview, see *Le Gaulois*, May 18, 1926.

2   *Lettres à une Amie*, p. 401.

3   Quoted in Maloon, "Monet's Posterity," in Shackleford, ed., *Monet and the Impressionists*, p. 185.

4   Gimpel, *Diary of an Art Dealer*, p. 59.

5   *Le Populaire*, May 19, 1926.

6   *Comoedia*, May 17, 1927, and *Le Petit Journal*, May 17, 1927.

7   Quoted in Terence Maloon, "Monet's Posterity," in Shackleford, ed., *Monet and the Impressionists*, p. 301. For Sickert's comments, see John House, *Nature into Art*, p. 108.

8   Gréard, *Meissonier: His Life and Art*, p. 345.

9   For these reviews, see Maloon, "Monet's Posterity," pp. 182–3 and 185.

10 *L'Art Vivant*, September 1927.

11 Martet, *Clemenceau*, p. 244.

12 Hoschedé, vol. 1, p. 97.

13 Albert Flament, cited in Romy Golan, "Oceanic Sensations: Monet's *Grandes Décorations* and Mural Painting in France from 1927 to 1952," in Paul Hayes Tucker et al., *Monet in the 20th Century*, p. 92.

14 See Golan, "Oceanic Sensations," pp. 86 and 96.

15 Quoted in Elizabeth W. Easton, "Monet: New York," *Burlington Magazine*, vol. 151 (December 2009), p. 867.

16 *Le Ménestrel*, October 18, 1929.

17 Fortuné d'Andigné, *Les Musées de Paris* (Paris: Éditions Alpina, 1931), p. 135.

18 *La Renaissance: Politique, Littéraire, Artistique*, January 14, 1928.

19 *Claude Monet: Exposition Rétrospective* (Paris: Musée de l'Orangerie, 1931), p. 8.

20 The doctoral dissertation of Robert Rey had been on the "rebirth of the classical" in the work of Degas, Renoir, Gauguin, Cézanne, and Seurat. Rey predicted, oddly, that had Monet lived and painted for another decade, the "clouds of water lilies would have assumed human form…and would have become geniuses and nymphs." Figures, in other words, would have reappeared in his landscapes, making it possible for Rey to claim that even Monet—had he lived longer—would ultimately have surrendered to "le grand art classique." See Rey, *La Renaissance du sentiment classique dans la peinture française à la fin du 19e siècle: Degas, Renoir, Gauguin, Cézanne, Seurat* (Paris: Les Beaux-Arts, Édition d'Études et de Documents, 1931), pp. 136–37.

21 *Claude Monet: Exposition Rétrospective*, p. 77.

22 Quoted in Golan, "Oceanic Sensations," p. 92.

23 *Formes* (May 1931), p. 75.

24 Quoted in Maloon, "Monet's Posterity," p. 184.

25 On the rural nostalgia after the Great War, see Romy Golan, *Modernity and Nostalgia: Art and Politics in France Between the Wars* (New Haven, CT: Yale University Press, 1995). She discusses the attacks on Monet's work at the Orangerie on pp. 39–40.

26 Quoted in Golan, *Modernity and Nostalgia*, p. 40.

27 *Paris-Normandie*, November 28, 1949.

28 André Masson, "Monet the Founder", trans. Terence Maloon in Shackleford, ed., *Monet and the Impressionists*, p. 190.

29   Paul Facchetti, quoted in Romy Golan, "Oceanic Sensations," p. 96.

30   *Sunday Times*, March 6, 1966.

31   Quoted in Jenny Gheith, "Tableau Vert," *Art Institute of Chicago Museum Studies* 35, no. 2 (2009), p. 45.

32   *Time*, January 16, 1956.

33   Quoted in Michael Plante, "Fashioning Nationality: Sam Francis, Joan Mitchell, and American Expatriate Artists in Paris in the 1950s," in Laura Felleman Fattal and Carol Salus, eds., *Out of Context: American Artists Abroad* (Westport, CT: Praeger, 2004), p. 143.

34   Quoted in Roald Nasgaard, *Abstract Painting in Canada* (Vancouver: Douglas & McIntyre, 2007), p. 82.

35   Jane Livingston, "The Paintings of Joan Mitchell," in *The Paintings of Joan Mitchell* (New York: Whitney Museum of American Art, 2002), p. 40. Art critics frequently make justifiable comparisons between the work of Monet and Mitchell, but Mitchell was anxious to disavow an influence. As a *New York Times* interview reported the year before her death: "'I bought this house because I liked the view, not out of any love for Monet,' she snaps, pointedly mispronouncing the painter's name so that it rhymes with the word 'bonnet'" (*New York Times*, November 24, 1991).

36   Quoted in Temkin and Lawrence, p. 18.

37   Quoted in Maloon, "Monet's Posterity," p. 186.

38   *Clement Greenberg: Collected Essays and Criticism*, vol. 4, ed. John O'Brian (Chicago: University of Chicago Press, 1993), p. 3.

39   Clement Greenberg, *Art and Culture: Critical Essays* (Boston: Beacon Press, 1961), p. 45.

40   Quoted in Wildenstein, *Monet, or the Triumph of Impressionism*, p. 446.

41   "Interview with William Wright," in Kristine Stiles and Peter Selz, eds., *Theories and Documents of Contemporary Art: A Sourcebook of Artists' Writings* (Berkeley and Los Angeles: University of California Press, 1996), p. 22.

42   Hoschedé, *Claude Monet, ce mal connu*, vol. 1, p. 83.

43   *Time*, July 19, 1971, and March 26, 1990.

44   Ibid., March 21, 1960.

45   Ibid., January 28, 1957.

46   Masson, "Monet the Founder," trans. Terence Maloon, p. 191.

47   Pascal Rousseau, "Monet, le cycle des Nymphéas," *Journal de l'année* (2000), p. 323. For the renovation project, see *Musée de l'Orangerie: Dossier de presse* (Paris: Ministère de la culture et de la communication, 2006).

48   *Le Petit Parisien*, February 12, 1922.

49   Personal e-mail communication, August 2, 2015.

CLAUDE MONET'S WATER LILIES IN PUBLIC COLLECTIONS

IN THE UNITED STATES

Museum of Fine Arts, Boston, MA
The Water Lily Pond, 1900
Water Lilies, 1905
Water Lilies, 1907

Worcester Art Museum, MA
Water Lilies, 1908

Museum of Modern Art, New York
Water Lilies (triptych), 1914–26
Water Lilies, 1914–26
Agapanthus, 1914–26
The Japanese Footbridge, c. 1920–22

Metropolitan Museum of Art, New York
Water Lilies, 1919
Water Lilies, 1914–26
Bridge Over a Pond of Water Lilies, 1899
The Path Through the Irises, 1914–17

Philadelphia Museum of Art, PA
Japanese Footbridge, Giverny, 1895
The Japanese Bridge, 1919–24

National Gallery, Washington, D.C.
The Japanese Footbridge, 1899

Museum of Fine Arts, Richmond, VA
Iris, 1914–17

Carnegie Museum of Art, Pittsburgh, PA
Water Lilies, c. 1915–26

Cleveland Museum of Art, OH
Water Lilies (Agapanthus), c. 1915–26

Allen Memorial Art Museum, Oberlin College, OH
Wisteria (Glycines), c. 1919–20

Columbus Museum of Art, OH
Weeping Willow, 1918

Dayton Art Institute, OH
Water Lilies, 1903

Toledo Museum of Art, OH
Nympheas, 1914–17

Art Institute of Chicago, IL
The Bridge Over the Water Lily Pond, 1900
Water Lilies, 1906

Minneapolis Institute of Arts, MN
The Japanese Bridge, c. 1919–24

St. Louis Art Museum, MO
Agapanthus, 1915–26 (The central part of a triptych, the other two canvases are at the Cleveland Art Museum and the Nelson-Atkins Museum of Art)

Nelson-Atkins Museum of Art, Kansas City, MO
Water Lilies, c. 1915–26

Dallas Museum of Art, TX
Water Lilies, 1908

Kimbell Art Museum, Fort Worth, TX
Weeping Willow, 1918–19

Museum of Fine Arts, Houston, TX
Water Lilies, 1907

Denver Art Museum, CO
Water Lilies, 1904

Phoenix Art Museum, AZ
Flowering Arches, Giverny, 1913

Portland Art Museum, OR
Nympheas, 1914–17

**Fine Arts Museums of
San Francisco, CA**
Nymphéas, 1914–17

**Los Angeles County
Museum of Art, CA**
Nympheas, c. 1897–98

Honolulu Museum of Art, HI
Water Lilies, 1917–19

OUTSIDE THE UNITED STATES

France
Musée d'Orsay, Paris
Water Lily Pond, Harmony in Green, 1899
Water Lily Pond, Harmony in Rose, 1900

Musée Marmottan Monet, Paris
Nymphéas, 1916–19
Nymphéas, 1916–19
Saule pleureur et basin aux nymphéas,
1916–19
Les Hémérocalles, 1914–17
Nymphéas, 1914–17
Nymphéas et agapanthes, 1914–17

Lycée Claude Monet, Paris
Nymphéas avec rameaux de saule, 1916–19

United Kingdom
National Gallery, London
Water Lilies, after 1916
Water Lilies, Setting Sun, c. 1907
The Water Lily Pond, 1899
Irises, 1914–17

**National Museum and Gallery,
Cardiff, Wales**
Water Lilies, 1908

Switzerland
Kunsthaus Zurich, Zurich
The Water Lily Pond (diptych),
c. 1915–26

Foundation E.G. Burhle, Zurich
Le Bassin aux nymphéas, reflets verts,
ca. 1920–26

Austria
Léopold Museum, Vienna
Nymphéas, 1916–19

Albertina Vienna
The Water Lily Pond, 1917–19

Germany
Neue Pinakothek, Munich
Nymphéas, 1914–17

Wallraf-Richartz-Museum, Cologne
Nymphéas, 1914–17

Sweden
Goteborg Museum of Art, Goteborg
Water Lilies, 1907

Australia
National Gallery, Canberra
Nymphéas, 1914–17

Japan
Chichu Art Museum, Naoshima
Water-Lily Pond (diptych), c. 1915–26
Water-Lilies, Cluster of Grass, 1914–17
Water Lilies, 1914–17
Water-Lily Pond, 1917–19
*Water Lilies, Reflections of Weeping
Willows*, 1916–19

**National Museum of Western Art,
Tokyo**
Water Lilies, 1914

Bridgestone Museum of Art, Tokyo
Water Lilies, 1907
Water Lilies, 1916

Tokyo Fuji Art Museum
Water Lilies, 1908

Museum of Modern Art, Gunma
Nymphéas, 1914–17

Oyamazaki Museum, Kyoto
Nymphéas, 1914–17

INDEX

A NOTE ON THE AUTHOR

Born and raised in Canada, Ross King has lived in England since 1992. Among his books are the bestselling *Brunelleschi's Dome*, *Michelangelo and the Pope's Ceiling* and *Leonardo and The Last Supper*.